Mrs. ~~Effie Ballance~~
R. R. 3, East Wellington Rd.
Nanaimo, B.C.

Revelation

Mrs. Effie Ballance
R. R. 3, East Wellington Rd.
Nanaimo, B.C.

Revelation

ILLUSTRATED AND MADE PLAIN
BY TIM LAHAYE

ZONDERVAN
PUBLISHING HOUSE
OF THE ZONDERVAN CORPORATION
GRAND RAPIDS, MICHIGAN 49506

This book is gratefully dedicated to my mother,
MARGARET LaHAYE
Child Evangelism Director, Lansing, Michigan.

Her consistent Christian life and earnest prayers helped guide me during my rebellious years and ultimately led me into the ministry. It was her keen interest in Bible prophecy that sparked my own. I could wish for every young man such a dedicated Christian mother.

REVELATION — Illustrated and Made Plain
Revised edition copyright © 1973, 1975 by Tim LaHaye

Third printing 1976

Library of Congress Catalog Card No. 74-9323

All rights reserved. No part of this publication may be reproduced, stored in a retrieval system, or transmitted in any form or by any means, electronic, mechanical, photocopy, recording, or otherwise, without the prior permission of the copyright owner.

Unless otherwise indicated, Scripture references are from the *New Scofield Reference Bible,* copyright © 1967 by Oxford University Press, Inc.

Printed in the United States of America

Grateful acknowledgment is made to the publishers for permission to quote from the following copyrighted material:

Halley's Bible Handbook by Henry H. Halley. Copyright © 1965 by Halley's Bible Handbook Inc. Reprinted by permission.

Lectures on the Book of Revelation by Harry A. Ironside. Used by permission of the publisher, Loizeaux Brothers, Inc.

Things to Come by Dwight J. Pentecost. Copyright © 1958 by Dunham Publishing Company. Reprinted by permission of the publisher, Zondervan Publishing House.

The Revelation of Jesus Christ by John F. Walvoord. Copyright 1966, Moody Press, Moody Bible Institute of Chicago. Used by permission.

CONTENTS

Part III   Christ and the Future

FOREWORD

The book of Revelation is the only book in the New Testament that presents Jesus Christ as He really is today. The gospels introduce Him as the "man of sorrows, acquainted with grief" during His incarnation. Revelation presents Him in His true glory and majesty after His resurrection and ascension into heaven, never again to be reviled, rebuked, and spat upon. No wonder John entitled it "The Revelation of Jesus Christ."

The study of this book will warm your heart as you perceive the true Christ and His ministry to the churches for the past two thousand years. You will thrill to see myriads of angels bowing before Him and singing His praises. You will also view His dynamic triumph over Satan and all the forces of evil.

The book of Revelation makes it clear that Christ and Christians are the ultimate winners in the game of life. In fact, a study of this book is essential for a comprehensive view of the rest of Scripture. It finalizes God's wonderful purposes for His favorite creatures — mankind.

A proper understanding of this book will help the Bible student know what God has in store for this world before it comes to pass, so he may prepare himself and not be taken unaware. It will also afford him a confident faith with which to confront the political, social, and religious chaos that is imminent. Only a biblical illiterate is unable to see that these are the last days.

No book in the Bible has been more discredited than Revelation except for its counterpart in the Old Testament, the book of Daniel. Because Revelation deals predominantly with prophecy and the future, and because it exposes Satan as a deceptive fraud, the archenemy of man has tried his hardest to discredit the book. The last thing he wants is for people to become aware of Christ's majesty, Satan's treachery, and the Christian's final triumph when this old world system ultimately fails.

I have found that the proper understanding of Revelation motivates Christians to consistent dedication and service. It lifts their spirits and gives them a hope in the future that no other book in the world provides. Most of all, the study of this book will give you a vital love for Jesus Christ and the souls of lost men about you, for it not only reveals the Lord and His wonderful plan to redeem His Church but also discloses the awful plight of this world and of those who reject Him.

Revelation — Illustrated and Made Plain is the fulfillment of a twenty-five-year dream. I have always wanted to write a commentary on this book that was clear and down-to-earth, one that young Christians could read and understand. It is my prayer that this book will stir the heart of every reader and inspire him to greater service and preparation for the rapidly approaching day when we will see Him who said, "Behold, I come suddenly!"

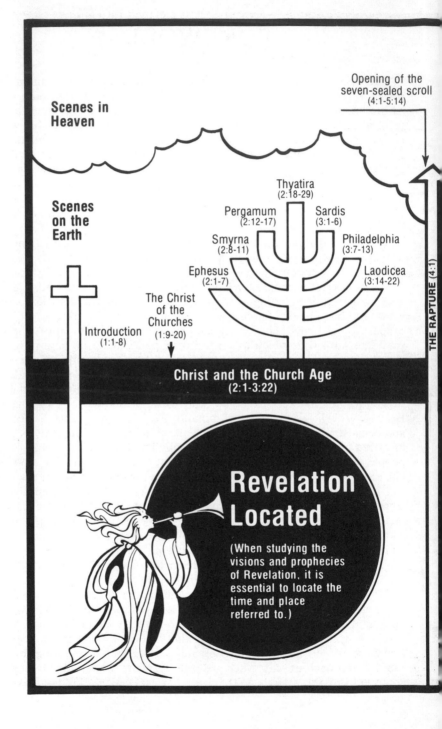

Scenes in
Heaven

Opening of the
seven-sealed scroll
(4:1-5:14)

Scenes
on the
Earth

Thyatira
(2:18-29)

Pergamum
(2:12-17)

Sardis
(3:1-6)

Smyrna
(2:8-11)

Philadelphia
(3:7-13)

Ephesus
(2:1-7)

Laodicea
(3:14-22)

THE RAPTURE (4:1)

The Christ
of the
Churches
(1:9-20)

Introduction
(1:1-8)

Christ and the Church Age
(2:1-3:22)

Revelation
Located

(When studying the
visions and prophecies
of Revelation, it is
essential to locate the
time and place
referred to.)

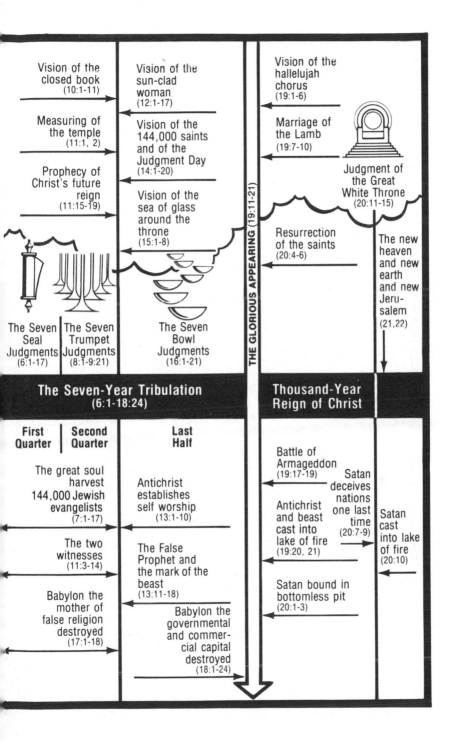

Vision of the
closed book
(10:1-11)

Vision of the
sun-clad
woman
(12:1-17)

Vision of the
hallelujah
chorus
(19:1-6)

Measuring of
the temple
(11:1, 2)

Vision of the
144,000 saints
and of the
Judgment Day
(14:1-20)

Marriage of
the Lamb
(19:7-10)

Prophecy of
Christ's future
reign
(11:15-19)

Vision of the
sea of glass
around the
throne
(15:1-8)

Judgment of
the Great
White Throne
(20:11-15)

Resurrection
of the saints
(20:4-6)

The new
heaven
and new
earth
and new
Jeru-
salem
(21,22)

THE GLORIOUS APPEARING (19:11-21)

The Seven
Seal
Judgments
(6:1-17)

The Seven
Trumpet
Judgments
(8:1-9:21)

The Seven
Bowl
Judgments
(16:1-21)

The Seven-Year Tribulation
(6:1-18:24)

**Thousand-Year
Reign of Christ**

First
Quarter

Second
Quarter

Last
Half

The great soul
harvest
144,000 Jewish
evangelists
(7:1-17)

Antichrist
establishes
self worship
(13:1-10)

Battle of
Armageddon
(19:17-19)

Satan
deceives
nations
one last
time
(20:7-9)

Antichrist
and beast
cast into
lake of fire
(19:20, 21)

Satan
cast
into lake
of fire
(20:10)

The two
witnesses
(11:3-14)

The False
Prophet and
the mark of the
beast
(13:11-18)

Babylon the
mother of
false religion
destroyed
(17:1-18)

Babylon the
governmental
and commer-
cial capital
destroyed
(18:1-24)

Satan bound in
bottomless pit
(20:1-3)

PRELIMINARY CONSIDERATIONS

Over fifty years ago, Dr. C. I. Scofield said in his notes on Revelation in the Scofield Reference Bible, "Doubtless, much which is designedly obscure to us will be clear to those for whom it was written as *the time approaches.*" That time is at hand, and many things are clearer than they were in Dr. Scofield's day. It is my hope that these notes and pictures gathered from writers new and old, plus the leading of the Holy Spirit, will further clarify these things for "those for whom they were written" — which could well be this generation.

The Value of Studying Revelation

To many, the book of Revelation is a closed book. More than one Bible teacher has taken a class from Matthew through the book of Jude, only to return to the book of Matthew rather than face the unusual teachings of the book of Revelation. It cannot be denied that it has confused many people. Nor can we deny that this book has been of immeasurable blessing to others. The following are some valuable reasons for studying this great book:

1. A special blessing is promised to those who read this book (Rev. 1:3). There is blessing in reading any portion of God's Word, but this is the only book that promises special blessing for those who read and hear its words. Keep in mind too that the book closes with a restatement of this blessing for those who, in addition to reading and hearing the Word, also keep it (Rev. 22:7).

2. It reveals God's Plan for the future. A keen interest in future events is a universal desire of man, particularly in days like ours when world conditions are so uncertain. Many people anxiously ask, "What does the future hold for me?" The student of the book of Revelation need not be taken unaware as these events unfold, for it is possible through the study of this book to know God's future plan.

3. This book gives clearer detail concerning Bible prophecy than any other book in the Bible. For example, John described the glorious appearing of Jesus Christ (Rev. 19); the governmental operation of the man of sin; the terrible events of the Tribulation Period; the ultimate end of Satan; the future glorification of the Church; the future position of the saints; and the city Christ has gone to prepare for His Church.

4. This book completes the circle of Bible truths. As the Word of God, the Scriptures predictably reveal superb planning and organization. We see that clearly in the book of Revelation, for it completes the great truths begun in Genesis and in other passages of the Bible. Here are some examples:

1

Genesis shows man's beginning in a beautiful paradise.
Revelation shows the wonderful paradise to come.

Genesis shows how man lost his chance to eat of the tree of life (3:22-24).
Revelation shows man will yet eat of that tree (22:2).

Genesis tells of man's first rebellion against God (3 and 4).
Revelation promises an end to man's rebellion against God.

Genesis records the first murderer, drunkard, and rebel.
Revelation promises a city where "there shall in no way enter into it any thing that defileth, neither he that worketh abomination, or maketh a lie, but they who are written in the Lamb's book of life" (21:27).

Genesis reveals the tragic sorrow that resulted from sin (3 and 4).
Revelation promises, "God shall wipe away all tears from their eyes" (21:4).

Genesis records the first death (4:8).
Revelation promises that "there shall be no more death" (21:4).

Genesis shows the beginning of the curse (3:15-18).
Revelation shows the curse lifted (22:3).

Genesis introduces the devil for the first time as the tempter of men (3:1-18).
Revelation shows the final doom of Satan (20:10).

Genesis promises that Satan's head would be bruised (3:15).
Revelation shows him bruised and defeated (19:20).

Genesis shows Satan's first attempt at discrediting the Word of God when he asked Eve, "Yea, hath God said?" and his first attempt at denying the Word of God, "Ye shall not surely die" (3:1-5). Sad to say, the thousands of years since then reveal man still believing Satan and not God. Today the Bible is not believed by the majority but rather is subjected to the criticism of skeptics in education, science, and even the ministry. This skepticism has tragically resulted in the doom of many unsuspecting souls.
Revelation promises a curse on all such infidels who detract from God's holy Word, "And if any man shall take away from the words of the book of this prophecy, God shall take away his part from the tree of life, and out of the holy city, and from the things which are written in this book" (22:19).

Special Suggestions for Studying This Book

1. Follow the golden rule of interpretation: When the plain sense of Scripture makes common sense, seek no other sense; therefore, take every word at its primary, ordinary, usual, literal meaning unless the facts of the immediate text, studied in the light of related passages and axiomatic and fundamental truths, clearly indicate otherwise. This rule, suggested by Dr. David L. Cooper, provides basic guidelines for properly interpreting the many signs and symbols in the book.

2. Locate the scene of activity. Hopeless confusion will be generated in the study of Revelation unless one keeps firmly in mind whether the scene under discussion takes place in heaven or on earth. The action should also be followed closely, for sometimes a scene in heaven results in activity on the earth. For example, chapters 4 and 5 are scenes in heaven, chapter 6 a scene on earth. The preceding chart, besides showing the chronology of Revelation, shows the scene of activity for each event.

3. Understand that the book is not written chronologically. It is impossible to understand this book properly if one expects it to fall into chronological sequence. This is particularly important in the events of the Tribulation. The student of the book of Revelation should memorize immediately the fact that the seal judgments of chapter 6 comprise the first quarter of the Tribulation and the trumpet judgments of chapters 8 and 9 comprise the second quarter of the Tribulation. The bowl judgments of chapter 16 comprise the last half, or three-and-a-half years of the Tribulation. Everything else has to be studied in the context of the period with which it coincides. Examine the chart below carefully before proceeding further.

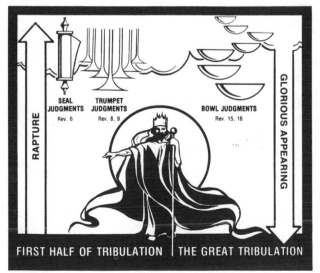

Four Interpretations

The interpretation one gives the book of Revelation will obviously determine its message to him. There are four basic interpretations that are worthy of note.

Preterist Interpretation

The preterist view holds that John was referring to events of his own day, about A.D. 96. This requires mental gymnastics that are quite unnecessary if one would apply the Golden Rule of Interpretation. The Roman emperors Nero or Domitian could scarcely fulfill the requirements of this book for the Antichrist.

Historical Interpretation

The historical view suggests that John was describing the major events that would take place during the history of the Church. It therefore suggests that we can see these events as we look back at history. This, of course, calls for the juggling of historical events to fit the prophecy. This is historically unsound and tends to distort the plain meaning.

Spiritualizing Interpretation

There are those who believe everything in the book should be taken figuratively or metaphorically, that John was talking about a spiritual conflict and not a physical experience. This view is held by most amillennialists and postmillennialists. Until the turn of the century, postmillennialism gained many followers with the idea that the world was getting better and better and we were about to usher in the kingdom. Man's perpetual degeneracy during this century has rendered this a most untenable position.

Futurist Interpretation

The futurist view, which seems to me to be the most satisfactory, accepts the book of Revelation as prophecy that primarily is yet to be fulfilled, particularly from chapter 4 on. This is the interpretation accepted by most premillennial Bible teachers.

A safe rule to follow in the study of the book of Revelation is to accept the book as literal unless the facts are obviously to the contrary.

An Outline of the Book of Revelation

Since the book of Revelation is the "Revelation of Jesus Christ," it should not seem strange that an outline of the book should revolve around the person, work and future plans of Jesus Christ.

    I.   CHRIST AND THE CHURCH AGE (chapters 1-3)

        A.   Introduction (1:1-8)

        B.   The Christ of the churches (1:9-20)

        C.   Christ's message to His churches (2,3)

           1. The church of Ephesus (2:1-7)

2. The church of Smyrna (2:8-11)
3. The church of Pergamum (2:12-17)
4. The church of Thyatira (2:18-29)
5. The church of Sardis (3:1-6)
6. The church of Philadelphia (3:7-13)
7. The church of Laodicea (3:14-22)

II. CHRIST AND THE TRIBULATION (chapters 4-18)
   A. John caught up to heaven (4)
   B. Christ receives glory in heaven (5)
   C. The seven seals — the first quarter of the Tribulation (6)
      1. Revival under the 144,000 Jewish witnesses (7)
      2. The preaching of the two witnesses (11:1-14)
   D. The trumpet judgments — the second quarter of the Tribulation (8, 9)
      1. Israel persecuted by Satan (12)
      2. The beast (Antichrist) and the False Prophet (13)
      3. Ecclesiastical Babylon destroyed by the kings of the earth (17)
   E. Heavenly visions
      1. Vision of the little scroll (10)
      2. Vision of the glorious appearing of Christ (11:15-19)
      3. Satan cast down to the earth (12:7-12)
      4. Vision of the martyrs secure with Christ; doom pronounced on the beast worshipers (14)
      5. Vision of the coming bowl judgments (17)
   F. The seven bowls — last half of the Great Tribulation (15, 16)
      1. The commercial city of Babylon destroyed by God (18)

III. CHRIST AND THE FUTURE (chapters 19-22)
   A. Christ's marriage to His Church (19:1-10)
   B. Christ's glorious appearing (19:11-21)
   C. Christ's millennial kingdom (20:1-11)
      1. Satan bound a thousand years (20:1-3)
      2. Resurrection of believers (20:4-6)
      3. Satan loosed to test man's will (20:7-9)
      4. Satan doomed (20:10)
   D. Christ's judgment of unbelievers (20:11-15)
   E. Christ's creation of new things
      1. New heaven and earth (21:1, 2)
      2. New conditions for men (21:3-8)
      3. New Jerusalem (21:9-27)
      4. The new paradise (22:1-7)
   F. Christ's last message (22:8-21)

Key Verse of Revelation

Revelation 1:19 is the key verse that unlocks the door to the entire outline of the book. It is further evidence of the threefold division of this great Revelation. John was told expressly by Christ to write —

1. the things which thou hast seen
2. the things which are
3. the things which shall be hereafter.

From this, it seems evident that the book is made up primarily of future events. It includes some things which existed in John's day (chapters 2 and 3), all based on the things he saw. From this, we see that the futurist interpretation of the book of Revelation is the valid one.

Part I

Christ and the
Church Age

THE SEVEN CHURCHES OF REVELATION

WHITE
HORSE OR 1ST ACK ALTERNATE WHOSR
CONQUER RED HORSE 13FOR SEPMET PT/YA0036
ANTICHRIST FEDPROM SPIRIT PUM COYOGE
ANTISPIRIT RISING 3CROOOOO

	EPHESUS The Apostolic Church Rev. 2:1-7	SMYRNA The Persecuted Church Rev. 2:8-11	PERGAMUM The Indulged Church Rev. 2:12-17	THYATIRA The Pagan Church Rev. 2:18-29	SARDIS The Dead Church Rev. 3:1-6	PHILADELPHIA The Church Christ Loved Rev. 3:7-13	LAODICEA The Lukewarm Church Rev. 3:14-22
	A.D. 30-100	A.D. 100-312	A.D. 312-606	A.D. 606-Tribulation	A.D.1520-Tribulation PROTESTANT REFORMATION	A.D. 1750-Rapture	A.D. 1900-Tribulation
COMMENDATION I know thy. . .	Good works, labor, patience. Hated Nicolaitans.	Works, tribulation, poverty.	Works. Held fast my name. Has not denied my faith.	Good works, love, service, faith, patience.	Works. A name that thou livest.	Works. Missions. Little strength. Kept my word. Not denied my name.	Not one word!
CONDEMNATION	Thou hast left thy first love.	Not one word!	Thou hast false teachers of Balaam and the Nicolaitans.	Thou allowest Jezebel to teach idolatry and compromise.	Thou art dead. Works not complete.	Not one word!	Thou art lukewarm, wretched, miserable, poor, blind, and naked.
COUNSEL I counsel thee. . .	Remember from where thou art fallen, and repent.	Fear not. Be faithful.	Repent.	Hold fast what you have till I come.	Watch. Strengthen the things that remain. Remember; hold fast, and repent.	Hold that fast which thou hast.	Buy gold tried by fire and white raiment. Anoint thine eyes. Be zealous and repent.
CHALLENGE To him that over-cometh. . .	Will I give to eat of the tree of life.	Shall not be hurt of the second death.	Will I give hidden manna and a white stone.	Will I give millennial leadership and the Morning Star.	Will be clothed in white raiment.I will not blot his name out of the book of life.	I will make him a pillar and write upon him the name of God and My new name.	Will I grant to sit with me in my throne.

RAPTURE OF THE CHURCH

LION   OX   MAN

Introduction

The Revelation of Jesus Christ, which God gave unto him, to show unto his servants things which must shortly come to pass; and he sent and signified it by his angel unto his servant, John, who bore witness of the word of God, and of the testimony of Jesus Christ, and of all things that he saw. Blessed is he that readeth, and they that hear the words of this prophecy, and keep those things which are written in it; for the time is at hand.

John, to the seven churches which are in Asia: Grace be unto you, and peace, from him who is, and who was, and who is to come, and from the seven spirits who are before his throne; and from Jesus Christ, who is the faithful witness, and the first begotten of the dead, and the prince of the kings of the earth. Unto him that loveth us, and washed us from our sins in his own blood, and hath made us a kingdom of priests unto God and his Father, to him be glory and dominion forever and ever. Amen. Behold, he cometh with clouds, and every eye shall see him, and they also who pierced him; and all kindreds of the earth shall wail because of him. Even so, Amen. I am Alpha and Omega, the beginning and the ending, saith the Lord, who is, and who was, and who is to come, the Almighty (Rev. 1:1-8).

The Subject of Revelation

"The Revelation of Jesus Christ . . ." The word "revelation" is a translation of the Greek word *apokalypsis,* which means "an unveiling." It is not a new word in the New Testament, for it occurs eighteen times (Luke 2:32; Gal. 1:12; 2 Thess. 1:7; 1 Pet. 1:7; etc.). The word means "to show or expose to view," as the unveiling of a painting is a "revelation." This book, then, is the unveiling of Jesus Christ. But not just Jesus Christ, for John has already presented Him very clearly as the divine Son of God in the gospel that bears his name. Further on in the verse we find that this is the Revelation of Jesus Christ "to show unto his servants things which must shortly come to pass." Again we see that the emphasis of the book is on future events.

9

". . . and signified it by his angel." The word "signify" has been abused by many godly scholars in their study of this book. Some suggest that it means "sign-ify," that is, to write in signs. True, there are some symbols in the book and God calls them symbols, for example, Revelation 12:1, 3, and 15:1. However, it is wrong to classify the entire book as a book of signs and symbols, suggesting that they cannot be taken literally. On the contrary, the figurative language of Revelation is figurative of fact. There is far more in the book of Revelation that should be accepted literally than should be spiritualized.

The Scribe of Revelation

". . . his servant, John." There has never been any serious question that the human writer of the book of Revelation was the Apostle John. This book is generally accepted as the last New Testament book, written when John was an elderly man banished to the Isle of Patmos, either by force or choice, bearing "record of the word of God, and of the testimony of Jesus Christ." The only serious consideration for questioning his authorship is that this book does not have the same style of writing as found in his gospel and his epistles. This is quickly understood, however, by anyone who comprehends the unique nature of the transmission of this book, for John was definitely just the scribe, recording the things that were audibly spoken to him during his heavenly visions; thus less of the writer's personality and style would naturally be reflected in the book. From earliest days, this book was received as divine writ from the pen of the revered apostle, who even at that point in his Christian experience referred to himself as "the servant of Jesus Christ."

The Spiritual Blessing of Revelation

We have already seen that a blessing is offered to those who read, hear, and keep the words of this book. The word "blessing" in Scripture is similar in meaning to the word "happy." As you know, happiness is not found in the things of this world but comes from God. The book of Revelation is a source of happiness to anyone who will read it, hear it in the depths of his heart, and obey its instructions. If ever a generation needed to study this book, it is ours. We are probably living at the time when these things will begin to come to pass.

The Source of Revelation

It is important that we keep in focus the true source of the book of Revelation. It did not originate with John but came to him through a fourfold sequence of transmission: *God — Christ — angel — John: to the Church*. The true source of the book of Revelation is God.

The Trinity

". . . from him who is, and who was, and who is to come." This is a reference to the Holy Trinity or the triune God. Whenever the word

God appears in Scripture, the context should be examined closely to determine whether it is referring to God the Father, God the Son, or God the Holy Spirit. It is erroneous to assume that the title God always refers to God the Father. Many times it refers to the triune God. The expression "who is, and who was, and who is to come" is an encompassing expression which connotes the eternity of God. It is significant to note that this great book has its origin in the Trinity. The triune nature of God is again revealed in verse 8 of this chapter.

The Salutation of Revelation

"Grace be unto you, and peace." *Grace* is the Greek method of greeting; *peace* is the Hebrew form of greeting. Both of these generate from God, not men. Grace and peace are not the prerogatives of men. One's relationship to God determines his possession of grace and peace.

This verse shows that the Trinity shares in the dispensing of grace and peace to man: God the Father — "from him who is, and who was, and who is to come"; God the Spirit — "and from the seven spirits who are before his throne"; and God the Son — "and from Jesus Christ." ("The seven spirits" is a reference to the sevenfold work of the Spirit as revealed in Isaiah 11:2, where He is called "the Spirit of the Lord, the Spirit of wisdom, the Spirit of understanding, the Spirit of counsel, the Spirit of might, the Spirit of knowledge, the Spirit of the fear of the Lord." The number seven denotes perfection or completeness; the term "seven spirits" does not mean seven Holy Spirits but the seven ministries of the Holy Spirit.)

The Savior of Revelation

Right here in the introduction we have the first of many descriptions of Jesus Christ in the glory and majesty befitting His person and nature. In our Lord's first coming, He was "despised and rejected of men; a man of sorrows, and acquainted with grief" (Isa. 53:3). In His next coming, He will be adored and worshipped, for He will come "with power and great glory" (Luke 21:27). The book of Revelation presents the Lord Jesus more magnificently than any book in the Bible. For a true picture of the whole nature of Jesus Christ, one must understand Him as He is revealed in this book. Verses 5, 6, and 7 describe the past, present, and future work of Christ Jesus, the Lord.

". . . the faithful witness . . ." The Lord Jesus Christ is the faithful witness. All that men need to know about God is revealed through Him. As He said to Philip, "He that hath seen me hath seen the Father" (John 14:9). Though there are other witnesses of the person of Christ, such as God the Father who spoke from heaven, John the Baptist, Jesus' miracles, and the Scriptures (John 5:31-39), His witness is sufficient. For this reason He could say of Himself, "I am the truth."

". . . the first begotten of the dead . . ." This literally means firstborn *from* the dead; as indicated in 1 Corinthians 15:23, it means that Christ is the "first fruits." Christ is not the first one raised from the dead, for Elisha and Elijah raised the dead, and Christ Himself raised three people from the dead. However, they all died natural deaths later. They were not raised in "incorruption." Christ is the first one ever to have been resurrected in His glorified body, an event which also guarantees our ultimate resurrection.

". . . the prince of the kings of the earth." Jesus Christ is in control of this world, though He is permitting men certain latitude; nevertheless, His control of the world rulers of this day is evident in the fact that He ultimately permits men to be put down. It seems that He permits world rulers certain latitudes which have kept one man from ever controlling this world since the time of Christ. For example, Napoleon met his Waterloo, Kaiser Wilhelm met his, and Adolph Hitler met his, just as the communist tyrants of our day will meet theirs. The ultimate meaning, of course, is in reference to that day when He will reign physically as King of Kings and Lord of Lords on this earth.

The Present Work of Christ

He "that loveth us" denotes continual action. Not only did He give Himself for us, but today He continues to love us with an everlasting love.

". . . and washed us from our sins in his own blood." All those who have received Christ Jesus by faith have been cleansed by His blood. This is not a universal experience but a unique washing by Christ of those who personally call on Him. The Bible tells us, "The blood of Jesus Christ, [God's] Son, cleanseth us from all sin" (1 John 1:7). But this is based on the condition that we confess our sin. Let me pause here to ask, Have you confessed your sin? Have you called personally on the name of the Lord Jesus Christ? Unless you have, you are still in your sins. However, the blood of Jesus Christ will be applied to those sins in cleansing power if you will but ask the Savior for His cleansing and turn your life over to Him.

"And hath made us a kingdom of priests unto God and his Father." Amazing as it may seem, Christ has made us kings and priests. We may not look like kings today, but there is a day coming when, because we are the children of God by faith, we will rule and reign with Him — that is, if we have been born into His spiritual kingdom, having been translated from the power of darkness into the kingdom of the Son of His love in whom we have redemption, the forgiveness of our sins (Col. 1:13, 14).

Our present condition does not accurately convey our future realization, but it is as certain as the eternal God. In the meantime, however, we are to do our work faithfully as "priests unto God," which means that we are to intercede on behalf of those who need Christ and cannot pray for themselves. One of the great needs of the Church of Jesus Christ today is to be actively engaged in the work of intercessory prayer.

The Future Work of Christ

Christ is coming again. Yes, Jesus is coming again! This is a certified, guaranteed promise. The angelic messengers in Acts 1:11 said, "This same Jesus, who is taken up from you into heaven, shall so come in like manner as ye have seen him go into heaven." This can only mean that He will come visibly to the earth. This is a reference to His coming at the end of the Tribulation Period to set up His millennial kingdom.

"Behold, he cometh with clouds." He ascended in a cloud (Acts 1:9) and will return in a cloud. Jesus Himself said that He would come in a cloud (Matt. 24:30).

". . . and every eye shall see him." This does not mean only those who are on the earth at that time. It means every eye. Jesus Himself said to Caiaphas, the high priest, "I say unto you, Hereafter ye shall see the Son of man sitting on the right hand of power, coming in the clouds of heaven" (Matt. 26:64). Caiaphas is now dead and, unless he repented with those on the day of Pentecost, is in Hades. Thus we see that even those in Hades will see Him along with those "which pierced him," meaning that all those who lent their assent to the crucifixion of Jesus will face Him again, for He is coming visibly in power and great glory. It could not be said more majestically than the manner in which the Lord Jesus Himself stated it in Matthew 24:30, 31:

> And then shall appear the sign of the Son of man in heaven; and then shall all the tribes of the earth mourn, and they shall see the Son of man coming in the clouds of heaven with power and great glory. And he shall send his angels with a great sound of a trumpet, and they shall gather together his elect from the four winds, from one end of heaven to the other.

It is no wonder that God predicts that "all kindreds of the earth shall wail because of him." The kindreds of the earth wail because they are earthly; that is, they have rejected the Christ and they are eternally lost. If the book of Revelation teaches us nothing else, it teaches that Jesus Christ is coming again to judge this world, and the basis of judgment will be whether or not men have received Him as Savior and Lord.

1

The Christ
of the Churches

Revelation 1:9-20

I, John, who also am your brother, and companion in tribulation,
and in the kingdom and patience of Jesus Christ, was in the isle that is
called Patmos, for the word of God, and for the testimony of Jesus
Christ. I was in the Spirit on the Lord's day, and heard behind me a
great voice, as of a trumpet, saying, I am Alpha and Omega, the first
and the last; and, What thou seest, write in a book, and send it unto
the seven churches which are in Asia: unto Ephesus, and unto Smyrna,
and unto Pergamos, and unto Thyatira, and unto Sardis, and unto
Philadelphia, and unto Laodicea (Rev. 1:9-11).

The Apostle John

The early church was not given to ecclesiasticism! This deadly teaching that has created a division between "clergy" and "laity" has done
much harm to the Church of Christ through the centuries. The Apostle
John was the oldest living apostle of our Lord at the time of this writing.
He was probably esteemed as the most revered saint of his day. Instead
of attracting attention to this, he immediately identified himself with the
people by stating, "I, John, who also am your brother and companion
in tribulation." This tribulation is to be differentiated from the Great
Tribulation that he was to speak of later as coming in the future (chapters 4-18). He was going through tribulation as a member of the early
church that was persecuted so unmercifully by the emperors of Rome,
who had already claimed the lives of Peter and Paul and probably most
of the other apostles.

He further identified himself as their companion "in the kingdom
and patience of Jesus Christ." The "kingdom" here is obviously the
spiritual kingdom which Jesus set up on the day of Pentecost, which is
in operation today and can be entered into only by being born again
(John 3:3). The "patience" of this kingdom is seen in our faithfully
"occupying till he come" at the end of this age.

Imprisoned at Patmos

The Isle of Patmos, located in the Mediterranean Sea just off the mainland of Asia from the city of Miletus, is a tiny island to which John had probably been banished by the Roman government "for the Word of God, and for the testimony of Jesus Christ." It is noteworthy that even at the venerable age of approximately ninety, John refused to compromise his faithful preaching concerning the resurrected, glorified Christ. One cannot resist the temptation of quoting the dying words of another Christian saint, Polycarp, who was burned at the stake, refusing to recant his faith in Jesus Christ and who, just as the torch was applied to the wood stacked at his feet, said, "Eighty and six years have I served Him, and He never did me any wrong. How could I blaspheme my King and my Savior now?" The history of the Christian Church is replete with countless thousands who chose death rather than faithlessness to the Word of God and the testimony of Jesus Christ. Who can say that the church age will not end the same way it began?

"In the Spirit on the Lord's Day"

John's reference to the Lord's day is considered by some to be the first time the term "the Lord's day" was applied to the first day of the week, when the Christians gathered together to worship. It is true that they were freed from the law as a testimony to Israel and that, to express their belief in the resurrection, they did not meet on the Sabbath but on Sunday. Many modern-day Christians do not realize that our Sunday is not a sabbath day, since to the Christian every day is a holy day. In fact, the Bible teaches that we are not to esteem one day above another. We should keep in mind Romans 14 and Colossians 2, which show that we go to the Lord's house on what we call "the Lord's day" as a testimony that we believe Jesus Christ rose bodily from the dead on the first day of the week.

Meaning of "the Lord's Day"

John's use of "the Lord's day" in this connection with being "in the Spirit" probably does not refer to being in the Spirit on the first day of the week. Rather, it is a reference to the fact that by the power of the Holy Spirit John was lifted in prophetic vision beyond the church age to "the day of the Lord." This specifically refers not only to the glorious appearing of Christ to the earth, but also incorporates the many events of the Tribulation Period, including the Rapture of the Church and the seven years of tribulation, and culminating with the glorious appearing of Christ and the establishment of His millennial kingdom.

The Seven Churches

The seven churches of Asia selected by Christ in verse 11 are worthy of close scrutiny. We will treat them individually when we come to

The Seven Churches

chapters 2 and 3, for there is a world of meaning contained in these messages. Opinion is divided as to the extent to which the teachings gained in the study of these messages to the churches can be taken. It is generally agreed, however, that these messages can have four applications.

1. The Seven Churches of John's Day

Obviously, these were literal churches with which John was familiar, for much of his ministry had been conducted throughout that area of Asia. The question that naturally comes to mind is: why of the hundreds of churches located in cities all over the world by this time (about sixty-three years after the day of Pentecost) were these seven churches selected? It is suggested that they also represent the seven basic divisions of church history.

2. The Seven Basic Divisions of Church History

A study of history reveals that the Church has gone through seven basic periods or stages. These will be dealt with in detail in subsequent chapters.

3. The Seven Types of Churches That Exist Today

Although most of these phases of church history are now concluded, nevertheless their influence still carries over from stage to stage, and some trends are still in existence even in our own day.

4. The Seven Characteristics That Can Exist in Any Church or Christian

This suggestion is merely the practical application of the messages to these churches on a personal and individual basis. As we come to them, we can readily see that these seven churches comprise seven methods of attack by Satan upon the Church or individual Christians within the Church, demanding that we take unto ourselves the whole armor of God (Eph. 6:10-18) and "resist the devil."

The Seven Lampstands

"I saw seven golden lampstands." We can be most dogmatic on the meaning of the seven candlesticks here because they are interpreted for us in verse 20, where the Lord Jesus Himself told John that "the seven lampstands which thou sawest are the seven churches." These seven churches were uniquely elected by Christ for the purposes which we have already designated. A lampstand is a fitting symbol for the church. While in this world, Jesus Christ was the light of the world; however, before departing from this earth, He told His disciples, "Ye are the light of the world" (Matt. 5:14). Though we give light, we do not originate light; just as a lampstand does not originate light, but gets its light from the oil or electricity generating through it, so the child of God is a means of light. Christ is the light, but He uses the churches and the children of God in the churches as lampstands to convey this light. We can either yield ourselves unstintingly to Christ and, by letting Christ shine through us, be used to illuminate the darkness that has engulfed humanity, or we can commit the sins of the churches of Asia and dim that light. Christ has ordained the Church to be His torch-bearer in this generation. The only limitation placed on the brilliance of the light is the yieldedness of the lampstand, the Church!

The Vision of the Christ of the Churches

And I turned to see the voice that spoke with me. And being turned, I saw seven golden lampstands. And in the midst of the seven lampstands one like the Son of man, clothed with a garment down to the foot, and girded about the breasts with a golden girdle. His head and his hair were white like wool, as white as snow; and his eyes were like a flame of fire; and his feet like fine bronze, as if they burned in a furnace; and his voice like the sound of many waters. And he had in his right hand seven stars; and out of his mouth went a sharp two-edged sword; and his countenance was as the sun shineth in its strength. And when I saw him, I fell at his feet as dead. And he laid his right hand upon me, saying unto me, Fear not; I am the first and the last; I am he that liveth, and was dead; and, behold, I am alive forevermore, Amen, and have the keys of hades and of death.

Write the things which thou hast seen, and the things which are, and the things which shall be hereafter: The mystery of the seven stars which thou sawest in my right hand, and the seven golden lampstands. The seven stars are the angels of the seven churches; and the seven lampstands which thou sawest are the seven churches (Rev. 1:12-20).

This vision of Christ is graphically descriptive, not only of Christ in His glory, but of His relationship to the churches of His day and churches of all ages.

The Ten Characteristics of Christ Envisioned by John

As John turned to see who it was that spoke to him, he saw seven golden lampstands and a personage in their midst. He lists ten details of that personage that are most descriptive. Notice that only the stars and the lampstands are interpreted for us. Nothing about the person of Christ is interpreted. One might ask, Why is this true? It is because the Holy Spirit has interpreted these details on other occasions in Holy Writ. As we contemplate this fact, we recognize the basic principle of Bible study that we should compare Scripture with Scripture. We shall take each of these characteristics of John's vision and note their meaning from the Scriptures.

1. ". . . one like the Son of man" indicates that this person was not a grotesque creature of the supernatural world; rather He was manlike in His appearance. "The Son of man" is one of the most frequent titles Jesus applied to Himself. It is used of the Messiah in all four gospels and also in Daniel 7:13.

2. ". . . clothed with a garment down to the foot." This was typical of the long robes of the high priests as they ministered in the Holy Place in the Temple.

3. ". . . girded about the breasts with a golden girdle" refers to a symbol of strength and authority common in the ancient world. The average working man wore a short tunic of loose-fitting clothes. Only those in authority wore a girdle.

4. "His head and his hair were white like wool, as white as snow" conveys the thought of antiquity and reminds us of the vision of Daniel 7:9-13, where Christ is called the "ancient of days." The whiteness here, of course, also speaks of the righteousness of God, who is from everlasting to everlasting.

5. ". . . his eyes were like a flame of fire." The Greek construction is literally "His eyes shot fire," indicating that Christ was indignant over something; as we progress with the vision, we find that He was indignant over the indifference, in some cases, of the apostate churches. Whenever the Church of Jesus Christ is not what it should be, we can be sure it arouses the indignation of the Christ.

6. " . . . his feet like fine bronze." The bronze speaks to us of judgment. It reminds us of the brazen altar of the tabernacle, where sin was judged.

7. " . . . his voice like the sound of many waters." This simile can best be illustrated by Niagara Falls. When you come to the edge of the great falls, all other sounds are eliminated from your hearing as you are engulfed by the deafening roar of the turbulent waters. This figure seems

to indicate the attitude of the Son of God as He comes on the Lord's day in judgment. Men cannot hear His voice today, but they will hear it then. The call of worldliness, materialism, science, education, psychology, and all other voices calling to the souls of men seem to take precedence over the voice of Jesus Christ today. In that day all other voices will be stilled by the deafening, overpowering voice of the Son of God, to whom all men will give heed, for they will be entering into their hour of judgment. The church or Christian that so desires can hear His voice today if he will but listen.

8. "And he had in his right hand seven stars." The Lord Himself interpreted to John the meaning of the seven stars. In verse 20 we find that "the seven stars are the angels of the seven churches." The meaning of the Greek word translated "angels" is literally "messengers."

Many godly Bible scholars believe this verse refers, not to supernatural angelic beings, but to the messengers divinely appointed by God to lead local congregations. For example, the spiritual leader or pastor at the church of Ephesus was addressed in Revelation 2:1: "unto the messenger of the church of Ephesus write." Once I heard Dr. J. Vernon McGee, the radio Bible teacher, say regarding this, "I like to think that it refers to the local pastors. It is good to hear a pastor being called an angel; sometimes we are called other things."

Another view is that the messenger is an actual angel, a supernaturally created being especially assigned to that church. This could mean that churches all have a guardian angel, just as Christ indicated that little children have a guardian angel (Matt. 18:10). The main objection to this suggestion is that some of the angels obviously failed in keeping their churches pure. However, in answer to that, even angels, though supernatural, are not divine. Nor can they supersede the will of man, because this is a liberty given by God. If Christ has subjected Himself to the position of being on the outside of the door of the church, knocking for entrance (Rev. 3:20), we can scarcely imagine the angels doing more. If a church has failed in its mission, it is not because its angel has been irresponsible, but because the church has rejected his leading.

Of the two views suggested, I lean to the thought that the meaning here is "angel." With all the enemies armed against the church, both natural and supernatural, I like to think that we have a specially assigned angel working for us. Certainly we need one!

9. " . . . out of his mouth went a sharp two-edged sword." Ephesians 6 refers to the Word of God as "the sword of the Spirit." Hebrews 4:12 tells us that the Word of God is "sharper than any two-edged sword." Evidently the spoken word of Christ will go forth as a sharp sword against which there will be no defense in the day of judgment. Thus we can see that there will really be no battle with the Antichrist, for he will be indefensible against the very presence of Christ at His coming (Rev. 19, 20).

10. " . . . his countenance was as the sun shineth in his strength." This speaks of the divine nature of Christ and reminds us of the event that took place on the Mount of Transfiguration, where Christ "was transfigured before them; and his face did shine like the sun, and his raiment was as white as the light" (Matt. 17:2). For just a moment during His earthly ministry, Peter, James, and John saw Jesus in His divine glory, as John saw Him here in this vision. Let there be no doubt about it: This is Jesus the Christ, the divine Son of God. Amen!

John's Reaction to His Vision of Christ

Although we are the sons of God, "joint heirs with Christ," let it be clearly understood that we will never be divine or "deities." Christ is so exalted beyond us that even in our glorified state we will willingly worship at his feet. This John who prostrated himself at the feet of the resurrected Christ is the same John who was familiar enough with the Lord Jesus to lay his head on His breast in the upper room. Now we find John falling at His feet "as dead," knocked cold by His glory. Anyone truly in touch with the Spirit of God instinctively bows in adoration to Jesus Christ. Any spirit that motivates one in defiance of Christ is not the Holy Spirit.

Four Reasons Why Christians Should Not Fear

Cold, naked fear is gripping the hearts of men everywhere today because of chaotic world conditions. This never should be the case for the child of God! "For God hath not given us the spirit of fear, but of power, and of love, and of a sound mind" (2 Tim. 1:7).

As Jesus laid His right hand upon John and said to him, "Fear not," He was enunciating in the form of His essential deity what He had announced to the disciples on many occasions while in His incarnate state. He often used the terms "fear not," "peace be unto you" and "let not your heart be troubled." These messages not only admonished the disciples of Jesus' day but reflect the attitude of life that should characterize His disciples in every age, for He said, in giving the Great Commission, "And lo, I am with you alway." The greatest cure for man's natural fear is the personal presence of Jesus Christ. Notice Jesus' four reasons why we need not fear:

"I am the first and the last" speaks of Christ's eternity. He is before all things; and after all things are through, He will still be in control.

"I am he that liveth, and was dead" speaks of Christ's sacrificial death for our sins and His resurrection. This phrase attests to the fact that we worship a risen, living Christ.

" . . . I am alive forevermore." The Scripture tells us that Christ died "once for sin." He will not die again. He will not change His state. He will always be! Oh, that men might realize the decision of accepting or rejecting Jesus Christ as an eternal decision; just as He is able to save "forevermore," so He is able to damn forevermore those who reject Him.

" . . . and have the keys of hades and of death." This is a detail that John did not record in his description, but Jesus stated that in His hand He held "the keys of hades and death." These keys were evidently purchased with His own blood, for according to Hebrews 2:14, 15, "through death he [nullified] him that had the power of death and [delivered] them who, through fear of death, were all their lifetime subject to bondage." The Christian need not fear death or hades. The unseen abode of the unbelieving dead currently is hades, often called "hell." After the Great White Throne Judgment of Revelation 20, death and hades will be "cast into the lake of fire. This is the second death." Men outside of Jesus Christ have every reason to fear that event! The child of God, however, should never fear death, hades, or the lake of fire. Why? Because Christ our Savior has the keys of hades and death, and a key is a symbol of release.

Years ago I was taken to see a prisoner by the special representative of the warden's office in the reformatory at St. Cloud, Minnesota. While there, I noted that new inmates obviously feared the institution and the long anticipated confinement; however, I did not fear the institution. Why? Because the representative of the warden's office held the key to the institution for me. In a similar manner, those who know Jesus Christ need never fear hades and death, for He holds the key that unlocks the door to this dreaded place.

The big question is, *do you know Him?* Is He your Savior? Though Jesus Christ died for the sins of the whole world, He has not saved all the people of the world, for He has chosen to leave it up to man's personal will whether or not he will accept or reject Him. When the Philippian jailer asked the Apostle Paul, "What must I do to be saved?" he received the emphatic reply, "Believe on the Lord Jesus Christ and thou shalt be saved." That is, trust on the Lord Jesus Christ. Have you trusted on Him? If not, I urge you to commit your soul, by faith, to Him today by asking Him to come into your heart, cleanse your sin, and save your soul.

2

The Church
of Ephesus

Revelation 2:1-7

The Church of Jesus Christ was founded on the testimony of His personal deity (Matt. 16:18). He said of it, "The gates of hades shall not prevail against it," He could speak prophetically of the future destiny of the Church because He intended to see to it personally that the Church He established would be protected. Nowhere is this seen more clearly than in John's heavenly vision, which we have already examined, portraying Christ walking among the lampstands (the churches), shining forth the light they received from Him to a lost world floundering in darkness.

Chapters 2 and 3 of Revelation give the message of Christ to the seven churches of Asia and go beyond them to the churches which "shall be hereafter." Christ's divine commendation, condemnation, counsel, and challenge are just as vital today as they were in the day they were written.

The Apostolic Church, A.D. 30 - 100

Commendation: "I know thy works, and thy labor, and thy patience, and how thou canst not bear them who are evil; and thou hast tried them who say they are apostles, and are not, and hast found them liars; and hast borne, and hast patience, and for my name's sake hast labored, and hast not fainted . . . Thou hatest the deeds of the Nicolaitans, which I also hate."

Condemnation: "Thou hast left thy first love."

Counsel: "Remember from where thou art fallen, and repent."

Challenge: "To him that overcometh will I give to eat of the tree of life, which is in the midst of the paradise of God."

Ephesus is considered by Bible scholars to have been one of the finest and largest churches of New Testament times. It was begun by the Apostle Paul on his second missionary journey. Located in a wicked city

22

given over to the worship of the goddess Diana, the church exhibited a spiritual vitality that carried over from Paul's habit of going "from house to house warning men with tears." For a good description of the founding of this church, read Acts 18-20. One cannot help being impressed with the deep spirituality of the Ephesian elders who came to Miletus to see Paul before he went to Jerusalem (Acts 20:17-38).

The Ephesian or Apostolic Period

Of the seven churches mentioned in chapters 2 and 3, this is the only one where reference is made to the apostles. This would bear out the thought that the message of Christ to the church at Ephesus was directed not only to one local church, but to the church of the first century, usually called "the early church" or "the apostolic church." This covered the period of time from the day of Pentecost (about A.D. 30) to A.D. 100.

The name Ephesus means "desired one." This was the most desirable of all the churches or church ages. It was characterized by fervent evangelism. One of the main reasons for this was the large percentage of Jewish converts that made up the church. The Church of Jesus Christ owes much to the Jew, through whom we have the Bible and our Savior, Jesus Christ. The success of the early church was due largely to a preponderance of Jewish leadership.

The Early Church Preached the Gospel Around the World

There is strong scriptural indication that the early church preached the gospel around the world. Romans 10:18 tells us, "But I say, Have they not heard? Yes, verily, their sound went into all the earth, and their words unto the ends of the world." Romans 16:26 relates that the gospel is "made known to all nations for the obedience of faith." In Colossians 1:6, speaking of the gospel, the Holy Spirit asserts through the Apostle Paul that it "is come unto you, as it is in all the world." In Colossians 1:23 we find, "If ye continue in the faith grounded and settled, and be not moved away from the hope of the gospel, which ye have heard, and which was preached to every creature that is under heaven, of which I, Paul, am made a minister."

Putting these four passages of Scripture together, we find that before the Scripture canon had been completed, the early church accomplished more widespread preaching of the Gospel through the ministry of the Jewish Christians than has ever been done since the Church has become predominantly led by Gentiles. In fact, even with our modern means of communication and jet travel today, we are not able to equal their evangelistic success. It is interesting to note that apostasy and indifference were characteristics of the Church of Jesus Christ under the administration of Gentiles, whereas evangelism was a characteristic of Jewish leadership. This is highlighted by the prophetic truth, found in Revelation 7, that the only other time the Gospel will be proclaimed around the world will again be under Jewish leadership when the 144,000 Jewish Christian witnesses will go forth, preaching the Gospel to reach "a great multitude which no man could number."

Christ's Commendation

A Working Church

The speaker in this vision, of course, is Christ, described by John as walking in the midst of the seven golden lampstands. This indicates that Christ and His power have always been available to the Church. He is thus fulfilling His words to the apostles in Matthew 28:20, "and, lo, I am with you always, even unto the end of the age."

"I know thy works, and thy labor, and thy patience." Christ commended this early church for its faithful works of Christian service. Service for Jesus Christ is work. It is a joyous labor of love for the child of God who is "abiding in Christ," but it is nonetheless a labor. Christ knows and records all faithful service. He said in Matthew 10:42, "And whosoever shall give to drink unto one of these little ones a cup of cold water only in the name of a disciple, verily I say unto you, he shall in no way lose his reward."

No act of service is too small to escape the Savior's notice. Dr. M. R. DeHaan, the great prophetic Bible teacher, once stated, "To come to Christ costs nothing, to follow Christ costs something, but to serve Christ costs everything." Jesus said, "He that findeth his life shall lose it; and he that loseth his life for my sake shall find it" (Matt. 10:39).

Every Christian should have a thorough understanding of Ephesians 2:8-10. We are all familiar with the principle of salvation by grace through faith as stated in verses 8 and 9; but few understand that after this transaction we go on "unto good works, which God hath before ordained that we should walk in them."

A Separated Church

"I know . . . how thou canst not bear them who are evil." The word for "church" in the Greek is "ecclesia," literally meaning "called-out ones." A true church is a church in the world but not of the world. One of the things that characterized the early church, but not some of the other churches, was the refusal to fraternize with loose Christians. The early church heeded the injunctions of the Holy Spirit to "mark them who cause divisions and offenses contrary to the doctrine which ye have learned; and avoid them" (Rom. 16:17). Church discipline is almost unheard of today. The early church practiced it, and the truly separated church that is filled with the Spirit today will still practice it.

Some years ago, while visiting the church of the Tzeltal Indians of southern Mexico, I saw what it meant for a group of believers to observe church discipline, having only the Bible to instruct them. One man was standing outside, watching while the services were being conducted. We were informed that this was because he had been going with an unsaved woman in the village, which compromised his Christian witness and was considered an offense by that church. They would not permit him to sit inside through the services until he repented. We were also informed that others of that church were not permitted to take communion or give their tithes and offerings if they were not in fellowship with the Lord. What a stir it would create in the modern church if such practices were conducted faithfully; but who can say they should not be?

A Pure Church

"I know . . . thou hast tried them who say they are apostles, and are not, and hast found them liars." Satan sowed tares in the Lord's wheat field immediately after the day of Pentecost. Some of these tares disguised themselves as apostles and went about deceiving some of the early churches in their innocence, for they had no written copy of the Scriptures. Of course, God is faithful, and those churches that truly looked to Him and tried the spirits, "to see if they are of God," were not deceived. The church at Ephesus was one of these and would not be taken in by "false apostles."

The current Church of Jesus Christ needs to heed this message, for there are many false apostles "going about disguised as servants of Jesus Christ" who are really enemies of the cross, seeking their own personal gain. The ecclesiastical sickness of "ecumania" (a one-world church regardless of one's faith), which has caught the fancy of many church leaders, has a deadening effect upon the true Church wherever it is found. We can expect this trend to continue with increasing ferocity until the Lord comes. We have every right today to test men to see if they are of God. If their teachings are not consistent with and faithful to the Word of God, they should be rejected. Because of the devil's use of semantics, we have to examine what men mean by the words they employ, as well as the words themselves.

An Enduring Church

"I know . . . thou hast borne, and hast patience, and for my name's sake hast labored, and hast not fainted." The structure of these words clearly indicates that the church at Ephesus was a consistent church, enduring through its entire history in faithful propagation of the gospel message, not being faint-hearted, but courageously presenting the Gospel of Christ. The entire commendation is a tribute to the faithfulness of this godly church.

An Autonomous Church

"I know . . . thou hatest the deeds of the Nicolaitans, which I also hate." The word "nicolaitans" comes from two Greek words: *niko,* meaning "to conquer, or overthrow," and *laos,* meaning "the people or the laity." It seems that in the early days of the church the followers of

Nicolai held two serious heretical views: they practiced sensuality by completely separating the spiritual and physical natures, thus giving themselves license to sin. And they tried to establish an ecclesiastical order. This latter heresy is known as "Nicolaitanism." Evidently an effort was made to set up bishops, archbishops, cardinals, and popes. This is an unscriptural idea that causes the local church to become enslaved by one man or a small group of men whose spiritual life can determine the spiritual success of the church. This is a most dangerous principle indeed, since every human being is dependent on an abiding relationship with Jesus Christ to maintain spiritual vitality. "Holy men" may cease "abiding" after taking office, to the great detriment of the church. Another evil of this practice is that it causes the local church to look to men for the solution to their problems rather than to the Holy Spirit. The Lord Jesus said that He would send the Holy Spirit and that "He will guide you into all truth."

Nicolaitanism, which is synonymous with modern day ecclesiasticism, is a concept which Jesus Christ said, "I also hate." Would to God that the Church of Jesus Christ could learn the valuable lesson that it is not by ecclesiasticism or organization or promotion or administration, but "by my Spirit saith the Lord." The greatest single curse in modern Christendom is ecclesiasticism. When men get control of the spiritual training of other people and are in a position to dominate the church, their theological position will eventually dominate that church. The history of the Church of Jesus Christ is a continuous cycle of autonomous churches amalgamating into great conventions or denominations of ecclesiastical hierarchies that eventually become apostate. This in turn caused a breaking away on the part of the minority group that sought to be faithful to the Scripture and to be autonomous, depending only on the Holy Spirit. Evidently the church at Ephesus and the early apostolic church were successful in withstanding the work of the Nicolaitans, which was accepted later by the church of Pergamum (Rev. 2:15).

Christ's Condemnation

"Nevertheless, I have somewhat against thee, because thou hast left thy first love." There was only one condemnation against this early church — but a serious one indeed. Although basically faithful, it had unconsciously succumbed to the natural tendency of letting even the most wonderful experience become commonplace. The generation of the apostles had passed from the scene, and their children had taken their places by the time this message was given. Although the Ephesians loved the Lord, they had lost the spontaneous sparkle of their love for Him. This has been illustrated many times in human experience by marriages which fall onto dangerous ground when the husband and wife begin taking each other for granted. Honeymoon love erodes and becomes just routine married life. As devastating as this is in marriage, it is many times worse in the relationship of an individual or a church with Christ.

The thrilling flush of new-found conversion and experience with Jesus Christ must be guarded by submission to the Holy Spirit all during one's Christian experience. Most Christians' lives consist of a "first love experience" that develops into a routine walk of having "left thy first love." During this latter period they take for granted "the marvelous grace of God" and the thrilling "new creation in Christ Jesus," which has resulted from their salvation. Many later come to heed the words in this message and return to a day-by-day intimate fellowship with and love for the Lord Jesus Christ. This is essential in experiencing the abundant Christian life.

The Counsel of Christ

The Christ of the churches counseled the church of Ephesus to do three things.

Remember Therefore From Where Thou Art Fallen

Christ sternly admonished them to recall their faithfulness of earlier years and to take inventory of their spiritual life. This is also a need of the twentieth-century church.

Repent

They were to turn back from their coldness and indifference to a vital relationship with Christ.

Do the First Works

This completes Christ's counsel and stands as a test of their love. The Lord Jesus said, "By their fruits ye shall know them"; so it is today that by a church's or an individual's "works" He shall know them. Those that truly love Jesus Christ with all their heart obey Him. The Savior Himself said, "If ye love me, keep my commandments." The child of God who excuses his indulgence and lack of consecration only proves by his conduct that he does not love the Lord Jesus Christ with all his heart, and all his soul, and with all his mind. The Christian who is unwilling to yield all his talents and capabilities to Jesus Christ has a love problem; that is, he does not sufficiently love Christ. It is safe to conclude that if our love for Christ Jesus is what it should be, no task is too great, no sacrifice too much for Him.

The Challenge of Christ

The challenge of Christ to the church of Ephesus falls into two main divisions: "Hear what the Spirit saith" and "To him that overcometh . . ."

Hear What the Spirit Saith

"He that hath an ear, let him hear what the Spirit saith unto the churches." This was an expression of the Lord Jesus Christ which appears in many of His parables (e.g., Matt. 13). The statement implies three kinds of individuals:

1. Those without ears. This, of course, could not refer to physical ears, for everyone is equipped with them. He is obviously referring to those who are not attuned to the Holy Spirit by the new birth — that is, those who have not been born again and thus are not anointed with the Holy Spirit. Consequently, they cannot hear the voice of God when He speaks.

2. Those who are dull of hearing. Not all born-again Christians are willing to hear the Spirit of God when He speaks. The Holy Spirit upbraided the Hebrew Christians for being "dull of hearing" (Heb. 5:11). This is in reference to those Christians who are in rebellion against the Spirit of God and His mastery of their lives — a most dangerous condition in which to live.

3. Those spiritually minded Christians who are willing to hear what the Spirit saith unto the churches. The test of this hearer is seen in his conduct, for the Scripture teaches that we should be "doers of the word and not hearers only."

Eternal Life for Overcomers

"To him that overcometh will I give to eat the tree of life, which is in the midst of the paradise of God." The Tree of Life, of which overcomers are given the opportunity to eat, is unquestionably the tree from which Adam and Eve were forbidden to eat after their sin. A symbol of eternal life, it is pictured as having a prominent place in the paradise of God that awaits those who put their trust in Him (Rev. 22:2).

The tree of eternal life will be eaten only by "overcomers." Who is an overcomer? 1 John 5:4, 5 gives us the answer. "For whatever is born of God overcometh the world; and this is the victory that overcometh the world, even our faith. Who is he that overcometh the world, but he that believeth that Jesus is the Son of God?"

Overcoming the world is the experience that takes place in the life of the individual who puts his faith in Jesus Christ. There is no other way by which a man or woman can become an overcomer.

3

The Church
of Smyrna

Revelation 2:8-11

The church in Smyrna was a much-persecuted church in a wealthy city that had little time for Christians. The city itself, founded about three centuries before Christ, was a well-planned accomplishment of Alexander the Great. The commercial center of Asia Minor, it was on the direct trade route from India and Persia to Rome. The large variety of coins found by archeologists in the city clearly indicates that it was a wealthy city. The Jewish segment of the population seems to have been most irreligious and neglectful of spiritual things. Few specific details are known of the history of the Smyrna church other than that which is given here in the book of Revelation. It can be safely deduced, however, that it was a most faithful church in the face of persecution. From the account here in Scripture, the known characteristics of the conditions in the church at Smyrna indicate that the judgment seat of Christ will reveal this church to be one of the most outstanding local bodies of believers in all of church history.

The Persecuted Church, A.D. 100 - 312

Commendation: "I know thy works and tribulation, and poverty (but thou art rich)."

Condemnation: Not one word!

Counsel: "Fear none of those things which thou shalt suffer . . . Be thou faithful unto death."

Challenge: "He that overcometh shall not be hurt of the second death."

The Smyrna period of church history was probably the greatest time of persecution the Church of Christ has ever known. Satan unleashed a violent attack on the church in an effort to obliterate it, for it became evident to him that the apostolic church, because of its faithful preaching

29

of the Gospel, had become a serious threat to his worldwide godless empire. That he was unsuccessful in this attempt is easily seen in a study of church history, for God overruled and Satan learned a valuable lesson. The more he persecuted the church during this period, the more the church overcame the one condemning characteristic of the apostolic age, that of having left its first love. Not one word of condemnation was hurled by Christ at this church. From this Satan learned a great secret: persecution will not stamp out the Church of Christ! Consequently, the age ended with the easing of persecution; then Satan used what turned out to be one of his most effective weapons to weaken the Church, that of indulgence or endorsement.

Some Persecutions of This Age

As predicted by the Lord Himself in verse 10, "Ye shall have tribulation ten days." This church age saw eight of the ten periods of persecution under Roman emperors.

Nero	A.D. 54 - 68	Paul beheaded and Peter crucified
Domitian	A.D. 81 - 96	John exiled
Trajan	A.D. 98 - 117	Ignatius burned at the stake
Marcus Aurelius	A.D. 161 - 180	Justin Martyr killed
Severus	A.D. 193 - 211	
Maximinius	A.D. 235 - 238	
Decius	A.D. 249 - 251	
Valerian	A.D. 253 - 260	
Aurelian	A.D. 270 - 275	
Diocletian	A.D. 284 - 305 [1]	

Diocletian is considered the worst emperor in Rome's history and the greatest antagonist of the Christian faith. He led a violent attempt to destroy the Bible from the face of the earth. Under his leadership many Roman cities had public burnings of the sacred Scriptures.

During the second and third centuries this persecution age saw hundreds of Christians brought into the amphitheaters of Rome to be fed to hungry lions while thousands of spectators cheered. Many were crucified; others were covered with animal skins and tortured to death by wild dogs. They were covered with tar and set on fire to serve as torches. They were boiled in oil and burned at the stake, as was Polycarp in the city of Smyrna itself in A.D. 156. One church historian has estimated that during this period, five million Christians were martyred for the testimony of Jesus Christ.

A Thriving Church

Evidence of the supernatural nature of the Church can be seen in the fact that the Church reached its greatest numbers in proportion to world population during this period of persecution. In addition to the establishment of churches in many parts of the world, this church age distinguished itself by its production of many hand-copied manuscripts of the sacred Scriptures and the translation of Scripture into many languages. Early in this period, the Bible was translated into Syriac and what is known as the Peshito manuscripts, which became the official scriptures of the Eastern churches and from which translations were made into Arabic, Persian, and Armenian. In the second century the Bible was translated into Latin in what is called the Old Latin Version. This became the Bible of the Western churches for more than a thousand years and has been translated into many different languages. The more the Scripture was disseminated and used by the people, even in the face of persecution, the more the Church advanced in numbers until it was such a dominant factor in the Roman Empire that Christianity was established as the state church by Emperor Constantine in A.D. 312. However, the cessation of persecution turned out to be a master stroke of Satan and a great tragedy to the Church. This will be borne out in Christ's next message to the church of Pergamum, which was assimilated by paganism, lost its fire, and received serious condemnation from our Lord.

The Message of Christ to Smyrna

"These things saith the first and the last, who was dead, and is alive." It is interesting to note that Christ introduced each message to the churches by reaching back to the vision of Himself in chapter 1 and picking out one of the characteristics of His nature. To Ephesus He referred to Himself as the one who "holdeth the seven stars in his right hand, who walketh in the midst of the seven golden candlesticks," emphasizing that He faithfully provides for the churches. To Smyrna He emphasized His eternal nature — "the first and the last"; His death for their sins — "who was dead"; and His resurrection — "and is alive."

Again we see the unique characteristic of Christianity in that we do not worship a dead man, as do the Mohammedans, the Buddhists, or the Confucianists, but a Christ who is alive. Because of this, He is able to work on behalf of His children in any age.

The Commendation of Christ

The message to the church of Smyrna is the shortest of all Christ's messages. However, one of the greatest commendations to this church is the fact that He does not condemn it. Christ's commendation highlights three characteristics of the church: tribulation, poverty, and affliction.

A Persecuted Church

"I know thy works, and tribulation." This was a severely persecuted church. Since the word "works" of verse 9 does not appear in the best manuscripts, the emphasis is placed here not on the faithful works of the church, which no doubt were many, but upon the fact that they had undergone much persecution.

A Poor Church

"I know thy . . . poverty (but thou art rich)." They were poor and yet rich. In addition to the physical persecution, it would seem that the church of Smyrna went through a severe period of financial persecution. Smyrna was not only a trade city but also a city of guilds which closely regulated the craftsmen of the day much as unions do today. Because of the intense hatred for Christians, when a man took a stand for Jesus Christ, his shop was boycotted or his employment was severed or some other means was used to limit his economic opportunity. Those Christians who were rich in this world's goods went bankrupt. Consequently, the church enjoyed few monetary assets. This was true not only of the church of Smyrna, but also of the second and third century churches.

Someone has said that the churches of the first three centuries were marked by material poverty and spiritual power, whereas the churches of our day are marked by material wealth and spiritual weakness. Sad to say, this seems to be true. Today Christians are cursed with material things that are not conducive to their spiritual development. Christians living under economic impoverishment should praise God that during such a time He will prove Himself faithful and, if they let Him, will bring them much spiritual blessing.

". . . but thou art rich." This highlights a divine principle that, regardless of one's economic state, knowing Jesus Christ brings wealth in this life and in the life to come! Many who are as poor as the proverbial "church mouse" are rich in this life in the things that money cannot buy: joy, peace, happiness, contentment, and eternal accomplishment.

This unseen wealth available to the child of God is seen in the statement of the Apostle Paul in 2 Corinthians 6:10, "As sorrowful, yet always rejoicing; as poor, yet making many rich; as having nothing, and yet possessing all things."

The Apostle Paul had not one thing in this world materially, but he was able to impart riches and said of himself, "yet possessing all things." Only the Christian is truly rich in those things that are important. Oh, that God's people in this twentieth century could realize the principle our Savior is here setting forth to the church of Smyrna. Riches can never be provided by this world! Our oneness with Jesus Christ determines the realization of our wealth in this world. The closer we are to Jesus Christ today, the richer we are. The further we are from Him, notwithstanding the balance of our bank account, the poorer we are. Christian, on this basis, how much are you worth?

An Afflicted Church

"I know the blasphemy of them who say they are Jews, and are not, but are the synagogue of Satan." They were an afflicted church, afflicted by false teachers who had claimed to be Jews but really were not. The New Testament definition of a Jew is one who is circumcised "of the heart, in the spirit and not in the letter" (Rom. 2:29). It is never sufficient to obey the teachings of the Word legalistically. Submission of the heart to God, not adherence to a prescribed set of rules, is His desire for men.

The Synagogue of Satan

Satan has his own religious faith. He also has his churches, called "synagogues of Satan." Any church that preaches a gospel other than the Gospel of Jesus Christ is a synagogue of Satan, regardless of what it is called. Many so-called "Christian" churches today are like the Jews at Smyrna — they are not Christians at all and are condemned by the Savior Himself because they preach a message other than the one laid down in the Word of God. In reality, they are the synagogue of Satan, not the Church of Jesus Christ.

Two Basic Heresies

The two basic heresies that emanate from the synagogue of Satan in the name of Christianity were apparent before the end of the second century. In fact, they existed at the time Christ gave His message to the churches of Ephesus and Smyrna. These heresies are first, a false doctrine of Christ, and second, mixing law and grace. The latter was the work of the Judaizers condemned by the Savior in verse 10.

Practically every false religious system and cult coming out of Christianity can be traced to one of these two heresies. Either they are confused about the personal deity of our blessed Lord, suggesting that though He was a good man, He was not the virgin-born Son of God who lived a sinless life, died a sacrificial death, rose bodily from the grave, ascended physically into heaven, and promised to return physically to this earth some day. Or they add to salvation "by grace through faith," saying that in addition to believing on Jesus, we should also keep the Sabbath, observe certain rites and ceremonies, eat or not eat certain kinds of meat, etc. The church of the first three centuries in large measure successfully withstood these two insidious teachings that are deceiving many people today in one cult or another.

The Counsel of Christ

The Christ of the churches counseled the church of Smyrna and the Smyrna age of the Church to two things — "fear nothing" and "be faithful unto death."

"Fear none of those things which thou shalt suffer." The Lord Jesus predicted the suffering that would come to this church, telling them, "the devil shall cast some of you into prison, that ye may be tried, and ye shall have tribulation ten days." These ten days are considered by many Bible teachers to be the ten periods of persecution referred to previously. Some Bible teachers suggest it refers to the last ten years of the age, A.D. 303-312, during which the Church suffered intense persecution under Diocletian.

The counsel of our Lord to this dear church was the same advice He gives the believers of every age when they fall into tribulation: "Fear not." The man that has Jesus Christ has enough, regardless of the intensity of his persecution! When grace is needed, grace is supplied; when courage is needed, courage is supplied; for we have the divine promise that our God is able to "supply all your need according to his riches in glory by Christ Jesus" (Phil. 4:19).

"Be thou faithful unto death, and I will give thee a crown of life." Future riches are involved in this promise of our Lord. We shall "reign with Him a thousand years" in direct proportion to our faithfulness in Christian service. The Lord Jesus said, "Lay up for yourselves treasures in heaven." Only Christians are permitted to "lay up" for eternity. A popular saying states, "You can't take it with you!" That is not entirely true for the Christian, because through the economy of God the Christian can send his riches ahead of him by laying up "treasures in heaven." In this connection, it would be good to study the judgment of the believer's works as described in 2 Corinthians 3:9-20 and our Lord's parable of the pounds in Luke 19:11-27.

The Challenge of Christ

Again, the challenge of Christ comes to those who have spiritual ears to "hear what the Spirit saith to the churches," and it is a challenge to overcome. As we have already seen, this is dependent upon one's personal faith in Jesus Christ.

"He that overcometh shall not be hurt of the second death." We have already seen in the vision of the Christ of the churches in Revelation 1:18 that Christ holds in His hand the keys of hell and death. The child of God has Christ's personal promise that he will never be hurt by the second death, which is described in Revelation 20 as the time when hades (the present abode of the unbelieving dead) and death are cast into the lake of fire. "This is the second death" (Rev. 20:14).

One must understand what the Bible means by death. It is the Bible's term for the complete ruin of a man in God's plan for his life, which is eternal. Death occurs when man is forever separated from God instead of united with God as was His intention. The second death is that state when men who have died in unbelief are resurrected and cast alive into an eternal state of separation from God in the place called the lake of fire (Rev. 20:15). This second death need never cause the child of God to fear, for it will have no power over him.

4

The Church
of Pergamum

Revelation 2:12-17

Pergamum was the capital city of Asia until the close of the first century. It was a city given over to the worship of many Greek idols. Local Roman rulership, unable to cope with the multitude of religious differences in the city, demanded the cooperation of all groups. Two of the most prominent religious systems of the city were the worship of Bacchus (the god of revelry) and the worship of Asclepius (the god of healing).

Verse 13 twice refers to the city as the place where "Satan's throne is" or "where Satan dwelleth." A detailed commentary on this condition could scarcely be given with accuracy, for we do not have access to the historical details. However, we can say that the following conjecture to a large degree is representative of the truth. Satan has a kingdom; Babylon has from earliest times been considered the capital of this kingdom. Idolatry gained its start in Babylon through Nimrod and his mother, inspired by Satan. As long as Babylon was a dominant world power, it made an excellent headquarters for Satan's attack on men. However, when Babylon's glory began to decline and it was left desolate, Satan looked for another location. He selected Pergamum because of its strong idolatrous religions. Missionaries have been in areas so pagan in their religions that it seemed as though the very atmosphere was charged with the presence of Satan. No doubt these were the conditions under which the little church of Pergamum was faithfully preaching the gospel of Jesus Christ.

The Indulged Church, A.D. 312 - 606

Commendation: "I know thy works, and where thou dwellest, even where Satan's throne is; and thou holdest fast my name, and hast not denied my faith, even in those days in which Antipas was my faithful martyr, who was slain among you, where Satan dwelleth."

Condemnation: "But I have a few things against thee, because thou hast there them that hold the doctrine of Balaam, who taught Balak to cast a stumbling block before the children of Israel, to eat things sacrificed unto idols, and to commit fornication. So hast thou also them that hold the doctrine of the Nicolaitans, which thing I hate."

Counsel: "Repent; or else I will come unto thee quickly, and will fight against them with the sword of my mouth."

Challenge: "To him that overcometh will I give to eat of the hidden manna, and will give him a white stone, and in the stone a new name written, which no man knoweth except he that receiveth it."

The Indulged Church Age

Satan learned from his attack on the church of Smyrna that persecution only caused the church to flourish and continue in a perpetual state of revival. After Diocletian's unsuccessful attack on the church, Constantine succeeded him as emperor of Rome. Constantine's ascendancy to the throne was not without controversy, and it had far-reaching effects on the Christian Church of the fourth, fifth, and sixth centuries.

Roman history tells us that Constantine contended for the throne with Maxentius after the death of Galerius. Both Roman history and church tradition indicate that Constantine, already attracted by Christianity, allegedly saw a vision of a fiery cross in the sky and heard a voice saying, "In this sign conquer."

Constantine believed this vision was a message from God that if he would embrace the Christian religion, he would be able to conquer his enemies. He accepted the Christian faith and declared himself to be its defender and protector. There are some who accept this as a bona fide conversion on the part of Constantine; however, a careful examination of his life indicates that either he had a poor concept of Christianity or he had never been truly born again by the Spirit of God. One commendable thing he did was to order Eusebius, bishop of Rome, to supervise the production of fifty copies of the Holy Scriptures to be used by the churches. Some of these manuscripts comprise our oldest existing copies of God's Word.

When Constantine became emperor of Rome, he became the virtual emperor of the Western world. As the self-styled "protector of the Christian faith," he issued an edict of toleration for Christianity and showered many favors on the Christian Church. The government provided money for the operation of the church, and many of the pagan temples were taken over by Christians. To please the emperor, these leaders adopted customs that were parallel to pagan practices. One compromise invariably leads to another, and what seemed at the start to be a great blessing ended up a great curse. During the succeeding three centuries of this period, many anti-Christian practices of pagan origin were adopted, which robbed the church of its fire and its evangelistic fervor.

Pagan Practices Introduced Into the Church

The influence of paganism on the Church increased over the years step by step. The Church began to shroud itself in "mystery" and ritualism that had a strong resemblance to Babylonian mysticism. The Chaldean tau, which was the elevation of a large "T" on the end of a pole, was changed to the sign of a cross. The rosary of pagan origin was introduced. Celibacy of priests and nuns, which has no scriptural verification, but finds a counterpart in the vestal virgins of paganism, was conceived. The following is a partial list of unscriptural changes introduced during this age. Gradually these changes became more prominent than the original teachings of Christianity.

A.D. 300 - Prayers for the dead
A.D. 300 - Making sign of the cross
A.D. 375 - Worship of saints and angels
A.D. 394 - Mass first instituted
A.D. 431 - Worship of Mary begun
A.D. 500 - Priests began dressing differently than laymen
A.D. 526 - Extreme unction
A.D. 593 - Doctrine of purgatory introduced
A.D. 600 - Worship services conducted in Latin
A.D. 600 - Prayers directed to Mary[2]

From A.D. 312 on, the Church became more Roman and less Christian in its practices. The Roman Catholic church of today is hard put to trace its ancestry beyond A.D. 312. Until that time the Church was an independent collection of local churches, working together whenever possible but not dominated by central authority. The name Pergamum literally means "marriage" or "elevation." As the Church became married to governmental authority and elevated to a place of acceptance, it declined in spiritual blessing and power.

Postmillennialism Introduced

The blessed doctrine of the imminent return of Christ, espoused by the Church of the first three centuries, producing an evangelistic, consecrated, fervent Church, began to change when Christianity was made the state religion. As the Church became rich and powerful, it was suggested that the world was getting better and better, that Christ's kingdom was already ushered in, and that He would come at the *end* of the thousand-years reign. This demanded a reinterpretation of the status of Israel, which was accomplished by suggesting that Israel had been "cast off forever" and the promises of Israel now applied to the

Church. Not until fourteen hundred years later was the coming of Jesus Christ reemphasized, and with it came a return to evangelistic fervor. Whenever a local church or denomination has maintained a strong emphasis on the second coming of our blessed Lord, it has been an evangelistic, missionary-sending station. Where this doctrine has been neglected, the church has become cold, indifferent, and worldly.

The Nature of Christ Revealed to Pergamum

"These things saith he who hath the sharp sword with two edges." We have previously seen that Christ selected one of the aspects of His nature as revealed to John in his vision and presented it to each individual church. To Pergamum He revealed the "sharp, two-edged sword," which, without question, refers to the Word of God. The cure for the problems of the local church at Pergamum, of the Pergamum age of the Church, or of any church is the Word of God. Christ used the Word of God to sanctify His Church (John 17:17); to clean it (John 15:3); to bring it joy (John 15:11); and to bring it peace (John 16:33). Had the church of Pergamum and the Pergamum age heeded the Word of God, the evils of the Dark Ages could well have been avoided.

Christ's Commendation to Pergamum

The commendation of our Lord to Pergamum, as recorded in verse 13, falls into three basic categories.

1. "I know thy works, and where thou dwellest, even where Satan's throne is." We have already seen the evil nature of this city where Satan made his headquarters. This headquarter was moved to Rome near the close of the first century. From there Satan directed the affairs of his worldwide kingdom, perverting the souls of men. Through the Roman emperors, as we have already seen, Satan had learned during the first three centuries that attacking Christians would never conquer them; thus, he changed his approach during the Pergamum period to one of indulgence and "elevation."

2. "Thou holdest fast my name." Criticism cannot be hurled against the doctrine of this church or church age, for they were doctrinally pure. But they sinned by taking in the ceremonies of paganism, which later were supported by artificial doctrines of an unscriptural nature that went on to pollute the true doctrines of the Church. The truth of the matter is that many outstanding leaders were produced during this Pergamum age . It was during this time that the Arian controversy was fought at the Council of Nicea in A.D. 325. Arius and his followers denied the personal deity of our Savior. Actually, their concept of Christ was much like that of modern-day Jehovah's Witnesses: Christ was the greatest of all created beings, but not one with the Father. At this council, presided over by Constantine himself, the question inspired heated debates. It must have seemed strange indeed for a governmental leader to preside

over a Christian assembly while at the same time bearing the title of previous emperors, namely, high priest of the heathen religions. Dr. H. A. Ironside, in his book *Lectures on the Book of Revelation,* tells this story. During the council, feelings ran so high that Constantine had to intervene on several occasions. At one point, the brilliant Arius seemed almost to have stopped all opposition

> when a hermit from the deserts of Africa sprang to his feet, clad chiefly in tiger's skin. This latter he tore from his back, disclosing great scars (the result of having been thrown into the arena among the wild beasts). With his back dreadfully disfigured by animal claws exposed to their view, he dramatically cried, "These are the brand marks of the Lord Jesus Christ, and I cannot hear this blasphemy." Then he proceeded to give so stirring an address, setting forth clearly the truth as to Christ's eternal deity, that the majority of the council realized in a moment that it was indeed the voice of the Holy Spirit.

Dr. Ironside continues,

> Whether this story be actually true or not, I cannot say; but it well sets forth the spirit pervading many who participated in the council, most of whom had passed through the terrible persecution of Diocletian. The final outcome of the Council of Nicea was that Jesus Christ was declared to be "very God of very God," "perfection of perfection," and "God and man in one person."[3]

Because this church held fast to Christ's name, the organized church did not teach anything but the personal deity of Jesus Christ for over a thousand years. Not until rationalism came in and produced nineteenth and twentieth century modernism could the Church be found guilty of a false doctrine regarding our Lord. The devil did succeed in subverting this teaching by making it merely a dogmatic doctrine rather than a vital relationship with a person. However, most so-called Christian churches today at least pay lip service to the deity of Christ.

3. ". . . and hast not denied my faith." Much of this has already been covered, related to the doctrinal purity of this church and church age. The Antipas referred to in verse 13 is unknown by Bible scholars. It is suggested that he was a local Christian in the city of Pergamum who had, like many during the first century, sealed the testimony of his faith with his own blood.

Condemnation

The condemnation of Christ given to the church of Pergamum reveals that, although their theological doctrine was correct, their practical doctrines were radically evil. These false doctrines fell into two main categories.

> But I have a few things against thee, because thou hast there them that hold the doctrine of Balaam, who taught Balak to cast a stumbling block before the children of Israel, to eat things sacrificed unto idols, and to commit fornication (Rev. 2:14).

1. The Doctrine of Balaam

To properly evaluate this doctrine, one should be familiar with the book of Numbers, chapters 22-31. In short, Balaam tried for filthy lucre's sake to prophesy a curse against Israel. Balak, the king of Moab, was afraid of the children of Israel as they were coming through his land. He hired Balaam to use his gift of prophecy against Israel, and Balaam sought every means at his disposal to do so. However, he encountered a major problem: God was with Israel! Every time Balaam opened his mouth to curse them, out came a blessing. Finally, in desperation, he gave the Israelites the suggestion of making an unholy alliance with the Moabites; thus we find fulfilled what is referred to in Revelation 2:14: ". . . Balaam, who taught Balak to cast a stumbling block before the children of Israel, to eat things sacrificed unto idols, and to commit fornication." At Balaam's suggestion, the Israelites intermarried with the Moabites, contrary to the will of God. Thus the people were polluted socially and spiritually.

This was typical of the church of Pergamum in that, although they were faithful to Christ's name and held the faith regarding theological doctrine, they did not remain separated from the world, but amalgamated with paganism. As we have already seen, paganism soon predominated, as it always does!

The only time a Christian has the unlimited power of the Holy Spirit at his disposal is when he is obedient to the will of God. When he disobeys God and makes alliances with the world, he is entering into a powerless state that will enmesh and ruin him. An illustration of this homogenized state that crept into the Church, here called the doctrine of Balaam, is seen in a coin that today resides in the British Museum in London, stamped during the days of Constantine. On one side are Christian emblems, on the other side emblems of heathen gods. Some early tradition suggests that when large heathen basilicas were given to the Christian Church for meeting places to satisfy the emperor, the pagan names where chiseled off idols and the names of Christian saints were inscribed; they were then used as statues. Whether or not this is true, the church that traces its origin back to Rome today bears evidence that somewhere in its history the idolatry of paganism crept in.

2. The Doctrine of the Nicolaitans

"So hast thou also them that hold the doctrine of the Nicolaitans, which thing I hate." The doctrine of the Nicolaitans has already been examined under the church of Ephesus, though the Ephesian church and the apostolic age rejected this heresy. It was, however, accepted by the church of Pergamum and the indulged or Pergamum Age. Nicolaitanism is the doctrine of a strong ecclesiastical hierarchy ruling over the laity; this has never been conducive to a strong spiritual condition in the church. Laymen were given no voice in church affairs, but were required to obey blindly the decrees of the clergy. The clergy then gradually seemed to gravitate to an impractical ivory tower type of existence that separated them more and more from the people. Whenever a minister loses contact with people, he ceases to be an effective tool in the hand of God.

In this modern age, the work of church administration and Christian promotion often demands so much of a pastor's time and effort that he does not devote the proper amount of time to meeting the unsaved man face to face. Although a faithful minister should "search the scriptures" so he can "preach the word of God," his work must always be flavored by Paul's admonition to Timothy to "do the work of an evangelist." This spirit of evangelism is most effective when the minister has been faithfully dealing personally with unsaved men. Some of the greatest Bible sermons ever preached have been occasioned by the inspiration of the Holy Spirit given to a man of God as he dealt with an unsaved soul.

The Lord Jesus gave His opinion of hierarchical systems of church government when He referred to the doctrine of the Nicolaitans as "which thing I hate." This teaching has ruined more churches and denominations than any other.

Counsel

The counsel of Christ to the church of Pergamum is a simple statement of a basic principle of God which, reduced to the barest minimum, states: repent or be judged by the Word of God. This principle, which has never been changed, applies to both individuals and churches. Unless we are willing to repent of our sins or our violations of the stated Word of God and return in obedience to the Word, we will be judged by the Word, "the two-edged sword." Be sure of this — if there is a principle in the Word of God to which you have refused to submit yourself in this life, you will face that principle when you stand before the Lord Jesus at His coming. It is better to heed the Word of God in 1 Corinthians 11:31, "For if we would judge ourselves, we should not be judged," thus guaranteeing that we will hear the Master's "well done thou good and faithful servant" instead of His condemnation.

Christ's Challenge to the Church of Pergamum

Our Lord's challenge to the church of Pergamum is directed to overcomers (1 John 5:4) and is divided into two beautiful symbols loaded with meaning — "hidden manna" and "a white stone."

The Hidden Manna

The hidden manna is a symbol that is readily understood by the Bible student. Manna was the heavenly food sent by God to the children of Israel in the wilderness. It typifies the spiritual food provided by God in His Word. It should be clearly understood that this is an individual feeding, not a church function. Just as the children of Israel had to individually go and gather the manna in the wilderness, so the child of God in the Pergamum church age or in any church age is dependent on God for his individual spiritual supply. No matter what life's dilemma, if God's children will only look to Him, their needs will be supplied: "But my God shall supply all your need according to his riches in glory by Christ Jesus" (Phil. 4:19).

The White Stone

The symbolic meaning of the white stone is not as easy to determine as the hidden manna. Bible commentators are not agreed on this subject, though there is a basic tone of agreement — that of assurance. White in the Bible refers to the righteousness of God. In this connection I like to think of an ancient custom as being the key that unlocks the meaning of this stone. It seems that in ancient times a white stone meant acquittal. For example, if a man had been tried by a court, the jurors published their vote on his case by laying down a white stone, signifying that they acquitted him of the crime. This would certainly be in accord with many other passages of Scripture which indicate that Christ has given an acquittal to the child of God who has called upon Him for forgiveness and salvation. He is, according to Romans 5:1, "justified by faith." The big difference, of course, is that we are guilty. Nevertheless, because Christ died guiltless, we receive the white stone of acquittal with a name for Christ upon it that is yet unknown to men. The white stone, then, stands as a beautiful symbol of the eternal acquittal we gain through faith in the Lord Jesus Christ.

5
The Church
of Thyatira

Revelation 2:18-29

The city of Thyatira was probably founded by Alexander some three-hundred years before Christ. It was a wealthy city in Macedonia, noted in the ancient world for its outstanding color dyes.

It has been suggested that the city was evangelized by the Ephesian church or perhaps by Paul's first convert in Philippi, Lydia (Acts 16:14). The main characteristic of this church seemed to be its "works" toward men rather than doctrinal belief. In fact, as we shall see, it was indicted for permitting a false teacher to spread her soul-damning heresy.

The Pagan Church, 606 to the Tribulation
(The Dark Ages)

Commendation: "I know thy works, and love, and service, and faith, and thy patience, and thy works, and the last to be more than the first."

Condemnation: "Thou allowest that woman, Jezebel, who calleth herself a prophetess, to teach and seduce my servants to commit fornication, and to eat things sacrificed unto idols."

Counsel: "That which ye have already, hold fast till I come."

Challenge: "And he that overcometh, and keepeth my works unto the end, to him will I give power over the nations; and he shall rule them with a rod of iron; as the vessels of a potter shall they be broken to shivers, even as I received of my Father. And I will give him the morning star."

The Church of the Dark Ages

The church age of Thyatira produced what is known in history as the Dark Ages. "Dark" indicates that the program of merging paganism with Christianity, begun under the church of Pergamum, increasingly emphasized paganism, which is darkness. The light which Jesus Christ entrusted to His Church all but flickered out during the Dark Ages and was not rekindled until the days of the Reformation.

Continuing where the church of Pergamum left off (see p. 37), the following changes and doctrines that have their source in paganism were added to the Church during this period.

A.D. 607 - Boniface III made first Pope
A.D. 709 - Kissing the Pope's foot
A.D. 786 - Worshiping of images and relics
A.D. 850 - Use of "holy water" begun
A.D. 995 - Canonization of dead saints
A.D. 998 - Fasting on Fridays and during Lent
A.D. 1079 - Celibacy of the priesthood
A.D. 1090 - Prayer beads
A.D. 1184 - The Inquisition
A.D. 1190 - Sale of Indulgences
A.D. 1215 - Transubstantiation
A.D. 1220 - Adoration of the wafer (Host)
A.D. 1229 - Bible forbidden to laymen
A.D. 1414 - Cup forbidden to people at communion
A.D. 1439 - Doctrine of purgatory decreed
A.D. 1439 - Doctrine of seven sacraments affirmed
A.D. 1508 - The Ave Maria approved
A.D. 1534 - Jesuit order founded
A.D. 1545 - Tradition granted equal authority with Bible
A.D. 1546 - Apocryphal books put into Bible
A.D. 1854 - Immaculate conception of Mary
A.D. 1864 - Syllabus of Errors proclaimed
A.D. 1870 - Infallibility of Pope declared
A.D. 1930 - Public schools condemned
A.D. 1950 - Assumption of the Virgin Mary
A.D. 1965 - Mary proclaimed Mother of the Church[4]

Since the above changes and additions have been made, as substantiated by history, it seems quite ironic that the church of Rome today likes to boast that "Rome is always the same." The ironic tragedy is that, in spite of the above historical facts, many Americans believe this assertion.

"Continual Sacrifice" — Rome's Greatest Heresy

"Thyatira" comes from two words meaning "sacrifice" and "continual"; this introduces the central heresy that has produced other false doctrines. That is, the church of Rome denies the finished work of Christ but believes in a continuing sacrifice which produces such things as sacraments and praying for the dead, burning candles, etc. All heresy falls into one of two basic categories: a false concept of the personal deity of Christ or mixing works with faith. The church of Rome can scarcely be accused of teaching a false concept of the personal deity of Christ; however, their emphasis on the "continual sacrifice" and rejection of our Lord's finished work breeds a concept that causes man to try to earn his own salvation by works, penance, indulgences, and many other satanically conceived ideas labeled by our Lord in Revelation 2:24 as "the depths of Satan."

Rome's Similarity to Paganism

A few years ago my wife and I had the privilege of flying to Mexico City where, together with another family in our church, we toured the largest Roman cathedral on the North American continent, the Shrine of Guadalupe. I was deeply impressed with the unscriptural conduct of the service and how similar their service was to pagan rituals which I had seen previously. For example:

Penance. Many were crawling on their hands and knees over hundreds of yards of concrete in an effort to punish themselves, whereas the Scripture teaches, "For by grace are ye saved through faith; and that not of yourselves, it is the gift of God — *not of works, lest any man should boast*" (Eph. 2:8, 9).

Darkness. The room was so dark that photographs could not be taken and everything was kept in a gloomy state; the Scriptures teach, "He that doeth truth cometh to the light . . ." (John 3:21).

Mystery. The mysterious nature of the service could be seen in the fact that individuals could not understand the Latin being spoken during the mass, and no message was given in a language they recognized. Parents came to the glass-encased form representing a dead saint, thinking that by rubbing the casket and placing an offering in the slot provided they could then rub blessing on the forehead of their infant children or other loved ones. In contrast, the Lord Jesus talked about those who hear the Word, and *understand it* (Matt. 13:23).

Idolatry. Prominently located on every wall were idols representative of Christ, the apostles, or other saints. I counted seventeen such idols. Though idolatry is typical of pagan worship, it is forbidden in the Bible. "Thou shalt not make unto thee any carved image, or any likeness of anything that is in heaven above, or that is in the earth beneath, or that is in the water under the earth" (Exod. 20:4).

Chanting. During the service much chanting was performed by the priests. Individuals who had come to worship prayed by saying the same words repetitiously, whether they knew the meaning or not. By contrast our Lord has warned that "When ye pray, use not vain repetitions, as the pagans do; for they think that they shall be heard for their much speaking" (Matt. 6:7).

Mary the Central Figure. A large picture of Mary framed in gold occupied the most prominent place in the cathedral, while the idol representing Christ was off to the left and not nearly so prominent. To the contrary, the Bible teaches "that in all things he (Christ) might have the pre-eminence" (Col. 1:18).

Crucifix. A crucifix, well known in Roman forms of worship, was all that could be seen of our blessed Lord, whereas the Scriptures speak not of "continual sacrifice" but, in the words of Christ Himself speaking of the sacrifice, "It is finished"; the angel on the day of resurrection said, "He is not here, for He is risen, as He said." Oh, that these people might recognize the principle conveyed in the words of our Lord: "I am he that liveth, and was dead; and, behold, I am alive for evermore, Amen, and have the keys of hades and of death" (Rev. 1:18).

Christ's Character Revealed

"These things saith the Son of God, who hath his eyes like a flame of fire, and his feet are like fine bronze." Our Lord's selection of the title "Son of God" for Himself is most instructive when compared to 1:13, where He selects the title "Son of Man." These titles are synonymous or interchangeable. This should be borne in mind in this day when false teachers are prone to advocate the human nature of Christ at the exclusion of His divine nature. Also, it is instructive to those in the church of Rome who are prone to think of Him as the "Son of Mary."

"Eyes like flame" and "feet like bronze" denote that Christ is looking with piercing judgment on the Church because she has permitted the false teaching to creep into her midst and "seduce my servants."

Christ's Commendation

Our Lord's commendation to the church of Thyatira comes in the form of six words. He commends them for their (1) "works" — indicating that many through Rome's long history have been faithfully serving Jesus Christ as a result of receiving Him; (2) "love" — a love for mankind has characterized this church, for in ancient times hospitals and sanitariums were almost exclusively the work of the church through its nuns and priests; (3) "service" means ministry; (4) "faith" — although it is not given the prominence of works and love, it nevertheless is a characteristic of that age and church with the main exception noted in the paragraph above; (5) "patience" means endurance and speaks of the long time period of this church; (6) "works; and the last to be more than the first" — the good works of the church of Rome (except for such periods as the Inquisition, when many were wantonly murdered) are quite commendable. It should also be borne in mind that, although the vast majority of members have been held in ignorance and darkness, many have been faithful to the Lord Jesus Christ. Some outstanding products of that period were John Wycliffe, John Huss, Savonarola, and many others who earned the martyr's crown because they refused to give up their adherence to the Word of God and Christ Jesus the Lord.

Christ's Condemnation

"Notwithstanding, I have a few things against thee, because thou allowest that women, Jezebel, who calleth herself a prophetess, to teach and to seduce my servants to commit fornication, and to eat things sacrificed unto idols." Our Lord's condemnation upon the church of Thyatira took two forms: (1) He condemned her for permitting a false teacher to enslave or to lead astray His servants, and (2) He condemned her for not repenting when she had opportunity.

Jezebel, the False Prophetess

The Lord Jesus reached back into the Old Testament for the name of a woman who brought Baalism into Israel and perverted the nation, using her as a point of comparison for those who brought paganism and its devilish teachings into the church. (Whenever a woman is used symbolically to convey a religious teaching, she always represents a false religion.) Our Lord's parable in Matthew 13:33-35 concerning the woman who took leaven (a symbol of evil) and hid it in three measures of meal "till the whole was leavened" is a prophetic glimpse of what took place during the false teaching of this period.

The teaching of the false prophetess, Jezebel, took two forms: (1) "to seduce (and lead into false teaching) my servants to commit fornication," which is a symbol of the idolatry brought in during this period, and (2) "to eat things sacrificed to idols," a symbol of the union of the church with the world. During this time Rome sought to bring the kingdom of the world under the domination of the pope in Rome. Though contrary to the teachings of our Lord, who said, "My kingdom is not of this world," they seriously attempted to make their kingdom of this world.

"And I gave her space to repent of her fornication, and she repented not." "Space" means time. Plenty of opportunity was given to this church to repent, almost a thousand years was granted, yet "she repented not."

Christ's Future Judgment of This Church

"Behold, I will cast her into a bed, and them that commit adultery with her into great tribulation, except they repent of their deeds." Our Lord here predicts that this church and those that are persuaded to follow her false teachings will go into the Great Tribulation, when she will, according to Revelation 17, be the church of the Tribulation. This warning should speak to every Bible-believing Christian in the world about having any entangling affiliation with the ecumenical movement. Pope John XXIII popularized through his ecumenical Council the concept that "they all shall be one." Protestant unbelievers and heretics are advancing this program on every hand. God's faithful followers should be careful to measure everything according to the stated Word of God and, if need be, to stand alone.

"I will kill her children with death; and all of the churches shall know that I am he who searcheth the minds and hearts; and I will give unto every one of you according to your works." "Death," according to Greek scholar Vincent, is literally a reference to the "second death" when all unbelievers regardless of religious affiliation will be cast into the lake of fire (Rev. 20:15).

"I will give unto every one of you according to your works" is an obvious reference to the equitable judgment of the Great White Throne, when all men will stand before Christ, as described in Revelation 20:11-15.

Christ's Counsel

Our Lord's counsel to the church at Thyatira was apparently directed to the faithful individuals within that church who rejected the false doctrines.

"Hold fast till I come" refers to the fact that many during the Tribulation will refuse to knuckle under to the false religious system, called "the harlot" in Revelation 17.

Christ's Challenge

"And he that overcometh, and keepeth my works unto the end, to him I will give power over the nations." There are two aspects of the challenge of our Lord to the individual overcomer of this period: (1) He will give him a position of leadership and authority during the millennial age if he is faithful in this age; (2) "and I will give him the morning star." This beautiful title is clearly understood in the light of our Lord's word in Revelation 22:16, where He explains that He is the "bright and morning star." This promise is clearly the promise of Christ to come and "abide" if you "overcome." Who is an overcomer? 1 John 5:1-4 clarifies that it is "whosoever believeth that Jesus is the Christ!"

6
The Church
of Sardis

Revelation 3:1-6

There is nothing worse than a dead church! It is like a man dying of thirst on the desert who sees a well off in the distance, only to find upon arrival that it is dry. Many thirsty souls stumble through the desert of this world and then finally see what they think is hope in the form of a church, only to find upon entering that it is completely dead. Such is the picture this text gives us of the church of Sardis and the age she represents — the Reformation.

Sardis, the capital city of Lydia, was prominent in Asia Minor. Noted for its carpet industry, it was a wealthy city that was finally destroyed by an earthquake. The local church there seems to have had an acceptable name in certain areas but was really dead. This is tragic in view of the fact that life is a characteristic of the born-again Christian. Jesus said, "I am come that ye might have life, and that ye might have it more abundantly."

There were, however, a few faithful believers there who refused to "defile their garments."

The Dead Church, 1520 to the Tribulation

Commendation: "I know thy works, that thou hast a name that thou livest . . ."

Condemnation: ". . . [thou] art dead . . . I have not found thy works perfect before God."

Counsel: "Be watchful, and strengthen the things which remain, that are ready to die . . . Remember, therefore, how thou hast received and heard, and hold fast and repent. If, therefore, thou shalt not watch, I will come on thee as a thief, and thou shalt not know what hour I will come upon thee."

49

Challenge: "He that overcometh, the same shall be clothed in white raiment; and I will not blot his name out of the book of life, but I will confess his name before my Father, and before his angels."

The Dead Church Age

Sardis means "escaping ones" or those who "come out." This name, together with our Lord's condemnation of the church, provides a perfect description of the Reformation churches. The Protestant Reformation was the result of the continued emphasis by the Roman church on pagan doctrines (see chapter 5) rather than adherence to scriptural principles. The basic emphasis of the Reformation churches originally was Martin Luther's watchword, taken from Scripture, "The just shall live by faith." They had recoiled from trying to make salvation the result of works and sparked a resurgence of interest in studying the Scriptures.

The tragedy of the Reformation churches that earned for them the condemnation by the Lord of being "dead" was two-fold.

1. They became state churches. Luther, for example, sought the approval of the political leaders, and eventually the Lutheran Church became the state church of Germany, as did others throughout Europe. The danger of this is that the church then includes the entire population, thus eliminating the need for personal acceptance of Jesus Christ and an emphasis on the individual's relationship to God.

2. The Reformation churches did not sufficiently change many customs and teachings of the Roman church. Infant baptism was continued, in spite of the fact that there is no scriptural verification for it. Sprinkling was also continued, and ritualism, including some elements of the sacraments, was perpetuated. Ritual and formality, characteristic of pagan forms of worship, are not conducive to genuine worship, for they appeal to the sensuous nature of man. The Bible teaches that God must be worshiped in *spirit* and in *truth*. Ritual that comes from paganism cannot be of the Holy Spirit and does not convey truth. The main purpose of a church is the propagation of the Gospel of Jesus Christ. This should be done in song and word. If people leave a church with the mysterious feeling of "worship" but have not been brought face to face with Jesus Christ in a personal way, they have been worshiping in a dead church.

Christ's Nature Revealed to Sardis

The aspect of Christ's nature revealed to Sardis is most instructive. Reaching back into the complete vision of His nature imparted to John in chapter 1, He selected two characteristics of Himself: seven spirits and seven stars.

"These things saith he that hath the seven spirits of God, and the seven stars." The seven spirits refer to the Holy Spirit, who Jesus said is truth. The stars are the angels of the churches. This church had more than adequate opportunity to know the truth and to obey the Lord *if* they had heeded His warning. The natural explanation of their deficiency appears to be that they preferred to trust the State in a time of economic need instead of God. Had Luther and other reformers depended solely on the Holy Spirit instead of governmental authorities and leaders, who can say but that the Reformation would not have been a far greater spiritual experience for millions more?

Christ's Commendation

The church of Sardis received the shortest commendation from our Lord of any of the churches. In fact, some Bible scholars do not include any commendation for this church, but list the commendation as a condemnation because of the way it ends.

"I know thy works." This could well refer to the early stages of the Reformation when Martin Luther and others chose to defy Roman authority, even at the risk of their own lives, to obey the Bible's teaching on salvation by faith.

"That thou hast a name" probably refers to the fact that they had a reputation as a church faithful to Christ, particularly in the earlier days of the Reformation.

"That thou livest" indicates that there was some life in the church. Certainly those who placed their faith in Jesus Christ "lived." It should be noted, however, that the act of placing one's trust in Jesus Christ and also receiving His salvation does not guarantee consistent obedience to the Holy Spirit. Steadfast obedience is a result of a day-by-day submission to the will of God.

Christ's Condemnation

"Thou . . . art dead." This has already been covered in the introduction to this chapter, indicating that the ritual and ceremony of the Reformation church often crowded out the true life underneath so that it was impotent and ineffective in the hand of God. This is defined in verse 2 by our Lord's statement, "for I have not found thy works perfect before God." The Greek word perfect means "complete." Although the Reformation leaders began well, they did not proceed to complete the works of reforming the church, but stopped far short of scriptural standards.

Christ's Counsel

Our Lord counseled the church of Sardis to do five things which, had they obeyed, would have made them acceptable to Him.

1. "Be watchful" is an expression that points up a serious deficiency in the teaching of the Reformation leaders. The word "watch" is used by our Lord in other passages of Scripture to indicate the attitude of life that should characterize His children in view of His promised return. The most serious deficiency in the Reformation teachings was that they

lacked instruction in Bible prophecy and separation. Prophetically instructed Christians are more apt to be separated, consecrated Christians than those who are not aware of the promises of our Lord's second coming.

2. ". . . and strengthen the things which remain." This evidently refers to the need for strengthening the good doctrinal teachings of the early days of the Reformation, which were limited to salvation by faith, the total depravity of man, and the authority of the Word of God.

3. "Remember therefore how thou hast received and heard" indicates the need to return to the days of blessing as a result of searching the Scriptures and depend upon God rather than on the state church and ritual.

4. "Hold fast" communicates a warning to adhere tenaciously to the doctrines clearly taught in the Scriptures they presently had. It was bad enough that they did not press far enough in the development of scriptural truth then, but it is even worse that the church of Sardis represents some of the denominations swept along in the advancing tide of neo-orthodoxy today, giving up or compromising the orthodox position that characterized the reformers.

5. ". . . and repent." Repentance involves not only an act of turning toward God, but a submissive heart. The Reformation churches needed to turn back to Christ, seeking His will and His Spirit's teaching, rather than to accept their own preconceived ideas about the interpretation of truth. Had they been willing to repent, doubtless the Holy Spirit would have guided them "into all truth."

Christ's Warning to Sardis

"If, therefore, thou shalt not watch, I will come on thee as a thief, and thou shalt not know what hour I will come upon thee." Because the Reformation churches have not heeded our Lord's warning, it is obvious that they are going to be taken unawares when our Lord comes. One of the many evidences of this prophetic ignorance on the part of Reformation churches is that they are leaders in the World Council of Churches' ecumenical program, which purposes to unite all Protestants, all Catholics, and eventually all religions. If they just understood the prophetic Word of God, they would realize that they are aiding and abetting the Antichrist's program, for that combined church will be his church during the first three-and-a-half years of the tribulation (Rev. 17).

Some Faithful Saints in Sardis

"Thou hast a few names even in Sardis that have not defiled their garments, and they shall walk with me in white; for they are worthy." As in all church ages, the Reformation had individuals who were faithful to their Lord. They saw through the pageantry of ornate religious sacraments and ritual and came to the personal acceptance of Christ as Savior and Lord. Because of this faith in Him and obedience to His

Word, they refused to "defile their garments," to compromise with the attitude and conduct of the world, and rather chose to live a separated and godly life.

The Lord has promised that all who are faithful to Him during persecution will "walk with me in white; for they are worthy." The story is told that years ago, when our country established relief camps to help Armenian refugees, one young girl came and waited outside the tent for medical assistance. Her dark eyes betrayed the tremendous pain that racked her body. Someone asked her, "Have you been hurt?" To which she answered, "I am bearing the cross. I bear in my body the cross of Jesus Christ. Now I know how He suffered." They did not understand, but the nurse who assisted her in the medical tent, when she slipped off her dress, saw the cross that had been branded on her shoulder with hot irons. The wound was swollen and burning with infection. The girl explained, "Every day they would say to me, 'Mohammed or Christ?' When I said 'Christ' on the last day, they branded my shoulder with this cross. Now as long as I live I will bear this cross, and someday when I see Jesus I will be glad."

Many of us who have never tasted the sting of persecution for the cause of Jesus Christ will stand aside and be thrilled at the Judgment Seat of Christ when those who have endured are rewarded.

Christ's Challenge to Sardis

Our Lord's challenge to this church, as to all the others, is directed to the individual. "He that overcometh," as we have already seen, is a direct reference to those who have been born again by faith in Christ (1 John 5:1-4). "The same shall be clothed in white raiment" is a reference to the righteousness of Christ with which we are clothed when we are born again (2 Cor. 5:21).

"I will not blot his name out of the book of life, but I will confess his name before my Father, and before his angels." This indicates the security with which a believer is held against the day of judgment described in Revelation 20:11-15. The Book of Life is that book which contains the names of all living individuals. It is possible to have one's name blotted out of that book for three reasons: (1) for sinning against God (Exod. 32:33); (2) for not being an overcomer, which is synonymous with being born again or putting one's trust in Christ Jesus (1 John 5:1-4); (3) for taking away from the words of the prophecy of Revelation 22:19. In short, then, anyone who has sinned against God has his name blotted out of the Book of Life when he dies.

Our Lord concludes, "He that hath an ear, let him hear what the Spirit saith unto the churches." Whether or not you have heard is determined by whether or not you have heeded His warning to be born again. The way to guarantee that your name will never be blotted out of the Book of Life is to get on your knees and ask God right now to cleanse your sin and save you.

7

The Church
of Philadelphia

Revelation 3:7-13

Having found the study of the three preceding churches somewhat depressing, we find it refreshing to consider the church of Philadelphia. This sixth church is a throwback to the first and second churches, Ephesus and Smyrna, of the first three centuries. Your heart will be stirred as you study this passage, and you will find yourself desiring to be identified with this kind of church.

The church of Philadelphia was located in a center of Greek civilization. Founded only 189 years before Christ, the city had a surprising influence on that area of the ancient world. This church must have been very vital, for Philadelphia remained an independent Christian city until the close of the fourteenth century, when it was conquered by the Turks.

The Church Christ Loved, 1750 to the Rapture

Commendation: "I know thy works; behold, I have set before thee an open door, and no man can shut it; for thou hast a little strength, and hast kept my word, and hast not denied my name."

Condemnation: Not one word!

Counsel: "Behold, I come quickly; hold that fast which thou hast, that no man take thy crown."

Challenge: "Him that overcometh will I make a pillar in the temple of my God, and he shall go no more out; and I will write upon him the name of my God, and the name of the city of my God, the new Jerusalem, which cometh down out of heaven from my God; and I will write upon him my new name. He that hath an ear, let him hear what the Spirit saith unto the churches."

54

The Philadelphia Age of Church History

The name Philadelphia literally means "brotherly love." Our Lord selected that church to describe the kind of church age that was initiated around the year 1750 and will continue to the Tribulation. Just as Sardis came out of Thyatira, so the Philadelphia age came out of Sardis. The Reformation church, as we saw in the preceding chapter, became dead and cold as a state church. Philadelphia, however, was marked by vitality of life. In this church age, God worked in a thrilling manner that produced revivals in Europe and the British Isles, spreading even to America. These revivals in turn produced what is known today as the modern missionary movement.

It was this moving of the Spirit of God on the part of His people that caused an English shoe cobbler to become so burdened for the lost of India that in 1793 he became the first foreign missionary. William Carey was followed by other young people whom the Spirit of God touched, and thus the present-day "Faith Missionary Movement" was begun. As our Lord said, "I will set before thee an open door." This open door found such men as Adoniram Judson, David Livingstone, Jonathan Goforth, and literally thousands of other people going out to Africa, China, Japan, Korea, India, South America, and the islands of the sea.

The Two Reasons for the Missionary Movement

One factor that led to the great missionary movement was the printing of the Bible in the language of the people and the natural tendency of the ordinary individual to take the Bible literally. Thus, when a young man like William Carey read our Lord's command, "Go ye into all the world, and preach the gospel to every creature" he was inclined to obey it.

The second factor that contributed to this missionary movement was the increased interest in the study of the doctrine of the second coming of our Lord. Around 1800 the doctrine of the premillennial return of Christ, which had been all but dead since the end of the third century, was revived. This teaching, as was pointed out in the previous chapter, contributed to a consecrated and separated church. In preparation for her Lord's return, she was willing to do whatever He commanded.

Christ's Nature Revealed

Four aspects of Christ's character are revealed to Philadelphia in verse 7, two of which are not found in His vision to John in chapter 1.

1. "Holy." Our Lord reminds this church of His holiness. It is good to be reminded at this point that He also said, "Be ye holy; for I am holy" (1 Pet. 1:16). This aspect of His nature may have been singled out to signify the practice of the church of Philadelphia in being separated from the world unto holiness.

2. "True." In several passages our Lord is referred to as Truth (John 14:6). Dr. J. Vernon McGee offers this interesting suggestion: "True

means genuine with an added note of perfection and completeness. Moses did not give the 'true bread.' Christ is the 'true bread'" (John 6:32-35). From this we see that Christ is not only truth, but the ultimate truth. No truth will be given to this world other than the truth revealed in Jesus Christ. This aspect of His nature may well have alluded to the movement toward doctrinal separation that characterized the age of Philadelphia.

3. "He that hath the key of David" is an obvious reference to the authority of Christ. It forecasts His eventual rulership of the world but still relates to Revelation 1:5: although He gives latitude to the kings of the world, He nevertheless controls the extent to which they can govern.

4. "He that openeth, and no man shutteth; and shutteth, and no man openeth." The Lord Jesus gave His disciples the commission to "Go into all the world and preach the gospel" on the basis of what He had already said in Matthew 28:18, "All authority is given unto me in heaven and in earth." The doors of opportunity for preaching the Gospel are controlled by the Lord Jesus Christ. Neither Leonid Brezhnev nor Mao Tse-tung nor any world dictator can close the door to the preaching of the Gospel unless Christ so wills it. This is not only true of the missionary movement of the Philadelphia church age, but also of the individual.

The late Dr. Henrietta C. Mears was a great leader of young people. She often used verse 7 in challenging young people called of God to obey His word without fear or reservation. God is not limited in His ability to open doors. This is a message much needed by the Lord's servants today. There is a tendency to compromise in order to gain opportunities, whereas in truth it is our responsibility to do right and God's responsibility to open the doors of opportunity.

Christ's Commendation

Our Lord commended the church of Philadelphia for four things, which in turn invoked a promise from Him.

1. "I know thy works; behold, I have set before thee an open door, and no man can shut it." This evidently refers to the doors of opportunity open to them for the proclamation of the Gospel, one of the chief characteristics of faithful service throughout this church age. 1 Corinthians 16:9 indicates that the Apostle Paul considered an open door an opportunity for Christian service.

2. ". . . for thou hast a little strength." This refers to the status of their minority group. Except for some churches in America, the Philadelphia church age is characterized by small congregations which, according to man's standards, are weak. This, of course, is real strength; for as the Holy Spirit tells us through Paul, "When I am weak, then am I strong."

3. " [Thou] hast kept my word." This indicates that this church not only believed the Word of God, but obeyed it. The Reformation

churches, past and present, believe the Word of God but are not characterized by obedience to it. The church of Philadelphia, a fitting contrast to this practice, is characterized by obedience to His Word.

4. "... and hast not denied my name." Satan always tries to counter an effective work of God. It is interesting to notice that the greatest increase in false Christs and false religions in the world's history began during this same period of time. One characteristic of this church age is that it refuses to deny the name of the Lord, thereby offering a challenge that needs to be presented to every faithful Christian as he approaches the end of the age.

Christ's Promise to a Commendable Church

This rather unique promise of Christ, resulting from the commendable attitude of this church, falls into two basic divisions: vindication and preservation.

1. Vindication: "Behold, I will make them of the synagogue of Satan, who say they are Jews, and are not, but do lie; behold, I will make them to come and worship before thy feet, and to know that I have loved thee." Christ promised that all the false religionists (religious imposters and false teachers) who claimed to be Jews, but were not, would someday be subdued before them. These heretics will realize that, in persecuting the faithful Church of Christ, they have turned their backs on Him.

2. Preservation: "Because thou hast kept the word of my patience, I also will keep thee from the hour of temptation, which shall come upon all the world, to try them that dwell upon the earth." The world has never known a universal period of tribulation. This passage is an obvious reference to the Tribulation Period of seven years that will be covered extensively in our study of Revelation 6 through 18. This promise, however, is to the church of Philadelphia: she will be raptured before that Tribulation begins. It seems difficult to understand why some false teachers suggest that the Church must go through the Tribulation in view of this clear-cut statement of our Lord.

Christ's Counsel

"Behold, I come quickly; hold that fast which thou hast, that no man take thy crown." Our Lord's counsel to the church of Philadelphia is based on the promise of His second coming. It is interesting to note that the challenge is made on the basis that the church of Philadelphia will be in existence at His coming. It is clear from history that this church age, now almost 300 years old, is one of the shorter periods of church history. Christ's counsel to them is to hold fast to what they have already been doing and to continue faithfully until the end. The church of Philadelphia is characterized by a spirit of revival that promotes evangelism and a missionary-minded church.

Dr. Oswald J. Smith suggested two basic essentials for building a spiritual church: evangelism and missions. His great ministry as pastor of the People's Church of Toronto, Canada, is a fitting witness to this formula. A third point which also contributed to his success and should characterize a faithful church is Bible teaching. These three character-istics must be maintained by the churches of Philadelphia until our Lord comes.

The churches that are following this formula today are enjoying un-precedented growth. In fact, we are currently witnessing the development of large Philadelphia-type churches in almost every major American city. These churches have life and vitality, mute evidence of the power of the Spirit upon them.

This is in sharp contrast to the Sardis or Laodicean churches, which are having a hard time maintaining the status quo — and many are losing more members than they take in. Their problem is that they have not "kept his word" and they have "denied his name."

The emptiness of our Western civilization because of its atheistic humanistic philosophy has given the Philadelphia churches their greatest opportunity in their almost three-hundred-year history to harvest the souls of men. For the first time in centuries man is not only philosophically empty but also aware of his emptiness. Faithful churches with a Bible-teaching, evangelistic, missionary-minded ministry are leading many out of their philosophical desert into the abundant life Christ came to offer all mankind.

Christ's Challenge

The challenge of our Lord to overcomers (those that are born again) is threefold:

1. "He that overcometh will I make a pillar in the temple of my God, and he shall go no more out." A pillar speaks of stability. A Christian has stability in this life only in Christ. He is often buffeted and rejected for his faith; however, in the life to come he will not be an outsider, but will be on the "in" with relation to Christ.

2. "And I will write upon him the name of my God, and the name of the city of my God, the new Jerusalem, which cometh down out of heaven from my God." The writing of the names of God is indicative of the fact that the believer is identified with Christ by the seal of the name of God, which entitles him to have entrance into the city of God. Christ promised to prepare a new Jerusalem that would come down to the new earth, as described in Revelation 21:9 through 22:6.

3. "And I will write upon him my new name." Believers of the church of Philadelphia will have not only the name of God, which entitles them to entrance into the city of God, but also the name of Christ, which according to Revelation 22:3, 4 entitles them to be "his servants . . . and they shall see his face." One of the blessed promises in the Word of God to His children is that one day we will see the one who is the object of our affection, the Lord Jesus Christ, whom we have worshipped

in spirit and in truth through the Word of God. That is, we shall see Him face to face. This is an exclusive experience for all those who are overcomers. Those who are just hearers of the Word of God are not justified before God, but they who have received the Lord Jesus and accordingly are prepared to meet Him at His coming are justified before God.

8

The Church
of Laodicea

Revelation 3:14-22

The last of the seven churches is the most disappointing. In fact, it is disgusting! Our Lord compares it to the nauseating experience of drinking anything lukewarm. In this sense it is a graphic prophecy of the modern-day apostate church.

Laodicea was a wealthy inland city about forty miles from Ephesus. Steeped in Greek culture and learning, it was a thriving center of industry. The local church must have been wealthy, as evidenced by the fact that among present day ruins are three churches dating back to the early days of Christianity. In spite of her wealth, nothing is known of the ministry of this church in preaching the Gospel throughout the region around it as was characteristic of the church of Ephesus.

The Apostate Church or the People's Church,
1900 to the Tribulation

Commendation: Not one word!

Condemnation: "Thou art neither cold nor hot; I would thou wert cold or hot. So, then, because thou art lukewarm, and neither cold nor hot, I will spew thee out of my mouth. Because thou sayest, I am rich, and increased with goods, and have need of nothing, and knowest not that thou art wretched, and miserable, and poor, and blind, and naked."

Counsel: "I counsel thee to buy of me gold tried in the fire, that thou mayest be rich; and white raiment, that thou mayest be clothed, and that the shame of thy nakedness do not appear; and anoint thine eyes with salve, that thou mayest see."

Challenge: "To him that overcometh will I grant to sit with me in my throne."

The Laodicean Church Age

It should be kept in mind that the first three church ages differ from the last four in that each of the former stopped at the beginning of the next church. Ephesus was replaced by Smyrna, Smyrna by Pergamum, and Pergamum by Thyatira. A look at the chart at the beginning of Part I will show that we have Thyatira, Sardis, and Philadelphia with us at the present time. Thus Laodicea adds to this church age by arising from the three that preceded it.

The Laodicean church age began around 1900 and is increasing in intensity at a breathtaking pace. Laodicea could well be called the apostate ecumenical church that is gathering momentum at this very hour. The characteristics of the Laodicean church age can best be seen by a detailed examination of Christ's condemnation upon her.

Christ's Description of Himself to Laodicea

Only one of the three titles our Lord used to describe His nature to Laodicea is found in John's vision of chapter 1. It is the first.

1. "Amen" is a Hebrew word which means "true" and carries with it the meaning of finality. In this sense, Christ is the final truth. That is, all God's revelations to man about Himself are found in the person of Jesus Christ. If you want to know about God, all you have to do is study the life of Jesus Christ. Dr. Merrill C. Tenney has very beautifully stated it, "Christ is the seal of God's revealed truth, the finality of all that the Father has spoken. Beyond Him, God has nothing more to say to man."

2. ". . . the faithful and true witness. . ." The Lord Jesus is truth and the faithful witness of Truth. Because He knows the end from the beginning, His Word can be accepted as absolute authority for two reasons. He is God, and "God giveth not the Spirit by measure unto him" (John 3:34).

3. ". . . the beginning of the creation of God." This title does not teach, as some false cults would have us believe, that Jesus is the first of God's creation. On the contrary, when considered in the light of the Word and parallel passages (Col. 1:15), this could well be translated, "the beginner of the creation of God." It is obvious that all things are created through His power when we consider John 1:3, "All things were made by him; and without him was not anything made that was made," and Colossians 1:16, 17, "For by him were all things created, that are in heaven, and that are in earth, visible and invisible, whether they be thrones, or dominions, or principalities, or powers — all things were created by him, and for him; and he is before all things, and by him all things consist."

Taken in reverse order, the three titles here selected by our Lord present Him as the beginner of creation, the faithful witness of everything which emanates from God, and the final authority (as He certainly will be at His second coming).

Christ's Commendation of Laodicea

The church of Laodicea has the distinction of being the only one whose conduct was so reprehensible that even the Christ of Glory, who knew all about her, could not find one thing upon which to commend her. This is a tragic indictment, indeed, on so-called Christianity in this twentieth century.

Christ's Condemnation of Laodicea

Our Lord's condemnation of Laodicea is twofold:

1. They are sickeningly lukewarm. "I know thy works, that thou art neither cold nor hot: I would thou wert cold or hot." Our Lord makes clear that He is fully aware of the neutral condition of the church in the last days. It was not "hot," meaning "zealous of good works," nor was it "cold," meaning "lifeless." Instead it was "lukewarm" or indifferent. What a description of the modern-day church! All kinds of organizations, programs, committees, activities, but no power. The Holy Spirit warned through Paul in 2 Timothy 3:5 that in the last days many would be characterized as "having a form of godliness, but denying the power thereof; from such turn away." This lukewarm church that claims to represent Jesus Christ never sees the transformation of a soul from darkness to life, but instead deceives many because they do not have the power of the Gospel of Christ. These churches are usually more interested in social action than Gospel action, more interested in reformation than transformation, more interested in planning than praying. Consequently, they are sickening to the Lord.

"So, then, because thou art lukewarm, and neither cold nor hot, I will spew thee out of my mouth." This statement indicates that the Lord Jesus Christ does not claim this church even though she may make broad her claim on Him.

2. They are deceived about themselves. "Because thou sayest, I am rich, and increased with goods, and have need of nothing, and knowest not that thou art wretched, and miserable, and poor, and blind, and naked." All deception is evil, but the most devastating deception is self-deception. The Laodicean church and the age she represents are deceived about themselves. This fact can easily be seen by a simple comparison of Laodicea's description of herself and the Lord's description of her.

Laodicea's Description of Herself

Laodicea said of herself, "I am rich, and increased with goods, and have need of nothing." Material abundance is not conducive to spiritual vitality. The Laodicean church of today is "rich." Her churches are the finest. She has fabulous architecture, million-dollar buildings, fund-raising organizations and a large but unconsecrated church membership. In saying, "I have need of nothing," she does not realize her poverty-stricken state. For Jesus said, "Without me ye can do nothing." Man can organize. Man can build. Man can promote. Man can preach. Man can teach. But only the Spirit of God can convict the souls of men. Only the Spirit of God can transform the lives of men. Only the Spirit of God can glorify Jesus Christ, who said of the Holy Spirit, "He shall glorify me . . ." (John 16:14). This offers a good test of any work claiming to be performed in the name of Jesus Christ. If it glorifies man, it is not the work of the Spirit! The unique test of the Spirit is: Does it glorify Jesus Christ? This church age does not!

The plight of the Laodicean church when she stands before Jesus Christ in the Judgment will be the same as that of the group of religionists described by our Lord Himself in Matthew 7:22, 23: "Many will say to me in that day, Lord, Lord, have we not prophesied in thy name? And in thy name have cast our demons? And in thy name done many wonderful works? And then will I profess unto them, I never knew you; depart from me, ye that work iniquity."

Christ's Description of Laodicea

The true state of the Laodicean church can be seen by noting in detail what Christ saw in this church. To Him she was —

1. "Wretched and miserable." Even though she gave herself lessons on positive thinking and read books on how to have peace, inwardly her people were an unhappy, wretched lot, for riches never satisfy the hungry heart of man.

2. "Poor." Even though rich in material things, they were poor because they knew not Christ. This is in accord with our Lord's statement in Mark 8:36, "For what shall it profit a man, if he shall gain the whole world, and lose his own soul?"

3. "Blind." Although they thought they knew and understood through their sophisticated education and appropriation of "wisdom," they did not understand the ways of God. This blindness is illustrated in twentieth-century Christendom's invasion of civil rights. The pulpits of churches are being used today as sounding boards for racial agitation, which depicts the blindness of these churches because they are striving to solve man's racial problems externally or by means of education. That is impossible! Man's nature must be changed internally, and only Jesus Christ can do that! The more man tries to solve these social problems without Christ, the more confused the problem will become.

4. "Naked." This twentieth-century Laodicean church is clothed with religion. She wraps her religious robes about her, burns her candles, waves her symbols, offers her chants, and reads her creeds; but Jesus Christ sees her as "naked," for she is not clothed by faith with the garments of righteousness. Oh, that this church age could realize that the name of Christ which she uses, but does not believe in as the divine Son of God, has been excluded from her midst and that without Him she is nothing.

Christ's Counsel to Laodicea

Our Lord counseled the church of Laodicea to do four things, all of which are part of the salvation experience, indicating that this was not a born-again church.

1. "I counsel thee to buy of me gold tried in the fire, that thou mayest be rich." Eternal riches are not appropriated by material possessions. Instead, they have been appropriated by the blood of Jesus Christ and are available by faith. 1 Peter 1:7 indicates that "the trial of your faith" is more precious than gold. It is interesting to note that the Laodicean church, labeled "poor," is asked to buy something. How is this to be understood?

In the book of the prophet Isaiah (55:1), we read God's invitation to men to come and buy what they need "without money and without price." Salvation is not purchased through man's efforts. It has been purchased for man by the death of Christ on Calvary's cross. Therefore, the poorest of the poor can pay the price, which is to humble oneself, calling upon the name of the Lord and believing by faith.

2. "I counsel thee to buy of me . . . white raiment." This indicates the righteousness required to come into God's presence (referred to in 3:5). He knew their nakedness and their need for the "white raiment" that represents righteousness. In Isaiah 61:10 we read of God's provision of "garments of salvation" and the "robe of righteousness" as a bride or groom would wear. Righteousness is imputed to men when they call upon the name of the Lord and are saved.

3. ". . . anoint thine eyes with salve, that thou mayest see." This is an indication of man's need of spiritual illumination. No matter how brilliant he is in the flesh, unless he is indwelt by the Spirit of Jesus Christ, he will never understand the ways of God. Only the Holy Spirit, whom Jesus said would be our teacher, can cause man to understand the ways of God. "But the natural man receiveth not the things of the Spirit of God: for they are foolishness unto him: neither can he know them, because they are spiritually discerned" (1 Cor. 2:14).

4. "Be zealous, therefore, and repent." This lukewarm, indifferent, materialistic church was challenged by our Lord, on the basis of His love for them even in that lost state, to repent of their sins and turn to Him.

Christ's Counsel to Individuals

Christ's message to Laodicea contains a most interesting counsel that is specifically directed to the individuals of this church age. Although the church has excluded Him, those who are willing to receive Him are given this special invitation which is also applicable to individuals of all church ages: "Behold, I stand at the door, and knock; if any man hear my voice, and open the door, I will come in to him, and will sup with him, and he with me."

This verse of Scripture has been beautifully described by one saint of God as "the simplest explanation of the plan of salvation encompassed in so brief a statement within the lids of God's Word." The door referred to here is obviously the door to man's heart or the center of his being. The Bible says, "Out of [the heart] are the issues of life" (Prov. 4:23). Consequently, we find Christ knocking at the door of this emotional center called the heart, asking entrance. He does not force His way, but patiently knocks. "If *any* man hear my voice, and open the door, I will come in to him. . . ."

For almost two thousand years our Lord has faithfully, patiently, wonderfully knocked on the door of man's heart. How does He knock? In many ways, four of which I would like to share with you.

1. Through His Word. The Lord Jesus said, "Verily, verily, I say unto you, He that heareth my word, and believeth on him that sent me, hath everlasting life, and shall not come into judgment; but is passed from death unto life" (John 5:24). Man must hear our blessed Lord's Word to be saved. Many a man has felt the gentle knock of the Savior at the door of his heart as he read some portion of the Word of God. Sometimes this knocking evidences itself by violent reaction and rejection, but that does not minimize the fact that Christ has knocked.

2. Through His people. Another method our Lord uses to knock at the door of men's hearts is through His children. The Scripture says, "How shall they hear without a preacher?" We usually think of the great preachers of the Church as men like D. L. Moody, Billy Sunday, Harry Ironside, and many others, but if the truth were known, and it will be when we stand before the Judgment Seat of Christ, Jesus knocks through the ordinary, everyday, often obscure people.

The late Dr. Lee Scarborough, the great preacher from Texas, told of the conversion of a well-to-do businessman who came forward at the close of a service. The pastor asked who it was that God used to speak to him about Christ. He had heard the preaching of D. L. Moody, Truett, and many other outstanding ministers, but said, "None of those great preachers moved me. About eight years ago God saved my wife. I have watched her now these eight years as she has been faithful to Jesus Christ in poverty and in riches. Night after night I've watched her kneel beside our bed to pray. I've watched her as she went faithfully to prayer meeting and church services, putting Jesus Christ first in every area of her life. Last night as we retired, when she kneeled to pray, I began to think of the difference between her life and mine. As I lay there, I thought of my life as a little molehill of nothing and her life as a great mountain for God and righteousness. I got up out of bed and for the first time in eight years asked her to pray for my soul. Last night, by my bedside, I was lead to Jesus Christ — not by D. L. Moody or George Truett, but by my wife." Yes, there is no question about it. Jesus knocks on the door of men's hearts through His people.

3. Through His Holy Spirit. The Lord Jesus made it clear in John 14 that He sent the Holy Spirit to convict the heart of man of "sin, righteousness, and judgment." Many a man who thought he had escaped the preacher and Word of God has been awakened in the middle of the night to toss restlessly on his bed at the conviction of God's Spirit, which is the gentle knocking of Jesus at his heart's door.

4. Through providence. Usually I don't use the word "providence," for it is often misused as a rather impersonal reference to God. I'm using it in this sense to mean God's gentle alignment of the affairs of a man's life that continually point him to his need of inviting Jesus into his heart. Many a man who has felt the hot breath of death upon him recognizes that he was saved by the providence of God. He may not have recognized that this was the gentle knock of Jesus at his heart's door, but it was just the same.

Years ago, in a small town in Texas, a German merchant and his entire family came forward at the close of a service to receive Christ as Savior and Lord. When the pastor asked him to tell his experience, this is what he said: "Yesterday I closed my store early and went for a ride with my family. We were crossing the railroad tracks when a train struck the back of our car. We went home and got out, all frightened. There was just one member of our family, little Mary, a member of your church, who was not frightened. We talked about it and Mary said, 'Daddy, if we had been one second later in crossing that track, all the family would have been in hell now but me.' As soon as Mary said that, I called the family to prayer and asked Mary to lead us to heaven."

It may be that you have heard the Lord Jesus knock at your heart's door in all of these ways: through His Word, His people, His Holy Spirit, His providence. They key question is: Have you opened the door and accepted His promise? "If any man open the door, I will come in to him, and will sup with him, and he with me." The word "sup" simply indicates fellowship. Man is incomplete until he has fellowship with God through His Son Jesus Christ, which is only possible by inviting Him into your heart.

Christ's Challenge to Laodicea

The challenge of Christ to Laodicea, like His six other challenges, is to "overcomers" or "born-again believers." The challenge is simply a promise to share His throne as He shares the Father's throne. This is a promise that we will rule and reign with Christ in His coming kingdom. The ultimate victory of the Christian, not seen in this life but in the life to come, is a challenge to faithfulness.

"He that hath an ear, let him hear what the Spirit saith unto the churches." Have you heard what our Lord has said to the churches?

The message of Christ to Laodicea indicates that as this age draws to a close, apostasy, deadness, and indifference will increase. It is no wonder our Lord asked of this age, "When the Son of Man cometh, shall He find faith on the earth?" We should not expect to see revival as in the days of Moody, Finney, and others, but an apostasy on the part of the Laodicean church. And who can deny that the ecumenical movings of this day clearly fulfill this prediction?

As we have come to the close of the messages of Christ to the seven churches, it is the burden of my heart that individuals will heed the Savior's invitation to open the door of their heart. The picture of Christ knocking at the heart's door is not only the picture of what He has been doing these past two thousand years but the picture of all He is going to do in this age to bring men to Him. If man refuses to voluntarily open the door of his heart, he rejects Jesus Christ!

9

Christ's Description of Himself

Revelation 1-3

The book of Revelation is the only document in the Bible that contains Jesus Christ's personal description of Himself. It is of particular importance to us because it describes Him as He is today, not as He was during His thirty-three years of self-limitation on earth, when He came to suffer and die for our sins.

It is exceedingly profitable for us to examine these statements. When placed together as a unit, they give a clear picture of the divine nature of our Lord. Let there be no doubt about it — Jesus Christ is God!

1:11 — "I am Alpha and Omega, the first and the last."

1:17 — "I am the first and the last." This speaks of Christ's eternity.

1:18 — "I am He that liveth, and was dead." This indicates His life on earth and crucifixion.

1:18 — "I am alive forevermore." This speaks of His resurrection and eternity.

1:18 — "I . . . have the keys of hades and of death." Christ controls who goes to hell and the future of all believers.

2: 1 — "These things saith he that holdeth the seven stars in his right hand." Christ controls the messengers of the churches.

2: 1 — "Who walketh in the midst of the seven golden lampstands." Christ walks among the churches, easily accessible to them if they desire.

2: 8 — "These things saith the first and the last, who was dead, and is alive." Here Christ combines a reference to His eternal nature with the fact of His death and resurrection.

2:12 — "He who hath the sharp sword with two edges." Christ presents the Word of God as His offensive weapon.

2:18 — "The Son of God." This asserts Christ's relationship to God as His divine Son.

2:18 — "Who hath his eyes like a flame of fire." This is an obvious reference to His searching gaze upon the work of His Church.

2:18 — "His feet are like fine bronze." Bronze, or brass, speaks of judgment. The Lord Jesus Christ will one day judge all men.

3: 1 — These things saith "he that hath the seven spirits of God, and the seven stars." The Holy Spirit will guide the "star" messengers of the churches. The Church has never been without guidance, if she would just look for it.

3: 7 — "These things saith he that is holy." His nature is holy.

3: 7 — "True." His testimony is right and can be relied upon.

3: 7 — "He that hath the key of David." Authority to rule over God's people is His.

3: 7 — "He that openeth, and no man shutteth; and shutteth, and no man openeth." Christ controls men's opportunities to serve Him.

3:14 — "These things saith the Amen." He has final authority.

3:14 — "The faithful and true witness." He is *the* revelation of God.

3:14 — "The beginning of the creation of God." Christ is the author and source of all God's creation.

3:20 — "Behold, I stand at the door and knock; if any man hear my voice, and open the door, I will come in to him, and will sup with him, and he with me." The Lord of glory pictures Himself standing without, knocking at the door of man's heart. He does not force His entrance, but leaves it to the individual to invite Him to come in.

Mr. Holman Hunt has painted a beautiful picture of Christ knocking at the heart's door. It is said that one day he unveiled this picture to a friend and asked, "What do you think of it?"

"It is a beautiful picture, but I think you have forgotten something," said the friend. "There is no latch on the door."

Mr. Hunt replied, "Ah, my friend, you have missed the point of the picture. The man at the door is the Lord Jesus Christ. The door is the entrance to the human heart and the latch is on the inside. Unless the one on the inside opens the door, Jesus will never come in.

A Description of Salvation by Christ Himself

Next to the person of Christ, the most important subject in the Bible is the doctrine of salvation. Since our Lord gave a descriptive phrase of salvation to each of the seven churches, we can combine them to produce the most complete picture of eternal life to be found in the Bible.

Each of Christ's definitions of salvation is given to him that "overcometh" or who is born again (1 John 5:4, 5; John 3:3, 7).

2: 7 — "To him that overcometh will I give to eat of the tree of life, which is in the midst of the paradise of God." Believers will live forever in God's paradise. This is suggestive of an eternal existence comparable to the Garden of Eden: no death, no sin, no heartache, nothing but the blessings of God.

2:11 — "He that overcometh shall not be hurt of the second death." Believers will not be "cast into the lake of fire" (Rev. 20:15) but are saved from eternal death, or separation from God.

2:17 — "To him that overcometh will I give . . . a white stone, and in the stone a new name written, which no man knoweth except he that receiveth it." The stone indicates acquittal from our sin and the new name, as Christ renamed Peter and Paul after their conversions, points to the new life we have in Him.

2:26, 27 — "To him will I give power over the nations; and he shall rule them with a rod of iron; as the vessels of a potter shall they be broken to shivers, even as I received of my Father." This indicates that believers will rule and reign with Christ in the millennium.

2:28 — "And I will give him the morning star." This is Christ's promise to come into the believer's heart and dwell with him.

3: 5 — "He that overcometh, the same shall be clothed in white raiment." The believer's sinful nature is covered by the righteousness of Christ.

3: 5 — "I will not blot his name out of the book of life." Only those whose names are *not* written in the Book of Life are "cast into the lake of fire." Believers need never fear hell, for Christ will see that our names remain in the Book of Life.

3: 5 — "I will confess his name before my Father and before his angels." Sinful men have no right to go to heaven in the presence of the Father and His angels; but Jesus will confess our names, thus giving us the right to be there.

3:12 — "Him that overcometh will I make a pillar in the temple of my God, and he shall go no more out." Believers will have access to the Holy Place of God.

3:12 — "I will write upon him the name of my God, and the name of the city of my God, the new Jerusalem, which cometh down out of heaven from my God." Believers will be eternally identified with Christ and thus have access to the Holy City that is to come down from heaven.

3:12 — "I will write upon him my new name." Believers will be eternally identified with Christ.

3:21 — "To him that overcometh will I grant to sit with me in my throne." Believers will have a share in the ruling of Christ's coming kingdom.

Part II

Christ and the Tribulation

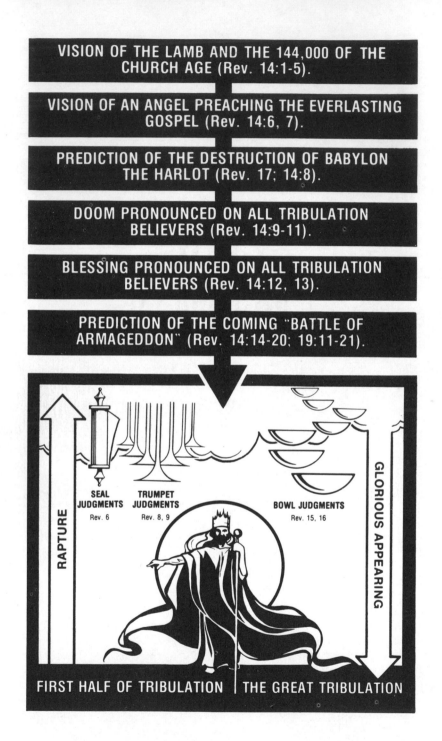

VISION OF THE LAMB AND THE 144,000 OF THE CHURCH AGE (Rev. 14:1-5).

VISION OF AN ANGEL PREACHING THE EVERLASTING GOSPEL (Rev. 14:6, 7).

PREDICTION OF THE DESTRUCTION OF BABYLON THE HARLOT (Rev. 17; 14:8).

DOOM PRONOUNCED ON ALL TRIBULATION BELIEVERS (Rev. 14:9-11).

BLESSING PRONOUNCED ON ALL TRIBULATION BELIEVERS (Rev. 14:12, 13).

PREDICTION OF THE COMING "BATTLE OF ARMAGEDDON" (Rev. 14:14-20; 19:11-21).

RAPTURE

SEAL JUDGMENTS
Rev. 6

TRUMPET JUDGMENTS
Rev. 8, 9

BOWL JUDGMENTS
Rev. 15, 16

GLORIOUS APPEARING

FIRST HALF OF TRIBULATION | THE GREAT TRIBULATION

10

The Throne
of God

Revelation 4, 5

> After this I looked and, behold, a door was opened in heaven; and
> the first voice that I heard was, as it were, of a trumpet talking with
> me; which said, Come up here, and I will show thee things which must
> be hereafter. And immediately I was in the Spirit and, behold, a
> throne was set in heaven, and one sat on the throne (Rev. 4:1, 2).

Somewhere, high in the heavens, out in the universe, a "throne is set"
which is the throne of God. This throne, described in the passage before
us, gives us a brief glimpse of the heaven of God.

The Bible teaches us that there are three heavens. The first, the atmospheric heaven where "the prince of the power of the air" holds forth,
will one day be destroyed. The second heaven is the stellar heaven,
known to us as the universe. The third heaven, into which John was
caught up in verse 1, is the heaven of God. This could be the "empty
place" referred to by Job in 26:7. Although the heavens are filled with
stars wherever the telescope can reach, it seems that behind the North
Star there is an empty place. For that reason it has been suggested that
this could be the third heaven, the heaven of God, where His "throne
is set."

John Raptured

The first thing after the close of the church age was the call to John
to "come up here," or be caught up into heaven. This has given impetus
to the suggestion that the Church will be raptured before the Tribulation.
If this were the only reason for believing in the pretribulation Rapture,
the concept would rest on rather shaky ground. There are several other
passages, however, that make this point clear. When this view of John's
rapture is added to the others, they make a good case. Consider the
following four reasons for this conclusion.

1. The location of this event is right for the Rapture. Chapters 2 and 3 deal with the seven successive periods of church history. Chapters 4 and 5 present a vision in heaven, and chapter 6 introduces the Tribulation Period. John, one of the first true members of the Church of Jesus Christ, is a fitting symbol of the Church being taken out of the world just before the Tribulation begins, as our Lord promised: "Because thou hast kept the word of my patience, I also will keep thee from the hour of temptation, which shall come upon all the world, to try them that dwell upon the earth" (Rev. 3:10).

2. The absence of any mention of the Church indicates that it is not on the earth during the Tribulation. There are sixteen references to the Church in the first three chapters of Revelation, whereas chapters 6 through 18, which cover the Tribulation, do not mention the Church once. The natural conclusion drawn from this is that the Church will be absent during the events of the Tribulation.

3. The extensive use of Old Testament language and symbols in chapters 4 to 18 is an indication of Israel, not the Church. This is understandable since the church age is the time of the Gentiles, whereas the Tribulation is the time of Jacob's trouble or the seventieth week of Daniel, determined by God for His dealing with Israel. Some of these Old Testament symbols are the tabernacle, the Ark of the Covenant, the altar, elders, censers, cherubim, seals, trumpets, plagues.

4. There is much similarity between the events of Revelation 4:1, 2 and other scriptural teaching on the Rapture, such as 1 Thessalonians 4:13-18.

None of the above four reasons is sufficient in itself to insist that Revelation 4:1, 2 refers to the Rapture of the Church. When, however, all of them are considered, we are inclined to believe that this inference could rightly be made.

The Rapture of the Church is not explicitly taught in Revelation 4 but definitely appears here chronologically at the end of the church age and before the Tribulation. We will turn to other passages of Scripture that specifically deal with the Rapture of the Church so that we might be clearly informed of what the Bible teaches on the subject.

Rapture — What Does It Mean?

The main Bible passage on the Rapture of the Church is 1 Thessalonians 4:13-18. Verse 17 tells us, "Then we who are alive and remain shall be *caught up* together with them in the clouds." "Caught up" is a translation of the Greek word which literally means to seize as a robber seizes a prize. The Latin word, from which we get the word "rapture," is *raptus,* meaning to seize by force. Thus we have as the meaning of rapture that one day Christ is coming to rob the world of His jewels (that is, His redeemed ones) to take them into heaven with Him. Therefore, when we refer to the Rapture of the Church, we mean it is a sudden snatching out of this world of the believers. It should be pointed out that this is not limited to certain denominations or religious groups but includes all those who have voluntarily invited the Lord Jesus Christ into their life. (For a more complete presentation of the second coming of Christ and of the Rapture of the Church, see chapters 1 and 2 of the author's book, *The Beginning of the End*.)

Before we peer into heaven, we should understand one basic principle. Whenever the Bible describes heaven to human beings, it has the problem of conveying the unfamiliar things of heaven to men. The difficulty of this can be seen when one considers the problem a native from a primitive tribe of Indians would have in writing to his tribesmen after being brought out to civilization. What words would he use to convey to people totally unfamiliar with civilization such things as automobiles, bicycles, refrigerators, TV sets, and ice cream cones? It is equally difficult to convey to human beings the marvels of heaven. For this reason, many things are presented symbolically. These symbols are not difficult to understand or deduce when one keeps in mind the background and understanding of the people to whom they are written. Most of the symbols in the book of Revelation depicting heaven have a counterpart in the Old Testament.

The Throne of God

The central object of heaven is the throne of God, referred to eight times in the first six verses of chapter 4 and eighteen times altogether in chapters 4 and 5. It seems to be a fixed point, with everything else in heaven located in relationship to it. We find such expressions as "about the throne," "out of the throne," "before the throne," "in the midst of the throne." The throne of God has been considered the fixed center of the universe, the immovable point of reference. Just as the North Star has been the ancient navigators' positional guide because of its fixed position among the stars, so is the throne of God the place of authority and the center of God's rulership for the activities of heaven.

Seven Things Around the Throne of God

The remainder of chapter 4 conveys to us seven distinct characteristics of the throne of God that are most interesting. We shall examine them individually.

1. The Triune God

"And immediately I was in the Spirit and, behold, a throne was set in heaven, and one sat on the throne." Verses 2 and 3, when carefully studied, reveal all three members of the triune God. When John said "immediately I was in the Spirit," he was referring to the Holy Spirit. The King James Version unfortunately does not always capitalize Spirit, but it should (see the American Standard Version, 1901, and also the New Scofield Reference Bible). This refers to the thought that John was filled with the person of the Holy Spirit. Also in verse 2 we have another unfortunate translation. "And one sat on the throne" should read "and there sat on the throne." The Greek does not denote singular or individual characteristics. Instead, it refers to the presence on the throne but does not denote how many. Consequently, we know that God the Father is there. However, verse 3 points out that God the Son is likewise present; as taught in other passages of Scripture, He is "seated at the right hand of God."

"And he that sat was to look upon like·a jasper and a sardius stone; and there was a rainbow round about the throne, in sight like an emerald." Verse 3 mentions and describes the Lord Jesus Christ, for John said, "and he that sat was to look upon . . ." We know from several passages of Scripture that God the Father cannot be seen (John 1:18; 6:46, 1 Tim. 6:16). The one John looked upon is none other than the only member of the Trinity that can be seen, the Lord Jesus Christ, who is described in two ways.

First, Christ is our High Priest. John's description of the one he looked upon as "like a jasper and a sardius stone" is most illuminating. Dr. Harry Ironside, in his book on Revelation, says this about John's description.

> The jasper of the Revelation is not the opaque stone we know by that name. It is later described as a crystal (chapter 21:11). It is probably the diamond, the most brilliant of all the precious jewels. The other stone is blood red, and may really be the ruby. Thus the two together give the idea of glory and sacrifice. Remembering that many of the first readers of the Revelation were converted Jews, we might ask, what would these stones suggest to them? Surely every instructed Hebrew would instantly recall that they were the first and last stones in the breastplate of the High Priest (Exodus 28:17-20). As these stones bore the names of the tribes of Israel, arranged according to the births of the twelve patriarchs, the one would suggest at once the name of Reuben, "behold a son," and the other Benjamin, "son of my right hand." It is Christ enthroned; the Son about to reign in power Who was before the seer's vision.[5]

One might well ask the question, Why is it that the first thing we notice about Christ here presents Him in His priestly role? The answer to that is seen in the location of this description. Coming right after the church age and before the Tribulation, it represents the first time Christ has had His entire priesthood together at one time. The priesthood of believers began at the day of Pentecost. Every member of the body of Christ is a member of the priesthood of believers; actually we are called in 1 Peter 2:9 "a royal priesthood." The Church of Jesus Christ, made up of "the royal priesthood," is not now in the presence of Christ, at least in its entirety. Only after the Rapture of the Church, when the dead in Christ are raised and we are changed, will the entire priesthood of Christ be united at one time. Therefore, the sardius and jasper stones are used to depict Christ as our High Priest.

Second, Christ is the Eternal One. Another phase of the description of Christ as seen by John is "a rainbow round about the throne, in sight like an emerald." This is not an ordinary rainbow but a perfectly circular rainbow. We only see half of the rainbow on earth, but in heaven we will see a perfectly circular rainbow which, like a green emerald, presents the eternal nature of Christ. Truly He is the Eternal One.

As we examine these two descriptions of Christ, the first to greet the Christian after the Rapture, they remind us that we are in heaven not because of anything we have done, but because Christ, our faithful High Priest, has given us a royal priesthood, freely, by His grace. And similarly, He has imparted of His eternal nature to us, entitling us to share His everlasting life. When we take this into consideration, certainly it should not be difficult for us to offer the "sacrifice of praise to God continually" (Heb. 13:15).

One of the most commonly neglected Bible subjects among Christians today is the priesthood of the believer — that is, that we today are priests of God. As His priests, we should be faithful in exercising our privileges and responsibilities. What are our responsibilities? Basically they are twofold: intercession and sacrifice.

Intercessory prayer should occupy much of the life of the believer (1 Tim. 2:1). If we really understood that non-believers cannot pray and that Christians out of fellowship with God cannot pray, then we would be very burdened to pray for our brothers in Christ and for the unsaved. The course of history could well have been changed had we Christians been faithful in this regard.

Another work of the priest in the Old Testament was to sacrifice. The New Testament tells us of four sacrifices that can be made by the Christian:

Romans 12:1,2 — your body
Hebrews 13:15 — the sacrifice of praise (worship)
Hebrews 13:16 — good works
Hebrews 13:16 — giving

2. The Twenty-Four Elders

"And round about the throne were four and twenty thrones, and upon the thrones I saw four and twenty elders sitting, clothed in white raiment; and they had on their heads crowns of gold." The next thing we see "round about the throne" are twenty-four thrones with "elders," in white raiment and crowns on their heads, sitting on the seats. One of the most controversial questions raised by this vision of the throne of God is the identity of the twenty-four elders. Some Bible scholars, good ones indeed, believe them to be men, whereas the others, equally competent, believe them to be angels. Let us examine both views.

John Darby, one of the first to write on this subject, said, "The number twenty-four represents twice twelve. One might perhaps see here the twelve patriarchs and the twelve apostles — the saints in the two dispensations." This is better than to make them "represent" the *Church;* but it leaves them symbolic rather than actual elders.[6]

Dr. Ironside explains,

> But now the fourth verse brings before us a sight never beheld in heaven on any previous occasion: twenty-four thrones (not merely "seats") surrounding the central throne, and upon them twenty-four elders seated, with victors' crowns (not diadems) upon their heads, and clothed in priestly robes of purest white. Who are these favored ones gathered around the glorious central Being? I do not think we need be in any doubt as to their identity, if we compare scripture with scripture and distrust our own imagination, which can but lead us astray.
>
> In 1 Chronicles, chapter 24, we read of something very similar; and again I would remind you that many of John's readers were Hebrews, thoroughly familiar with the Old Testament. Can we question for a moment that every Jewish believer would instantly remember the twenty-four elders appointed by King David to represent the entire Levitical priesthood? He divided the priests into twenty-four courses, each course to serve for two weeks at a time in the temple which Solomon was to build. The same arrangement was in force when our Lord's forerunner was announced. Zacharias was "of the course of Abiah," the eighth in order (Luke 1:5).
>
> The priests were many thousands in number; they could not all come together at one time, but *when the twenty-four elders met* in the temple precincts in Jerusalem, *the whole priestly house* was represented. And this is the explanation, I submit, of the symbol here. The elders in heaven represent the whole heavenly priesthood — that is, all the redeemed who have died in the past, or who shall be living at the Lord's return. In vision they were seen — not as a multitudinous host of millions of saved worshipers, but just twenty-four elders, symbolizing the entire company. The church of the present age and Old Testament saints are alike included. All are priests. All worship. There were twelve patriarchs in Israel, and twelve apostles introducing the new dispensation. The two together would give the complete four and twenty.
>
> Then, observe further: these persons are not angels. They are redeemed men who have overcome in the conflict with Satan and the world, for they wear victors' wreaths upon their brows. Angels are never said to be "crowned," nor have they known redemption.
>
> There are two kinds of crowns mentioned in this book: the victor's crown, and the ruler's diadem. The former is the word here used.[7]

Thus two of numerous great men of God believe that the elders are men.

When I studied with Dr. David L. Cooper some years ago, he said of these twenty-four elders that nothing in the context would indicate that these elders are used representatively. Never should one resort to a figurative, symbolic, or secondary meaning of any passage of Scripture unless there is a warrant for the same in the context. One will seek in vain for such justification. There is nothing that suggests the idea of representation. The language simply states that there were twenty-four thrones and twenty-four elders who were seated upon their thrones, and who had crowns of gold upon their heads. These are heavenly beings. The most rational interpretation of them is that they are celestial beings of an especially high order who, under God, are assisting in the administration of the universe.

Dr. William R. Newell explains,

> We can only assume, not prove, that the "elders" are not of our race at all. The cherubim are not; nor the seraphim nor the "chief princes" (Daniel 10:13). Because the term "elders" is so often mentioned (over 200 times) in Scripture, both in connection with Israel and the Church, many are willing to assume that the elders are human beings. But the elders do not testify of their own *salvation* at all: although they celebrate that of *others*, as in Revelation 5:8, 9 (R.V.).
>
> Inasmuch as God had "elders" over His people *Israel*, and "elders" were also to be appointed in each *Church*, (Titus 1:15); and inasmuch as twenty-four seems God's governmental order, we do not see why it may not be that there are "elders" over God's creation; that they were created so; and they are twenty-four in number . . . so these "elders" were created and associated by God with His government. When Christ, with His Bride, the Church, comes to reign in power, in Revelation 19, we hear no more of these twenty-four elders: for God then subjects *all* to the *Man;* Psalm 8 is fulfilled. The elders, as all other heavenly beings, have their place, but under Christ and the Church.[8]

The above quotations clearly point out the vast difference of opinion on this subject. It does seem to me, however, that when we take the term "elders" into consideration and understand that there is a mistaken rendering of a passage in the King James (Rev. 5:8-12), we may properly conclude that these elders are angels.

The word "elder" means leader. Actually it is a title of rank. It has been pointed out that, militarily speaking, we have a similar expression in English. The commanding officer of any unit is often called "the old man." This has nothing to do with his age or the size unit that he heads, for he may be the commanding general of an entire army. On the other hand, he may be a twenty-four-year-old first lieutenant who is a company commander. Both are more or less affectionately referred to as "the old man." Essentially that is what the word "elder" means: "the old man." This word is used of pastors and church leaders to indicate leadership.

The most significant thing we learn about these elders is found in Revelation 5:8-12, where the twenty-four elders fall down before the Lamb and sing a new song. The King James Version reads (and probably this is what has given rise to the idea that they were men), "and hath redeemed us to God by thy blood out of every kindred, and tongue, and people, and nation." This is an unfortunate translation, for the original text does not say "redeemed *us*." The American Standard Version translates this verse, "and didst purchase unto God with thy blood men of every tribe, and tongue, and people, and nation." The very fact that these elders do not include themselves with the song of redemption indicates that they are not redeemed men. Therefore, like the other beings around the throne, they are supernatural beings or angels. The function of these twenty-four angels, then, is to lead a vast group of angels in the service of God, in the administration of his universe. We have already seen that the Lord Jesus Christ indicated in Matthew 18:10 that little children have guardian angels. It could well be that these twenty-four angels are the leaders of the angels that work with men. It should be understood, however, that these angels are limited to the will of the individual. Though men have guardian angels, if they rebel against God and refuse to walk with God, they are not guaranteed protective custody or watchful care by their angel.

3. The Signs of Judgment

"And out of the throne proceeded lightnings and thunderclaps and voices." Three things are mentioned here: "lightnings," "voices," and "thunderclaps," all proceeding from the throne of God. Lightning and thunder have long been associated with the concept of judgment; thus we conclude, since they come from the throne of God, that they are a prelude to the judgment that is about to fall upon the earth, as described in chapters 6 through 19. It should be remembered that the tribulation judgments come from the throne of God. They are not due to man's evil against man, but appear as the direct judgment of God.

4. The Seven Spirits of God

"And there were seven lamps of fire burning before the throne, which are the seven spirits of God." The seven lamps of fire, burning before the throne, are defined as "the seven spirits of God." We have already seen this description in Revelation 1:4, where John was apparently referring to the sevenfold characteristics of the Holy Spirit as revealed in Isaiah 11:2 —

1. the Spirit of the Lord
2. the Spirit of wisdom
3. the Spirit of understanding
4. the Spirit of council
5. the Spirit of might
6. the Spirit of knowledge
7. the Spirit of the fear of the Lord.

The seven Spirits do not mean seven different Spirits, but the seven characteristics of the one Holy Spirit. It should be borne in mind, however, that these characteristics are not limited to His role in heaven, or His role during the Tribulation, or His role during the church age, but are an eternal part of the Holy Spirit. Therefore, when we are filled with the Holy Spirit, in addition to the fruit of the Spirit found in Galatians 5:22, we should expect to manifest these characteristics —

wisdom, understanding, council, might, knowledge, and reverence for the Lord.

5. The Sea of Glass

"And before the throne there was a sea of glass like crystal." It is impossible to be dogmatic as to the meaning of the sea of glass, though one can conclude it is meant to convey stability, for a glassy sea is a calm sea, untroubled by winds and storms. Two suggestions for the sea itself are (1) the Church at rest or (2) the Word of God, the latter taken from the sea of glass in Solomon's Temple, which symbolized the Word of God for the means of sanctification. So we are cleansed by "the washing of water by the Word" (Eph. 5:26).

A sea in Scripture usually refers to people, and this is in accord with what we find in Revelation 15, where the tribulation saints that have been martyred by the Antichrist stand on the sea of glass.

It would seem that the sea of glass represents the sure foundation, the Word of God, our means of cleansing. The stability speaks of the completed sanctification and security of the believer. One of the things that shakes our confidence or our feeling of security is sin. The strife that goes on in the life of the believer between his old nature and his new nature causes him to yearn for ultimate sanctification, when he will no longer be tossed about by the winds of life. Here we see the tribulation believers after the Rapture standing on a solid, untroubled foundation, the sea of glass.

6. The Four Living Creatures

"And in the midst of the throne, and round about the throne, were four living creatures full of eyes in front and behind." It is most unfortunate that the King James Version translates this Greek word "beast." Actually, it is the word *zoa,* from which we get our word "zoology," which means a study of living creatures or animals. As we look at the description of these creatures, we find that they take on animallike characteristics. These four living creatures are seraphim, described by Isaiah in his vision of the throne of God (Isa. 6:1-3). They have six wings and cry, "Holy, holy, holy, Lord, God Almighty."

There are many orders of angels of which the elders are leaders, but over the elders we have seraphim, which number only four. It seems that they are engaged in the worship of God constantly, but their form would indicate that they also have other duties to perform. Because of their characteristics, it may well be that they are leaders of the realm they depict. For example, note their forms:

A lion — leader of the kingdom of wild beasts

A calf — leader of domestic animals

A man — leader of the angelic hosts responsible for the human race

A flying eagle — leader of the kingdom of the fowls of the air

7. The Heavenly Worship of Christ

"And when those living creatures give glory and honor and thanks to him that is seated on the throne, who liveth forever and ever . . ." This describes the fact that the Lord Jesus Christ is the object of worship in heaven. He is the one who sits on the throne, the object of their affections. The cause for this worship could well be linked with the fact that the Church will be raptured at this point, and for the first time they will be gathered together before the throne in resurrected bodies, thus bringing to fulfillment the purpose of Christ's incarnation. Only the Lord Jesus Christ could have left the glories of heaven to take on the form of a man, identify himself with man, become his sin, and thus pay the penalty for his sin, as He did on Calvary's cross. As mighty as these celestial beings of the angelic order are, none of them could have qualified to redeem men from their sin. The blood of a celestial being could never have cleansed us from our sin. However, the blood of God's own Son could — and did!

These angelic beings seem to be responsible to God for mankind and were no doubt frustrated because Satan had perverted himself and subverted God's plan by bringing sin into the world. They stood by helplessly while generation after generation of men fell into sin and lost fellowship with God. This act of worship seems to be their expression of devotion and adoration to the Lord Jesus Christ for redeeming from the earth what they could not redeem.

"Thou art worthy, O Lord, to receive glory and honor and power; for thou hast created all things, and for thy pleasure they are and were created." The song these celestial beings sing is a song of glory and honor to God because He is the Creator of all things. This, of course, on the basis of John 1:3, is another evidence that it is the Lord Jesus Christ who is being worshiped.

One cannot help but be moved at the loving concern and the feeling of adoration and worship in the heart of celestial beings because the Lord Jesus Christ redeemed men from sin. How much more should our hearts rejoice as we worship Him? We are the recipients of His redemption!

11

The Seven - Sealed Scroll

Revelation 5

"And I saw in the right hand of him that sat on the throne a scroll written within and on the back, sealed with seven seals" (Rev. 5:1). Whenever a chapter in the Bible opens with the word "and," we know it should be joined to the preceding chapter. This is not only true in subject matter but also in chronology.

It is as if after John had seen the throne of God, his attention focused on an object in the hand of God, which brings us to the seven-sealed scroll.

Although the word "book" is used in the King James Version, we should bear in mind that there were no hard-covered flat books during the lifetime of John. In those days and in the days of the Old Testament all books were scrolls of either papyrus or vellum.

There are three characteristics of this scroll. First, it was in the right hand of God; second, it was written "within" (on the inside) and on the "back" (outside); and three, it was closed by seven seals.

Someone has said, "The little seven-sealed book in the hand of the one on the throne mentioned in Revelation 5 contains the secret of the chapter which follows and is the key which opens the entire book of Revelation." There can be no question that this is a most significant scroll, as determined by the events which follow.

The Cause of John's Weeping

John saw "a strong angel proclaiming with a loud voice, Who is worthy to open the scroll, and to loose its seals? And no man in heaven, nor in earth, neither under the earth, was able to open the scroll, neither to look on it" (Rev. 5:2, 3).

It is evident at the outset that this is a scroll intensely related to man, for angelic beings are excluded from opening it. Instead the angel is looking for a man. We therefore conclude that the book has something to do with mankind and his relationship to the earth, the home of man. In spite of that fact, no redeemed man in heaven, no man on earth, nor any man under the earth (in hades) is considered worthy to open the book.

The importance of the book is seen in the fact that John wept when it was discovered that "no man was found worthy to open and to read the book, neither to look thereon."

What could cause a Spirit-filled man like John, lifted into heaven, to weep? These were not idle tears, induced because John just couldn't satisfy his curiosity. No, his tears had a far deeper meaning!

The prophet Jeremiah warned Israel that if they did not repent of their sin and turn to God, they would go down into captivity for seventy years. Because they refused to heed the warning of God, their judgment was imminent. Through the same prophet of judgment, God promised that they would go down into captivity for seventy years but would one day return to the land. To prove to them that they would return, God told Jeremiah to do a strange thing. Hanamel, Jeremiah's cousin, had a piece of ground that he knew would soon be worthless. Since Nebuchadnezzar was about to capture Jerusalem, God caused Hanamel to go to Jeremiah and offer to see it. Jeremiah bought the property for

> seventeen shekels of silver. And I signed the deed, and sealed it, and took witnesses, and weighed him the money in the balances. So I took the deed of the purchase, both that which was sealed according to the law and custom, and that which was open. And I gave the deed of the purchase unto Baruch, the son of Neriah . . . in the sight of Hanamel, mine uncle's son, and in the presence of the witnesses that signed the deed of the purchase, before all the Jews that sat in the court of the prison (Jer. 32:9-12).

The prophet then instructed his secretary, Baruch, to place the sealed scroll in an earthen jar, thus preserving it for his heirs. It was placed with the other papers, verifying the legal owners of property.

Although Jeremiah never lived to see the day when Israel went back into the land, his legal heir one day went before the proper authorities and, on the basis of his kinship to Jeremiah, proved that he was "worthy to open the book" and to own the property.

Essentially that is the scene in heaven. For all intents and purposes the seven-sealed scroll is the title deed to the earth. This title deed was given by God to Adam, who lost it through sin to Satan; for that reason Satan is in control of the world from the time of Adam until the glorious appearing of Christ. John wept because he knew that this scroll represented the title deed to the earth and that as long as it was left sealed, Satan would remain in control of the earth.

The Lion-Lamb Is Worthy

> And one of the elders saith unto me, Weep not; behold, the Lion of the tribe of Judah, the Root of David, hath prevailed to open the scroll.

and to loose its seven seals. And I beheld and, lo, in the midst of the throne and of the four living creatures, and in the midst of the elders, stood a Lamb as though it had been slain, having seven horns and seven eyes, which are the seven spirits of God sent forth into all the earth (Rev. 5:5, 6).

As John looked, he saw a Lamb that appeared as if it had been sacrificed already, possessing seven horns, seven eyes and seven spirits. This gives us five characteristics of the Lord.

". . . the Lion of the tribe of Judah." The names of our Lord are never given by accident, but all convey a part of His nature. Since the lion is the king of beasts and since Judah is the ruling tribe of Israel, this indicates that Christ is to come as King to reign over the affairs of men.

". . . the Root of David." This, of course, refers to Jesus' incarnation or His first birth with His roots in the family of David.

". . . a Lamb as though it had been slain." When Christ completed the work of redemption, He earned the title deed to the earth; as by Adam came sin, by Christ came redemption. It is a beautiful picture that we see here! Even though the angel refers to our Lord in His glory as a Lion, indicating His power and might, John sees Him as a sacrificial Lamb, for John sees Him through eyes of faith. Men who reject Christ will see Him as a Lion when He comes to judge and to reign over them. Men who believe in Him will see Him as their sacrificial Lamb.

". . . having seven horns." This indicates that the Lamb was not weak. A horn in Scripture indicates power (see Zech. 1:18 and the little horn of Dan. 7). The Lord Jesus said of himself, "All authority is given unto me in heaven and in earth" (Matt. 28:18). When Christ came the first time, as a Lamb, though He displayed certain powers, He did not manifest all of His power. When He comes the next time, as a Lion, at His glorious appearing, it will be in the manifestation of His omnipotence, His all-consuming power.

". . . having. . . seven eyes, which are the seven spirits of God sent forth into all the earth." These eyes speak of the judgment of our Lord, including the seven characteristics of the Holy Spirit that rests upon Him without measure (John 3:34). When our Lord comes, He will know all that men have ever thought or done. Every deed will be brought into judgment. It should be pointed out that seven is God's number of perfection; therefore when Christ, the Lion of the tribe of Judah, comes to judge the world at the end of the Tribulation, it will be as the perfect judge who has all power and who knows all about mankind. It should also be borne in mind that He was the sacrificial Lamb, but men rejected Him. The unsaved man rarely contemplates that the one who will judge him in eternity is the very one he spurns by his rejection of Christ Jesus as Savior and Lord today.

The moment Christ takes the seven-sealed scroll, all the angelic beings in heaven fall down before Him: the four living creatures and the four and twenty elders. Almost as a footnote, they are mentioned as having two things in their hands: (1) harps, indicating the music of heaven, and (2) golden bowls filled with the prayers of the saints. Although it is impossible to be dogmatic about these prayers, one is almost led to believe that they are unanswered prayers that will be answered at the glorious appearing of Christ. Many a Christian has gone out into eternity with the prayer of the Apostle John, "Even so, come, Lord Jesus," still unanswered; this prayer will be answered in that day. Many a Christian has prayed as our Lord taught us to pray, "Thy will be done on earth as it is in heaven." This will not be accomplished until Christ comes to set up His millennial rule. This is another indication that all prayer is answered, though we may not receive the answer in our lifetime.

A new song is sung by the heavenly singers that is not clear in the King James Version. Therefore I quote from the American Standard Version.

> Worthy art thou to take the book, and to open the seals thereof: for thou wast slain, and didst purchase unto God with thy blood *men* of every tribe, and tongue, and people, and nation, and madest them to be unto our God a kingdom and priests; and they reign upon the earth (Rev. 5:9, 10).

As was pointed out in our discussion of the identity of the twenty-four elders, these elders are not singing about themselves, but about the worthy one who has redeemed men on the earth.

We must keep in perspective the dramatic scene in heaven. When John sees the book and discovers what it represents, the title deed to the earth, he sorrows because no one is worthy to open the book. Suddenly he finds that "the Lamb of God which taketh away the sins of the world" is worthy to open the book on the basis of what He has done for men. The angels' song indicates that He is worthy for three reasons:

1. "For thou wast slain." This refers, of course, to Christ's mediatorial work on Calvary's cross.

2. ". . . and didst purchase unto God with thy blood men of every tribe, and tongue, and people, and nation." Since someone from every tribe and nation and tongue will be included in redemption, the 270 million people in the world today that do not have the Bible in their own mother tongue will hear about the Savior and His love. (More will be said concerning this in our study of chapter 7.) This verse is particularly delightful for me when I think of the ministry of Mr. and Mrs. Phil Bair, Wycliffe Bible translators to the Lacondone Indians of Mexico. When I was in their home many years ago, they had been ministering to these Indians for eighteen years. One of the promises of God that spurred them on was the assurance that one day a Lacondone Indian would be included in the redeemed. They have the promise of Almighty God as found in this verse.

3. ". . . and madest them to be unto our God a kingdom and priests; and they reign upon the earth." This, of course, refers to the fact that we are members of God's spiritual kingdom into which we are born when we believe on the Lord Jesus Christ. It bears repeating that we are His priests, doing the work of priests, conveying to men the Gospel in this age. When Christ comes again in His glory, we believers will be with Him "to rule and reign with him."

The Description of Christ by Angels

And I beheld, and I heard the voice of many angels round about the throne and the living creatures and the elders . . . saying with a loud voice, Worthy is the Lamb that was slain to receive power, and riches, and wisdom, and strength, and honor, and glory, and blessing (Rev. 5:11, 12).

In a day when humanistic men are unwilling to acknowledge Jesus Christ as more than a good man or a model example, we should hear what the angels of heaven, who know Him best, say of Him. They proclaim Him worthy to receive seven things — power, riches, wisdom, strength, honor, glory, and blessing — which far outshadows any obeisance due to mortal men. I joyfully accept the description of the angels as the only authentic portrait of Christ.

The Universal Worship of Christ

And every creature that is in heaven, and on the earth, and under the earth, and such as are in the sea, and all that are in them, heard I saying, Blessing, and honor, and glory, and power be unto him that sitteth upon the throne, and unto the Lamb forever and ever. And the four living creatures said, Amen. And the four and twenty elders fell down and worshiped him that liveth forever and ever (Rev. 5:13, 14).

These verses, which almost seem like the second stanza of the song of the heavenly hosts, carry John beyond the Tribulation, beyond the glorious appearing, to the end of the millennium, to the time of the Great White Throne Judgment, when every living creature will worship Christ. This passage of Scripture should be studied in connection with Philippians 2:9-11:

Wherefore, God also hath highly exalted him, and given him a name which is above every name, that at the name of Jesus every knee should bow, of things in heaven, and things in earth, and things under the earth, and that every tongue should confess that Jesus Christ is Lord, to the glory of God, the Father.

Both of these passages of Scripture indicate very clearly that every living creature in heaven, on earth, under the earth, or in the sea, awaiting the day of judgment, will one day worship Jesus Christ. That includes all those who in this life voluntarily reject Him. All those on earth will worship Him; all those under the earth and those in the sea, awaiting judgment, will at their resurrection be forced to worship Him just before they are cast into the lake of fire. What a tragedy!

12

The Tribulation
Period

Daniel 9:24-27

As we come to the sixth chapter of the book of Revelation, it becomes immediately apparent that we have reached the very heart of the book. As John beholds the Lord Jesus Christ, represented by a lamb, breaking the first seal, we encounter the first of a long series of events that begin in heaven and are consummated on earth. A seal is broken in heaven and a horseman appears on earth. Each seal broken in heaven introduces a tragedy on earth.

With the breaking of the seal and the appearance of the horseman the dreaded period of time known as the Tribulation Period begins. This seven-year span of future world history, graphically described in Revelation 6:1 - 19:21, will be the darkest time the world has ever known.

To understand the Tribulation Period as described in the book of Revelation, one should understand that it is a very special day in the plan of God for His nation, Israel. To see this clearly, we must turn to the book of Daniel and examine Daniel's seventy weeks of years.

The Seventy Weeks of Daniel

The ninth chapter of Daniel reveals that after the nation of Israel had been in captivity about sixty-eight years, Daniel was diligently studying the prophetic word of God. He saw in Jeremiah 25:11, 12 that Israel would serve the king of Babylon for 70 years:

> And this whole land shall be a desolation, and an horror; and these nations shall serve the king of Babylon seventy years.
> And it shall come to pass, when seventy years are accomplished, that I will punish the king of Babylon, and that nation, saith the LORD, for their iniquity, and the land of the Chaldeans, and will make it perpetual desolations.

Daniel tells us in 9:2, after the Chaldeans had conquered the Babylonians, "I, Daniel, understood by books the number of the years, concerning which the word of the LORD came to Jeremiah, the prophet, that he would accomplish seventy years in the desolations of Jerusalem." At this point Daniel began to pray, confessing his sins and the sins of the nation of Israel. After that the Lord sent the angel Gabriel with a special message to Daniel, which according to verses 22 and 23 was to "give thee skill and understanding" that he should, "therefore, understand the matter, and consider the vision." Here is the exact vision given to Daniel.

> *Seventy weeks* are determined upon *thy people* and upon thy *holy city*, to finish the transgression, and to make an end of sins, and to make reconciliation for iniquity, and to bring in everlasting righteousness, and to seal up the vision and prophecy, and to anoint the most Holy. Know, therefore, and understand, that from the going forth of the commandment to restore and to build Jerusalem unto the Messiah, the Prince, shall be seven weeks, and threescore and two weeks; the street shall be built again, and the wall, even in troublous times. And after threescore and two weeks shall Messiah be cut off, but not for himself; and the people of the prince that shall come shall destroy the city and the sanctuary, and the end of it shall be with a flood, and unto the end of the war desolations are determined. And he shall confirm the covenant with many for one week; and in the midst of the week he shall cause the sacrifice and the oblation to cease, and for the overspreading of abominations he shall make it desolate, even until the consummation, and that determined shall be poured upon the desolate (Dan. 9:24-27).

Seventy Weeks Means Seventy Years

It is most important to understand the time element involved. The Hebrew word translated "week" actually means a unit of seven rather than seven days and only the context reveals how much time is involved. The word should literally be translated "sevens" or "heptads."

We have a similar expression in English. For example, if I say a dozen, I could mean a dozen weeks or a dozen years; or I could say a gross, which limits me to a unit of 144 but does not tell me what that 144 is. The same is true of this Hebrew word.

This is not as complicated as it may seem. For if we study the context, it is clear from both Daniel and Revelation 12 that these sevens are weeks of years or heptads of years. Thus we find that Daniel's 70 weeks are literally 70 units of 7 years, or 490 years.

The Three Divisions of the Seventy Weeks of Years

Verse 25 of Daniel 9 tells us that these 490 years are divided into three groupings which we must understand in order to comprehend the time element.

1. Seven weeks of years equals forty-nine years. "Know, therefore, and understand, that from the going forth of the commandment to restore and build Jerusalem unto the Messiah, the Prince, shall be . . ." seven haptads or forty-nine years. A study of Jewish history reveals that from the going forth of the decree of Cyrus, it took the Jews under both

Ezra and Nehemiah forty-nine years to complete the building of the walls of the city of Jerusalem. Thus we have the first unit predicted.

2. Sixty-two weeks of years equals 434 years. These next 434 years, described as 62 heptads, were predicted to be "troublous times," and certainly that is accurate. It was a period of silence from God until John the Baptist came on the scene. It was a time of weakness in Israel, culminating in Roman domination at the time of Christ. This period was predicted to end when "Messiah shall be cut off, but not for Himself . . ." Thus we see that this second period of time extended from the rebuilding of the Temple to the crucifixion of Christ, a total of 434 years. Verification of the exact dates is impossible, since the Medo-Persians were notoriously poor historians. The best evidence we have is fulfilled prophecy. Since all other prophecies about Christ have been fulfilled without deviation, we can well assume the fulfillment of this one. Sir Robert Anderson's masterful book, *The Coming Prince,* shows that Christ's coming into Jerusalem the Sunday before His crucifixion occurred in exactly the right year. To my knowledge, his book has never been refuted.

3. One week equals seven years. Verse 27 predicts that *he* ("the prince that shall come," or the Antichrist, who will obviously be a Roman, since he will be of the people that were to destroy Jerusalem) will make a covenant with Israel for one week. That covenant, which will cover seven years, has not been made since the crucifixion of Christ but is a covenant that will be made in the days of the Antichrist. Even though he will break the covenant in the midst of the seven years, it will still be part of the period of time that Gabriel predicted would be "determined upon thy people and upon thy holy city" (Dan. 9:24).

The first two periods of these 70 units of years total 483 years. Please see the chart on the next page and note that from the going forth of the decree of Cyrus to the crucifixion of Jesus Christ, the Messiah, was 483 years. Thus all but one "week," or heptad, of Israel's prophetically determined history has been accomplished. The final period of time will be such a time in history that the people of God are referred to as "the desolate."

The latter part of verse 26 of Daniel's prophecy indicates that there will be a predicted time of interruption in this prophetic calendar: "unto the end of the war desolations are determined." This corresponds with Isaiah's reference to "the year of Jehovah's favor" (Isa. 61:2, ASV), which is the Christian dispensation, the year of God's grace to the Gentiles. This, however, culminates in Isaiah 61:2 with "the day of vengeance of our God," which is the resumption of God's prophetic calendar for Israel, called the seventieth week of Daniel or the Tribulation Period.

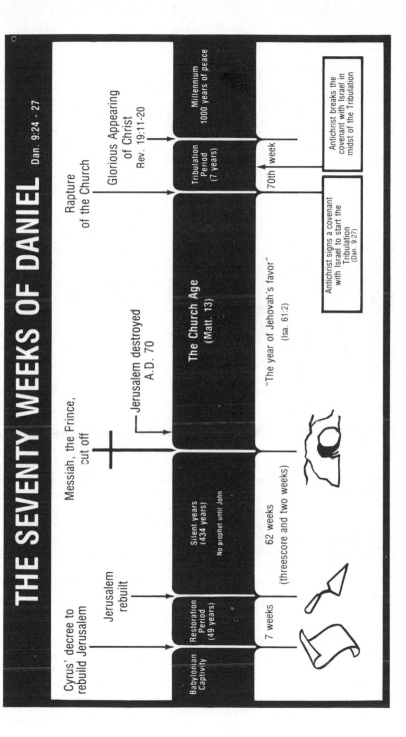

THE SEVENTY WEEKS OF DANIEL
Dan. 9:24 - 27

Cyrus' decree to rebuild Jerusalem

Jerusalem rebuilt

Messiah, the Prince, cut off

Jerusalem destroyed A.D. 70

Rapture of the Church

Glorious Appearing of Christ
Rev. 19:11-20

Babylonian Captivity

Restoration Period (49 years)

Silent years (434 years)
No prophet until John

The Church Age (Matt. 13)

Tribulation Period (7 years)

Millennium 1000 years of peace

7 weeks

62 weeks (threescore and two weeks)

"The year of Jehovah's favor" (Isa. 61:2)

70th week

Antichrist signs a covenant with Israel to start the Tribulation (Dan. 9:27)

Antichrist breaks the covenant with Israel in midst of the Tribulation

Man Will Never Destroy the World

We hear a great deal of speculation as to whether or not man will ever destroy the world. That this could never happen is seen by the fact that God projects seven years in the future, destined for His people Israel, that will be consummated in the physical coming of Christ to the earth to set up His millennial kingdom. Everything God determines and predicts in His Word will happen. Therefore we can say without reservation that man will not destroy the world.

The Chronology of Revelation

Turning again to Revelation 6, which introduces the Tribulation Period, we must examine this book carefully for the chronology, or sequence of events. To assume that the book of Revelation is intended to unfold step by step is to prepare oneself for hopeless confusion. Because of the variety of subjects dealt with, there must be some overlapping, but because the first six chapters fall into a natural sequence, some readers are inclined to assume that this is true of the entire book.

Chapters 6, 8, 9, and 16 Are the Keys

Chapter 6 introduces the seal judgments, which make up the first quarter of the Tribulation Period. The seventh seal then introduces the seven trumpets, which indicates that we are carried into the second quarter of the Tribulation, as described in chapters 8 and 9. The seventh trumpet, in turn, introduces the seven bowl judgments, which comprise the last half of the Tribulation Period. Everything else between chapters 7 and 8 must be placed within the consecutive events of these three judgments. An illustration often used by the late Bible teacher, Dr. David L. Cooper, will explain this. He suggested that in a fireworks display, bright objects will scatter through the heavens in proper sequence and then suddenly one will explode into several others. Then, just when they are almost gone, one of them bursts into several more. John saw the seven seals broken one at a time; then the seventh one introduced the seven trumpets, and finally the seventh trumpet introduced the seven bowls. Each of these judgments, whether breaking a seal, blowing a trumpet, or pouring out a bowl, is a symbolic announcement in heaven of an event that actually takes place on earth. By examining the following chart, the reader can see that these judgments take place consecutively.

The Purpose of the Tribulation

Having pointed out the fact of the seven-year Tribulation Period which will yet come upon this earth, we should examine God's purpose in sending it. We are not left to conjecture, for it was revealed to Daniel at the same time he received the prediction of the "seventy weeks." (Note Dan. 9:24.) God never does anything without a purpose, and here we find that He had six things in mind.

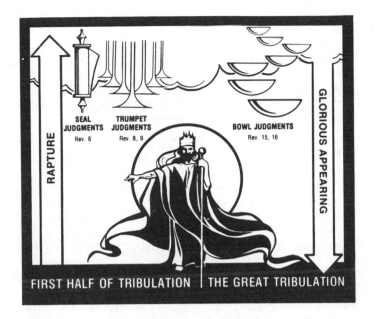

SEAL JUDGMENTS
Rev. 6

TRUMPET JUDGMENTS
Rev. 8, 9

BOWL JUDGMENTS
Rev. 15, 16

RAPTURE

GLORIOUS APPEARING

FIRST HALF OF TRIBULATION | THE GREAT TRIBULATION

1. "To finish the transgression." This time of suffering will finish the transgression of Israel, which is the rejection of her Messiah. During the Tribulation, the people of Israel will turn to Christ in great revival and will become witnesses who will go forth and preach the Gospel around the world, as we will see in the study of chapter 7. Actually, the Tribulation Period will help cause a great revival in Israel.

2. "To make an end of sins." The words "make an end" litcrally mean "to seal up." This period of time will end with the binding of Satan, which will "seal up" sin. Man's cup of iniquity is filled to overflowing, and God brings judgment upon the earth for man's rejection of His Son.

3. "To make reconciliation for iniquity." Again, this is a reference to the revival of Israel, when they will be reconciled to God through Him whom they rejected and whom they asked Pilate to crucify.

4. "To bring in everlasting righteousness." When Israel experiences her revival, the age of righteousness or the millennial kingdom of Christ will be ushered in. Though there will be a brief insurrection at the end, it will be so short-lived as not to interrupt this final period of everlasting righteousness that will lead into the new era of the future, described in Revelation 21 and 22.

5. "To seal up the vision and prophecy." When Israel has turned to Christ, there will no longer be a need for prophets' visions and prophecy.

6. "To anoint the most Holy." This could refer to the holy place on Mt. Moriah where Solomon's Temple was built over the place where

Abraham had prepared to offer Isaac as a sacrifice, symbolically preparing the way for Israel to have her sins cleansed through the anticipation of the eventual death of Christ on the cross. It could also refer to the millennial kingdom that will consummate the Tribulation and usher in that age of righteousness that all Christians yearn for, the only answer to the heartaches and problems of this world.

What Begins the Tribulation Period

Some Christians have the erroneous idea that the Rapture of the Church will occur at the end of the Tribulation. There is no Scripture to support this view other than the slight suggestion of 1 Thessalonians 4:16 that accompanying Christ, who will shout from heaven, will be the voice of the archangel and the trump of God, indicating that as Christ comes to take His Church, possibly the angel Michael will come back to the earth to again lead the children of Israel as he did in Old Testament days.

The actual event inaugurating the Tribulation is found in Daniel 9:27 when the Antichrist, "the prince that shall come," makes a covenant with Israel for seven years. Even though he will break that covenant, his signing will trigger the prophetic clock of God, and from that moment on only seven years will be left for man on the earth. One of the reasons we know Christ is coming *before* the Tribulation to rapture His Church is because the Rapture is a secret thing. The glorious appearing will not be secret but well known, for exactly seven years will elapse from the signing of the covenant to the glorious appearing of Christ on the earth.

It may be that when Christ raptures the Church, the Antichrist will make a covenant with Israel the next day, the next week, or who knows how much later. There are sufficient signs existing today to indicate that this event could take place soon: for example, Israel's return into the land of Palestine to become a nation, with whom the Antichrist will deal; the one-world church that will dominate the first half of the Tribulation Period; and the craze for one-world government, already in existence and continuing to gather momentum until it culminates in the signing of the covenant between the Antichrist and Israel. From that point God's prophetic clock will begin to tick and man will have only seven years left.

Who Will Be in the Tribulation

Since it seems evident that the coming of Christ is close at hand, men living today are keenly interested in whether or not they will have to live under the Antichrist during the Tribulation. In all probability most of the present generation *will* go into the Tribulation.

The great exception to that is the Church of Jesus Christ. If you are a member of the body of Christ — that is, if you have personally invited Jesus Christ into your heart — you will *not* go into the Tribulation. The Bible tells us in 1 Thessalonians 1:10 that the Lord Jesus has "delivered us from the wrath to come," referring to the Tribulation Period. Revelation 3:10 also clarifies that the church of Philadelphia, which is the present-day church of true believers, will be delivered from the Tribulation: "Because thou hast kept the word of my patience, *I also will keep thee from the hour of temptation, which shall come upon all the world, to try them that dwell upon the earth.*"

In the final analysis, then, *you* decide whether or not you will go into the Tribulation. Your acceptance or rejection of Jesus Christ determines your relation to that time of great misery and heartache. If you accept Jesus Christ, you will be raptured out before it begins. If you have rejected Him, then according to all that the Bible teaches you will be one of those unfortunate individuals who will live at the time of the greatest misery in all the history of mankind.

13

The Seal Judgments

Revelation 6

This tired old planet has come under cruel times of famine, catastrophe, dictatorship, and many other causes of suffering. But the sixth chapter of Revelation introduces the most awesome period of time the world has ever known. This seven-year period decreed by God is for the primary purpose of shaking man loose from a false sense of security. Then he may call upon the name of the Lord just before the end of the age. How well God achieves this purpose will be seen in our study of chapter 7.

The first of the three chronological judgments — seals, trumpets, and bowls — is set forth in chapter 6. Some Bible teachers see enough similarity in these judgments to suggest that they run concurrently. That is, the first seal will occur at the same time as the blowing of the first trumpet and the pouring of the first bowl. Certainly all three sets of judgments tend to build up intensity as they get to numbers five, six, and seven. The problem with that idea is that it completely overlooks the fact that the opening of the seventh seal introduces the trumpet judgments of chapters 8 and 9 and the blowing of the seventh trumpet introduces the seven bowls of chapter 16. Therefore we may conclude that the three judgments run chronologically and represent periods of the Tribulation.

The seal judgments cover approximately the first quarter of the Tribulation or the first twenty-one months.

The Four Horsemen of the Apocalypse

The first four seals reveal horses and riders in the form of striking imagery. An examination of the context indicates that it is clearly a dramatic presentation of literal facts. It is not God's intent to convey individual personality through these horsemen but world conditions. That

The
Seven-Sealed
Scroll

they all do not refer to specific people can readily be seen by noting that the fourth horseman is called death, and death is not a person.

The four horsemen present the picture of man's inhumanity to man. They seem to be a divine prediction of the affairs of man which will cause much human suffering. This is not new, for man in control of the affairs of this world has a history of causing his fellow creatures much suffering, with false hopes of peace followed by wars, famines, and death.

The First Seal — the Rider on the White Horse

And I saw when the Lamb opened one of the seals, and I heard, as it were, the noise of thunder, one of the four living creatures saying, Come. And I saw and, behold, a white horse; and he that sat on him had a bow; and a crown was given unto him, and he went forth conquering, and to conquer (Rev. 6:1, 2).

Immediately after the Lamb opens one of the seals, the first of the prophetically well-known "Four Horsemen of the Apocalypse" appears. Since there are three more horses and riders to follow with the successive breaking of the other seals, it is important that we identify this first rider, as a key to understanding the three that follow him.

The Antichrist

The Antichrist and his kingdom are obviously what is symbolized by the rider on the white horse. Emperors such as Napoleon, Alexander the Great, and many other would-be conquerors ride on horses. The purpose

of this rider is clearly stated: "conquering and to conquer." This is none other than "the little horn," that "willful king" that Bible students have been anticipating for many years. One interesting characteristic of his coming is that he has a bow in his hand, symbolic of aggressive warfare, but no arrow, indicating that he will conquer by diplomacy rather than by war. Ushering in a false peace, he will be the superman who promises to solve all the world's problems. That he will be ultimately victorious is seen by the fact that he has a crown upon his head.

Interdependence among nations today is increasing at a rapid pace. In spite of the obvious and flagrant uselessness of the United Nations, it is being heralded by many world leaders as the only answer to world peace. The international hysteria of nuclear warfare has created a phobia in the minds of men who will never be satisfied until they have a one-world government. The stupidity of such a possibility is completely ignored by the idealistic aspirations of millions. The fact that Communist thinking and subversive activity dominates the U.N. does not deter the advocates of one-world government. Their enthusiasm has not abated, although many small new nations are given equal vote with mature nations like our own, and two-thirds of the voting power resides in the hands of 10 percent of the world's population, which owns 5 percent of the world's land area. Dr. J. Vernon McGee once told of a woman in Arkansas who named the U.N. as the beneficiary of her $700,000 estate in the fervent hope that this relatively small contribution could be of some effect in bringing about universal peace on earth and good will among men. Doubtless this poor woman never dreamed that her money would be used for a spying headquarters by Communists against her own nation. Nor did she ever dream that her money would be used to help finance the butchery of innocent victims in Katanga in an effort to force the typical Communist coalition government upon the people. In all probability, she was not aware that the U.N., the so-called International Peace Organization, by private agreement has always had a Communist in charge of the Security Commission. In spite of all these things, some of the wealthiest foundations in the United States are doing everything humanly possible to brainwash the population through television and other mass communication with the idea that the only solution to the world's problems is the United Nations. If this is not setting up the U.N. in a perfect position to make room for the Antichrist and his one-world government, it is at least preparing the thinking of the people for Antichrist's eventual government.

Russia to Be Destroyed

The way this master diplomat, the Antichrist, *could* conquer the world through his sudden diplomacy is to offer peace and prosperity to mankind. In all likelihood, this could be accomplished if Russia and her cohorts were out of the way. Ezekiel 38 and 39 tells us that Russia will conceive of the idea of conquering Israel. Just at the moment when she is preparing to do so, God will supernaturally destroy Russia. In the wake of this destruction, the Antichrist could very well offer peace to all men in order to avoid any further wars between nations.

When will Russia be destroyed? It is impossible to be dogmatic in answering this question. At the latest, it will occur at the beginning of the Tribulation, for it will take seven years to burn the implements of war after God has wrought His destruction on Russia (Ezek. 39:9). It is unthinkable that this would go on during the Millennium; therefore it must come at the very beginning of the Tribulation or even before it.

It is *possible* that Russia will be destroyed before the Rapture of the Church. There is nothing that demands it, for the Lord could come at any time. However, there is no reason to believe that Russia would not be destroyed before the Rapture of the Church. If the Antichrist signs a covenant with Israel immediately after the Rapture of the Church, thus beginning the Tribulation, it is highly probable that Russia will be destroyed *before* the Rapture. However, if there is a period of time between the Rapture of the Church and the beginning of the Tribulation, the Church could be raptured, Russia destroyed, and then the Antichrist set up his one-world government. (For further information on this subject, see the author's book, *The Beginning of the End,* chapter 5.)

Although all the world leaders promise peace to the masses, man does not have the capacity to fulfill that promise, no matter who he is or what nation he represents. The Antichrist will be no exception! For we will see that his false promises of peace, though giving him control of the world, are impossible for him to fulfill.

The Second Seal — the Rider on the Red Horse

And when he had opened the second seal, I heard the second living creature say, Come. And there went out another horse that was red; and power was given to him that sat on it to take peace from the earth, and that they should kill one another; and there was given unto him a great sword (Rev. 6:3, 4).

The red horse is obviously a symbol of war, for he has the ability to "take peace from the earth, and that they should kill one another." This is also evidenced by the fact that a great sword is given unto him. Obviously, in the Antichrist's takeover of the world, some dissatisfied nations will have waited too long to make their play to avoid his domination. Yet, rather than remain slaves, they will revolt, thus inaugurating a world war. Although their attempt to throw off the shackles of the Antichrist will be unsuccessful, it is evident from the opening of the next seals that this will be a widespread and bloody war.

The Third Seal — the Rider on the Black Horse

And when he had opened the third seal, I heard the third living creature say, Come. And I beheld and, lo, a black horse; and he that sat on him had a pair of balances in his hand. And I heard a voice in the midst of the four living creatures say, A measure of wheat for a denarius, and three measures of barley for a denarius, and see thou hurt not the oil and the wine (Rev. 6:5, 6).

The black horse is an evident symbol of famine. Black is used to depict famine in other portions of Scripture (Jer. 4:28; Lam. 4:8, 9), and famine often follows war as it did after World War I.

Inflation also tends to grip the world right after a world war. Such will be the case during the Tribulation. The balances in the hand of the rider on the black horse indicate the scarcity of food. In fact, a penny is the biblical reference to the equivalent of a man's wage for one day (Matt. 20:2, 9). Three measures of barley are about a pint, a minimum daily sustenance diet. This, then, indicates that a man will have to work for a whole day just to earn enough money to live, which will leave nothing for his family or the elderly. On this basis we can predict that all Social Security and other means of "preparing for our old age" will come to an untimely and unsuccessful end.

The rich, however, are not so injured, as indicated by the fact that the rider on the black horse was instructed not to "hurt the oil and the wine," which are traditionally foods of the rich. As in the case of all war and resulting famine, this famine will take a heavy toll on the common people.

The Fourth Seal — the Rider on the Pale Horse

And when he had opened the fourth seal. I heard the voice of the fourth living creature say. Come. And I looked and, behold, a pale horse, and his name that sat on him was Death, and Hades followed with him. And power was given unto them over the fourth part of the earth, to kill with sword, and with hunger, and with death, and with the beasts of the earth (Rev. 6:7, 8).

The pale horse is literally livid or corpse-like, signifying death. The death rate of the first twenty-one months of the Tribulation Period will be tremendously high as a result of war, famine, and inflation. In fact, one-fourth of all the world's population will die. According to the present world census, that would total between 600 and 700 million people — some killed by the edge of the sword, some by hunger, and some by "wild beasts of the earth." This could mean literally a revolt against man on the part of the animal kingdom, or it could be a symbolic use of the term "beasts," relating to governments of men. In the book of Daniel, we find that kingdoms of men are pictured by God as beasts. Also in Revelation 13, the beast that comes up out of the sea symbolizes the Antichrist and his government. In any event, one-fourth of the world's population will be wiped out as a result of the Antichrist's greedy confiscation of world power.

The fact that hades follows the pale horse of death indicates that these are unsaved dead. A believer who receives Christ during the Tribulation Period will not go to hades, which is a place reserved for unbelievers as they await the Great White Throne Judgment (Rev. 20). Without being dogmatic, I suggest for your consideration that individuals who receive the mark of the beast (Rev. 13) will be those who die during this period. My reason for stating so will be given more clearly when we get to the thirteenth chapter.

The Fifth Seal — the Martyred Tribulation Saints

And when he had opened the fifth seal, I saw under the altar the souls of them that were slain for the word of God, and for the testimony which they held. And they cried with a loud voice, saying, How long, O Lord, holy and true, dost thou not judge and avenge our blood on them that dwell on the earth? And white robes were given unto every one of them; and it was said unto them that they should rest yet for a little season, until their fellow servants also and their brethren, that should be killed as they were, should be fulfilled (Rev. 6:9-11).

Chapter 7 will introduce the fact that at the beginning of the Tribulation there will be a great soul harvest throughout the world. The opening of this fifth seal clearly teaches that after this has begun, there will be a time of great personal persecution for the children of God. These, then, are tribulation saints, individuals who had not received Christ at the time of the Rapture, before the Tribulation began, but did receive Him as a result of the faithful witnesses who are depicted in chapter 7. They will be martyred "for the word of God and for the testimony which they held." The world despises a clear-cut testimony based on the Word of God, and that hatred will be given free reign during the Tribulation Period, resulting in an agonizing time of persecution for God's people. Even though these saints inquire of the Lord, "How long, O Lord . . . ," others will be killed for their testimony. Their prayer will not deter persecution, because it is a time that must be "fulfilled." We know that these are believers, for verse 11 indicates that they are clothed in "white robes." It is comforting to know that although this time must be "fulfilled," it is also "yet for a little season." This will probably be the greatest period of cruelty to Christians the world has ever known. Many of the believers referred to in Revelation 7:9 as "a great multitude, which no man could number," will probably be slain.

The Sixth Seal — Catastrophe on Earth

"And I beheld, when he had opened the sixth seal and, lo, there was a great earthquake, and the sun became black as sackcloth of hair; and the moon became like blood" (Rev. 6:12). When the sixth seal is opened, the earth is violently shaken by a giant earthquake, indicating that it is the great day of God's wrath. Following the persecution of His saints, He will show His displeasure on the earth for this persecution.

Although there is some conjecture to the contrary, this would seem to be a description of a physical shaking of the earth caused by earthquakes and volcanic eruptions. Such things have happened before. Earthquakes in Northern Peru in 1970 took almost 67,000 lives. A professor once stated that in the last 4,000 years earthquakes have caused a loss of 13 million lives, and he claimed the most awful earthquake is yet to come. Dr. Robert Thieme tells of the eruption on August 27, 1883, of Krakatau on an island in the Dutch East Indies. The explosion was heard in Rodriguez, South America, 3,000 miles away. As a result of the earthquake, the sun was blotted out. Volcanic ash seems to make the moon look red and blots out the sun, for after the eruption of Krakatau, it is said that the sun was blotted from view at Batavia, 100 miles away. At Bondune, 150 miles away, the sun was blotted out and the moon appeared red. Tidal waves traveled as far as Cape Horn, 7,000 miles away, and in all 36,000 people were killed.

"And the stars of heaven fell unto the earth, even as a fig tree casteth her untimely figs, when she is shaken of a mighty wind" (Rev. 6:13). Verse 13 indicates that meteors will fall to the ground and hit as hard, unripe things.

"And the heaven departed as a scroll when it is rolled together; and every mountain and island were moved out of their places" (Rev. 6:14). This catastrophe will apparently bring about fantastic changes on the physical earth.

"And the kings of the earth, and the great men, and the rich men, and the chief captains, and the mighty men, and every slave, and every free man, hid themselves in the dens and in the rocks of the mountains" (Rev. 6:15). Great fear will grip the hearts of men, but because of their stubborn, willful, rebellious ways, instead of turning to God in the hour of peril they will hide in the rocks and the dens of the earth. The cataclysm will be so gigantic in proportions that even the great men of the earth will have no place to hide. Who knows what will happen to the poor?

"And said to the mountains and rocks, Fall on us, and hide us from the face of him that sitteth on the throne, and from the wrath of the Lamb; for the great day of his wrath is come, and who shall be able to stand?" (Rev. 6:16, 17). It seems evident from these verses that the world will know that this is a judgment from the Lord Jesus Christ, for they refer to Him as the Lamb. They are also fully aware that they are in the Tribulation Period. The fact that the fifth seal delineates the large scale persecution of Christians during the Tribulation prepares us for the opening of the sixth seal. That is followed suddenly by this great catastrophe, which in turn leads the world to recognize that this is the judgment of God because they have persecuted the followers of the Lamb of God. Suddenly they will recognize that they are being judged and will be conscious that there is no place to hide. Oh, that men in that day will have enough sense to recognize that the Lord is their defense, as did the people in Nahum's day (Nah. 1:5-7) in a similar experience. These sixth-seal catastrophes are only an introduction to the great cataclysms that will come upon the earth during the remainder of the Tribulation Period.

The first twenty-one months of the Tribulation Period consist of horrifying events. After the Antichrist assumes world-wide control, world war, famine, inflation, and the death of 25 percent of the world's population will follow. Then will occur a great persecution of God's people, followed by the catastrophic judgment of God. If this passage of Scripture teaches anything, it instructs us that the Tribulation is a period no man should enter. The wonderful thing is, you don't have to! If you have received the Lord Jesus Christ as your Savior, you will never go into the Tribulation Period.

14
The 144,000
Servants of God

Every spiritually minded Christian is interested in revival! One of the most frequent questions I am asked when holding prophetic conferences is, "Do you think there will ever be a great worldwide revival?" My answer to this is always an unqualified "Yes, but not as you think." I then go on to explain the biblical teaching that until the time of the Rapture of the Church, there will be a falling away, apostasy, a decline in the moving of the Spirit of God, so much so that the Lord Jesus said of those days, "When the Son of man cometh, shall he find faith on the earth?" (Luke 18:8).

The greatest revival the world has ever known is yet to come. It will not occur within the church age but during the Tribulation Period. This coming worldwide revival is prophetically described in Revelation 7, appearing right after the seal judgments to indicate that it will take place during the first twenty-one months of the Tribulation. Evidently, while the Antichrist is making his political advance, the Holy Spirit will move in the hearts of millions of people, leading them to a saving knowledge of Christ.

The Work of Angels

A detailed study of the work of angels in the book of Revelation would reveal that they are the special ministers of God, administering His plans for the earth. In chapters 2 and 3 they are seen as messengers assigned to the individual churches. In chapter 8 they are observed presenting the trumpet judgments. Here we find that they control the forces of nature. Actually, in the seventh chapter the angels supervise the administration of two things:

1. They control the wind from the four corners of the earth. "And after these things I saw four angels standing on the four corners of the

earth, holding the four winds of the earth, that the wind should not blow on the earth, nor on the sea, nor on any tree" (Rev. 7:1).

2. They seal the servants of GOD, the 144,000 tribulation witnesses. Since the sixth seal takes place toward the end of the first quarter of the Tribulation, we find that the destroying angel is ordered to wait until the works of sealing are finished. This would indicate that at the beginning of the Tribulation, the 144,000 servants of God will be sealed and begin their ministry of preaching the Gospel, attended by a mighty worldwide soul harvest which will culminate in a severe time of persecution for believers, inspired by the Antichrist. This would accord with the breaking of the fifth seal; at this time the sealing angel will have finished his work and the destroying angel will be permitted to hurt the earth and the sea, ushering in the sixth seal.

The 144,000 Servants of God

Few passages of Bible prophecy have been so misunderstood and distorted as to their proper meaning as verse 4. Dr. Harry A. Ironside gives this explanation:

> I am sure that many of my hearers have often been perplexed by conflicting theories regarding the 144,000. The way in which so many unscriptural and often positively heretical sects arrogate to themselves this title would be amusing, if it were not so sad. You are perhaps aware that the Seventh-Day Adventists apply it to the faithful of their communion, who will be found observing the Jewish Sabbath at the Lord's return. They suppose that these will be raptured when the Lord descends, and judgment poured out upon the rest of the church. Then we have the followers of the late Pastor Russell (Jehovah's Witnesses) who teach that the 144,000 include only the "overcomers" of their persuasion who continue faithful to the end, following the teaching of the system commonly called "Millennial Dawnism." That very absurd and weird cult known as "The Flying Roll" makes claim to the same thing; only with them, the 144,000 are those who will have their blood so cleansed that they cannot die, but will have immortal life on this earth! Besides these, there are many other sects, whose leaders consider their own peculiar followers will be the 144,000 sealed ones at the end time. All of these, however, overlook a very simple fact, which if observed, would save them from their folly. That is, *the 144,000 are composed of 12,000 from each tribe of the children of Israel. There is not a Gentile among them* . . . Whenever I meet people who tell me they belong to the 144,000, I always ask them, "Which tribe, please?" and they are invariably put to confusion for want of an answer.[9]

Who Are the 144,000?

Due to widespread confusion in regard to these 144,000, we must take time to examine the subject. If we let the "plain sense of Scripture make common sense," it becomes clear that the 144,000 are Jews. For John specifically states, "And I heard the number of them which were sealed; and there were sealed an hundred and forty and four thousand of all the tribes of the children of Israel" (Rev. 7:4).

Twelve thousand from each of the 12 tribes means exactly 12,000! 1 Kings 19 tells us that in Elijah's day God had kept for Himself 7,000 prophets who had not bowed their knees to Baal. No one seems to question the fact that He had "7,000 prophets." Why should there be any difference regarding the 144,000? It simplifies the Bible interpretation greatly if we accept God's Word at face value and do not try to force upon it any other meaning than that which it naturally conveys. There will be 12,000 Jews from each of the 12 tribes of Israel, making a total of 144,000.

The word "servants," from the Greek word *doulos,* is the same word employed by the Apostle Paul and by James when referring to themselves as the "servants" or bond-slaves of Jesus Christ. The chief function of a servant of Jesus Christ, no matter what his occupation or dispensation, is to communicate the Gospel of the grace of God. That these "servants of God" will be faithful in communicating His message is seen from the fact that they experience such fantastic results, as will be described from verse 9 of our text.

They will be inspired by the fact that they will understand the book of Revelation, which is given of God "to show unto his servants things which must shortly come to pass" (Rev. 1:1). Although they will go through a great time of persecution, they will have the comfort of knowing the duration of the Tribulation and can actually anticipate the astounding events that will take place through a study of this last book in God's revealed plan for man.

God's Seal on Their Foreheads

In some manner, these servants will have the seal of God in their foreheads (Rev. 7:3). We do not know of what this seal will consist, but the text suggests it will be visible. It is interesting to note that during this same period of time, men will be forced to receive the "mark of the beast" in their foreheads (Rev. 13:14-18). It may be that believers will have the mark of God on their foreheads, whereas unbelievers will feature the mark of the Antichrist. I am inclined to believe that both marks are final. Once a man receives the Antichrist as his master, he will have made his decision for eternity. The same will be true when one believes on the Lord Jesus Christ. The evangelization of the 144,000 will proceed among those who have not yet had the opportunity to succumb to the "lying wonders and deceitfulness" of the Antichrist. This suggests that there could well be vigorous campaigning on the part of the followers of the Antichrist and the 144,000 to get men to voluntarily submit to the mark of their master during the early days of the Tribulation. After the Antichrist instigates a wave of persecution against all Christians (the fifth seal), and after he sets himself up as God in the midst of the Tribulation Period, there will be few on the earth who are uncommitted, one way or the other. That there will be some is seen in the teaching of our Lord from Matthew 25:31-46. Those individuals referred to as "sheep" will have befriended the Jews during the Tribulation at the risk of their own lives, thus earning the right to enter the millennial kingdom in the flesh. They will be the ones who populate the millennial earth.

The Holy Spirit and the 144,000

A good deal of confusion exists among many splendid Christian people relative to the ministry of the Holy Spirit during the Tribulation Period. Much of the confusion is caused by the footnote in the Scofield Reference Bible on 2 Thessalonians 2:1-12. This footnote indicates that the Holy Spirit, the restraining influence on the devil today, will be taken out of the world when the Church is raptured just before the Tribulation begins. However, the restrainer in this passage is not the Holy Spirit; the reference is to three of the kings of the revived Roman Empire who will restrain the Antichrist during the first three-and-a-half years of the Tribulation. When the Antichrist finally subdues them, he will gain complete control of the world. That will take place during the second half of the Tribulation Period.

The Holy Spirit will most assuredly be here to empower the ministry of the 144,000. The prophet Joel foresaw this ministry of the Spirit of God in Joel 2:28, 29:

> And it shall come to pass afterward, that I will pour out my Spirit upon all flesh; and your sons and your daughters shall prophesy, your old men shall dream dreams, your young men shall see visions; and, also, upon the servants and upon the handmaids in those days will I pour out my Spirit.

This passage makes it clear that the outpouring of the Holy Spirit experienced on the day of Pentecost (referred to by Peter in Acts 2) will be the type of outpouring experienced by the 144,000 witnesses of the Tribulation. Although it did occur on the day of Pentecost, as Peter said, the primary teaching of Joel 2:28, 29 concerns the work of God on the earth during the Tribulation Period. "And it shall come to pass afterward" is a direct reference to the Tribulation.

Jews Everywhere

One can scarcely imagine a country in the world where Jews are not scattered throughout the leading cities and, in many cases, hold prominent positions of leadership. The 144,000 witnesses will not have to learn the language of the people to whom they communicate the Gospel message, for they will already be citizens of those countries and will suddenly leave all to follow Jesus Christ. No mission boards of deputation programs will be needed, for these Jews will immediately put everything else aside in their spontaneous desire to preach. It will be like having 144,000 Apostle Pauls proclaiming the Gospel of Christ.

What Message Will the 144,000 Preach?

For some strange reason, good and able Bible scholars have been confused about the kind of message the 144,000 will preach. Some have suggested that they will preach "the Gospel of the kingdom," meaning they will revert to the same message that John the Baptist preached. This cannot be so, for since Jesus Christ died on Calvary's cross and rose again, there has only been one way and one person of salvation!

Some have tried to stipulate that several gospels are referred to in the Scriptures. Let us look at some of them:

1. "The gospel of the grace of God" (Acts 20:24)
2. "My gospel" (Rom. 2:16)
3. "The gospel of God" (Rom. 15:16)
4. "The gospel of peace" (Eph. 6:15)
5. "The gospel of Christ" (Rom. 1:16)
6. "The everlasting gospel" (Rev. 14:6).

A careful examination of these passages will indicate that these terms are interchangeable and refer consistently to *one* Gospel. In fact, at the close of the book of Acts (28:30, 31) we find, "And Paul dwelt two whole years in his own hired house, and received all that came in unto him, *preaching the kingdom of God,* and teaching those things which concern the Lord Jesus Christ, with all confidence, no man forbidding him." The text does not say that Paul was preaching the Gospel, but "the kingdom of God," which *is* the Gospel of Jesus Christ! "There is no other name under heaven given among men, whereby we must be saved" (Acts 4:12).

If the terms for the Gospel as listed above are not interchangeable, then the Apostle Paul would be guilty of his own indictment, for he insisted in his epistle to the Galatians that there is just one Gospel.

> But though we, or an angel from heaven, preach any other gospel unto you than that which we have preached unto you, let him be accursed. As we said before, so say I now again, If any man preach any other gospel unto you than that we have received, let him be accursed (Gal. 1:8, 9).

It is apparent from this that the 144,000 witnesses will be preaching the same message that the Apostle Paul or the Apostle Peter preached, the same message that we preach. This so-called sophisticated society in which we live must bear in mind that the Church of Jesus Christ dare not alter its Gospel one iota nor try to adapt it to the traditions of men. Like the 144,000 witnesses, we will one day stand before God to give an account of how we have *preached* the Gospel. The great need of the ministry and the laity today is to say with Paul, "Woe is unto me, if I preach not the gospel!"

The Great Soul Harvest of the Tribulation

After this I beheld and, lo, a great multitude, which no man could number, of all nations, and kindreds, and people, and tongues, stood before the throne, and before the Lamb, clothed with white robes, and palms in their hands (Rev. 7:9).

Uppermost in the mind of God is the salvation of souls. 2 Peter 3:9 makes it clear that it is not God's will that any should perish. The same principle is found in other Bible passages, notably Matthew 18:14. As a special climax to God's ministry of salvation, Revelation 7:9 indicates that during the first part of tribulation the greatest soul harvest in all history will take place. In fact, it is this writer's belief that more people will accept Christ during the early months of the tribulation, before the Antichrist really has a chance to consolidate his one-world government and set up his one-world religion of self-worship (Rev. 13:5-7), than have been converted in the entire 1900 + years of the church age.

To assert that a soul harvest of such gigantic proportions is scheduled to take place in the future is admittedly to controvert the thinking of most prophetic students. It is nevertheless exciting to think that more people will be saved during that time than responded under the preaching of the apostles, the early church fathers, the reformation preachers, modern missions, fragmented denominationalism, radio and television preaching, and even the present day, when Bible-teaching local churches seem to be gathering in such a large number of souls. This concept is more than an optimistic dream, for it is a reasonable conclusion of a number of prophetic realities, all climaxing with the text of Revelation 7:9, "a great multitude, which no man could number, of all nations, and kindreds, and peoples, and tongues . . ."

Very infrequently can a prophetic concept be reduced to an equation, but the charted formula on the next page indicates that the soul harvest during the tribulation will exceed in number all the conversions of the almost two millenniums of church history. I challenge you to study it and the succeeding explanation to see if you agree.

The Effects of the Rapture on the World

Although the Antichrist and his followers will be delighted that the Church has been taken out of this world, many thoughtful individuals will be seriously impressed by the mysterious evacuation of millions of people. Some have suggested, and I think rightly, that the Rapture will leave its mark on mankind. Consider for a moment what would happen if the Rapture took place while Christian airline pilots were flying their 747's or DC10's loaded with people. Or think of the impact on humanity when hundreds of Christian train engineers and bus and automobile drivers are suddenly snatched from the controls of their moving vehicles.

Because Christians have invaded almost every legitimate profession known to man, the Rapture will leave an unprecedented vacancy and

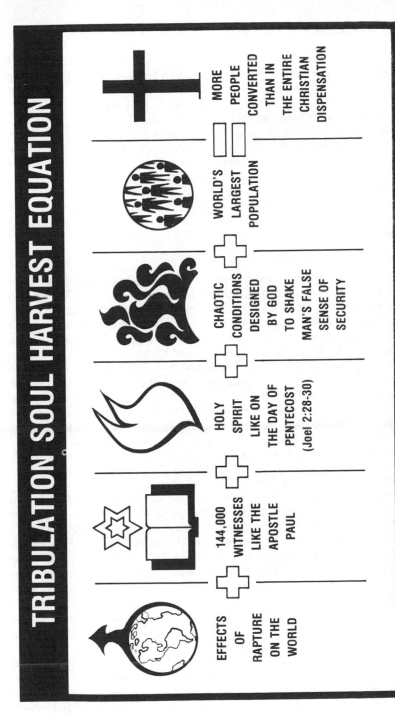

cause the most chaotic and disruptive consequences that have ever been created by a single event. Yes, the world will be fully aware of the supernatural aspect of the Rapture of millions from all over the world, particularly when they discover that the only common denominator of those raptured is their personal faith in Christ.

The impact of these strange events will soon be forgotten by the majority of those living in the tribulation due to the lies and deceit of the Antichrist, who will sign a covenant with Israel and start his diplomatic conquest of world government. But many reflective, perceptive individuals will not forget the effects created by this strange rapture, which will doubtless stir a revival of interest in prophetic studies among them. Such a mental climate will provide fertile ground for the 144,000 Jewish evangelists.

The 144,000 Apostle Pauls

We have already examined the identity of the 144,000 Jewish witnesses of the Lord Jehovah who go out to serve Him during the first few months of the tribulation. Their zeal to serve God can only be compared to that of the Apostle Paul, who was such a successful harvester of souls. As a result of their preaching, an innumerable multitude will respond from "all nations, and kindreds, and peoples, and tongues."

To appreciate the impact of these 144,000 Spirit-filled preachers on the earth, one need only compare them with the approximately 25,000 or so Spirit-filled missionaries in the world today. Add to that an equal number of Spirit-filled ministers (admittedly these are only estimates — personally, I think they are somewhat high), and we gain almost three times as many Spirit-filled, zealous soul winners going out during those early tribulation months, harvesting a myriad of converts.

A Return of the Day of Pentecost

Contrary to popular opinion among prophecy students, the Holy Spirit will not be taken out of the world when the Church is raptured. Although widely accepted, this erroneous idea (caused largely by footnotes in the Scofield Reference Bible interpreting the "restrainer" of 2 Thessalonians 2:3-8) creates more problems than it solves. First, it is not a good translation of the Greek text, which really has in view the restraining kings of Daniel 11, not the Holy Spirit. Second, the Holy Spirit is omnipresent and thus will not leave the world. Third, no man can be saved without the Holy Spirit, and since our text clearly states there will be countless conversions during the tribulation (Rev. 7:9, 14), it is evident that He will be on earth at that time in great power.

To further prove our point, we must consider Joel 2:28-32 in context and in the light of the Apostle Peter's statement on the day of Pentecost.

> Ye men of Judaea, and all ye that dwell at Jerusalem, be this known unto you, and harken to my words: for these are not drunk, as ye

suppose, seeing it is but the third hour of the day. But this is that which was spoken through the prophet Joel: And it shall come to pass in the last days, saith God, I will pour out of my Spirit upon all flesh; and your sons and your daughters shall prophesy, and your young men shall see visions, and your old men shall dream dreams; and on my servants and on my hand-maidens I will pour out in those days of my Spirit, and they shall prophesy: and I will show wonders in heaven above, and signs in the earth beneath; blood, and fire, and vapor of smoke. The sun shall be turned into darkness, and the moon into blood, before that great and notable day of the Lord come; and it shall come to pass that whosoever shall call on the name of the Lord shall be saved (Acts 2:14-21).

Although the Apostle Peter's text here was the passage from Joel, the prophecy will be more completely fulfilled during the tribulation period. The great soul harvest on the day of Pentecost was *like* that which is yet to come, but it was not the complete fulfillment. For there was no evidence of "wonders in the heaven above, and signs in the earth beneath; blood, and fire, and vapor of smoke." Joel prophesied, "The sun shall be turned into blackness and the moon into blood, *before* the great and glorious day of the Lord shall come." Pentecost did not experience these phenomena — but the tribulation period *will* culminate with these events (Matt. 24:29). We see, then, that the soul harvest of the day of Pentecost was only a type or first installment of what God has scheduled for the tribulation period.

Chaotic World Conditions

The main purpose of the tribulation is to compress into seven years of trauma, conditions that will be conducive to bringing every man to a decision about Jesus Christ or Antichrist. We will see in subsequent studies that the majority of men will accept the mark of the beast as followers of Antichrist. But in the early days of the tribulation period many other millions will decide for Christ.

The sixth seal judgment which we studied in the previous chapter, contains the description of the conditions designed by God to shake man from his false sense of security that the earth is a permanent structure, so he will be more prone to look to God for help. As long as man can stand on "terra firma," he maintains a self-sufficient attitude toward God. But when a great earthquake occurs, stars fall from heaven, the sky rolls back like a scroll, and every mountain and island are moved out of their places (Rev. 6:12-14), many terrified men will look to God for help.

A miniature illustration of this occurred in San Diego some years ago. I had been invited to address the Lions Club December luncheon meeting by the president, who had recently become a Christian. As I stood up, I sensed the usual "ho hum" attitude that often greets gospel preachers at such events. About five minutes later we felt an earthquake! The ground shook, lights went out for a moment, and the chandeliers swung to and fro. When I commenced my message a moment later, I was impressed with the fact that I now had their undivided attention. Never have I addressed a more attentive secular audience. If such a change could be created by a minor earth tremor, can you imagine the transformation after all the chaotic conditions of the sixth seal judgment occur? But keep in mind that they will come after war, pestilence, famine, and death — certainly no time to foster independence from God!

When all of these momentous occurrences are added together, we find that the ideal mental climate created in the minds of millions by the Rapture, plus 144,000 Apostle Paul types, plus an outpouring of the Holy Spirit, as in the day of Pentecost, plus chaotic conditions designed by God to shake man from his false sense of security, will certainly produce conversions double or possibly triple the percentage of those who have accepted Christ throughout the history of the church. By multiplying all this by the unprecedented population that will exist at that time, we can easily conceive of a greater ingathering of souls than have been won to Christ during the entire church age.

Unprecedented Population

Most people are acquainted with the effects of today's population explosion, but few have applied it to the spread of the gospel in the end time. The chart below has been based on accepted population statistics, past, present, and future. By studying it, you discover that there are probably more people living in the world today than have lived from the time of Christ to the generation before this present generation. If the population continues to grow as expected, and if, as suggested above, the spiritual conditions during the first half of the tribulation more than double the percentage of people won to Christ during that period, because of the enormous population, this will result in more souls harvested to Christ than have been saved during the entire history of the church. From all this we can realize the full significance of verse 9 when it says, "After this I beheld and, lo, a great multitude, which no man could number, of all nations, and kindreds, and peoples, and tongues, stood before the throne, and before the Lamb, clothed with white robes, and palms in their hands, and cried with a loud voice, saying, Salvation to our God which sitteth upon the throne, and unto the Lamb . . . These are they who came out of the great tribulation, and have washed their robes, and made them white in the blood of the Lamb" (Rev. 7:9-10, 14).

The Redeemed Multitude

Verse 9 gives us a small picture of this vast crowd of people who will be saved during the Tribulation Period, a crowd so vast that it is described as "a great multitude, which no man could number." This mighty soul harvest shows the power of God's Holy Spirit working through dedicated vessels who are already scattered around the world.

The people will be from "all nations, and kindreds, and peoples, and tongues." This indicates that the extent of the revival will approximate

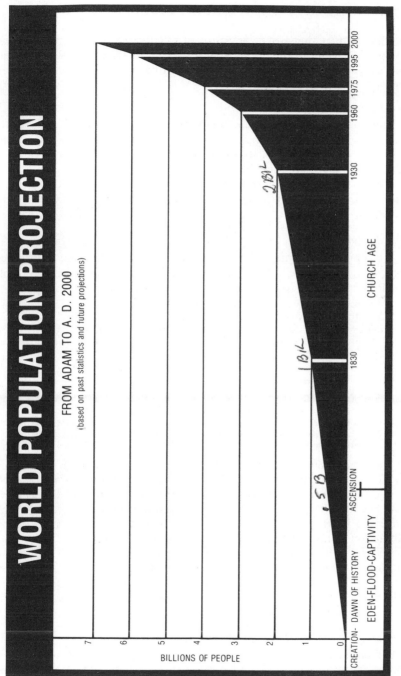

WORLD POPULATION PROJECTION

FROM ADAM TO A. D. 2000
(based on past statistics and future projections)

BILLIONS OF PEOPLE

7
6
5
4
3
2
1
0

CREATION– DAWN OF HISTORY

EDEN-FLOOD-CAPTIVITY

ASCENSION

CHURCH AGE

1830   1930   1960   1975   1995   2000

the first-century moving of the Spirit of God, when "every creature that is under heaven" heard the Gospel (Col. 1:23). However, here we find that every tribe will not only hear, but will have some of its members respond. Praise His name!

The Multitude Before the Throne

The fact that this multitude stands before the throne and before the Lamb clothed in white robes shows that they are redeemed ones from the earth who now are in the presence of the Lord, the palm branches indicating their victory in Christ.

Their song, "Salvation to our God who sitteth upon the throne, and unto the Lamb" (v. 10), indicates that they are the recipients of personal salvation.

Angels Rejoice When Men Are Saved

We often hear it said, "The angels of heaven rejoice when one sinner comes to repentance." Note the attitude of these angels as they look upon the redeemed from the earth while praising God.

> And all the angels stood round about the throne, and about the elders and the four living creatures, and fell before the throne on their faces, and worshiped God, saying, Amen! Blessing, and glory, and wisdom, and thanksgiving, and honor, and power, and might be unto our God forever and ever. Amen (Rev. 7:11, 12).

Identity of the Multitude

> And one of the elders answered, saying unto me, Who are these who are arrayed in white robes? And from where did they come? And I said unto him, Sir, thou knowest. And he said to me, These are they who came out of the great tribulation, and have washed their robes, and made them white in the blood of the Lamb (Rev. 7:13, 14).

The exact identity of this multitude is carefully spelled out. The elder asked the question as to the identity of the multitude. John did not recognize them, indicating that if they had been members of the Church or of the Old Testament, he could have identified them. Since they were redeemed from the Tribulation, however, he did not know them. These tribulation saints constitute a distinctive category, just as the Church and Israel or Old Testament saints form a special company. Each group has its own relationship to Christ, depending on the period of time in which these individuals were converted. That these are believers is unquestionable in view of the fact that they have "washed their robes and made them white in the blood of the Lamb."

Eternal Rewards for This Multitude

Eternal rewards are to be given this multitude. "Therefore are they before the throne of God, and serve him day and night in his temple; and he that sitteth on the throne shall dwell among them" (Rev. 7:15).

1. "They [are] before the throne of God, and serve him day and night in his temple." These people, like the Apostle Paul, are "absent from the body, and present with the Lord." They are not on the earth, but in heaven; in order to be there, they had to die. Their position before the throne makes it clear that they have just as much eternal blessing as the believers of the other periods.

2. ". . . and he that sitteth on the throne shall dwell among them." This is the same promise given to us in 1 Thessalonians 4:17: ". . . and so shall we ever be with the Lord." One of the promises imparted to all those who put their faith in Christ is that in the next life they will forever be with the Lord.

3. Their every need will be supplied. "They shall hunger no more, neither thirst any more; neither shall the sun light on them, nor any heat. For the Lamb who is in the midst of the throne shall feed them, and shall lead them unto living fountains of waters" (Rev. 7:16, 17). These verses suggest that the tribulation saints will sustain much personal suffering and human deprivation. They evidently will hunger and thirst during the Tribulation and will undergo excruciating exposure to the elements, but they will endure "to the end" and thus be "delivered" by the Savior.

4. ". . . and God shall wipe away all tears from their eyes" (Rev. 7:17b). This promise to "wipe all tears from their eyes," offered to His children in the life to come, is similarly extended to the Church after the Great White Throne Judgment in Revelation 21:4. Although it is impossible to say exactly what is meant by "wiping away all tears," I am inclined to believe it relates to removing our capacity to recall unpleasant things, including those eternally lost. If we could remember our loved ones suffering the torments of the damned in hell, the joy of heaven would be extinguished unless God in His marvelous grace removed the capacity for such suffering. And this further points out the seriousness of man's need of salvation and the blessings God has prepared for them that love Him.

The Great Multitude Individually Saved

One consistent principle throughout the Scriptures is graphically illustrated in regard to this multitude that no man can number: men must choose individually to accept or reject Jesus Christ. Regardless of the period of time in which a man lives, he must make his own decision.

In the Lord Jesus' day, "He was in the world, and the world was made by him, and the world knew him not. He came unto his own, and his own received him not. But as many as received him, to them gave he power to become the children of God, even to them that believe on his name" (John 1:10-12).

The same is true during the present period of God's working with men, and it will continue in the Tribulation. The multitude is not merely composed of people from every tongue and kindred and nation, but those, as stated in verse 14, who "have washed their robes, and made them white in the blood of the Lamb." That they stand before God appears in the words of verse 15. They are permitted to stand before the throne of God because they did voluntarily "wash their robes, and made them white in the blood of the Lamb."

This expression offers a beautiful picture of our personal acceptance of salvation. When man is willing to come to God by the blood of His Son, acknowledging his personal sin, then his filthy rags are cleansed by the blood of the Lamb, Jesus Christ, and he is made white as snow.

15
The Seven Trumpet
Judgments

Revelation 8, 9

"And when he had opened the seventh seal, there was silence in heaven about the space of half an hour" (Rev. 8:1). "Silence is golden," people tell us. But there will be a silence in heaven so ominous that its very nature foreshadows enormous difficulties that are about to come upon the earth. The significance of this silence is twofold: (1) it is entirely opposite the usual sound pattern of heaven, and (2) it is the result of the revelation by Jesus Christ to the angelic hosts concerning what is about to fall upon the earth.

The usual sound pattern of heaven, as we have seen in chapters 4 and 5, is one of great joy and worship. John heard "a voice as of a trumpet speaking," thunder, celestial beings crying out continually, "Holy, holy, holy, Lord God, Almighty," and the twenty-four elders crying out, "Thou art worthy, O Lord." He heard over a billion angels join in songs of praise to the "Lamb of God," the Lord Jesus Christ, saying, "Worthy is the Lamb that was slain to receive power, and riches, and wisdom, and strength, and honor, and glory, and blessing." Suddenly, amid all this crescendo of sound, there comes universal silence. This may aptly be described as "the lull before the storm."

Opening the Seventh Seal

We have already seen that the seven-sealed scroll represents the title deed to the earth. But it also contains the awful future that awaits those who reject the Lamb of God who came to take away the sin of the world. The opening of the first five seals reveals the activities of man, bringing about great misery on the earth. The opening of the sixth seal seems to be God's reaction against the people for their cruel persecution of His saints. The opening of the seventh seal introduces the seven trumpet judgments, which are all judgments of God sent upon the earth. In these

The Seven
Trumpet
Judgments

judgments, God is exclusively the sender and man is exclusively the receiver.

These judgments are so terrible that the angels stand breathless in wonder. Would to God that men today who so easily reject Jesus Christ would stand still and heed the voice of God. They, too, would be "silent" if they just knew the horrible doom of judgment that is coming upon this earth because men are rejecting God's Redeemer, the Lord Jesus Christ.

The Seven Angels

As the seventh seal is broken, the seven angels receive trumpets. Since the covenant between the Antichrist and Israel will start the Tribulation and the first seal is the Antichrist, the first six seals cover the first twenty-one months of the Tribulation. The breaking of the seventh seal may very well occur at the close of the twenty-first month; it introduces the second quarter, or the seven trumpets.

"And I saw the seven angels which stood before God, and to them were given seven trumpets" (Rev. 8:2). The reading of this text indicates that the opening of the seventh seal does not make the seven angels stand before God. Apparently they are always there, awaiting a special assignment from their Creator. The opening of the seal results in each one being given a trumpet that will be blown in proper sequence, introducing a future form of judgment. One of these seven angels is the angel Gabriel. We learn this from Luke 1:19, for when he appeared to Zacharias, the father of John the Baptist, he said, "I am Gabriel, who stands in the presence of God." Again, we find this angel, Gabriel, sent by God to bring a message to the prophet Daniel (Dan. 9:21). Since Gabriel has been named as one of the seven angels who stands before God, carrying out His bidding to man, it could be that the other six serve the same purpose, though we do not have any Scripture to identify them.

Worship in Heaven

And another angel came and stood at the altar, having a golden censer; and there was given unto him much incense, that he should offer it with the prayers of all saints upon the golden altar which was before the throne. And the smoke of the incense, which came with the prayers of the saints, ascended up before God out of the angel's hand. And the angel took the censer, and filled it with fire from the altar, and cast it upon the earth; and there were voices, and thunderclaps, and lightnings, and an earthquake. (Rev. 8:3-5).

This description of another angel taking the golden censer to make incense and "offer it with the prayers of all saints upon the golden altar" presents to us a beautiful picture that the prayers of God's people continually go up before Him. These prayers, like the prayers of the saints under the altar in chapter 6:9, are probably the prayers that have been kept in heaven awaiting this very day. For two thousand years, God's people have been praying that God would avenge Himself on those who

blaspheme against Him, revile His Son, and abuse His people. The fact that this censer is filled with fire from the altar (which stands before the throne) and is cast into the earth indicates that these prayers of vengeance are about to be answered. The action takes place in heaven but causes a response on earth of "voices, and thunderclaps, and lightnings, and an earthquake." All of this signifies that mankind is about to feel the hot blast of the wrath of God.

Who Is This Angel?

There is some disagreement among Bible scholars concerning the identity of this angel. Some say that the other angel of verse 3 is the Lord Jesus Christ, for only He is worthy to receive the prayers of saints. Since He is the only "mediator between God and men" (1 Tim. 2:5), no one else would be qualified to receive the prayers of the saints. Actually, all are agreed that Christ is the only mediator to God and that prayer should be made directly to God, through Jesus Christ the Son. However, Revelation 5:8 indicates that the four living creatures and the four and twenty elders have "golden bowls full of incense, which are the prayers of the saints," indicating that prayers are directed to God, but when unanswerable, may be stored by these administrative angels until the time for their answer, at which time they are used in the worship of heaven.

Although it is impossible to be dogmatic, it is doubtful that this "other angel" is the Lord Jesus Christ, even though He is our great High Priest. This is not an act of redemption or propitiation, and nothing is said here about blood being sprinkled on the mercy seat. Instead, I would suggest two reasons why this is not a reference to the Lord Jesus Christ.

The Lord Jesus, when appearing in the Old Testament to the children of God, was never referred to as "an angel." Instead, he was always introduced as "the Angel of Jehovah" or "the Angel of God." Also, we have no record of the Lord Jesus appearing on earth as an angel after the incarnation and ascension to heaven. Here we view Him in heaven, where He is seen as a member of the triune God. Though He appears as "the Son of man," the "Lamb that was slain," He is also uniquely, with the other two members of the Trinity, "in the midst of the throne of God." It is more likely that this "other angel" is one more of the angels (in addition to the seven) that lead in the worship of God before His throne and that help administer His universe.

"The smoke of the incense, which came with the prayers of the saints" is a beautiful symbol that expresses the fact that our prayers are always heard by God. From our point of view, sometimes we think the heavens are as brass and that we are not getting through; but from God's viewpoint, our prayers always come before "Him that sitteth upon the throne."

"And the angel took the censer, and filled it with fire of the altar, and cast it into the earth: and there were voices, and thunderclaps, and lightnings, and an earthquake" (Rev. 8:5). The voices, and thunderclaps, and lightnings, and earthquake are the result of the fire from the altar, indicating that the action of heaven initiates a responsive action on earth. As the prayers of the saints for vengeance are taken from the altar, there are frightening sounds, flashes of light, and an earthquake on the earth, introducing the fact that the seven angels are about to sound their trumpets: "And the seven angels who had the seven trumpets prepared themselves to sound" (Rev. 8:6).

Are the Trumpet Judgments Literal Judgments?

The best way to decide whether the trumpet judgments are literal or symbolic is to study them in connection with the plagues of Egypt, as found in Exodus 1-11. There we see Moses performing the symbolic act of waving his rod over the waters of Egypt, which physically turn to blood. Here we see an angel performing the symbolic act of blowing a trumpet. Why should the result on earth be less physical than the event in Moses' day? Likewise, Aaron put out his rod and smote the dust of the ground; as a result of that symbolic act, physical lice appeared. Why should it be different when these angels perform their symbolic act of blowing the trumpet? Note also that five of the plagues of Egypt are repeated in the book of Revelation. No one suggests that what happened in Egypt was not literal in its form of judgment on the rebellious Egyptians; so we can conclude that the same thing applies during the Tribulation Period and that the trumpet judgments introduce physical judgment upon the earth. The only exception are those trumpets that introduce events beyond human understanding, and even they affect men physically.

The First Trumpet

"The first angel sounded, and there followed hail and fire mixed with blood, and they were cast upon the earth; and the third part of trees was burnt up, and all green grass was burnt up" (Rev. 8:7). The hail and fire are literal judgments that fall upon one-third of the earth's surface, burning up all the vegetation they light upon. It should not strike us as strange that this is a literal cataclysm, for such things have happened before. God rained down fire and brimstone upon Sodom and Gomorrah (Gen. 19), and, as we have already seen, Egypt's water turned to blood. In fact, just such a disaster was predicted for the earth just before the "day of the Lord": "And I will show wonders in the heavens and in the earth: blood, and fire, and pillars of smoke. The sun shall be turned into darkness, and the moon into blood, before the great and the terrible day of the Lord come" (Joel 2:30, 31).

The Second Trumpet

And the second angel sounded, and, as it were, a great mountain burning with fire was cast into the sea; and the third part of the sea became blood; and the third part of the creatures which were in the sea, and had life, died; and the third part of the ships were destroyed (Rev. 8:8, 9).

A biblical allusion to "the sea" usually has reference to the sea that was prominent to the land of Palestine, the Mediterranean Sea. What appeared to John as "a great mountain" is probably a giant burning meteorite which falls into the Mediterranean Sea, killing one-third of the living creatures and destroying one-third of the ships. The result of the death and the chemical composition of the meteorite turn the water to blood.

There certainly would be an ample supply of ships in the Mediterranean Sea, since that is the permanent home of the U.S. Sixth Fleet, plus representative fleets from many other countries of the world. Since Revelation 18 indicates that Babylon will be rebuilt and become the commercial center of the world, there will no doubt be several hundred ships on the "sea" when that meteorite falls, adding further devastating details to the time of Tribulation.

The Third Trumpet

And the third angel sounded, and there fell a great star from heaven, burning as though it were a lamp, and it fell upon the third part of the rivers, and upon the fountains of waters. And the name of the star is called Wormwood; and the third part of the waters became wormwood; and many men died of the waters, because they were made bitter (Rev. 8:10, 11).

The third trumpet judgment introduces us to a shining "torch" (ASV) that visibly falls from heaven, indicating it is another meteorite and must bury itself so deep at just the right spot that it pollutes the water supply of three rivers. Evidently there is a place in the earth where the headwaters of three great rivers come together. When this "Wormwood" meteorite strikes that place, it will embitter three great rivers, and those dependent on them will die.

The Fourth Trumpet

And the fourth angel sounded, and the third part of the sun was smitten, and the third part of the moon, and the third part of the stars, so that the third part of them was darkened, and the day shone not for a third part of it, and the night likewise (Rev. 8:12).

The fourth trumpet deals with the luminous bodies as they affect this earth. It is rather interesting that on the fourth day of creation God said, "Let there by light, and there was light." The same God that created light in the first place is able to diminish it to one-third. Actually, day and night will seem to be reversed, for there will be sixteen hours of darkness and eight hours of daylight. This corresponds to the ninth plague of Egypt as seen in Exodus 10 and the prediction of our Lord in Luke 21:25, 26: "And there shall be signs in the sun, and in the moon, and in the stars; and upon the earth distress of nations, with perplexity; the sea and the waves roaring; men's hearts failing them for fear, and for looking after those things which are coming on the earth; for the powers of heaven shall be shaken." Our finite minds can hardly fathom the tremendous forces that will be unleashed upon this earth as a result of the blowing of this fourth trumpet.

The Warning Angel

"And I beheld, and heard an angel flying through the midst of heaven, saying with a loud voice. Woe, woe, woe, to the inhabiters of the earth by reason of the three angels, which are yet to sound!" (Rev. 8:13). This verse introduces the three woes of the book of Revelation, which in turn inform us that as horrible as the first four trumpets have been, they will be surpassed in misery by that which is to follow. Man's rebellion against God strangely enough gets progressively worse. Aware that he has sinned against God and is in the midst of judgments placed upon him by the Lamb, he knows he cannot stand in the "great day of his wrath" (6:17), yet he persists in his stubborn self-will against God. This clearly answers the question often asked by people, "Will there be a second chance after death?" My answer is always the same, "What good would that do? Men would make the same decision a second time."

The warning of verse 13, sounded by a special angel, threatens that worse things are yet to come. The three woes of the Tribulation Period are actually the fifth, sixth, and seventh trumpet judgments. The seventh trumpet introduces the last half of the tribulation, or the bowl judgments. The seventh trumpet and the third woe, then, are synonymous. The first woe or fifth trumpet (for they are the same) covers five months. The second woe or sixth trumpet may cover a similar period. Even a casual reading of the fifth, sixth, and seventh trumpet judgments will acquaint the reader with the fact that they are distinguished from the previous judgments since they predict such an increase in the destructive powers to be unleashed upon men. Someone has aptly described this period as "hell let loose on earth."

The Fifth Trumpet

"And the fifth angel sounded, and I saw a star fall from heaven unto the earth: and to him was given the key to the bottomless pit" (Rev. 9:1). Whenever possible, we seek to interpret words in the book of Revelation literally. However, the use of the word "star" in Revelation 9:1 is obviously intended figuratively rather than literally, for the "star" is referred to as "him," thus clearly possessing personality. A "key to the bottomless pit" could not be given to a thing or object, but to a person. The word "star" parallels our customary reference to a "baseball star" or some other well-known individual. It indicates an angel to whom is given, at this point in the Tribulation Period, "the key to the bottomless pit."

This usage coincides with that in Revelation 20:1, where we find that at the end of the Tribulation Period an angel comes down from heaven "having the key of the bottomless pit and a great chain in his hand," indicating that the angel retains the key during the Tribulation Period and that the awful spiritual forces about to be unleashed from the "pit of the abyss" are controlled by the angel. This must be a good angel to whom God can entrust such grave responsibility. His location in heaven would further indicate that he is a good angel, for fallen angels do not reside in heaven.

The Bottomless Pit

The bottomless pit is literally, in the Greek, "the pit of the abyss," not hell or hades. It has been suggested that it may be at the bottom of the great gulf fixed in hades which separates the place of torment and the place of comfort, described as the abode of the dead by the Lord Jesus in Luke 16:19-31.

A study of Scripture indicates two kinds of demons: those that are free, living in a spiritual realm and seeking to indwell the bodies of men, and those that are confined "into chains of darkness, to be reserved unto judgment" (2 Pet. 2:4) — evidently for some great sin.

Free Evil Spirits

The free spirits were described by the Lord Jesus in Matthew 12:43-45. He indicated that some unclean spirits seek rest in human bodies. If a man who has such spirits gets rid of them, he must exercise great caution that they do not return at a later time and even bring their friends with them. Evidently they travel in groups, and more than one unclean spirit can abide in a man at a time. Apparently over a thousand unclean spirits possessed the wild man of Gerasa of Luke 8, for they said, "We are Legion." This may indicate that one unclean spirit is not sufficient to *dominate* a man's behavior. A number of spirits, however, can affect behavior, giving rise to irritable or irrational behavior on certain occasions. It would seem that the more numerous the unclean spirits in a man, the more control they can exercise over his body for evil.

Where did these unclean spirits come from? The best suggestion is that they are the angels who fell with Satan in his original rebellion against God, described in Ezekiel 28:11-19 and Isaiah 14. More will be mentioned about these when we get to chapter 12. These fallen angels, sometimes referred to as "disembodied spirits," make up the kingdom of Satan and under his leadership go about seeking to lead men in the defiance of the will of God, just as Satan tempted Adam and Eve in the Garden. The success or failure of their objective is dependent on the number of spirits in a man's body and whether or not he flees for deliverance to Jesus Christ, man's only defense against the attacks of Satan.

Christians need not fear these unclean spirits, although they should be warned about them. The Apostle John said of those who possess the Lord Jesus, "Greater is he that is in you, than he that is in the world." If Jesus Christ is resident within us, we do not have to fear anything that man or Satan can hurl against us. He is our adequate defense! Many Christians seem to have a phobia about demon possession and a great fear of being controlled by evil spirits. This should not be our main concern, for if we remain in an abiding relationship with Jesus Christ, according to John 15:1-11 we never need fear being indwelt or oppressed by evil spirits. If we are to be marked by an obsession, let it be to abide in Christ as a branch abides in the vine. Satan's kingdom of evil spirits who reside in the air or "high places," according to Ephesians 6:10-12, seeking constantly to indwell the human race, seem to be somewhat limited in their possession of men in Christian lands. Those who have traveled in pagan countries can tell of supernatural phenomena taking place that can only be accounted for by an evil spiritual force. Much of the superstitious fear generated in the many religions of the world can be basically traced back to the work of demons. According to 2 Thessalonians 2:9-12 we can expect a great increase in the expression of this evil spiritual effect on the affairs of men as we get closer to the Tribulation Period. As the Antichrist comes on the world scene, he will be able to work "signs and lying wonders, with all power and with all deceitfulness of unrighteousness." This power is given him by the free evil spirits. It is probable that some of the increasing tendencies toward spirit phenomena these days may indicate that we are getting closer to the end time.

Imprisoned Evil Spirits

Jude 6 tells us, "And the angels who kept not their first estate, but left their own habitation, he hath reserved in everlasting chains under darkness unto the judgment of the great day," It seems evident from this verse that there are imprisoned angels now kept in darkness, which could well be the "pit of the abyss," until the day of the Lord. These angels are probably those that violated the laws of God in that they came in unto the daughters of men and cohabited with them, producing a strange mixtured race that had to be destroyed by the flood (Gen. 6). This is further confirmed by 2 Peter 2:1-10, which refers to the fact that God "spared not the angels that sinned, but cast them down to hell [tartaros], and delivered them into chains of darkness, to be reserved unto judgment." *Tartaros* could be the "pit of the abyss" or the bottomless pit referred to here, which could well be at the bottom of "the great gulf fixed." Evil-spirit angels, already having manifested their evil tendencies and capabilities by almost destroying a race of men, are chained there. They will be unleashed on the earth for a time of spirit persecution, the like of which the world has never known. The description of this event is seen in the fifth and sixth trumpet judgments or, as they are also called, the first two woes.

The First Woe

> And he opened the bottomless pit, and there arose a smoke out of the pit, like the smoke of a great furnace; and the sun and the air were darkened by reason of the smoke of the pit. And there came out of the smoke locusts upon the earth, and unto them was given power, as the scorpions of the earth have power (Rev. 9:2, 3).

When the bottomless pit was opened, smoke arose out of the pit until the air became saturated with a smoglike condition worse than anything Los Angeles or any other city has ever experienced. Out of this smog will come locustlike scorpion creatures that have no counterpart in all history. They have been aptly called "infernal cherubim." Shaped like locusts, and like unto horses, they have faces like men, hair like women, and teeth as lions; they have breastplates of iron, their wings are as a sound of "chariots of many horses running to battle," and they possess stings in their tails as scorpions.

Years ago someone suggested that these are B-29s because they are well-protected but have the capacity to sting from the tail. This is a fanciful suggestion, for in reality these are spirit beings that probably will not be seen by men but whose effects will be strongly felt. These evidently fulfill the locusttype judgment the Lord predicted would come upon the earth during the Tribulation (Joel 1, 2). They are not to be interpreted literally, nor symbolically, but spiritually, for they depict a spirit creature able to effect a physical response on men. These awful creatures that come upon the earth for the purpose of persecuting men are beyond our comprehension. If men could see these creatures, their hearts would no doubt fail them for fear.

Apollyon — "Destroyer"

"And they had a king over them, who is the angel of the bottomless pit, whose name in the Hebrew tongue is Abaddon, but in the Greek tongue hath his name Apollyon" (Rev. 9:11). The leading angel of these evil spirits from out of the pit of the abyss is, in the Hebrew, Abaddon, and in the Greek, Apollyon, meaning "destroyer." (It is interesting to note that different generations have tried to identify this being with some particular world personage. A number of years ago I read in the *Pulpit Commentary* on the book of Revelation that this was no doubt Napoleon because of the similarity of names.) Actually this is a special angelic being of a fallen state who assists Satan in his evil spirit kingdom. It is probably not Satan himself, since he is not today confined in chains of darkness in the pit of the abyss. He is probably comparable in Satan's kingdom to the archangel Michael of the heavenly hosts. His actual name is destroyer, typical of the followers of Satan: they do not build or construct, but ever work to destroy.

Torment Five Months

Unlike any kind of locusts that have existed before them, these are not going to harm vegetation but men. They will not be able to kill them, but they will torment them five months. This torment is described as "the torment of a scorpion, when he striketh a man" (9:5). It has been said that the sting of a scorpion, though seldom fatal, is one of the most painful stings known. The venom seems to set the veins and nervous system on fire, and the effects last for several days. By contrast, the effects of this sting will extend five months.

Verse 6 speaks of pain so intense that "men [shall] seek death, and shall not find it; and shall desire to die, and death shall flee from them." Although these infernal creatures will not be observed by the human eye, they will cause such physical pain that men will seek death, but

death will be removed from them. This is a description of almost un-
imaginable suffering.

Believers Exempt From This Judgment

The power of God over the spirit world will protect believers from
these evil-spirit creatures. Verse 4 tells us that they have power to hurt
"only those men who have *not* the seal of God in their foreheads." Just
as God protected the children of Israel in the land of Goshen from the
plagues of Egypt, so He will protect His children during the Tribulation
Period. As the Lord Jesus said, "But he that shall endure unto the end,
the same shall be saved [delivered]" (Matt. 24:13). God will preserve
believers from the Tribulation judgments inflicting the earth. So far the
only means by which Christians will die is martyrdom. "I saw under the
altar the souls of them that were slain . . . for the testimony which they
held" (Rev. 6:9). This further confirms the faithfulness of our God, who
will give dying grace to His children in that hour and grant them the
crown of life (Rev. 2:10; cf. James 1:12), which will give them great
position in the millennium.

The fact that these terrible spirit beings have power to hurt "only
those men which have not the seal of God in their foreheads" (9:4) may
serve as a clue to part of God's purpose in this fifth trumpet judgment.
It may serve in the hand of God to help some uncommitted individuals
during the Tribulation Period realize the power of God and turn in faith
to receive the Messiah.

If this seems like a terrible way for God to bring men to repentance,
one should remember the seriousness of being eternally lost. The Lord
Jesus Himself said, "Fear not them who kill the body, but are not able
to kill the soul; but rather fear him who is able to destroy both soul and
body in hell' (Matt. 10:28). It would be an act of mercy on God's part
to permit a man to be tormented five months in an effort to bring him
to Christ so that he might avoid the torments of the damned for eternity.

Verse 12 indicates that although one woe is past, "there come two
woes more hereafter." As terrible as is this judgment that will come
upon the earth, lasting five months, it will be eclipsed by the terror of
the sixth trumpet judgment, which introduces the second woe. The sixth
trumpet judgment reveals another army of evil spirit beings to be unleashed upon men from the "pit of the abyss." This time the judgment
is far more severe to the inhabitants of the earth because the spirits are
not only able to inflict pain on men but also physical death.

The Sixth Trumpet

The Second Woe

> And the sixth angel sounded, and I heard a voice from the four horns of the golden altar which is before God, saying to the sixth angel who had the trumpet, Loose the four angels who are bound in the great river, Euphrates. And the four angels were loosed, who were prepared for an hour, and a day, and a month, and a year, to slay the third part of men (Rev. 9:13-15).

At the blowing of the sixth trumpet, John heard a voice from the horns of the golden altar which is before God saying, "Loose the four angels who are bound in the great river, Euphrates." This is our first introduction to these four bound angels. That they are evil angels seems obvious because they are bound. Evidently they are anxious to bring havoc upon mankind but have been bound by God, prohibiting the fulfillment of their intent. Why they hate man we are not told; perhaps it is because man is the special object of God's love (John 3:16). There is a day coming, however, when God will permit these awful creatures to come forth, indicating that He has a yet unfulfilled purpose and plan that will be unveiled according to His good pleasure. For it states that they had been "prepared for an hour, and a day, and a month, and a year, to slay the third part of men." Those that will be slain are no doubt incorrigibles that would never accept Christ and would only serve as a hindrance to "undecided" people (those who have neither the mark of the Father nor the mark of the beast).

The Euphrates River in Scripture

There is no need to spiritualize "the great river Euphrates," considered by Bible scholars to be the greatest river of boundaries in the Bible. No doubt the most prominent river referred to in the Scriptures, it formed one of the boundaries of the Garden of Eden. It was also a boundary for Israel (Gen. 15:18), the easternmost boundary of Egypt, and the boundary of the Persian Empire. It is used in Scripture as a symbol of Israel's enemies.

That these four evil angels are today bound in that area of the world is no accident, for it seems that some of the world's greatest events took place near the Euphrates River. Since it was a boundary for the Garden of Eden, near this river man's first sin was committed. It was evidently near here that the first murder was committed, the first war fought, and the tower of Babel erected in defiance against God. It was near the river Euphrates that Nimrod built the city of Babylon, where idolatry received its origin and surged through the world. It was to Babylon that the children of Israel were taken captive, and it will be in this area of the world that the final sin of man will culminate. Here, according to Revelation 18, the city of Babylon will be rebuilt and become the head-quarters of the commercial, religious, and military activities of the world under the Antichrist's rule. (More of this in Rev. 17 and 18.)

An Evil Army of 200 Million

"And the number of the horsemen were two hundred thousand thousand; and I heard the number of them" (Rev. 9:16). An army of 200 million men would be an awesome host to confront mankind. This will be an evil army of 200 million horselike creatures with riders on their backs called "horsemen." The four angels bound at the Euphrates River seem to be leaders of these evil spirits, riding on horselike creatures, having heads of lions and emitting fire, smoke, and brimstone. They have tails like serpents, from which their power is sent forth.

It is quite obvious that these are not to be taken as humans, for horsemen do not wear "breastplates of jacinth and brimstone," nor do horses have mouths that emit "fire and smoke and brimstone." Instead, this is a literal description of unnatural, demonlike evil spirits that come out of the abyss, advancing under the leadership of the four bound angels.

One-Third of Men Killed

By the power of their tail and the "brimstone and fire and smoke" which proceeds out of their mouths, the horsemen will kill one-third of the world's population. We have already seen that 25 percent of the population will be killed by the fourth horseman of the Apocalypse (Rev. 6:8) as a result of the pestilence following the world war at the beginning of the Tribulation Period. According to today's population figures, that would be seven hundred million to one billion people, depending on when the Tribulation takes place. This one-third would again involve a similar number of people, approximately six hundred or seven hundred million to one billion people.

Only Unrepentant Killed by This Judgment

"And the rest of the men who were not killed by these plagues yet repented not of the works of their hands" (Rev. 9:20). We can assume from this verse that the men killed by the evil spirits will be men who have received the mark of the beast during the Tribulation period, having rejected Christ and accepted the Antichrist to rule over them. This is not clearly stated, therefore we say it is assumed. However, we know that unrepentant men are so killed. Thus it is those with the mark of the beast, or possibly the undecided, who will be killed. Once again we find that believers are exempt from the awful judgment that awaits the earth.

It would seem that the purpose of this judgment, like the preceding one, is to rid the world of the incorrigibles in the Tribulation who reject the Lord Jesus Christ and salvation through Him. Since this trumpet judgment brings us close to the middle of the Tribulation Period, we find that about 50 percent of the world's unregenerate population will have died. It would seem, then, that God is ridding the earth of those who will never receive Him. These people could not possibly populate the millennial kingdom and therefore must be purged from the earth. God's judgment is seen here to be unchanged from His acts of judgment in the Old Testament. God's love is expressed in the gift of His Son as the means of redemption, but if man rejects this love gift, he falls under the judgment of God. This points out once again the need for man to receive Jesus Christ.

The Unregeneracy of the Human Heart

The Bible tells us that "the heart is deceitful above all things, and desperately wicked; who can know it?" (Jer. 17:9) The book of Revelation certainly answers the oft-stated suggestion of individuals that "what man needs is a second chance after death." During the Tribulation man will have unprecedented opportunity to see the omnipotent hand of God working in the affairs of men, yet he will stubbornly persist in his rebellion against God and his rejection of Jesus Christ. That is seen by the fact that, in spite of the destruction of half of the world's population and one-third of the world's vegetation, light, and water supply, man will not repent of his stubborn heart and sinful practices. He refuses to make the decision of Moses, who chose not to "enjoy the pleasures of sin for a season" (Heb. 11:25) but chose to believe in the Lord and suffer with His people. The tribulation population instead will embrace the pleasures of sin for a season and damn their immortal souls in the process.

Sins That Keep Men From Repentance

Instead of turning to God during the Tribulation Period, man will turn in rebellion away from God. What are the sins that keep men from coming in repentance to a saving knowledge of the Lord Jesus Christ? The same sins that keep men from coming to Him today!

1. Idolatry. Verse 20 states that they "repented not of the works of their hands, that they should not worship demons, and idols of gold, and silver, and bronze, and stone, and wood, which neither can see, nor hear, nor walk." Man has a built-in desire for God. He will never be happy unless he has communion with God. Because of this, the devil, the master of deceit, has used idolatry to deceive men ever since the days of Nimrod. Not that men have always worshiped that which they have made with their hands, but they use the images to worship the spirits that they think will indwell the images. Sometimes men have worshiped trees, but in reality it is the spirit in the tree that they worship. This leads to demon oppression and activity producing mystical phenomena, which in turn causes men to be superstitious and fraught with fear. If they had only turned to God, believing, in faith they could have enjoyed peace; instead they turned to idolatry and reaped its consequent fear.

2. Murder. Someone has said, "Wherever the influence of the Gospel is unknown, human life is cheap." This is certainly the case in Buddhist and Hindu countries of the world, not to mention unreached tribes in remote jungle areas. That is one of the reasons it is hard for the Western mind to understand the attitude of pagans toward human life. Pagans have no compunction about taking another man's life if it serves their purpose. Thus violent murders will be a common practice during the Tribulation Period.

3. Sorcery. As already mentioned, superstition is a product of idolatry. Another meaning of this word, sorcery, also indicates that there will be a widespread use of drugs for evil purposes — drunkenness and drug addiction will be widespread. No doubt those bitten by the scorpions of the fifth trumpet will seek relief in any conceivable medication, whether from a good or evil source. In the process, drug addiction will abound.

4. Fornication. Even during the Tribulation Period, when life is cheap and the world is in a state of chaos, sexual promiscuity will still be a rampant disease of man. Who could question the fact that we are observing a wave of lust that is sweeping across the world, preparing man for the day of complete moral breakdown that will reach its culmination during the time of the Tribulation?

5. Thefts. The thievery here mentioned substantiates the lawlessness that will abound in this hour of great tribulation upon the earth, when men will get money or things by any means possible. The book of Revelation teaches that the Tribulation Period will be a time when man will give in to the fulfillment of the desires and lusts of the flesh. In his mad quest for peace or contentment, he will turn further and further from

God. Not only will he damn his immortal soul, but he will bring upon himself all the heartache of his misspent life, for it will be just as true in the days of the Tribulation as in our own day, "Whatever a man soweth, that shall he also reap" (Gal. 6:7).

16

The Mighty Angel and
the Little Scroll

The first nine chapters of the book of Revelation have brought us almost to the middle of the Tribulation. The seven seal judgments covered the first quarter, the seventh seal introduced the next quarter, or the trumpet judgments, and now chapters 10 and 11:1-14 comprise a parenthetical section given to John just before the prophecy concerning the last half of the Tribulation. Revelation 10:1-11:14 is to the trumpet judgments what chapter 7 was to the seal judgments: a description of conditions that existed during the particular period of time covered by the preceding judgments.

The Mighty Angel

The identity of this strong angel is debated by Bible teachers. Some contend that this is Christ. Since Christ appeared as the angel of God in the Old Testament, this would be another occasion in which He appears to the nation of Israel. Others say it is not Christ but an unidentified angel.

The Lord Jesus Christ does not appear in the book of Revelation as an angel. In fact, we will look in vain for a presentation of Him as an angel after the incarnation. Ever since Jesus took on flesh, died for the sins of men, was crucified, was resurrected, and ascended into heaven, He has always appeared as the Son of God in His essential deity. Although this angel possesses some Godlike characteristics, he is not God. Part of the problem could well be a failure to understand the nature of angels. Although far beneath the character of God, they are created beings of an unusually high order.

It is rather interesting to see that angels play a prominent part in the book of Revelation. They are mentioned more than sixty-six times throughout the book, always in a position of service. They do not create things, but fulfill the administration of God in the affairs of men. This is not the first time we have been introduced to a mighty angel, for in chapter 5:2 we find the same word used, though there it is translated "strong."

Don't be deceived by the glorious description of this angel — "clothed with a cloud; and a rainbow was upon his head, and his face was as though it were the sun, and his feet as pillars of fire" (10:1). Actually, in 18:1 we find another angel, pronouncing doom on Babylon, having great power and so much glory that "the earth was made bright with his glory." No one seems pressed to identify this angel as the Lord Jesus Christ; consequently we should not think it strange that God could have other mighty angels that could easily fit the description of the one in our text.

This mighty angel has in his hand a little scroll which we will describe in connection with verse 8. He stands with his right foot in the sea and his left foot on the earth, indicating that he has authority over all land and sea surfaces. He then cries with a "loud voice," the signal for seven thunderlike voices.

Seven Thunderlike Voices

The voices that sounded like seven thunders are a unique feature in the book of Revelation. John was prepared to write down what these thunderlike voices said when he heard another voice: "Seal up those things which the seven thunders uttered, and write them not." This is the only proclamation in the entire book of Revelation that is sealed up. These voices could be the voices of other angels that sounded in such mighty volume as to resemble thunder, but since we are not told in the Scripture the exact identity of the voices, it is dangerous to speculate further. Even more important to man's curiosity is what these voices said. Dr. J. Vernon McGee, in his book, *Reveling Through Revelation,* points out that many ridiculous guesses and wild speculations have been proposed. For example, "Vitringa interpreted them as the seven crusades; Danbuz made them the seven nations that received the Reformation; Elliott makes them the pope's bull against Luther; and Seventh-Day Adventism has presumed to reveal the things which were uttered."[10] Since the Apostle John was commanded by the voice to "seal up" their utterances, it is foolish to conjecture any further.

The Mighty Angel Proves He Is Not the Lord Jesus Christ

The unusual action of lifting his hand toward heaven and swearing "by him that liveth forever and ever, who created heaven and the things that are in it, and the earth and the things that are in it, and the sea and the things which are in it" certainly indicates that this mighty angel is not the Lord Jesus Christ. The angel is making an oath by the only sure guarantee, that is, God Himself. Hebrews 6:13 tells us of an Old Testament promise made by God to Abraham in which "because he could swear by no greater, he swore by himself." This angel swore by someone greater than himself, for he lifted up his hand toward heaven and cried and swore by the Creator, the Lord Jesus Christ (John 1:3), who obviously he was not. This angel, then, is swearing or giving oath on the authority of the Lord Jesus Christ that "there should be delay no longer." The Greek word *kronos* has two meanings, "time" and "delay." It is obvious that time is not the exact meaning, for there *is* time after this event. In fact, three-and-a-half years of tribulation follow the utterance made here, plus the one thousand years of the millennial kingdom.

The American Standard Version has correctly translated this word "delay": there will be delay no longer. Man has been living in the time of God's delay for centuries, but this angel warns mankind that God is about to conclude His patience in the face of man's rebellion against His will, and that soon the final consummation will take place. This consummation occurs three-and-a-half years after the utterance is made, for it is given at approximately the middle of the Tribulation Period.

The Mystery of God

". . . the mystery of God should be finished, as he has declared to his servants, the prophets" (10:7). The word "mystery" appears several times in the Bible, meaning that God is going to disclose a truth that is only possible to know in the Word of God. Man's wisdom never has comprehended nor ever will be able to deduce these truths apart from the Word of God.

"The mystery of God" here referred to can only mean salvation. One of the characteristics of salvation involves a mystery that a Holy God could love sinful men sufficiently to send His only Son into the world to die for their sins. This was made known to the prophets and His servants in the Old Testament and also in the New Testament. For all these thousands of years men have been living under the mystery of God, where it is possible for sinful, fallen men to be reinstated into fellowship with God by being born into His family without works but by faith. That this mystery is soon coming to a close is apparent by the fact that 42 months of the Tribulation Period have expired when the statement is given, and, as we will see in the twelfth chapter, at this point there are only 1,260 days of man's known history left, apart from the kingdom age (Rev. 12:6).

Revelation 10:2 tells us that the mighty angel held a little scroll open in his hand. Verse 8 tells us that John was to take this scroll from the mighty angel.

What Is the Little Scroll?

Several suggestions have been made as to the identity of the little scroll. Some say it is the seven-sealed scroll taken from the hand of God by the nail-scarred hand of Christ, given to the mighty angel, who in turn gave it to John. If this is true, the little scroll is the title deed to the earth, with the title description on one side and the seven seal judgments on the other. Since the seven seals were broken and it was revealed what the seven seals are, it is possible that there was no longer need for this book. Thus John was told to eat it.

Another suggestion is that the little scroll is the new revelation to John of events from this point on to chapter 19 in the book of Revelation. In either case it is the prophecy of God concerning future events. Since the mighty angel is pictured as standing with one foot in the sea and one foot on the land, John must no longer be in heaven. He apparently returned to the earth to take the little scroll. It is a scroll, therefore, that has to do with events that are to come upon the earth.

After John asked the angel for the little scroll, he was told to take it and eat it, though warned that it would be sweet to the taste and bitter to the belly. Eating a scroll is a symbolic reference in the Scriptures to digesting a scroll. Jeremiah 15:16 states, "Thy words were found, and I did eat them, and thy word was unto me the joy and rejoicing of my heart; for I am called by thy name, O LORD God of hosts." Ezekiel 3:1-3 contains the admonition of the Lord to the Old Testament prophet to "eat this scroll," and it was in his "mouth like honey for sweetness." After he had eaten the book, he was told to go speak to the house of Israel. The obvious meaning of these symbolic references to "eating the word of God" is that before a man can be a spokesman for God, he must digest the Word of God. He obviously does not eat mechanically, but mentally feeds upon the Word of God. One of the reasons for so much sterility and stagnation in the Church of Jesus Christ today is that in spite of all the translations and vernacular writings available, God's people are not "digesting the word of God." If they read, they have a tendency to read more about what men have said concerning the Word of God than to read the Word of God itself.

After John had eaten the scroll, the mighty angel said unto him, "Thou must prophesy again about many peoples, and nations, and tongues, and kings." Through the written book of Revelation, this command to the apostle John has been fulfilled, for the book of Revelation has been studied by "peoples and nations and tongues and kings."

The picture of sweetness in the mouth and bitterness in the belly indicates the typical quality of the Word of God, which is sharper than a two-edged sword. The sweetness comes to John in the predictions concerning our blessed Lord's return; the bitterness comes to John in being confronted by the fact that judgment is pronounced upon the earth.

The Gospel is much like this. It is sweet to those who hear and respond, thus being guaranteed eternal salvation as the free gift of God. It is bitter to men who reject it, however, for the same Gospel that guarantees salvation to those who receive it, guarantees judgment and damnation to those who do not.

17
Two Super
Witnesses

Revelation 11:1-14

Revelation 11 is an integral part of the small parenthesis which began in Revelation 10:1 and continues to 11:14. Chapter 11 has to do with the spiritual life of Israel; chapter 12 concerns the coming persecution of Israel. In this eleventh chapter we find that Israel will revert to the Old Testament form of worship. They will rebuild the temple apart from the Messiah since they believe He has not come. Thus they will construct the temple of rejection. In addition, this chapter unfolds the revelation that two supernatural witnesses will be recalled from Old Testament days to convey God's message to the Jerusalem area. In spite of these witnesses and the 144,000 of chapter 7, Israel will basically remain in unbelief until the time of her great persecution described in chapter 12. Before proceeding any further, you should read the entire eleventh chapter.

History of the Jewish Temple
After Israel was established in the land of Palestine, David, the "man after God's own heart," desired to build a great temple for the Lord God, but David had bloodied his hands in wars to the degree that it was impossible for God to use him for that purpose. He was permitted instead to raise much of the money and material that later went into the building of what came to be known as Solomon's Temple.

The temple was built in Jerusalem at God's command, for Jerusalem was to be the city where He would place His name and where His people would come to worship (Pss. 71:65-72; 87:1-3; 132:13-15). The Shekinah Glory of God appeared in the temple and became a symbol of the protecting hand of God upon the nation Israel. In their apostate days, toward the end of the kingdom era, the nation thought itself impregnable as long as the temple stood. They were deaf to the cries of Jeremiah and

148

Ezekiel, even after some had been taken away into Babylonian captivity. Finally, the temple and the city of Jerusalem were destroyed by Nebuchadnezzar. Seventy years later a decree was given for the rebuilding of the city and eventually the temple. This temple, under the direction of Zerubbabel and Joshua, the high priest, was much inferior to the Temple of Solomon — so much so that some of the elders that recalled the Temple of Solomon wept when they saw the foundation of the new temple. This temple served Israel until it was desecrated by Antiochus Epiphanes, one of the Greco-Syrian rulers. This desecration was a type of the desecration of the temple by the Antichrist at the end time, or Tribulation Period. About forty years before Christ, Herod the Great had this whole temple destroyed piecemeal and rebuilt. That temple was known during New Testament days as Herod's Temple (John 2:20).

Matthew 24:2 contains the prediction of the Lord that the temple would be destroyed: "there shall not be left here one stone upon another that shall not be thrown down." This prophecy was fulfilled during the time of Titus, the Roman general who laid siege to the city of Jerusalem. Although he gave orders that the Temple should not be destroyed, the Jews burned it rather than allow it to fall into pagan hands. Jesus' prophecy was fulfilled exactly, for today the site of the old Jewish Temple is occupied by the Mohammedans, who built the Moslem mosque called the "dome of the Rock." One will look in vain for a single stone of the Temple of Herod resting upon another that has not been thrown down, for the Dome of the Rock which now occupies that space is made entirely of different material. Because of the Moslems' present-day hatred for Israel, it is very likely that not one stone has been left upon another.

The Temple to Be Rebuilt

Several passages of Scripture refer to the temple of the end time. In Matthew 24:15 the Lord Jesus referred to the "abomination of desolation, spoken of by Daniel the prophet," indicating that at the end time, in the middle of the Tribulation Period as Daniel predicted, a temple would be desecrated by the Antichrist. In order for this to be fulfilled it first must be rebuilt.

In 2 Thessalonians 2:1-13 the Apostle Paul predicted that the Antichrist, in the middle of the Tribulation, would defy God by sitting in the temple of God and presenting himself to the world as God. In order for him to do this that temple has to be rebuilt.

Ever since Jews have been returning to the land of Palestine, rumors have circulated concerning the accumulation of materials for the eventual rebuilding of the temple. The one piece of ground that the Jews want most is the site now occupied by the Dome of the Rock, the second most holy shrine in the Moslem world — second only to Mecca, the birthplace of Mohammed. Jewish interest has been aroused, because the Dome of the Rock is built right over Mt. Moriah, the place considered to be the site of Abraham's willingness to offer Isaac as a sacrifice in obedience to God. It is difficult to substantiate any of the rumors about the planned temple rebuilding. Some years ago a friend gave me a clipping from the *San Francisco Chronicle* entitled "Jerusalem is talking about rebuilding the temple," but it gave no specific details. In addition to this it stated, "Sometime ago the wife of a Chicago lawyer, Anna Ravens, left a legacy of $50,000 to be used toward the rebuilding of the Jewish temple in Jerusalem." No doubt her case has been repeated hundreds of times, and when the day comes that Israel can send a call to the Jews all over the world for this rebuilding, be assured that there will be millions of dollars pouring into Jerusalem immediately.

Rebuilding the Temple Is a Rejection of Christ

Believers in the Lord Jesus Christ are not taught to build a temple; on the contrary, we are taught that God does not dwell in temples made with hands, but that the Holy Spirit uses man's body as a tabernacle or dwelling place (1 Cor. 6:19, 20). The fact that Israel will rebuild the temple indicates that she has not received the Messiah. Therefore we suggest the following chronology of events:

The act that will start the Tribulation Period is the signing of the covenant with the Antichrist (Dan. 9:27), which will become an ungodly league with an evil power, indicating that Israel at the beginning of the Tribulation will not be predominately Christian. Then 144,000 servants of the Lord will go forth witnessing, reaching a multitude of Gentiles that no man can number; but they represent the remnant, not a major portion of the Jewish nation. Instead, the Jews will make this ungodly league with the Antichrist, permitting them to take the city of Jerusalem from the hands of the Arabs. They will build the temple and once again institute the sacrificial system, rejecting Christ.

The fact that John was told to measure the temple is an indication that he would find it woefully inadequate as compared with the Temple of Solomon, which was inspired by God. The word "measure" could well be a reference to the fact that Israel will be severely judged for her rejection of the Messiah in view of the astounding light she has and will have. This temple, then, will be built at the beginning of the Tribulation, for in the middle of it, as we shall see in chapter 13:2, the Antichrist will break his league with the Jews and set up his idol in the midst of the temple, indicating that the outer court is to be unmeasured, for it is in the hands of the nations (Gentiles). Two periods of time are measured here: 42 months and 1260 days. Since they are identical, they could well refer to the equal division of the Tribulation Period. These two measurements of time could refer to the first half of the Tribulation Period; those mentioned in Revelation 12:16 and 13:5 probably refer to the last half, since here again both types of description are used.

The Two Witnesses

"And I will give power unto my two witnesses, and they shall prophesy a thousand two hundred and threescore days, clothed in sackcloth" (Rev. 11:3). At this point, colorful and dynamic individuals come on the scene as the special witnesses of God. God will give *power* to them. These two witnesses will have the power to send fire out of their mouths and to kill those that try to persecute them. They also will have the power to shut up the heavens "that it rain not," that the earth might be covered with a great drought. They also will have power over waters to turn them to blood and to smite the earth with all manner of plagues. This power is for the purpose of witnessing the power of God in distinction to the power of the Antichrist.

Who Are These Two Witnesses?

A variety of fanciful suggestions have been offered as to the identity of these two witnesses. Because God has not chosen to tell us exactly who they are, we can only offer a suggestion. Some of the most reliable suggestions are Elijah and Enoch; or Elijah and John the Baptist; or Elijah and Moses.

Malachi 4:5, 6 predicted that Elijah would come before "the coming of the great and terrible day of the LORD." In addition to this, we find that the use of fire in the Old Testament was limited to Elijah, who called down fire to consume the altar in the days of Ahab (2 Kings 18:20-40). He also withheld rain from the earth for three years. Therefore it seems more than likely that Elijah is one of the two witnesses.

We do not find that John the Baptist demonstrated the power of Elijah, and he freely admitted he was not Elijah. Both he and the angel Gabriel made that clear. In Luke 1:17 Gabriel told Zacharias, the father of John the Baptist, that John would come "in the spirit and power of Elijah"; but that does not mean he would be Elijah. John was asked by the priests and Levites from Jerusalem, "Art thou Elijah? And he saith, I am not" (John 1:21). John wore sackcloth and was a type of Elijah, but he did not minister to the Jewish nation as Elijah did.

There are only two good reasons for suggesting Enoch. First, he did not die, whereas Hebrews 9:27 tells us "it is appointed unto men once to die, but after this the judgment." Second, Jude 14 and 15 state that Enoch prophesied that "the Lord cometh with ten thousands of his saints, to execute judgment upon all." Although these are good, there are reasons to the contrary sufficient to eliminate Enoch from consideration.

Enoch was a Gentile who lived hundreds of years before Abraham; therefore he is not identified in any way with Israel. The fact that Enoch and Elijah never died is not sufficient evidence to suggest they will be the two witnesses, for all believers living at the time of the Rapture of the Church will be exceptions to Hebrews 9:27. When the Lord comes, we "shall be raised incorruptible." (1 Cor. 15:52-58). At the Rapture, believers will be snatched out of the world and taken to be with the Lord without ever tasting of death (1 Thess. 4:13-18). According to Hebrews 11:5 the purpose of Enoch's translation was "that he should not see death." The two witnesses of Revelation 11:3-14 do taste death; therefore, it would seem that Enoch could not be one of these witnesses.

There are three good reasons why Moses is the second witness during the first part of the Tribulation Period.

1. In Matthew 17:1-5, when the Lord Jesus was transfigured before His Jewish witnesses — Peter, James, and John — two representatives of the Old Testament were brought before their view. These men were Moses and Elijah. Their purpose was to discuss with Christ His impending death.

2. Moses manifested power to bring plagues on the earth and to turn water into blood during the days of Pharaoh. Elijah did not do these things, but had power to call down fire from heaven and to stop rain. Therefore it would reasonably follow that these two men be given the miraculous powers which they already demonstrated on the earth.

3. Moses is an integral part of Jewish family tradition. It would seem logical, therefore, that he become one of the witnesses, for Moses and Elijah combined represent the entire Old Testament to the Jewish nation. When the rich man asked Abraham to send Lazarus back to his father's house to warn his five brethren to repent, "lest they also come to this place of torment," Abraham embraced the Jewish concept of the entire Old Testament by saying, "They have Moses and the prophets; let them hear them" (Luke 16:27-29). Moses represents the first five books; Elijah, the outstanding prophet of Israel, represents the prophetic books. "Moses and the prophets" includes almost all those who had a hand in writing the Old Testament. Thus the two men in Jewish history who most speak of God's dealing with the nation Israel are Moses and Elijah.

The Work of the Two Witnesses

The work of the two witnesses is outlined in our text. They will primarily be witnesses of God. This is seen by virtue of the fact that they are likened to the two lampstands and the two olive trees of the book of Zechariah. Since this Old Testament symbol is used to convey the message of two men proclaiming God's faithfulness, we assume Elijah and Moses will do the same. They will be on the scene during the first half of the Tribulation Period to counteract the lying wonders of the Antichrist. They will also "prophesy," which means they will preach concerning the things to come. No doubt they will be warning people on the basis of the book of Revelation concerning events and interpreting them as they relate to the people. Malachi 4:6 tells us that Elijah's ministry will be to "turn the heart of the fathers to the children, and the heart of the children to their fathers." This seems like normal living to us, but we should remember that the Antichrist will be deceiving the people, turning the fathers against the children and the children against the fathers. Therefore the witness of these two men will be helping those who receive the Lord to return to normal thinking. It is quite probable that they will be the special witnesses of God to the Holy Land, whereas the 144,000 are witnesses throughout the entire earth (Rev. 7:9). We find further that they will testify, for Revelation 11:7 tells us that "they shall have finished their testimony." Evidently this indicates the preaching of the Gospel. True testifying is preaching the Gospel, whether it be in the church age, the Tribulation, or the millennium.

The Witnesses Killed

"And when they shall have finished their testimony, the beast that ascendeth out of the bottomless pit shall make war against them, and shall overcome them, and kill them" (Rev. 11:7). "The beast that ascendeth out of the bottomless pit" refers to the beast described in Revelation 13:1-7. "The beast" is an expression used here for the first time; the fact that he will come up out of the abyss is a reference to the death and resurrection of the Antichrist, as we will see in more detail in chapter 13. The beast or Antichrist, the man of sin, will hate the two witnesses, make war against them, and kill them. However, it should be noted that he will have no power over them until "they shall have finished their testimony." In other words, they will be "immortal until

their work is done" — which could be said of all God's servants who walk in obedience to His will. The completely degenerate and inhuman characteristics of people living during the Tribulation Period can be seen in Revelation 11:8, which tells us that the bodies of the two witnesses will be left open in the streets of Jerusalem. The Holy City will be so degenerate spiritually that she will be called Sodom and Egypt, Sodom being a symbol of immorality and Egypt a symbol of materialism. The lives of the people going back to occupy the Holy Land today are anything but holy. They seldom even attend synagogues on the Sabbath.

"And they of the peoples and kindreds and tongues and nations shall see their dead bodies three days and a half, and shall not permit their dead bodies to be put in graves" (Rev. 11:9). Someone has suggested that the modern medium of television makes possible the fulfillment of Revelation 11:9. The only way in which people all over the world could see two bodies lying in the streets of a city over a three-day period of time would be through the medium of television; in fact, in recent years it has been possible by the launching of television satellites for many parts of the world to view the same sight at the same time. This is one more indication that we are coming closer to the end of the age, because it would have been humanly impossible just a few years ago for the entire world to see these two witnesses in the streets at a given moment of time. Not content to look upon them, according to verse 10 people throughout the world will enjoy a Christmaslike celebration, giving and receiving gifts because these preachers of righteousness and holiness are now dead.

The Witnesses Resurrected

> And after three days and a half the spirit of life from God entered into them, and they stood upon their feet, and great fear fell upon them who saw them. And they heard a great voice from heaven saying unto them, Come up here. And they ascended up to heaven in a cloud (Rev. 11:11, 12).

Then suddenly the "spirit of life from God entered into them, and they stood upon their feet." As our Lord was crucified, buried, and in three days rose from the dead, these men, after being slain and exposed to the eyes of the world, will hear the voice of God resurrecting them. A cloud will receive them out of sight in the face of their enemies. It is no wonder that "great fear fell upon them who saw them." The resurrection of these men will be the final confirmation that they were men of God, another illustration that God does not forget His own.

God's Judgment on Jerusalem

> And the same hour was there a great earthquake, and the tenth part of the city fell, and in the earthquake were slain of men seven thousand; and the remnant were terrified, and gave glory to the God of heaven (Rev. 11:13).

Here we find that as a result of the shocking treatment of these two faithful witnesses of God by the inhabitants of the city of Jerusalem, the Lord will send a great earthquake, destroying a tenth part of the city and slaying seven thousand men. This cataclysmic judgment of God upon the city of Jerusalem could be the event which triggers the revival that will sweep across Israel during the latter half of the Tribulation, for the passage reads, "and the remnant were terrified, and gave glory to the God of heaven." This remnant may refer to the Jewish inhabitants of the city who, after seeing the judging hand of God slay seven thousand of their residents and destroy a tenth part of their city, will turn in faith to embrace the message of the two witnesses so recently resurrected. All of these events take place before the third woe is sounded in verse 14, which identifies these two witnesses who live, preach, die, and are resurrected during the first half of the Tribulation Period. In addition to closing this second parenthetical passage, it also sets the stage for the events of the latter half of the Tribulation Period.

18

The Seventh
Trumpet Judgment

Revelation 11:15-19

The blowing of the seventh trumpet (which is the third woe) does not initiate anything on the earth. Instead, it is much like the breaking of the seventh seal of Revelation 8:1. It merely introduces the next series of judgments, the seven bowls. Occurring exclusively in heaven, the scene introduces activities that project a meaning to the earth to be disclosed later.

In order to comprehend the chronological events of this passage of Scripture, one should understand that immediately after this heavenly introduction to the seven bowls, there is another lengthy parenthetical passage which extends from Revelation 12:1 to 15:4. This parenthetical passage conveys details of events that will take place during the entire Tribulation Period. These events include the persecution of God's children (chapter 12); the Antichrist, or the "beast that came out of the sea," and the "false prophet" (chapter 13); also the heavenly vision of chapter 14 and the introduction to the last half of the Tribulation (chapter 15). This is a heavenly setting, announcing the great events that will come upon the earth. Awesome beyond description, it is called "Great Tribulation" because it reveals the most fantastic events the world has ever known.

The First Angelic Chorus
And the seventh angel sounded; and there were great voices in heaven, saying, The kingdom of this world is become the kingdom of our Lord, and of his Christ, and he shall reign forever and ever (Rev. 11:15).

John heard "great voices" singing in heaven, evidently angelic voices in chorus. They announced two things:

1. "The kingdom of the world has become the kingdom of our Lord, and of his Christ." The King James Version erroneously introduces

these kingdoms in the plural, whereas the American Standard and other recent translations translate it correctly as singular, for John has in view the kingdom of the Antichrist at the time of the glorious appearing (Rev. 19:11). Thus the angels will announce in heaven at the beginning of the last half of the Tribulation Period that the one-world kingdom of the Antichrist will be conquered by the kingdom of Christ.

2. "And he shall reign forever and ever." In the Greek language this is the strongest term possible for "ages of ages," indicating that once Christ comes to earth, there will be no interruption of His government. Rebellion will break out at the end of the millennium when Satan is loosed "for a season," but our glorified Lord will quell it so quickly that it will not interfere with His kingdom.

The Song of the Twenty-Four Elders

And the four and twenty elders, who sat before God on their thrones, fell upon their faces, and worshiped God, saying, We give thee thanks, O Lord God Almighty, who art, and wast, and art to come, because thou hast taken to thee thy great power, and hast reigned. And the nations were angry, and thy wrath is come, and the time of the dead, that they should be judged, and that thou shouldest give reward unto thy servants, the prophets, and to the saints, and them that fear thy name, small and great, and shouldest destroy them who destroy the earth (Rev. 11:16-18).

We have already seen that the twenty-four elders are twenty-four leading angelic beings that carry out the administration of God's universe. These representative angelic leaders fall on their faces before God and worship Him, announcing His eternity with the words, "who art, and wast, and art to come."

This is a song of thanksgiving ("We give thee thanks, O Lord God Almighty"). The elders use the prophetic perfect tense, indicating that they anticipate in heaven the final stage of God's activity on the earth before the coming of Christ, and they rejoice over the eventual consummation of His kingdom ("because thou hast taken to thee thy great power, and hast reigned"). Christ will not reign until the end of the Tribulation, but He certainly reigns then! The twenty-four elders proceed to make three predictions on the basis of the coming of Christ:

1. "The nations were angry, and thy wrath is come" indicates that at the time of His coming the nations will resent His coming and rebel against Him. Psalm 2 should be studied in this connection.

2. "And the time of the dead, that they should be judged" refers to the Old Testament saints and tribulation saints who have been slain. This does not refer to unbelievers, who will be judged a thousand years later at the end of the millennium (Rev. 11:20-15). The resurrection of Old Testament saints and the rapture of tribulation saints will take place at the end of the Tribulation, at the glorious appearing of our Lord. That subject is described in Psalm 50:1-6:

The mighty God, even the LORD, hath spoken, and called the earth from the rising of the sun unto the going down thereof. Out of Zion, the perfection of beauty, God hath shined. Our God shall come, and shall not keep silence; a fire shall devour before him, and it shall be very tempestuous round about him. *He shall call to the heavens from above, and to the earth,* that he may judge his people. Gather my saints together unto me, those who have made a covenant with me by sacrifice. And the heavens shall declare his righteousness; for God is judge himself.

Here the Lord is seen, not in heaven, but in the air, calling to His Old Testament saints who are still in heaven. The Church will not be in heaven at this point, since they will have been "caught up . . . to meet the Lord in the air" (1 Thess. 4:17) before the Tribulation. This will be a call, then, for the Old Testament saints who are still in heaven to be joined with the tribulation saints in rapture and resurrection. Just as our Lord Himself has a "shout" for the Church at the beginning of the Tribulation, He has a "cry" for the Old Testament saints who will be resurrected and the Tribulation saints who will be raptured: "Gather my saints together unto me."

3. "And shouldest destroy them who destroy the earth" indicates that Christ will take the Antichrist (the beast) and the False Prophet alive and throw them into the lake of fire. Their followers also will be killed (Rev. 19:20). This text teaches that the followers of Antichrist, like all human beings who die without Christ, will go in soul and spirit to the "place of torment" (as did the rich man in Luke 16) until the Great White Throne Judgment, when they will appear for the final judgment and be cast into the lake of fire. This fact again indicates the eternal seriousness of a rebellious attitude against Almighty God and His divine offer of salvation.

The Temple of God in Heaven

And the temple of God was opened in heaven, and there was seen in his temple the ark of his covenant; and there were lightnings, and voices, and thunderclaps, and an earthquake, and great hail (Rev. 11:19).

We should keep in mind that the subject of this passage is the rapture of Israel and Tribulation saints, who are redeemed because they have entered into a covenant with Him by sacrifice (Ps. 50:5). The Church does not have a temple or tabernacle, but Israel did. The vision of the Ark of the Covenant could be a reminder to Israel that they are dealing with a covenant-keeping God, and on the basis of His past faithfulness their redemption is guaranteed.

Israel, Christians, and tribulation saints share in common this essential: they enter into a covenant with God by sacrifice, the covenant of a blood sacrifice — Israel temporarily by animal sacrifices; Christians and the tribulation saints through the Lord Jesus Christ, who sacrificed Himself "once for all."

The "lightnings, voices, thunderclaps, earthquake, and great hail" indicate that the scene in heaven is over and events are about to be disclosed that have to do with the affairs of men. These catastrophes bespeak the mounting confusion and terror that will come upon the earth in the latter half of the Tribulation Period. In view of the destruction that awaits the earth, any intelligent being is left with only one decision, and that is to avoid that awful period in the world's future through receiving Jesus Christ as Savior and Lord by personal invitation.

19

Satan Versus Israel

Revelation 12

It should not come as a surprise that so much space is given in the book of Revelation to the nation of Israel. She dominates the pages of the Old Testament because she is God's nation of destiny. That He is not through with her is seen in the prophetic "time of Jacob's trouble" outlined in chapter 13 and described in Daniel 9:24-27. The "seventieth week of Daniel" or Tribulation Period is covered in Revelation 6-18. It would naturally include an extensive prediction of Israel's part in that time that will "try the whole earth."

So far in our study we have discovered that Israel will make a league or covenant with the Antichrist for seven years (Dan. 9:27). Revelation 7 indicates that 144,000 servants of God will go forth to preach the Gospel of Christ. Because of (1) the effects of the Rapture of the Church on men, (2) the outpouring of the Spirit of God as on the day of Pentecost (Joel 2:28-31), making them like 144,000 Apostle Pauls, (3) world conditions of chaos designed by God to lead men to Christ, and (4) the population explosion, placing more people on the earth than ever before in the history of the world, these 144,000 servants might well reach more people for Christ than have been won during the entire Christian dispensation. Such a host is described in Revelation 7:9: "a great multitude, which no man could number, of all nations, and kindreds, and people, and tongues, stood before the throne." It should be kept in mind that the 144,000 Jewish witnesses represent a remnant of Israel, for according to Revelation 11 the Jews will rebuild the temple in Jerusalem, indicating that they return to the land in unbelief. We also have found that God will send two special witnesses with supernatural powers like those of Elijah and Moses to counteract in Palestine the supernatural powers of Antichrist (2 Thess. 2:9-12).

Four Key Personages

Chapter 12 introduces the fact that in the middle of the Tribulation Period Israel will be confronted with the worst wave of anti-Semitism the world has ever seen. Yet "God is faithful" as usual! Four key personages appear in this chapter. We shall examine them carefully.

1. The Sun-Clothed Woman

> And there appeared a great wonder in heaven — a woman clothed with the sun, and the moon under her feet, and upon her head a crown of twelve stars. And she, being with child, cried, travailing in birth, and pained to be delivered (Rev. 12:1, 2).

Many suggestions have been offered to identify this "woman clothed with the sun." The church of Rome has maintained that she represents the Virgin Mary. In 1678 the Spanish artist Murillo created his famous painting "Mystery of the Immaculate Conception," a painting of the "woman clothed with the sun." For some reason he did not show her standing on the moon with a crown of twelve stars on her head. Thus the passage has been used to teach Mary's bodily assumption into heaven.

Others have proposed that the sun-clad woman is the Church, and still others have tried to use it to define themselves. In his *Book of Revelation,* Dr. Lehman Strauss writes,

> Then there is the blasphemous teaching of Mary Baker Glover Patterson Eddy, who was conceited enough to claim that this woman of Revelation 12 represented herself. She added that the "man child" that she brought forth is Christian Science; that the "dragon is mortal mind" (whatever that is) attempting to destroy her new religion. I shall not go beyond Dr. Ironside's answer to Mrs. Eddy's interpretation: ". . . I need not take up the time of sane people."[11]

Dr. J. Vernon McGee further notes, "A female preacher in California, who became famous or infamous — however you care to express it — toyed with the idea that she might be the woman mentioned in this chapter."[12]

The importance of the identity of this woman is stressed in Dr. H. A. Ironside's commentary on Revelation.

> I think I may say without exaggeration that I have read or carefully examined several hundred books purporting to expound the Revelation. I have learned to look upon this twelfth chapter as the crucial test in regard to the correct prophetic outline. If the interpreters are wrong as to the woman and the man-child, it necessarily follows that they will be wrong as to many things connected with them.[13]

The woman is referred to as "a great wonder in heaven" (Rev. 12:1). The word "wonder," literally translated from the Greek "sign" and appearing for the first time in the book of Revelation, indicates that the woman is not to be taken literally as a woman but as a symbolic representation of something. Furthermore, it is impossible to conceive of Mary giving birth to her child "in heaven," and this woman is pictured in heaven.

Joseph, the son of Israel (Jacob), related a dream to his father and brothers.

> He dreamed yet another dream, and told it to his brethren, and said, Behold, I have dreamed a dream more; and, behold, the sun and the moon and the eleven stars made obeisance to me. And he told it to his father, and to his brethren: and his father rebuked him, and said unto him, What is this dream thou hast dreamed? Shall I and thy mother and thy brethren indeed come to bow down ourselves to thee to the earth? And his brethren envied him; but his father observed the saying (Gen. 37:9-11).

As will be shown shortly, the man child (Rev. 12:5, 6) is none other than Jesus Christ the Lord. Religions such as Christian Science, or even the Church, will not qualify as the mother of Christ. Instead, this is a reference to the nation of Israel, which begat the Messiah. From Abraham to the days of Mary, the nation of Israel was preparing to bring forth a man child that would bless the entire world.

The fact that the woman is seen "clothed with the sun, and the moon" is most illuminating. These objects are light-conveying objects: the moon is a reflector, the sun, a source of light. They are symbolic of Israel as God's light-bearer to mankind. This she was in Old Testament days, for God intended that she propagate His message from the Holy Land to the entire world. Unfaithful in the dissemination of this message, she has fallen under the judgments of God. However, she will be God's light-bearer in the form of the 144,000 witnesses during the Tribulation. It should be noted from Revelation 2 and 3 that today the Church, God's "lampstand," is His torch-bearer to get His message out to this generation.

2. The Devil

"And there appeared another wonder in heaven; and, behold, a great red dragon, having seven heads and ten horns, and seven crowns upon his heads" (Rev. 12:3). The world today does not believe in a literal devil, accepting merely "an evil principle from without." But the Bible teaches an evil *personality* from without called the devil. This passage alone details several things about him.

Names Used for the Devil

Verse 3 — "a great red dragon." He is red because he is the motivating force behind much of the bloodshed in man's history, beginning with Cain and continuing to the present.

Verse 9 — "that old serpent." This refers to the first time the devil is seen in the Bible, in the Garden of Eden.

— "the devil." This is the name used for the devil in the gospels. It means "slanderer" or "accuser."

— "Satan." This name means "adversary." The devil is the adversary of all God's children.

Verse 10 —"the accuser of our brethren." This indicates his work before the throne of God today, seeking to discredit the saints before God.

Satan's Governmental Operation

Satan is revealed as a "great red dragon" having seven heads and ten horns and seven crowns upon his heads. More details related to Satan's governmental operations will be revealed as we study the Antichrist in chapter 13, but the seven crowned heads probably refer to the seven stages of the Roman Empire, the embodiment of evil government. Just because Rome has sunk beneath the sands of time does not mean that Roman government is not in force today. In fact, Roman government or Caesarean imperialism is in its sixth stage (head) and today covers a vast amount of the earth's population. Any dictatorial government belongs to this category. The ten horns refer to the ten kings who will be dominant during the Tribulation, from whom the Antichrist (the seventh head) will receive his power and authority. Antichrist is the human pawn or tool of Satan himself, for Satan uses the governments of man. Many modern governments and governmental leaders are his pawns today, which is the main reason for so much chaos in the world! Nothing has caused more havoc and evil to humanity than government. Power in the hands of evil men in the form of government has given license to murders, wars, famine, heartache, and suffering beyond human comprehension. This can be attributed to Satan, who by using world dictators and key leaders has manipulated the affairs of man, all to man's harm. The combination of such practices will reach a climax during the Tribulation Period.

The Fall of Satan

The great red dragon appears as "another wonder in heaven." Verse 4 tells us that "his tail drew the third part of the stars of heaven and did cast them to the earth." This probably refers to the original fall of Satan described in Isaiah 14. Some have suggested that the glacial age was a period of judgment on the earth long before man ever came into being because of Satan's pride, which induced rebellion and the casting from heaven of one-third of the angels, those who chose to follow him. The original casting of Satan out of heaven was not a final overthrow, for although his forces have been limited to the atmospheric heaven around the earth, Satan himself still has access to the throne of God to accuse the brethren (v. 10).

Satan's Conflict With the Seed of the Woman

The vision of Satan standing before the woman "who was ready to be delivered, to devour her child as soon as it was born" refers to the attitude of Satan ever since Genesis 3:15. This promise was given to humanity, predicting eventual deliverance from the domination of Satan.

God guaranteed deliverance through the "seed of the woman." In response, Satan initiated what Bible scholars call "the conflict of the ages," attempting to stamp out the seed of the woman from the time of Adam and Eve to the Tribulation Period, from Genesis to Revelation.

Satan tried to stop the seed by the murder of Abel by Cain (Gen. 4); by his effort to pollute the human race (Gen. 6); by his attempt to cut off the Hebrew nation in Egypt (Exod. 1, 2); and by the decree of Haman (Esth. 3:8-15). Several times during the life of Christ he tried to destroy the "seed of the woman" — Herod's decree to kill babies, the storm on the Sea of Galilee, and the attempts to throw Christ over a cliff.

During the Christian dispensation the conflict is seen in Satan's persecution of the Church; his propagation of Mohammedanism; the Dark Ages, when the Word of God was kept from men; and false religions that spring up everywhere but offer no remedy for sin. This conflict will reach its climax during the Tribulation when Satan through the Antichrist will seek to get men to worship him.

3. The Man Child — Christ

The identity of the man child should not be difficult for anyone familiar with the Word of God, for only Jesus Christ fits this description. The man child "was to rule all nations with a rod of iron," referring to the millennial kingdom when Jesus Christ will be the absolute ruler of the world and will "rule with a rod of iron." The man child's identity is further clarified in the statement, "her child was caught up unto God, and to his throne," which is exactly what happened to Jesus Christ after the resurrection. He was caught up to heaven, where He is now seated at the right hand of God; John reveals Him in chapters 4 and 5 as at the throne of God. It should be noted that He is the only one who has "ascended into heaven."

The entire picture of the sun-clad woman is best understood when one keeps in mind that the Christian dispensation of almost 2,000 years is entirely omitted. Not even a hint of it is found in our text. This parallels the seventy weeks of Daniel, which predicts 483 years until "Messiah the Prince shall be cut off" and then, making no reference to the Gentile church age, goes right on to the Jewish seven-year Tribulation Period, completing the seventy weeks of years. Between verses 5 and 6 have occurred 2,000 years of Church history. Just like Daniel 9, they are Gentile in scope, whereas this passage concerns Israel. Verse 6 refers to the Tribulation Period when it says "the woman fled into the wilderness" where God had prepared a place for her. As He provided for the nation Israel for forty years in the wilderness, so He will feed Israel during the Tribulation's 1,260 days. The eleventh chapter of Daniel speaks of a world war during the middle of the Tribulation which will affect all the countries of the world except Edom, Moab, and Ammon. These ancient countries, which now constitute Jordan, may well be the place God has prepared for the nation Israel to hide. In any case, they will flee during the last half of the Tribulation Period, persecuted by the greatest anti-Semitic campaign that Satan has ever unleashed against them. God, however, will be faithful to His children during that period and will provide for them. Isaiah 33:15, 16 indicates that during that time He will so supply for them that of Israel it will be said, "Bread shall be given to him; his waters shall be sure." No matter what the generation, to them that look for Him, God is faithful.

4. The Archangel Michael

"And there was war in heaven; Michael and his angels fought against the dragon; and the dragon fought and his angels" (Rev. 12:7). That Satan will make one final attempt to wrest control of the universe from Almighty God is suggested by the coming war in heaven between the holy angels, led by the archangel Michael, and the fallen angels, led by Satan. Before we review that coming war in heaven, let us examine the fourth key personage of this passage. The two angels whose names are given in Scripture are Gabriel and Michael. Gabriel is the "announcing angel"; Michael seems to be the "commanding general" of the heavenly hosts. It is suggested on the basis of Isaiah 14 and Ezekiel 28 that Michael is superior to the majority of the angels, but somewhat lower in created order than Satan himself. He has had previous confrontations with Satan, as noted in Jude 9, where he contended with the devil and disputed about the body of Moses. Satan wanted the body of Moses, no doubt to use as a sacred shrine or relic or object of worship to further mislead the children of Israel. Michael preserved the body of Moses against that eventuality, but even he "dared not bring against him [Satan] a railing accusation, but said, The Lord rebuke thee." Michael does not seem able to cope with Satan himself but must rely on the power of God for his defense. This is an excellent object lesson to Christians! If the archangel Michael, commander of God's heavenly host, is not adequate to take on Satan in conflict, neither are we! Our only defense against the devil is to flee to God. "Submit yourself unto God."

Daniel 10 reveals that Michael was hindered by "the prince of the kingdom of Persia," either a reference to Satan himself or someone on Michael's own level who was in charge of the demonic forces. Daniel 12:1 predicts that "at that time shall Michael stand up, the great prince who standeth for the children of thy people, and there shall be a time of trouble, such as never was since there was a nation even to that same time." We see from this that Michael was the angel specially assigned by God to work for the protection of Israel as a nation.

The War in Heaven

It has been suggested by Bible scholars that the war in heaven is not a single battle but a series of battles that culminate in the middle of the

Tribulation Period with the expulsion of Satan from the court of God. Satan and his hosts will battle vigorously with Michael and the heavenly hosts immediately after the Rapture of the Church, for when Christ comes for His Church "with a shout," He will come with "the voice of the archangel" (1 Thess. 4:16). The Tribulation, then, will not only be a time of war on the earth, in which men are the participants, but, unseen by men, battles will be fought between the hosts of God and the hosts of Satan. In a sense, this will parallel what must have occurred during the days of Christ, for when Satan did his best to slay Christ or to tempt Him, Christ was "ministered" to by the angels. One cannot help but surmise that the atmosphere around the cross was "charged" with conflicting spiritual forces, the holy angels on behalf of Christ conflicting with the demons who exulted in triumph over Him. The resurrection of Jesus Christ on the third day after His crucifixion was a devastating blow to the plans and aspirations of Satan and his host of demons!

In the middle of the Tribulation Period the conflicts between Michael and his hosts and Satan and his hosts will reach a climax. When God gives the order, Michael will cast the great dragon down to the earth, and "his angels were cast out with him." We can scarcely imagine the effect this will have on Satan, who for all these years has maintained access to the throne of God "day and night" to accuse the brethren. Suddenly, halfway through the Tribulation Period, he will be banished to the earth and confined there. His fury will know no limitations, except the power of God. Three-and-a-half years later, at the glorious appearing of Christ (Rev. 19:1 - 20:3), he will be cast into the bottomless pit for one thousand years.

The fact that Satan is once and for all cast from the throne of God along with his evil hosts, who will no longer be the "principalities and powers of the air" but beings limited to the earth, will be cause for "great rejoicing" in heaven. "And I heard a loud voice saying in heaven, Now is come salvation, and strength, and the kingdom of God, and the power of his Christ" (v. 10). The first giant step toward the eventual establishment of the kingdom of Christ will be the banishment of Satan from heaven. The fact that Satan no longer can accuse the brethren will be cause for great rejoicing. "Therefore rejoice, ye heavens, and ye that dwell in them" (v. 12).

Verse 10 states that Satan's particular ministry in this age is to appear before the throne of God "day and night" to accuse the saints of sin or weakness, much the same function as a prosecutor before a judge. The saints have overcome these accusations by the three sources of victory over the devil (v. 11).

1. "They overcame him — by the blood of the Lamb." Whether in casting out demons or victory over sin, the blood of the Lamb of God which takes away the sins of the world is the only true means of victory.

This certainly emphasizes the power of the blood of Jesus Christ. No wonder the hymn writer was inspired to write,

> Would you be free from your burden of sin?
> There's power in the blood, power in the blood,
> Would you o'er evil a victory win?
> There's wonderful power in the blood.

2. "They overcame him . . . by the word of their testimony." Another way to overcome Satan is a decisive testimony for Jesus Christ. The fact that these people who overcame Satan loved not their lives unto death emphasizes that their supreme desire was to serve Jesus Christ (Matt. 6:33). The Lord Jesus Christ promised, "He that findeth his life shall lose it: but he that loseth his life for my sake shall find it" (Matt. 10:39). Satan would have us reverse the procedure and think more highly of our lives than they really are worth in comparison to our eternal soul.

3. "And they loved not their lives unto death." Whenever man tries to save his life, he loses it. Only a Christian who can assert with Paul that he has "a desire to depart, and to be with Christ, which is far better" is ready to "resist the devil." Overcomers are more concerned with pleasing their Lord than saving their lives.

Satan's Final Anti-Semitic Crusade

> Woe to the inhabiters of the earth and of the sea! For the devil is come down unto you, having great wrath, because he knoweth that he hath but a short time. And when the dragon saw that he was cast unto the earth, he persecuted the woman who brought forth the male child (Rev. 12:12, 13).

Although heaven will rejoice because Satan is out, earth will not share this rejoicing, for he personally will take command of the earth and its operations against his greatest enemy, the nation Israel. Knowing he has but a short time (three-and-a-half years), he will be filled with wrath and hatred. The extent of his activities are sketched for us in the remaining verses of the chapter.

> And to the woman were given two wings of a great eagle, that she might fly into the wilderness, into her place, where she is nourished for a time, and times, and half a time, from the face of the serpent (Rev. 12:14).

The faithfulness of God to the woman is seen in the fact that she is given two wings of a great eagle that she might fly into the wilderness to a place prepared for her (v. 6) where for three-and-a-half years God will supernaturally protect her.

"And the serpent cast out of his mouth water like a flood after the woman, that he might cause her to be carried away by the flood" (Rev. 12:15). It is hard to establish the identity of this "flood." The best three suggestions are as follows:

1. Satan will divert rivers and bodies of water into the wilderness, where Israel will be kept by God, and will try to drown her.

2. He will attempt to flood her with false teachings.

3. Since this passage has already referred to symbols of "the woman" and the "great red dragon," the word "flood" could be a symbol similar to the one used in Isaiah 59:19, which speaks of an army as it invades a country. It seems quite likely that the latter is the best definition. The Antichrist will marshall a great horde of men, arm them, and send them into the wilderness to kill the children of Israel.

"And the earth helped the woman, and the earth opened her mouth and swallowed up the flood which the dragon cast out of his mouth," (Rev. 12:16). God will protect Israel supernaturally. As in the days of the rebellion of Korah (Num. 16) out in the wilderness, when the earth opened and swallowed those who were serving Satan and rebelling against the known will of God, so in the Tribulation the earth will swallow up the anti-Semitic armies of the Antichrist.

Dr. Seiss, in his classic commentary on the book of Revelation, suggests,

> It is the region and time of miracle when this drinking up of the river which the Dragon sends against the woman occurs. It is the region and time when there is to be a renewal of wonders, "like as it was to Israel in the day that he came up out of the land of Egypt." (Isaiah 11:15, 16.) It is the region and time of great earthquakes and disturbances in the economy of nature. (Zechariah 14:4; Luke 21:25, 26; Revelation 11:13, 19.) And there is reason to think that it is by some great and sudden rending of the earth that these pursuing hosts are arrested in their course, if not en masse buried up in the convulsion. At least, the object of their bloody expedition is thwarted. They fail to reach the Woman in her place of refuge. The very ground yawns to stop them in their hellish madness.[14]

Whatever the enemy, it is apparent that God will use the earth to preserve Israel supernaturally.

"And the dragon was angry with the woman, and went to make war with the remnant of her seed, who keep the commandments of God, and have the testimony of Jesus Christ" (Rev. 12:17). This verse indicates that even though Satan will be thwarted in his attempt to exterminate the Jews, not until the end of the Tribulation when he is cast into the bottomless pit will he stop trying. A glance at history reveals a foreglimpse of his consistent hatred and diabolical wrath against God's chosen people. It would almost seem that all the animosity and hatred he directs toward God in the last days of his freedom will be hurled against the nation Israel.

That Israel will be saved during the latter half of the Tribulation Period is clarified by this reference to the "remnant of her seed," denoting the last generation of the "seed of the woman" living during the Tribulation Period. Their faith is seen in that they (1) keep the commandments of God and (2) have the testimony of Jesus Christ. They will turn to God in complete obedience (something Israel has not done since the days of David), accepting their Messiah, Jesus Christ.

The final act of anti-Semitism on the part of Satan will be used of God to cause a worldwide revival to spread throughout Israel. Would to God that Israel two thousand years ago had accepted the offer of her Messiah and started then to "have the testimony of Jesus Christ." How this would have altered the course of human history!

20
The Antichrist

Revelation 13

Revelation 13 introduces a personage well known to the student of Bible prophecy. Called by at least twenty names, he is most commonly referred to as Antichrist. In an effort to thoroughly understand the detailed description of his activities during the Tribulation Period given in Revelation 13, we shall devote this chapter to a compilation of other Bible passages relative to his person, his work, and ultimate end. Then, by comparing this introductory study with chapter 13, we will gain a comprehensive picture of the work of the Antichrist.

The Fact of the Antichrist

Just as Jesus Christ is the promised "seed of the woman" (Gen. 3:15), the Antichrist is the promised "seed of the serpent." Counterfeiting the work of God has ever been the work of Satan, the master enemy of the soul of man. For six thousand years he has tried to counterfeit everything God has done for man. The crowning piece of counterfeit will appear when Satan raises up a man to be a substitute for the Lord Jesus Christ — a man referred to as the Antichrist. It should be pointed out that this term which has been universally accepted by fundamental Bible teachers and prophetic students is nowhere in the Bible used in connection with a specific person. The title is employed by the Apostle John in his first epistle but repeatedly refers to one who opposes Christ, particularly one teaching anything contrary to the deity of Christ. The Bible repeatedly predicts, however, that one will arise as the embodiment of all anti-Christian attitudes, purposes, and motives that Satan has implanted in his emissaries throughout past centuries. We call him Antichrist because he is opposed to everything which Christ represents.

170

Titles of Antichrist

Many titles are given to Antichrist in the Scriptures — at least twenty in number. Some are given below as examples:

Isaiah 14:4 — "king of Babylon"
Isaiah 14:12 — "Lucifer"
Daniel 7:8; 8:9 — "little horn"
Daniel 8:23 — "a king of fierce countenance"
Daniel 9:26 — "the prince that shall come"
Daniel 11:36 — "the willful king"
2 Thessalonians 2:3-8 — "that man of sin," "the son of perdition," "that wicked one"
1 John 2:18 — "antichrist"
Revelation 13:1 — "a beast."

Of all the titles given to him, the one used by the Apostle Paul in 2 Thessalonians 2:3, "the man of sin," is the most descriptive. As "the man of sin" he will come on the scene in the last days as the embodiment of all the sinful men who have ever lived. 2 Thessalonians 2:4 offers an appropriate description of his conduct: "Who opposeth and exalteth himself above all that is called God, or that is worshiped, so that he, as God, sitteth in the temple of God, showing himself that he is God."

A Contrast to Jesus Christ

In his masterful book, *Dispensational Truth,* Dr. Clarence Larkin has listed the following fourteen contrasts between the Antichrist and the Lord Jesus Christ.[15]

1. Christ came from above — John 6:38
   Antichrist will ascend from the pit — Revelation 11:7
2. Christ came in His Father's name — John 5:43
   Antichrist will come in his own name — John 5:43
3. Christ humbled Himself — Philippians 2:8
   Antichrist will exalt himself — 2 Thessalonians 2:4
4. Christ was despised — Isaiah 53:3; Luke 23:18
   Antichrist will be admired — Revelation 13:3, 4
5. Christ will be exalted — Philippians 2:9
   Antichrist will be cast down to hell — Isaiah 14:14, 15; Revelation 19:20
6. Christ came to do His Father's will — John 6:38
   Antichrist will come to do his own will — Daniel 11:36
7. Christ came to save — Luke 19:10
   Antichrist will come to destroy — Daniel 8:24
8. Christ is the good shepherd — John 10:1-15
   Antichrist is the "idol [evil] shepherd" — Zechariah 11:16, 17
9. Christ is the "true vine" — John 15:1
   Antichrist is the "vine of the earth" — Revelation 14:18
10. Christ is the "truth" — John 14:6
    Antichrist is the "lie" — 2 Thessalonians 2:11 (ASV)

11. Christ is the "holy one" — Mark 1:24
Antichrist is the "lawless one" — 2 Thessalonians 2:8 (ASV)
12. Christ is the "man of sorrows" — Isaiah 53:3
Antichrist is the "man of sin" — 2 Thessalonians 2:3
13. Christ is the "Son of God" — Luke 1:35
Antichrist is the "son of perdition" — 2 Thessalonians 2:3
14. Christ is "the mystery of godliness: God . . . manifest in the flesh" — 1 Timothy 3:16
Antichrist will be "the mystery of iniquity," Satan manifest in the flesh — 2 Thessalonians 2:7

Nationality of the Antichrist

One of the most frequently asked questions about the Antichrist concerns his nationality. Revelation 13:1 indicates that he "rises up out of the sea," meaning the sea of peoples around the Mediterranean. From this we gather that he will be a Gentile. Daniel 8:8, 9 suggests that he is the "little horn" that came out of the four Grecian horns, signaling that he will be part Greek. Daniel 9:26 refers to him as the prince of the people that shall come, meaning that he will be of the royal lineage of the race that destroyed Jerusalem. Historically this was the Roman Empire; therefore he will be predominantly Roman. Daniel 11:36, 37 tells us that he regards not "the God of his fathers" (KJV). Taken in context, this suggests he will be a Jew. In all probability the Antichrist will appear to be a Gentile and, like Adolph Hitler and others who feared to reveal Jewish blood, will keep his Jewish ancestry a secret. It may be known only to God, but the Bible teaches that he will be a Roman-Grecian Jew, a composite man representing the peoples of the earth. This technically qualifies him to be the embodiment of all evil men.

Future Activities of Antichrist

There is ample description of the work of Antichrist in Revelation 13 to warn the entire world of this awful personage who will come upon the earth to assume control. With characteristic biblical inspiration, these principles harmonize with other teachings in the Word concerning this person. We shall consider these teachings particularly in the light of the following seven events.

1. His rise to Power. As already seen in Revelation 6:2, the Antichrist will come on the scene in the "latter times" and assume power by the stealth of diplomacy. He will not gain control by war but by tricking the leaders of the world into the idea that he can offer peace and by gaining enough support from each of the ten kings of the earth. Eventually he will end up with control of all of them. This subtle method of diplomacy is confirmed by an examination of Daniel 8:25. "And through his policy also he shall cause deceit to prosper in his hand; and he shall magnify himself in his heart, and by peace shall destroy many; he shall also stand up against the Prince of princes, but he shall be broken without hand."

2. His one-world government. This one-world government is predicted in the image of Nebuchadnezzar (Dan. 2). The ten toes of the image represent an amalgamation of the ten kings under the dominance of the Antichrist. Revelation 17:12-15 reveals that the kings of the earth will finally come to the conclusion that they are not capable of governing themselves in peace with other nations of the world; thus they "shall give their power and strength unto the beast." Verse 13 suggests that for the sake of world peace they will establish a world government that they will consider the solution to the world's problems. That we have already entered into a day when man's political concept of government is one world in scope can scarcely be doubted. The monstrosity on Manhattan Island known as the United Nations, already having deceived the American people and robbed the U.S. Treasury, is a classic example.

3. The Antichrist will dominate world economy. When Revelation 17:13 states that the kings of the earth "shall give their power . . . unto the beast," this means not only their armies but also their economic power. It is inconceivable that a one-world government be established without an interrelated one-world economy. Such an economy has been suggested in the European Common Market. Although it is still in its infancy, because of economic necessity it could spread throughout the entire world and eventually become the type of instrument used by the Antichrist to control the monetary and financial affairs of the world.

4. The Antichrist's atheistic religion. The religion of the Antichrist appears in several places in Scripture, primarily Daniel 11:36-39 and 2 Thessalonians 2:1-12. These passages teach that the Antichrist will exalt himself "above all that is called God, or that is worshiped, so that he, as God, sitteth in the temple of God, showing himself that he is God" (2 Thess. 2:4). This evil personage will be a master of deceit even in the religious realm.

According to Revelation 17 he will give tacit approval to the ecumenical church, not because he believes in it, but because of its tremendous political overtones and his aspiration to control the world. He apparently will be dominated by the ecumenical church, as we will see in Revelation 17, since the harlot (the ecumenical church) rides the beast, indicating that she will actually limit or dominate many of his governmental activities. But this will all be subterfuge on his part until he can gather sufficient control to throw her off and kill this idolatrous ecumenical religion that is gathering momentum in our own generation.

Antichrist's true religion will be atheism, which has been increasing in prominence since the early days of German rationalism and today is given the respectability of intellectualism. Antichrist's religion of atheism is rapidly increasing already, particularly in key positions of influence. It is well known that the headwaters of the educational system in America rise from Columbia University which, thanks to John Dewey and others, is predominantly atheistic in philosophy. The atheists have propagated and enforced a purely secular education for our young people, contrary to all American principles.

All of these things fitted together are merely pieces of a puzzle that will spread the philosophies of atheism. This does not even include the fact that the foundation stone of communism and socialism is atheism. Wherever these "isms" are propagated (and they cover a third of the world today and are rapidly spreading), we find the seeds of atheism that will in the last days spring up in the worship of the Antichrist.

5. His covenant with Israel. Daniel 9:27 indicates that he will make a covenant with Israel for seven years which, as we have already seen, will be broken in the middle of the Tribulation when it suits his purposes. This covenant will only serve to keep the children of Israel from seeking God; just as they looked to Egypt in the Old Testament, they will look for help and alliance to the Antichrist for the first three and one-half years of the Tribulation.

6. His death and resurrection. As already seen, Antichrist will die and be resurrected. Revelation 17:8 states that "The beast that thou sawest was, and is not; and shall ascend out of the bottomless pit, and go into perdition; and they that dwell in the earth shall wonder, whose names were not written in the book of life from the foundation of the world, when they behold the beast that was, and is not, and yet is." This verse indicates that the Antichrist will die in the middle of the Tribulation. Since we have already seen that Satan will be cast out of heaven, aware that his time is short, he will indwell the Antichrist and duplicate the resurrection. Thus he will come up out of perdition and again contrast the supernatural work of Christ. From that point on, indwelt by Satan himself, he will have power to perform "signs and lying wonders" (2 Thess. 2:9-12) and could potentially deceive "even the very elect." He will have absolute authority by virtue of his supernatural powers and the submission of the kings of the earth to his control and dominance. It is then that he will unleash his attack on the nation or Israel. It will be the greatest anti-Semitic movement the world has ever known. He will seek to put to death all those who do not bear his mark or bow down and worship him as God.

7. The ultimate destruction of the Antichrist. 2 Thessalonians 2:8 declares, "And then shall that wicked one be revealed, whom the Lord shall consume with the spirit of his mouth, and shall destroy with the brightness of his coming." This destruction of Satan by our Lord at His coming is graphically described in Revelation 19:11-20. Christ will destroy Satan and his armies all at one time and will cast him alive into the lake of fire burning with brimstone. We have no record of his judgment. Only the Antichrist and the false prophet will not be judged, but because of their activities they will be cast alive into the lake of fire.

Thus we have prophesied the bitter end of the man of sin, the Antichrist. But consider the millions deceived by him who will share his fate — the lake of fire.

We shall see how these basic practices of the Antichrist are further confirmed in chapter 13, and later we will encounter his own private religious leader called the False Prophet. Of all the names used for Antichrist, the most significant is that in the original language of 2 Thessalonians 2:8, where he is called "the lawless one" (ASV). The present generation is preparing for the rule of Antichrist by its insistent, contagious desire for lawlessness. One of the plaguing problems of the younger generation is that of rebellion against law and order and a desire to reject restraint. Instead of morality, honesty, and decency based on the fixed standard of God's Word, we find immorality and self-expression. Self-indulgence is the watchword of life today! The Bible defines the spirit of lawlessness as sin in 1 John 3:4. The root word is identical: "Whosoever committeth sin transgresseth also the law; for sin is the transgression of the law [LAWLESSNESS, ASV]." The spirit of rebellion in the heart of any man signifies that he is a subject of the Antichrist even before he arrives. The spirit of submission to the Law of God is a supernatural result of having invited Jesus Christ into one's life.

21
The Beast
Out of the Sea

Revelation 13:1-10

Just as God uses men to accomplish His objective for mankind, so Satan uses men. The thirteenth chapter of Revelation is a good example of that fact, for in it we meet two men, referred to as beasts, who will be used by Satan during the Tribulation Period.

> And I stood upon the sand of the sea, and saw a beast rise up out of the sea, having seven heads and ten horns, and upon his horns ten crowns, and upon his heads the name of blasphemy. And the beast which I saw was like a leopard, and his feet were like the feet of a bear, and his mouth like the mouth of a lion; and the dragon gave him his power, and his throne, and great authority (Rev. 13:1, 2).

The best manuscripts use "he" instead of the pronoun "I" at the beginning of this verse, indicating that this verse belongs with chapter 12, verse 17, and refers to the dragon, or Satan. In other words, Satan is standing on the sand of the sea, which gives rise to this fearsome beast that will come on the world scene in latter times.

A Description of the Beast

This beast is obviously unlike any animal we have ever seen. Therefore we apply the golden rule of interpretation: "when the plain sense of the Scripture makes common sense, seek no other sense." Because the plain sense of this passage does not make common sense, we naturally seek another sense. Since there are no seven-headed animals, this composite picture of a leopard, lion, and bear must be a symbol.

There is much controversy as to the identity of this beast. Some would have us believe that it is a religious organization, because in chapter 17 we find the scarlet woman astride a similar beast. Others would have us believe that this beast is a kingdom, not a king. This is not the first time that the Holy Spirit has used the symbol of a beast to describe either a

king or a kingdom. In Daniel 7 we find that several beasts are employed
to convey the meaning of coming world governments, with the lion referring not only to the Babylonian Empire, but to Nebuchadnezzar himself
(Dan. 2). This is significant because Daniel said to Nebuchadnezzar,
"Thou art this head of gold." The late Dr. David L. Cooper noted that
the symbol of the beast can refer either to a king or his kingdom, depending on the Holy Spirit's point of view. He used the illustration of a
floodlight and a spotlight: when the spotlight is on, the king was in focus,
but when the floodlight is on, the Holy Spirit would have us look at the
entire kingdom. Such is the case in Revelation 13. Some details about
this beast can apply only to an individual, whereas others apply to his
kingdom. [16] We find that the beast opens his mouth and speaks blasphemy,
indicating a reference not only to a kingdom but to a specific personage.
We have already examined in detail the other Scripture passages about
the Antichrist. Now we find in Revelation 13 the description of the end-
time king and his kingdom.

The Seven Heads

The characteristics of this beast, as observed by John, are strange indeed. He has seven heads, ten horns, and crowns on each horn. Each
head has on it a "name of blasphemy." The beast has a body like a
leopard, feet like a bear, and a mouth like a lion. The source of his
power and authority is the devil himself. The seven heads are probably

the most difficult part of this beast to describe. The ten horns obviously correspond to the ten toes of the vision of Daniel 2 and the ten horns of the nondescript beast which represents the Roman Empire in Daniel 7. They are the ten kings who give the Antichrist their power during the Tribulation Period. The features of a leopard, a bear, and a lion characterizing the animal are most informative. In fact, they afford a model indication of the absolute accuracy of Scripture.

Daniel's four beasts in chapter 7 represented future kingdoms, beginning with the lion that represented the Babylonian Empire. Then he saw a bear that represented the Medo-Persian Empire, followed by a leopard representing the Grecian Empire, followed by a nondescript beast portraying the Roman Empire. These four animals, representing the four world kingdoms, are most interesting, for no world powers have existed other than the four described by Daniel, who wrote at the beginning of this chain of conquests. John penned his description when the last governmental beast was in control; therefore his description is in reverse order. Daniel began with the lion, whereas John ended with the lion. Because the prophets lived some six hundred years apart, Daniel was looking forward to what would come to pass in relationship to these world kingdoms, but John was looking backward, for the Babylonian, Medo-Persian, Grecian, and Roman Empires had already appeared on the scene.

The seven heads of this beast are mentioned in Revelation 17 as kings of the Roman Empire (17:10). The best definition I have heard is that they represent five kings to the time of John; the sixth, Domitian, was the Roman king at the time of John, who then skipped forward to the end time for the seventh head, Antichrist. Others suggest that these are the seven phases of Roman type of government through which the nondescript beast, which represents Caesarean imperialism, passed. In either case the whole animal represents a bestial kingdom that will be in dominant control of the earth during the Tribulation.

A rather interesting side note regarding the Holy Spirit's description of the beast to represent kingdoms appears in the contrasts in the book of Daniel. When man thinks of world governments, they take on a beautiful shape, as did Nebuchadnezzar's image in Daniel 2. Each section of that image represented one of the four coming world kingdoms. However, when God describes the coming world kingdoms, He uses beasts to symbolize them. Man looks favorably on government as a great help to him, whereas God looks upon government as a great hindrance to man, as does anyone who has studied history and observed government's bestial treatment of humanity.

The time of the setting of this beast, as described in Revelation 13, should be noted on the chart of this period (see below). Chapter 13 describes the work of Antichrist during the seven years of Tribulation. It is a parenthetical insertion coming between the trumpet and bowl judgments, not to indicate that he will begin his reign in the middle of the Tribulation Period but that his governmental reign will run through the entire period and reach its climax at the middle of the Tribulation. The first three-and-a-half years will be spent in trying to gain control of the world; they are described in Revelation 17. Antichrist will lead the governmental organization that will be dominated by the religious system of the day, which we will cover in our discussion of Revelation 17, but in the middle of Tribulation he will throw off the scarlet woman and assume absolute control of the world.

Verse 1 indicates that the beast rose "up out of the sea." Whenever the Bible refers to the "sea," it means the Mediterranean Sea, unless the sea is used symbolically as it is here. Sometimes "sea" is used to describe people, a sea of people. The meaning, then, would be that the Antichrist arises from among the people around the Mediterranean Sea, which is in accord with the nationality description we saw in the previous chapter. It is no wonder that Dr. Wilbur Smith describes this period of time rapidly coming upon the world as "the darkest hour of human history."

The Death and Resurrection of the Beast

"And I saw one of his heads as though it were wounded to death; and his deadly wound was healed, and all the world wondered after the beast" (Rev. 13:3). Verse 3 indicates that the beast, or Antichrist, will be given a deadly wound. It is quite possible that at the midway point of the Tribulation Period, in the great war referred to as the second war of the Tribulation Period, the Antichrist will be killed. (Apparently of the ten kings the three not in unanimity with the Antichrist will try to wrest control from him, probably at the same time the scarlet woman of chapter 17 is thrown out of control.) Revelation 17:8 indicates that his spirit will go down into the pit of the abyss where it belongs, but he will be resurrected. One must keep in mind that this beast is the Antichrist. In other words, he will try to duplicate everything Jesus Christ has done. This is significant in view of the fact that the sign of our Lord's deity appears in His resurrection. He said that no sign would be given unto men except "the sign of the prophet, Jonah; for as Jonah was three days and three nights in the belly of the great fish, so shall the Son of man be three days and three nights in the heart of the earth" (Matt. 12:39, 40). Christianity is unique in that we worship a resurrected, living Lord. The power of this testimony is beyond description to men who are real seekers after truth. This power will be all but nullified by the nefarious work of Satan through the resurrection of the Antichrist. As far as I know, this will be the first time that Satan has ever been able to raise the dead. His power and control of man is limited by God, but according to His wise providence He will permit Satan on this one occasion to have the power to raise the dead. When studied in the light of 2 Thessalonians 2, it may well be the tool he will use to deceive men.

"And they worshiped the dragon who gave power unto the beast; and they worshiped the beast, saying, Who is like the beast? Who is able to make war with him?" (Rev. 13:4). It would seem that after his resurrection thousands of individuals across the world, previously undecided about the Antichrist, will make him an object of worship and fall down before him.

The Blasphemies of the Beast

And there was given unto him a mouth speaking great things and blasphemies, and power was given unto him to continue forty and two months. And he opened his mouth in blasphemy against God, to blaspheme his name, and his tabernacle, and them that dwell in heaven (Rev. 13:5, 6).

Satan has long been the author of blasphemy against God. That blasphemy will reach its climax when, not content just to damn or curse in the name of God, he will set up a form of worship that leads men to fall down before him as though he were a god. This accords with Isaiah 14, which describes Satan's secret desire to have other creatures worship him. The Jews accused Jesus of blasphemy because He said He was God. Jesus was crucified for blasphemy. But declaring that one is God is blasphemous only when untrue. In the case of Antichrist during the Tribulation Period, it will be untrue, but such supernatural powers will be given him by the devil himself that he will appear to have Godlike characteristics and thus deceive many human beings.

Some Bible teachers suggest that when chapter 13 is compared with chapter 12, where Satan is cast out of heaven in the middle of the Tribulation Period, it appears that Satan will actually indwell the body of the Antichrist. This would account for the Antichrist's resurrection. Thus during the first three-and-a-half years of the Tribulation the Antichrist will be merely a man endowed with satanic power, but during the last three-and-a-half years, he will actually be Satan himself, clothed with the Antichrist's body.

The Power of the Beast

"And it was given unto him to make war with the saints, and to overcome them; and power was given him over all kindreds, and tongues, and nations" (Rev. 13:7). Today the world is prepared for a one-world governmental philosophy. That philosophy, propagated by Satan and advocated by the intellectual, godless, atheistic leading of world governments today, is rapidly spreading across the earth. As already seen, man has just about come to the conclusion that the only solution to the problem of continuous war is a one-world government. That government will be the devil's government, established during the Tribulation. In the midst of that time he will assume control himself and, as verse 7 tells us, will exercise power over "all kindreds and nations." During that period he will do two things: exert power over all kindreds and nations and persecute the saints. In accord with the fifth seal judgment, the latter half of the Tribulation will be a time of increased persecution of saints, and we have already seen from Chapter 12 that the devil will also persecute Israel. Therefore, we may conclude that Satan will try to control all the people of the world and will launch a gigantic anti-Christian, anti-Semitic crusade.

One comforting truth gleaned from the book of Revelation is that although Antichrist will have power over all kindreds and tongues, he will not deceive every individual; Revelation 7:9 makes it clear that the preaching of the Gospel by the 144,000 Jewish witnesses will reach a multitude which no man can number, from every tongue and tribe and people. Therefore, even Satan's control will not keep men from receiving Christ individually. This is in accord with the way it has been all during the Christian dispensation. Nations and peoples have rejected Christ, but individuals have received Him. According to John 1:10, 11, "He was in the world, and the world was made by him, and the world knew him not. He came unto his own, and his own received him not." But the text continues: "as many as received him, to them gave he power to become the children of God, even to them that believe on his name" (v. 12).

The Worship of the Beast

And all that dwell upon the earth shall worship him, whose names are not written in the book of life of the Lamb slain from the foundation of the world. If any man have an ear, let him hear. He that leadeth into captivity shall go into captivity; he that killeth with the sword must be killed with the sword. Here is the patience and the faith of the saints (Rev. 13:8-10).

It is evident even today that men seek to worship what they can see. This is reflected in the widespread use of idols and holy relics in conjunction with the worship of the religions of the world. During the Tribulation Period, Satan will provide a visible god with seemingly divine powers. Those who prefer a comfortable religion which does not demand righteous behavior will find just what they are looking for. On the basis of verse 8 alone it would seem that the majority of the people on the earth, even during the Tribulation Period, will worship the Antichrist rather than Christ Jesus the Lord. However, some will refuse to bow down and worship Antichrist. We will see shortly that he will set up an image of himself to be worshiped by men. Just as the three Hebrews refused to worship Nebuchadnezzar's image, which foreshadowed the day when during the Tribulation all men will be commanded to worship the beast, so there will be some faithful who refuse. In this text it is those whose names are "written in the book of life of the Lamb."

The significance of this expression cannot be bypassed. The Book of Life is introduced in several passages of Scripture, particularly in Revelation 20:15: "And whosoever was not found written in the book of life was cast into the lake of fire." The Book of Life contains the names of the living. It is God's book of anticipation. That is, whenever a human being is born, God writes his name in that book; if he dies without receiving Christ (Rev. 3:5), his name is blotted out of the book so that in eternity the only people whose names remain in the Book of Life are those who have received Christ by faith while they lived.

The Lamb's Book of Life is quite a different matter! There is no doubt as to the identity of the Lamb, for John the Baptist pointed to Jesus Christ as "the Lamb of God, who taketh away the sin of the world" (John 1:29). The Lamb's Book of Life includes only those who have come to the Lamb for life. Jesus said that He came to give unto men "eternal life," and many times He stated that His believers would have life everlasting. In fact, He proclaimed that those who believe on Him will "never die." He was not, of course, referring to the flesh, but to the real man of the heart, the eternal soul. We conclude, then, that the Lamb's Book of Life contains the names of those who have by faith received the Lamb of God and thus had their names "written in the book of life of the Lamb."

Not everyone has his name written in the Lamb's Book of Life! One's name is not written in at birth, nor does he have it written in by the sovereign choice of God. A man's name is written in the Lamb's Book of Life because he chooses to ask God to place it there. Jesus Christ offers men eternal life if they will receive Him, if they will invite Him into their hearts. If they heed His call and ask Him to come in as Lord and Savior, He enters their lives (Rev. 3:20) and the recording angel writes their names into the Lamb's Book of Life, from which it can never be blotted. Is your name written in the Lamb's Book of Life? If not, may I urge you to choose to invite Jesus Christ into your life right now and let Him write it there.

22

The False Prophet

Revelation 13:11-18

The Lord Jesus Christ predicted that in the last days "there shall arise false Christs, and false prophets, and shall show great signs and wonders, insomuch that, if it were possible, they shall deceive the very elect" (Matt. 24:24). Although many false prophets have arisen, seeking to deceive men, and though many exist in this present day, there has never been an adequate fulfillment to our Lord's prediction quite like that which will culminate during the Tribulation.

Since man is incurably religious, a world dictator must provide man with an outlet for his religious inclinations. We have already seen that Antichrist will come on the scene during the Tribulation Period to take control of world government. We shall soon observe that the ecumenical church, described in Revelation 17, will exert such power that it will dominate him during the first three-and-a-half years while he is solidifying the power of his empire. That he will resent her and attempt to throw off these shackles is clear from the fact that he will destroy her in the middle of the Tribulation Period and set up his own form of worship. To propagate that worship, the devil will provide a special man on the scene, the other awesome personage described in Revelation 13 as the "beast coming up out of the earth."

That these two beasts (the first beast that comes up out of the sea, the Antichrist, and this beast that comes up out of the earth) are men is clear from what will happen to them when our Lord returns at the end of the Tribulation Period.

> And the beast was taken, and with him the false prophet that wrought miracles before him, with which he deceived them that had received the mark of the beast, and them that worshiped his image. These both were cast alive into a lake of fire burning with brimstone (Rev. 19:20).

184

This verse can apply only to the two beasts described in Revelation 13. The first is the governmental leader, called the Antichrist, who will set himself up as God; the second is his religious leader, who will incite men to worship Antichrist.

Characteristics of the False Prophet

And I beheld another beast coming up out of the earth; and he had two horns like a lamb, and he spoke like a dragon. And he exerciseth all the power of the first beast before him, and causeth the earth and them who dwell on it to worship the first beast, whose deadly wound was healed (Rev. 13:11, 12).

In these two verses five characteristics chart the role of the False Prophet.

1. "And I beheld another beast coming up out of the earth." Many Bible teachers suggest that his coming up out of the earth indicates that he will not come up out of the sea of peoples, as will the first beast. That is, he will not be of mixed nationality; that he comes out of the earth (around Palestine) may indicate that he will be a Jew. This would point to an apostate Jew who during the first three-and-a-half years will lead Israel to make a covenant with Antichrist and deceive them by hiding his apostasy until the middle of the Tribulation Period, at which time he will serve his purpose by revealing his apostate beliefs and practices.

2. "He had two horns like a lamb." The Lord Jesus Christ is often referred to in the gospels and in the book of Revelation as "the Lamb of God." As such He has taken away the sins of the world. The False Prophet coming on the earth will look like a lamb with two horns. Lambs do not have horns, which are symbols of authority, but instead are meek and mild animals. The Lord Jesus said in the Sermon on the Mount, "Beware of false prophets that come unto you as wolves in sheep's clothing." The False Prophet will come to Israel in sheep's clothing, but God terms him "a beast."

3. "He spake as a dragon" suggests that he will derive power of speech from the devil who, as we found in chapter 12, is the dragon. This False Prophet, then, will deceive men by acting like a lamb; but really he will speak the words of Satan. Let it be understood that Satan is not against religion. He is, however, against personal faith in Jesus Christ. Therefore, the beast will be one of the chief spokesmen in the Holy Land for the ecumenical power described in Revelation 17.

4. "And he exerciseth all the power [authority] of the first beast before him." The close relationship between these two world leaders is seen in the fact that the False Prophet will be given power by the Antichrist himself. His whole purpose will be to work toward the complete dominance of the earth by the Antichrist, including a form of religion satisfactory to the Antichrist.

5. "And causeth the earth and them who dwell on it to worship the first beast." The False Prophet's basic purpose and operation with all of

this power from the Antichrist and speech from the devil will be to drive men to worship the Antichrist. When indwelt by Satan in the midst of the Tribulation, the Antichrist will be so deceived about himself that he will deem himself God and seek the worship of men (2 Thess. 2:3-8). This form of worship will be propagated by the second beast or False Prophet. He could well be described as the high priest of the Antichrist's religious system during the Tribulation Period.

The Satanic Trinity

Verses 11 and 12 couple the three evil personages of the Tribulation Period that counterpart the person of God. Just as the dragon has already been anti-God, and the first beast will be anti-Christ, so the second beast will be anti-Spirit. His capacity in working for the worship of the Antichrist will correspond with the present ministry of the Holy Spirit. He will not seek to cause men to worship himself. He will not court his own personal prestige but will work purely for the purpose of getting men to worship Antichrist. This evil scheme will be used by the devil and his two cohorts to deceive men during the Tribulation. They will victimize many individuals because they will traffic in amorality.

Supernatural Powers of the False Prophet

Every tribal witch doctor, false religious teacher, and false prophet has tried by magic, voodoo, trickery, or demonic power to deceive men by a display of supernaturalism. Religions of the world are bound by superstition. Only Jesus Christ is able to give peace and confidence before God to men of fearful temperaments, and this is not dependent on supernatural displays or signs.

None of the false teachers to this time has ever possessed the supernatural powers that will be exhibited by the False Prophet on behalf of the Antichrist during the Tribulation Period. Notice their description in this text.

"And he doeth great wonders" (Rev. 13:13). This word "wonders," translated in the American Standard Version as "signs," is the same word used by the Apostle John in his gospel, describing the ministry of Jesus. It is translated in verse 14 as "miracles." This would lead us to believe that the False Prophet will be equipped by Satan and the Antichrist with authority and power to do such supernatural signs as to "deceive the very elect." This should not come as a surprise to Bible students, for the devil has great power. When Moses threw down his rod before Pharaoh, it turned into a serpent. The false prophets of Pharaoh, however, were also empowered to make their rods turn into serpents, thus duplicating the miracle of the man of God. However, God caused Moses' serpent to eat up their serpents. Missionaries have told us of phenomena so fantastic that they could only be explained on the basis of supernatural power.

During the Tribulation Period the Antichrist, according to 2 Thessalonians 2:9, 10, will have the power to perform "signs and lying wonders, and with all deceivableness of unrighteousness." It does not seem surprising that the False Prophet will be able to reproduce everything that the special witnesses of God, described in Revelation 11, will be able to do, even to the point of reproducing the miracles of Jesus. This predicted demonstration of supernatural, miraculous power should warn us of the significant truth that the mere display of supernatural power does not suffice as evidence that a matter or practice originates with God. All supernatural power is for the purpose of giving credentials to a person or a teaching. We have something far more important to stand as a test of all teaching, regardless of its accompanied signs — the Word of God. If a teaching is not in accord with the Word of God, it is false!

"He maketh fire come down from heaven on the earth in the sight of men." The fire test of Elijah the prophet, which proved to the children of Israel that the prophets of Baal were powerless to communicate with God, will probably be repeated during the Tribulation Period. That may be one of the reasons for the coming of Elijah at the time. The difference between this confrontation and the previous one will be that the false prophet will be able to call down fire from heaven. Lest this take us by surprise, we should be reminded that Satan, the real force behind the false prophet, brought fire down from heaven and burned up Job's sheep and servants in Job 1:16. We could well ask ourselves, Why will God permit such power to be in Satan's hands? It is because even during the Tribulation Period men will be forced to worship God by faith. If all the supernatural power were on one side, it would not take faith but merely common sense to recognize the source of power. But the principle of salvation as a gift of God will still rest on the basis of faith: "Without faith it is impossible to please him" (Heb. 11:6).

The False Prophet will cause an image of the Antichrist to be built and will have power to "give life unto the image of the beast" (Rev. 13:14, 15). In the midst of the Tribulation Period, after the Antichrist has been slain and resurrected, the false prophet will cause men to build an image like Nebuchadnezzar's image and will demand that it be worshiped. By some mysterious means unknown in the previous history of the world, he will give life to this image. How long it will manifest life we are not told. What characteristics it will have we are not told. Possibly the only characteristic it will manifest is that it will "speak" (v. 15). This verse indicates that its speech will be caused by the False Prophet, who in turn will get his authority from the Antichrist and the dragon Satan himself. He will issue an order that all who do not worship him will be killed. Revelation 20:4 tells us that many will be slain by the guillotine.

This scene is so similar to that which happened to the children of Israel as a result of Nebuchadnezzar's image that we begin to realize that Satan's tactics do not vary significantly. Once again, an order will be given that those who do not bow down and worship him will be killed; instead of confronting a fiery furnace, they will be guillotined. This certainly establishes the high cost of knowing Christ as personal Savior during the Tribulation Period. I have heard unthinking men make such statements as "I am going to wait until the Tribulation to receive Christ." What they do not understand is the personal suffering and persecution that believers will endure during the Tribulation Period because of the animosity of Satan against God and those who worship Him. Both the fifth seal and Revelation 20:4 indicate that a martyrdom of true believers will exceed even that of the Dark Ages, when the Roman Catholic Church persecuted those who held to a personal faith in Jesus Christ.

Many things coincide with the middle of the Tribulation Period, one of which is Satan's persecution of the nation Israel. It may be persecution that will awaken Israel to the fact that the Antichrist is its enemy. It may, however, be the disclosure of the False Prophet's true theological persuasion that will awaken Israel. The Holy Spirit through the pen of Moses in Deuteronomy 13 determined the test of all prophets. As stated above, it was not sufficient merely to regard the manifestation of supernatural power, but to hear what the prophet said. And if the prophet declared, "Let us go after other gods, which thou hast not known, and let us serve them, thou shalt not hearken unto the words of that prophet, or that dreamer of dreams; for the LORD your God testeth you" (Deut. 13:2, 3). When the False Prophet erects his idol worship, it may be that Israel, who does not seem to embrace Christ the Messiah in the first half of the Tribulation, will embrace Him in the second half, thus rejecting the deceiving, idolatrous religion of the Antichrist.

As we approach the end of the age and these signs in their initial stages begin to come to pass, we should not let miraculous power deceive us, but judge everything according to the Word of God.

The False Prophet's Use of the Mark of the Beast

And he causeth all, both small and great, rich and poor, free and en-slaved, to receive a mark in their right hand, or in their foreheads, and that no man might buy or sell, except he that had the mark, or the name of the beast, or the number of his name. Here is wisdom. Let him that hath understanding count the number of the beast; for it is the number of a man; and his number is six hundred threescore and six (Rev. 13:16-18).

What is the mark of the beast? It is much easier to state what the mark of the beast is than what it means. The plain sense of Scripture tells us that it comprises the numbers, six, six, six. Perhaps some of the most fanciful suggestions for prophetic interpretation revolve around the meaning of this number. Some have by mathematical computations come to the conclusion that the name of Adolph Hitler, Mussolini, and many others equaled six, six, six. It is most dangerous to make such suggestions. Actually, we only know that six is the number of man. It is one short of the perfect number seven, and man was created on the sixth day; therefore in Bible numerology it is used to refer to man. Why three digits are used we do not know. Someone has suggested that it is the concentration of all that is human. The text does indicate that it somehow will mathematically speak the name of Antichrist. Since so many mistakes have been made in this regard, it behooves us not to offer any further suggestions. Since the number will not be revealed until the middle of the Tribulation Period and the Church will be raptured before the Tribulation, it seems more than likely that we will not be given a hint as to the full meaning or even the name of the Antichrist.

More important than the meaning is the use of these three numbers, six, six, six. The False Prophet will use them as a means of forcing men to worship Antichrist. He will demand that all men have this mark on their foreheads or on their hands in order to buy or sell. This economic pressure will be instrumental in causing many weak, worldly individuals to succumb to the establishment of this monarch, which will be tantamount to the personal rejection of Christ and acceptance of Antichrist. One can scarcely imagine the pressures of having to possess such a mark in order to secure the necessary food for his family. The U.S. government in World War II furnished a device of this kind in the form of food rationing. It was not enough to have money sufficient to pay for an item, for one had to have food stamps. The same will be true during the Tribulation Period, for the Antichrist will so control the economy that men cannot live if they do not worship him.

Physically speaking, it will be necessary for men to have the mark of the beast. Spiritually speaking, it will be fatal. For we have repeatedly seen that those who are redeemed by the Lamb, those who have the seal of God, do not have the mark of the beast. But those who receive the Antichrist's mark will have made the final decisions for eternity to reject Christ and worship his archenemy. This fact alone should cause men to fall down before the Lord Jesus Christ and worship Him today. For He has promised to save us from the hour of Tribulation, "which shall try the whole earth," if we put our faith in Him.

23

Another 144,000
Servants

Revelation 14

Anyone who would accurately interpret the book of Revelation must locate the scene of the activity before he begins his interpretation. Chapter 14 is a good illustration of that fact. Many Bible scholars consider this to be a scene in heaven, while others regard it as a scene taking place on earth. The difference in viewpoint will seriously affect one's interpretation.

Another rule to be kept in mind is that the time should be pinpointed. This passage, which falls within the "great parenthesis" that covers Revelation 11:16 - 15:4, takes place in heaven at the middle of the Tribulation Period. An examination of the chart on page 74 will show that the seventh seal judgment at the end of the first quarter of the Tribulation Period opens up into the seven trumpet judgments, which we have already seen in chapters 8 and 9. Chapters 12 and 13 describe events that culminate in the middle of the Tribulation Period. Now, before we begin the bowl judgments that come out of the seventh trumpet, covering the last half of the Tribulation Period, we are about to look upon the upheaval that will take place at the end of the three-and-a-half year period, or the middle of the Tribulation. Actually, several things will occur at that time. The ecumenical church, or the harlot of Revelation 17, will be thrown off by Antichrist and the ten kings of the earth. He will break his covenant with Israel and drive her out of the Holy Land. The revival under the witnessing of the 144,000 servants of God (chap. 7) will come to a close. The great persecution of tribulation saints, referred to in the fifth seal of chapter 6, prior to the middle of the Tribulation, will evidently come under the auspices of the ecumenical church, which will function much like the National Council of Churches today in that it will not oppose evil such as communism, secularism, or immorality, but will persecute those who believe in the supernatural resurrected Christ and salvation in His name. It will be violently overthrown by Antichrist, as we shall see in chapter 17. This chapter introduces a scene in heaven in the middle of the Tribulation.

Christ and 144,000 Outstanding Christians

And I looked and, lo, a Lamb stood on Mount Zion, and with him an hundred forty and four thousand, having his Father's name written in their foreheads. And I heard a voice from heaven, like the voice of many waters, and like the voice of a great thunder; and I heard the voice of harpers harping with their harps. And they sang, as it were, a new song before the throne, and before the four living creatures and the elders; and no man could learn that song but the hundred and forty and four thousand, who were redeemed from the earth. These are they who were not defiled with women; for they are virgins. These are they who follow the Lamb wherever he goeth. These were redeemed from among men, the firstfruits unto God and to the Lamb. And in their mouth was found no guile; for they are without fault before the throne of God (Rev. 14:1-5).

The contrast between chapters 13 and 14 is remarkable. From the fleshly, debased scene of earth, we are lifted to the lofty heights of heaven where Jesus Christ's name is honored rather than profaned, where He is the central figure before whom all bow and to whom all voices are raised in adoration.

Each time we are given a new glimpse of heaven, we gain additional knowledge of the details surrounding the throne. Such is the case on this occasion, for we are introduced to the 144,000 outstanding Christians from all ages standing before the throne. We know that this is a scene in heaven because John sees "the Lamb standing on Mount Zion." There are only two possible meanings for Mount Zion in the Scripture. One is the Mount Zion at the earthly site of Jerusalem; the other is the Mount Zion of the heavenly Jerusalem. That the Lamb of God will not be on the earth in the midst of the Tribulation Period is apparent from chapter 13. This must be a scene in the heavenly Jerusalem, described by the Holy Spirit in Hebrews 12:12-24.

But ye are come unto Mount Zion, and unto the city of the living God, the heavenly Jerusalem, and to an innumerable company of angels, to the general assembly and church of the first-born, who are written in heaven, and to God, the Judge of all, and to the spirits of just men made perfect, and to Jesus the mediator of the new covenant, and to the blood of sprinkling, that speaketh better things than that of Abel.

The identity of this group of 144,000 subjects has for some reason eluded many outstanding Bible scholars. Most commentators have a tendency to assume that they are identical with the 144,000 described in chapter 7. Therefore we must examine them in detail.

A Comparison of the 144,000 in Chapter 7
and the 144,000 in Chapter 14

144,000 of Rev. 7:1-9	*144,000 of Rev. 14:1-5*
vv. 1-3 A scene on earth.	v. 1 A scene in heaven. The Lamb is with them on Mount Zion.
v. 3 Servants of our God, sealed in their foreheads.	v. 1b "Having his name and the name of his Father written in their foreheads" (ASV).
v. 4 144,000 of all the tribes of Israel.	v. 3 Sing a new song before the elders and the four living creatures which only they knew.
vv. 5-8 12,000 from each tribe.	v. 3b "Who were redeemed from the earth."
	v. 4 "They are not defiled with women; for they are virgins."
	v. 4 "They follow the Lamb wherever he goeth."
	v. 4b "These were redeemed from among men."
	v. 4c "The first fruits unto God and to the Lamb."
	v. 5 "In their mouth was found guile."
	v. 5b "They are without fault before the throne of God."

The Similarities of the Two Groups

Two basic reasons are usually advanced for considering the two groups similar: (1) both groups total 144,000, and (2) both groups have something written on their foreheads.

The Differences of the Two Groups

1. The Revelation 7 group is specifically Jewish — 12,000 from each of the 12 tribes. The Revelation 14 group comes "from the earth" or "from among men."

2. The Revelation 7 group is sealed with the Father's seal. The Revelation 14 group has the name of both the Father and the Son.

3. The scene of chapter 7 occurs on the earth. Chapter 14 takes place in heaven, but only halfway through the Tribulation. This can be explained in that the 144,000 witnesses of Revelation 7, like their converts of verse 9, are slain and under the altar by the middle of the Tribulation Period. Thus they are described in chapter 14 as before the throne, in

their spirit or "soulish" state — "absent from the body, and . . . present with the Lord" (2 Cor. 5:8).

4. The additional qualifications for being a member of this group, found in verses 4 and 5, are not recorded in Chapter 7. The 144,000 of chapter 7 are "servants of our God"; the 144,000 of chapter 14 are "redeemed from among men, the first fruits unto God and to the Lamb." This indicates that their selection was not for the propagation of the Gospel on the earth during the Tribulation, but for a special position at the throne of God before Him and the Lord Jesus Christ.

5. Verse 4 tells us "these are they who follow the Lamb wherever He goeth." which could well indicate that as a select group, they have been faithful in completely abandoning their will to the will of Christ during their lifetimes.

Not Jews — Christians

Since only two similarities and several differences exist between these two groups, we can safely conclude that they are not the same. The fact that the numbers are the same — 144,000 — is not so overpowering when one bears in mind a statement by Dr. William R. Newell in his book on Revelation: "The repetition of the number 144,000, one of governmental completeness and fullness, is not necessarily conclusive proof that the two companies are one and the same."[17] This would indicate that for God's perfect governmental operation He has selected multiples of twelve to be His special servants in the Tribulation and another group, on the same basis, to enjoy a relationship with Him in heaven, the difference being that those in chapter 14 have earned their position because of their faithfulness in doing whatever the Lord commissioned them to do. That both have something in their foreheads is certainly not conclusive evidence one way or the other. The chapter 7 group is "sealed unto God"; the chapter 14 group have the name of Christ and the Father written in their foreheads. This could be a spiritual thing, exemplified by people of the stripe of the Apostle Paul, whose mind (behind the forehead) was filled with a desire to serve Jesus Christ and God the Father all the days of his life. If anyone is permitted into that group, certainly the Apostle Paul would be qualified.

The differences between the two groups seem to limit our assuming that they are the same, particularly when one bears in mind that the scene in chapter 14 is in heaven and that these are taken from among men, indicating they come from all nations, rather than just from among the Jews. Dr. Newell identifies the two as Israel, but he also makes the following statement:

> For, although we have thus spoken of them. we cannot but leave the question open for further light. Because in all other Scripture we can recall Israel's victors are always named as belonging to that elect nation. and the favor of God is seen as arising from that national election.

Whereas, these of Revelation 14 do not have that mark, but rather seem to be from a larger circle than Israel — even "from among men"; and their peculiar distinction appears to be a reward for their utter self-abnegation. As Dean Alford says, "We are perhaps more like that which the Lord intended us to be; but they are more like the Lord Himself."[18]

Considering the above statements carefully, I present the following possibility, not dogmatically, but with a sincere conviction that this is a more accurate interpretation than those I have come upon so far. The 144,000 found in chapter 14 are probably the most outstanding 144,000 saints of the Church from the early days of the spread of the Gospel to the Rapture of the Church. For this consecrated and devoted service to our Master they will enjoy a special position before the throne of God from death until the glorious appearing of Christ, at which time all saints will come with Him. This position doubtless signifies that they will have great responsibility while reigning with Him during the millennial kingdom.

Qualifications for This Elite Group of Christians

1. They are redeemed from the earth by faith in Christ, "having his name, and the name of his Father, written on their foreheads" (14:1b, ASV); "redeemed from the earth" (14:3b); "redeemed from among men" (14:4b). Obviously these men were first born again by receiving Jesus Christ as their personal Savior and Lord.

2. They are morally pure. "These are they who were not defiled with women; for they are virgins" (14:4). Much has been said by commentators about this qualification, suggesting that only unmarried men would qualify. There is no scriptural certainty to indicate that Paul was ever married, so that he very easily fits the pattern here, and to my knowledge we have no record of John having been married, though it is possible it is just not mentioned. In any case, there could well have been 144,000 in the last 1900 plus years of the Christian Church who have remained single for the Lord's sake; having met the other qualifications, they will share in that elite position with Paul, possibly John, and others. I would not insist upon a literal interpretation of this expression for the following reason. Nowhere does the Bible teach that sexual intercourse in marriage is defiling. On the contrary, Hebrews 13:4 clearly announces, "Marriage is honorable in all, and the bed undefiled, but fornicators and adulterers God will judge." Even the Apostle Paul, in 1 Corinthians 7, when encouraging consecrated young men to "abide even as I," was doing so not for moral reasons, but that they might give themselves more completely to serving the Lord and not be encumbered with concerns for the desires and tastes of a wife. In addition to this, we find Boaz in the book of Ruth addressing Ruth as "a virtuous woman," even though she had been married to his kinsman who had died (3:11). There is no indication that physical relations did not exist between Ruth and her first husband, and

to assume so merely because she did not have children could be taking unwarranted license in interpretation. I do not find where a faithful married woman is considered any less virtuous in the Scripture than an unmarried virgin. Anything else than this would mean that God's commandment to be fruitful and multiply and replenish the earth would connote defilement in the act of obedience, which contradicts other principles in Scripture that indicate that God does not tempt men with evil. On the contrary, the Revelation text probably does not mean unmarried men, but men who are undefiled by women; that is, they have either kept the marriage contract or have never known a woman, and thus in the eyes of God are considered virgins. It is interesting that this passage of Scripture is the only one in the Bible referring to men as virgins. The Bible does not teach celibacy; in fact, no hint of it is found in Scripture. The Bible everywhere advocates that Christians be holy and virtuous, undefiled by the world. Misuse of sex has always been one of man's greatest problems, infidelity and immorality one of man's greatest temptations. Therefore the elite group of 144,000 who qualify to stand before the throne of God in heaven are those who have kept themselves undefiled. That is, they kept their marriage vows or remained unmarried.

3. They are obedient and available. "These are they who follow the Lamb wherever he goeth" (14:4b). It is obvious that all of God's children, in fact, all of His servants, are not completely yielded to His will. Some have known years of yieldedness and faithful service, only to go back and "walk no more with him," whereas others have had on-again off-again periods of obedience. This elite group of 144,000 is unusually marked by obedience. Their attitude is epitomized by the statement of the Apostle Paul immediately upon recognizing Jesus, when he said, "Lord, what wilt thou have me to do?"

4. They tell the truth. "And in their mouth was found no guile" (14:5). These men are characterized by a contrast to Satan. They are faithful witnesses, always telling the truth. Lying is a part of man's nature when he follows Satan, "the father of all lies." One characteristic of an obedient Christian is that he tells the truth.

5. They live blameless lives. "They are without fault" (14:5b). This does not indicate that they are perfect, for they too had to be redeemed from among men; they were lost sinners and had to be born again. It does not mean sinless perfection, that they have never sinned since their salvation, but reasserts what the Apostle Paul meant in 1 Thessalonians 2:10 when he said, "Ye are witnesses, and God also, how holily and justly and unblamably we behaved ourselves among you that believe." These are men who, in their desire to serve Jesus Christ and walk with Him, leaned on His power to live holy, consecrated lives. They are men who can say with Paul, "I am crucified with Christ: nevertheless I live; yet not I, but Christ liveth in me; and the life which I now live in the

flesh I live by the faith of the Son of God, who loved me and gave himself for me" (Gal. 2:20).

The Reward of the 144,000 Christians

1. They are "the first fruits unto God and to the Lamb" (14:4b). This would suggest that they are the outstanding believers of the Lamb and are given a special position, as indicated in verse 1, in standing with the Lamb on Mount Zion, before the throne, and before the four living creatures and the elders.

2. They will sing a new song which no man can learn save the 144,000 (14:3). These two rewards suggest that they will enjoy a special relationship with God the Son and God the Father from the time of their death after a life of faithful, holy service until they come with Christ to the earth. Verse 4 states, "These are they that follow the Lamb wherever He goeth," perhaps indicating that in addition to being in a privileged position before the resurrection, they will always be in a special position of service for Christ after the resurrection.

Admittedly, the above interpretation places me in the minority among commentators of the book of Revelation. With due respect to faithful men of God who have sought the Holy Spirit for their interpretation, the above is not presented dogmatically, but prayerfully, with the desire that it be given consideration. A comparison of this interpretation with the popular view that chapters 14 and 7 refer to the same group will reveal that my view creates fewer problems than the others.

An Angel Preaching the Everlasting Gospel

And I saw another angel fly in the midst of heaven, having the everlasting gospel to preach unto them that dwell on the earth, and to every nation, and kindred, and tongue, and people, saying with a loud voice, Fear God, and give glory to him; for the hour of his judgment is come; and worship him that made heaven, and earth, and the sea, and the fountains of waters (Rev. 14:6, 7).

Verse 6 introduces the first of five angels who convey a special message concerning the middle of the end time, or Tribulation Period.

It is astounding that an angel is commissioned to go forth preaching the everlasting Gospel, for the preaching of the Gospel has not been committed to angels but to men. *This astounding state of affairs could only be an indication of the severity of the circumstances.* If we keep in view the setting of this passage, we will be able to understand readily why this will be necessary. Prior to the Tribulation, the Church will have been raptured. The 144,000 Israelite witnesses from all over the world will be converted through the printed page left behind by the departing church. These witnesses will harvest a multitude which no man can number according to Revelation 7:9. This would indicate, as we saw in our study of chapter 7, that the early days of the Tribulation will experience the greatest revival in world history.

Accompanying this revival, however, is the opening of the fifth seal, indicating that there will be a great time of persecution during the Tribulation, instigated by Antichrist and in all probability administered by the ecumenical church. As we will see in our study of chapter 17, the ecumenical or harlot church will be so powerful during the first three-and-a-half years of the Tribulation that it will actually exercise restraining power over Antichrist. Therefore any persecution of true believers during that time would obviously be pursued within the framework of her administration and approval. This should not take us by surprise, for when the Babylonian influence of the Church was greatest during the Dark Ages, millions of Christians were persecuted to death. This period of history is well named the "Inquisition." An overwhelming majority of believers will be eliminated; thus few will remain to propagate the Gospel after the middle of the Tribulation Period. We have already seen in our study of chapter 12 that Israel will not experience a revival in the first part of the Tribulation; instead, a Gentile revival will occur through the preaching of the 144,000, who are indicative of the minority of Israel, not the majority. Israel's revival, according to Habakkuk 3:2, will take place in "the midst of the years"; thus it would seem that only the persecution of Israel will bring about her national repentance.

One of God's faithful practices in all generations has been to send adequate warning prior to judgment. The case of Noah was one example. Before God sent the flood, Noah was a preacher of righteousness for 120 years. Before God destroyed Sodom and Gomorrah, He sent Lot who, instead of being a faithful preacher, became corrupted by the immorality of the city. Thus we find in the middle of the Tribulation Period, just before the greatest suffering inflicted upon the human race, and in the absence or deficiency of adequate human Gospel witnesses, God will make an omnipotent exception to His overall plan of committing the Gospel to men by commissioning an angel to go forth preaching the everlasting Gospel.

The Everlasting Gospel

What is the everlasting Gospel? Is this a different Gospel than that preached today? On the basis of the Word of God, absolutely not! This is the *same* Gospel that we preach, the same that was "once delivered unto the saints" (Jude 3). We have already seen in our study of Revelation 7 that there are several terms for the Gospel, but only one Gospel. It is evident from the text that the whole message committed to the angel is not here expressed, but that is not uncommon in Scripture. The message this angel preaches is one of warning!

Whenever the Holy Spirit through the Word informs us of individuals preaching the Gospel, the whole message is not necessarily given. The prophet Jonah went into that pagan city, Nineveh, and the Scripture tells us in Jonah 3:4 that he simply preached, "Yet forty days, and Nineveh shall be overthrown." As we read the text, we find this simple message caused the king and the people to repent of their sin and turn to God. The only conclusion we can come to is that in addition to preaching a message of warning, Jonah also told the people how to repent, for otherwise these pagans would not have known how to approach God in sackcloth and ashes. The same picture appears in the New Testament when Philip went down to preach to the Ethiopian eunuch. In Acts 8:35 the Scripture tells us, "Then Philip opened his mouth, . . . and preached unto him Jesus." The first question we hear the Ethiopian asking is, "See, here is water. What doth hinder me to be baptized?" Obviously, then, in preaching Jesus, Philip explained that it was necessary to call upon the name of the Lord to be saved and to give evidence of that act of faith through baptism.

In like manner, this angel will warn the people to fear God instead of Antichrist, to give glory to God instead of Antichrist, and he will instruct them how to do it. Otherwise, he would be proclaiming a message of doom instead of good tidings. The word Gospel means "good tidings," and the only way we can offer men eternal good tidings is to show them how to receive the Lord Jesus Christ by faith. A message concerning the judgment of God is only a partial presentation of the Gospel of Christ. The complete story of the Gospel not only clarifies that man is a sinner, but according to 1 Corinthians 15:3, 4 also includes God's remedy for sin through Christ, who died for our sins "according to the scriptures; and that he was buried, and that he rose again the third day."

The extent of this Gospel should be noted, for it will be preached "to them that dwell on the earth, and to every nation, and kindred, and tongue, and people." This seems to be God's last offer to mankind to flee the wrath to come before they accept Antichrist. We have already seen that Antichrist and the False Prophet will mount a great campaign, after having killed the harlot, ecumenical, Babylonian church, and will seek to get all men to worship Antichrist. This blasphemous idolatry will forfeit man's claim to eternal life; thus we will be eternally lost. As a prelude to that decision, the angel will make known the Gospel message to all the world so that no man can stand before God at the judgment and maintain that he accepted Antichrist without due warning from God.

There is no evidence that this angel will be any more successful in preaching the eternal Gospel than was Noah, the preacher of righteousness before the flood. On the contrary, it seems that man will pit his will against God and succumb to the lying tongues of Satan's chief tools during that period, Antichrist and the False Prophet. We will discover in chapter 16 that the angel's announcement will introduce the darkest days of human history.

Some have suggested that the message preached to every nation, kindred, and tongue would indicate a universal language at the middle of the Tribulation Period. This, however, is certainly not conclusive and would imply that we are some time away from the beginning of the Tribulation, for three-and-a-half years would not be adequate time to teach a common language to all peoples of the earth. It is much easier to assume that since an angel, a supernatural being, will be doing the preaching, he could very easily use the language of the people to whom he is preaching.

The Fall of Religious Babylon

"And there followed another angel, saying, Babylon is fallen, is fallen, that great city, because she made all nations drink of the wine of the wrath of her fornication" (Rev. 14:8). The message of the five angels we are presently studying should be considered in light of the fact that this scene takes place in heaven, not on earth, and is an anticipatory announcement of what will soon come to pass. As with the first angel's message, this event will take place in the middle of the Tribulation Period and offers a foreglimpse of the destruction of the ecumenical, Babylonian, harlot religion detailed in Revelation 17.

Bible students are well aware of the fact that two Babylons are referred to in the book of Revelation, both termed "Babylon the Great." Destruction is predicted for both because they will cause men to drink of the wine of the wrath of their fornication. We may understand that this foreglimpse refers to religious Babylon because it will take place in the middle of the Tribulation Period. The prediction of the destruction of the literal city of Babylon is found in Revelation 16:18, 19. That the city of Babylon will be rebuilt and become the commercial center of the world is seen from such passages as Isaiah 13 and 14, together with Jeremiah 50 and 51. As we will explain in detail in our discussion of chapters 17 and 18, the city of Babylon has never been destroyed according to the Old Testament predictions; thus we may only conclude that it will be rebuilt and become the commercial center of Antichrist's kingdom; then it will be destroyed at the end of the Tribulation Period. This again points to the fact that Babylon will become the center of the world. Future studies will reveal that the two Babylons begun by Nimrod in the city of Babylon, which have brought more misery and heartache on humanity than any other concepts, will be destroyed at the end time. More individuals have been ruined in the plan of God for their lives because of the two Babylons than for any other reason. These two Babylons begun by Nimrod are (1) false religion, which emphasizes idolatry, and (2) commercialization, which causes men to become materialistically oriented. These concepts that are playing such havoc in the world today will be destroyed — one in the middle of the Tribulation Period by Antichrist, the other at the end by the supernatural hand of God.

The Doom of Antichrist's Worshipers

And the third angel followed them, saying with a loud voice, If any man worship the beast and his image, and receive his mark in his forehead, or in his hand, the same shall drink of the wine of the wrath of

God, which is poured out without mixture into the cup of his indignation; and he shall be tormented with fire and brimstone in the presence
of the holy angels, and in the presence of the Lamb; and the smoke of
their torment ascendeth up forever and ever; and they have no rest day
nor night, who worship the beast and his image, and whosoever receiveth
the mark of his name (Rev. 14:9-11).

The third angel will pronounce doom on the worshipers of Antichrist
during the Tribulation Period. It may be, since he follows them, that he
will come to the earth and, like the angel who preached the eternal
Gospel, warn men of the consequences of worshiping the beast. His is
not called the Gospel message. On the contrary, his message issues a
warning of the awful consequences of accepting the mark of the Antichrist and becoming his worshiper. We have already seen that during the
Tribulation Period a man will be required to worship the Antichrist
image and receive his mark (666) in his forehead or in his hand. When
a man does this, he will "drink of the wine of the wrath of God, which
is poured out without mixture into the cup of his indignation"; that is,
he will have turned his back on God's method of salvation and taken to
himself man's method. This will incur the displeasure of Almighty God
and bring upon men judgment and destruction.

We have already seen that at the breaking of the fourth seal 25 percent
of the earth's population will be destroyed (Rev. 6:8) and during the
blowing of the sixth trumpet (Rev. 9:18) a third part of the earth's
population will be destroyed. Dr. David L. Cooper used to say that these
were the "incorrigibles of the Tribulation Period." That is, these are the
ones who turn their backs on the Messiah and become the worshipers of
Antichrist, thus forfeiting their chance for eternal life. Rather than be
allowed to pollute others of like mind, they will be destroyed in these
two great purges of the first half of the Tribulation Period. During the
latter half, as we will see in our study of the bowl judgments, great
persecution will fall on all those who take the mark of the beast and
become worshipers of Antichrist. Fire and brimstone will be their lot
while they live, and they will be tormented forever and ever and have
no rest day or night (Rev. 14:11). This, of course, refers to their eternal
judgment. Not all ungodly men will receive judgment during this life,
though all will receive it in the next. The followers of Antichrist, however, will be different, for all who worship the Antichrist during the
latter half of the Tribulation Period will receive the judgment of fire
and brimstone, plus the many other cataclysmic judgments sent by God
upon the Antichrist worshipers outlined in the bowl judgments. In addition, they will also be in torment for eternity.

Dr. Clarence Larkin, in his commentary on the book of Revelation,
stated "If 'eternal punishment' is taught nowhere else in the Bible it is
taught here, and if here, why is it not true as to other classes of sinners?"
This is only one of the many passages in the Bible that clearly teaches the

eternal suffering of the damned. I don't enjoy teaching eternal damnation for lost men, but as a faithful teacher of the Word, I can do nothing else. Satan tries to discredit the Word of God and minimize the importance of turning from one's sin to the Lord Jesus Christ, and he does not lack for false teachers to assist him in deceiving men.

Many today attempt to teach a no-judgment concept, including the annihilationists. These heretics take many forms in the various cults or "isms" of our day. It is well to remember that even matter cannot be annihilated, as any scientist will confirm. Elements can be changed, but they cannot be annihilated! If matter cannot be annihilated, how much less the immortal soul of man.

The marvels and blessings of heaven are so magnificent that it is a great tragedy and loss indeed just to miss that marvelous place. However, according to the Bible, just missing heaven is not hell. I wish I could report that the Bible teaches that hell is a place where men will suffer for a little while and then be burned up, never to be remembered again, or where they will be given a second chance to get into heaven, but I could not be honest to the Word of God and make such a statement. Not the slightest suggestion of this is found in the Bible, nor does it hint of a second chance after death! The Bible presents no picture other than that the lake of fire is absolutely eternal and that the populace of the lake of fire will be "tormented day and night forever and ever."

The Blessed State of Tribulation Saints

Here is the patience of the saints; here are they that keep the commandments of God, and the faith of Jesus. And I heard a voice from heaven saying unto me, Write, Blessed are the dead who die in the Lord from henceforth. Yea, saith the Spirit, that they may rest from their labors, and their works do follow them (Rev. 14:12, 13).

One of the consistent chords of the Scripture is the concept that present-day sufferings are inconsequential in view of the eternal blessings prepared for them that love the Lord. This passage of Scripture certainly teaches that fact, for it refers to the patience (endurance) of the saints who are characterized by obedience during the Tribulation. Jesus said, "If ye love me, keep my commandments" (John 14:15). Therefore, one who loves Him is obedient, as these saints will be obedient, even at the expense of great personal suffering at the hands of Antichrist. Because of their patience or endurance, they will be eternally "blessed" or "contented of heart," for this is the true meaning of the word blessed. Because they have "died in the Lord" or died in saving faith, they "rest from their labors [of the Tribulation Period], and their works do follow them." Here we see again that a day is coming when believers will be rewarded because of their faithfulness to the Lord. A just God will bring forth justice and equity in eternity.

The principle that "their works do follow them" is a blessed truth to the child of God. The Word clearly teaches that our investment of faithfulness to Jesus Christ today will earn eternal dividends. This conforms with the Savior's challenge to "lay up for yourselves treasures in heaven, where neither moth nor rust doth corrupt, and where thieves do not break through nor steal" (Matt. 6:20). The tribulation saints will be given special blessing for their faithfulness to Christ during that awful time of tribulation.

The Prediction of the Battle of the Great Day of God the Almighty

And I looked and, behold, a white cloud, and upon the cloud one sat, like the Son of man, having on his head a golden crown, and in his hand a sharp sickle. And another angel came out of the temple, crying with a loud voice to him that sat on the cloud, Thrust in thy sickle, and reap; for the time is come for thee to reap; for the harvest of the earth is ripe. And he that sat on the cloud thrust in his sickle on the earth, and the earth was reaped. And another angel came out of the temple which is in heaven, he also having a sharp sickle. And another angel came out from the altar, who had power over fire, and cried with a loud cry to him that had the sharp sickle, saying, Thrust in thy sharp sickle, and gather the clusters of the vine of the earth; for her grapes are fully ripe. And the angel thrust in his sickle into the earth, and gathered the vine of the earth, and cast in into the great winepress of the wrath of God. And the winepress was trodden outside the city, and blood came out of the winepress, even unto the horse bridles, by the space of a thousand and six hundred furlongs (Rev. 14:14-20).

The fourth and fifth angels of this chapter introduce the events following our Lord's return to destroy Antichrist and all his followers. This, like the passages before it, is a prophetic foreglimpse of what is to come, details of which will be found in Revelation 16:12-16 and 19:11-20. We will reserve more exhaustive comment on this passage until we get to the bowl judgments, particularly the sixth vial.

We will pause, however, to point out in this text that it is not difficult to identify what the Holy Spirit is revealing to us. The one sitting on the white cloud "like unto the Son of man, having on his head a golden crown, and in his hand a sharp sickle" can be none other than the Lord Jesus Christ appearing in judgment. The timing is important, for we find that it is when "the time is come for thee to reap; for the harvest of the earth is ripe." What makes the harvest of the earth ripe? The fullness of the cup of God's wrath is pictured by the harvest time of grapes. The "winepress of the wrath of God" can be nothing other than the last three-and-a-half years of the Tribulation Period, when man's rejection of God will have reached its ultimate and God will bring upon him His almighty wrath, culminating in the war of the day of God the Almighty and the triumph of Christ over Antichrist.

In concluding this chapter, we must stress that the prediction that Christ will bring judgment on the earth comes only after three angelic warnings: (1) in the preaching of the everlasting Gospel; (2) in the warning that the Babylonian religion will eventually be destroyed; and (3) in the assurance that worshipers of Antichrist will be judged in this life and the life to come. We can only conclude that those who are thus harvested and pressed into the winepress of the wrath of God are the incorrigibles who stumble over all kinds of divine warning against following Antichrist.

This tragic picture of the culmination of all things is another indication of the depravity of the human heart. With such supernatural warnings one would think that ungodly men would fall down and worship Jesus Christ, but nothing could be further from the truth. This is another reminder to us that when men reject the Lord, their problem is one of the will.

24

Another Glimpse
of Heaven

Revelation 15

Chapter 15 is the shortest chapter in the book of Revelation. Its size should not be taken as an indication of its importance, however, for it reveals three things:

1. It concludes the events revealed in chapters 10 through 15 concerning visions in heaven or conditions on the earth to the middle of the Tribulation Period.

2. It serves as an introduction to the Great Tribulation, the latter half of the Tribulation Period described in chapter 16, when the seven angels pour out the bowls of the wrath of God.

3. It reveals important truths concerning the wrath of God.

John said, "And I saw another sign in heaven, great and marvelous" (v. 1). The word "another" relates back to the two signs revealed to John in chapter 12, the woman representing Israel and the great red dragon representing Satan. This third sign is described by John as "great and marvelous," indicating that it is the most significant of all the signs revealed to this point. When we bear in mind that it is the sign revealing the final act of God's judgment upon earth, we will understand that it has great spiritual significance. God has inflicted judgment many times: His judgment on the tower of Babel; His judgment on the world in sending a universal flood; His judgment on Sodom and Gomorrah; His judgment on Jerusalem in A.D. 70; and His judgment on Israel for almost two thousand years. This will be God's final judgment, the result of His wrath being "filled up."

The word "sign" should not confound or disturb us, for it occurs seventh-seven times in the New Testament. An examination of the use of this word would certainly put an end to the lie that the book of Revelation is clouded with "signs and symbols" impossible for the average person to understand. John used this term in reference to our Lord's prediction of his death: "And I, if I be lifted up from the earth, will draw all men unto me. This he said, *signifying* what death he should die" (John 12:32, 33). This is not mysterious or hidden, but a plain statement of fact that Christ would be lifted up on the cross. John used this word again in John 18:32 and in John 21:19 in reference to Christ's prophecy of the death of Peter. He utilized this same word when referring to His own death, burial, and resurrection as covering a period of three days and three nights (Matt. 12:38-40). The book of Revelation becomes much more understandable when one recognizes that the word "sign" really means a "symbol of revelation." That is, it is a symbol or picture or prophetic event that conveys some great truth or principle of God that He wants to convey to His people. As one studies this book and begins to understand the meaning of these signs, he receives the fulfillment of chapter 1, verse 3: "Blessed [happy] is he that readeth, and they that hear the words of this prophecy, and keep those things which are written in it; for the time is at hand." As we shall see in the next chapter, the sign of these seven angels before the throne of God results in literal events of judgment emanating from the throne of God to the earth.

> And I saw, as it were, a sea of glass mingled with fire, and them that had gotten the victory over the beast, and over his image, and over his mark, and over the number of his name, standing on the sea of glass, having the harps of God (Rev. 15:2).

This sea of glass is probably the same sea observed before the throne of God in chapter 4, verse 6. The fire may refer to the trials of fire endured by the tribulation saints. On this sea of glass before God's throne are people described as "them that had gotten the victory over the beast, and over his image, and over his mark, and over the number of his name," who stand "on the sea of glass, having the harps of God." These are believers in Jesus Christ, for otherwise they would not be in the presence of God. They are not the saints of the church age who were raptured before the Tribulation Period, however, but the saints of the Tribulation who are victorious over the beast. Most Bible commentators suggest that these people have been martyred by the beast during the Tribulation because of their personal faith in Christ. In Revelation 13 we saw that the beast and the False Prophet will come on the scene in the midst of the Tribulation Period, seeking to make men worship Antichrist. The complete tyranny of the Tribulation Period is seen in the fact that during the first three-and-a-half years the ecumenical church of Revelation 17 will be so powerful it will dominate Antichrist and kill all believers who refuse to join with it. During the second half of the Tribulation Period it will be Antichrist and the False Prophet who will kill those that refuse to worship his image and receive his mark. Therefore, this group may be those who are saved out of the last half of the Tribulation Period, because Revelation 7:9 states that there will be a mighty harvest of souls during the first half of the Tribulation Period under the preaching of the 144,000 servants of God. This passage may suggest there will also be a great host of martyrs who will be victorious over Antichrist.

Death is Victory for Christians

How could these folks standing on the sea of glass in the presence of God be victorious when they will have been killed during the Tribulation Period by the wave of persecution inspired by Antichrist? The answer is found in 1 Corinthians 15:55-57: "O death, where is thy sting? O grave, where is thy victory? The sting of death is sin; and the strength of sin is the law. But thanks be to God, which giveth us the victory through our Lord Jesus Christ." Death at the hands of a murderous dictator or anti-Christian persecutor is only defeat as man looks upon the situation. People living during the Tribulation will think the Antichrist is overcoming the saints, but in reality he will be sending them out into eternity to be with their Lord. Man's vision when unenlightened by the Holy Spirit renders him incapable of understanding the eternal blessings of God. If man does not incur blessings in this life, he considers that defeat, not realizing that what man gains in this life is inconsequential in comparison to what he gains in the life to come. One great blessing bestowed upon these souls is the martyr's crown (James 1:12; Rev. 2:10), which will provide them with a special position of authority during the millennial kingdom and probably throughout the eternal ages to come.

"Having the harps of God" would indicate that they are playing the heavenly instrument in a beautiful symphony of praise and worship. In addition to the heavenly harp, they will also sing "the song of Moses . . . and the song of the Lamb."

The Song of Moses and the Lamb

These tribulation saints sing "the song of Moses, the servant of God, and the song of the Lamb" (v. 3). This does not mean that they are Israelites; instead, it signifies that they are singing the song of victory over their enemy, which is the song of Moses in Exodus 15:1-21. They couple this with the song of praise to the Lamb of God.

To understand the song of Moses, we must remember that after Pharaoh released the children of Israel, he repented of his decision and pursued them furiously with a host of Egyptian troops. When the children of Israel saw their plight, the Red Sea in front of them and Egyptian troops behind them, Moses looked to God, who had instructed him to put his rod upon the water. Thus the people walked over on dry land. It must have been a harrowing experience when the people barely got across the supernaturally created channel with the Egyptian army in hot pursuit. No sooner had the people safely arrived on the opposite shore when God permitted the channel to close and drown the Egyptians. The people were naturally overwhelmed, because what looked like complete disaster at the hands of a cruel, satanically inspired king (a brief likeness of Antichrist) was suddenly turned into victory, and they lifted their hearts in gratitude to God. That exactly parallels the response of these tribulation saints standing before the throne of God, realizing that they are out of the clutches of Antichrist and Satan. Their hearts are filled with rapturous joy at His deliverance. Since they are not Old Testament saints, they are not content to sing just the song of deliverance, as were the children of Israel, who were merely delivered physically from an oppressor, but a song of eternal redemption by the blood of the Lamb.

Christ Worshiped in Heaven as God

In a day when men have been deceived about the true nature of Jesus Christ, it behooves us to remember that heaven is not one iota confused about His identity. Understood in the light of Exodus 15 and the song of Moses, this verse makes plain that the God Moses and the children of Israel addressed in the face of their great earthly victory was none other than Jesus Christ. For confirmation of this fact we quote selected portions of that great psalm.

> Then sang Moses and the children of Israel this song unto the LORD, and spoke, saying, I will sing unto the LORD, for he hath triumphed gloriously: the horse and his rider hath he thrown into the sea. The Lord is my strength and song, and he is become my salvation: he is my God, and I will prepare him an habitation; my father's God, and I will exalt him. The LORD is a man of war; the LORD is his name . . . Thou shalt bring them in, and plant them in the mountain of thine inheritance, in the place, O LORD, which thou hast made for thee to dwell in, in the sanctuary, O Lord, which thy hands have established. The LORD shall reign forever and ever (Exod. 15:1-3, 17, 18).

The fact that they combine this song and the song of the Lamb can only be explained on the basis that Jesus Christ is Almighty God. The song of Moses and the Lamb in verses 3 and 4 clearly identifies Jesus Christ with the attributes of God Himself. No man or created being has ever been addressed like this. Note the characteristics attributed to Him:

1. Creation — "Great and marvelous are thy works, Lord God Almighty."
2. Justice — "Just and true are thy ways."
3. Object of worship — ". . . thou King of saints. Who shall not fear thee, O Lord, and glorify thy name?"
4. Holiness — "For *thou only* art holy."
5. Omnipotence and eternity — ". . . for all nations shall come and worship before thee; for thy judgments are made manifest." This song is a prophetic foreglimpse of the true treatment of Jesus Christ at the end of the Tribulation that will exist for the entire millennium and eternal order.

The most pitiful people in all the world are the religionists who, representing modernistic liberalism or the cults and isms, do not understand who Jesus Christ is. The book of Revelation certainly clarifies His identity, and, if for no other reason, it is worthy of our study because it does what its introduction predicted. Chapter 1, verse 1 announces "The Revelation of Jesus Christ." It is the only book in the world that truly presents Jesus Christ as He really is.

The Temple of the Tabernacle of God

"And after that I looked, and, behold, the temple of the tabernacle of the testimony in heaven was opened" (Rev. 15:5). The tabernacle of the temple of God is the Holy of Holies. Great significance should be attached to this scene. Dr. J. Vernon McGee points out in his commentary on Revelation:

> The temple is referred to 15 times in the Revelation. Its prominence cannot be ignored. Each reference is either to the temple in Heaven or to the absence of the temple in the New Jerusalem. In this instance the reference is specifically to the tabernacle, and the Holy of Holies in which the ark of the testimony was kept. In the ark were the tables of stone. Both the tabernacle and the tables of stone were duplicates of originals in Heaven.[19]

The testimony that emanates from the tabernacle is seen in the Ark of the Covenant. God has always kept His covenant with Israel, or with any to whom He has entered into a covenant relationship, including the members of the Church of Christ, who have entered into the "new covenant" through the blood of Christ.

The Seven Angels Before the Throne

> And the seven angels came out of the temple, having the seven plagues, clothed in pure and white linen, and having their breasts girded with golden girdles. And one of the four living creatures gave unto the seven angels seven golden bowls full of the wrath of God, who liveth forever and ever (Rev. 15:6, 7).

This is the third time we have encountered a group of seven angels at once. There were seven angels assigned, one each, to the seven churches in chapters 2 and 3. Then each of the seven angels was given a trumpet to blow in revealing the second quarter of the tribulation judgments. Now we see the seven angels to whom the judgments of the last half of the Tribulation Period are given.

Since these angels come out of the temple, it seems that angels are given access to the presence of God. Created holy beings, angels are permitted entrance into the presence of God in the true temple in heaven, of which the Old Testament tabernacle and temple were merely patterns or symbols. In those earthly dwelling places of God, men were not permitted except the high priest once a year, and then only after the most scrupulous preparation in righteousness. As these angels leave the temple, having worshiped the Lord, one of the four living creatures gives them each a bowl that will be poured out on the earth, the significance of which is revealed in chapter 16. As soon as the angels come out of the temple, great smoke from the glory of the presence of God and His power fills the temple so that neither angels nor men can go back into worship until "the seven plagues of the seven angels were fulfilled" (v. 8). In other words, from the middle of the Tribulation Period neither angels nor man will have access to the presence of God at His throne until the end of the Tribulation, for He will not be dealing with men in mercy, as is His usual custom. During the latter three-and-a-half years of the Tribulation, He will deal with men in judgment.

The Wrath of God

This brief section of eight verses in the middle of the book of Revelation opens and closes with the wrath of God. It depicts the scene in heaven of God sending out His angels of judgment to perform His last act of bringing men to Himself. He uses mercy, love, circumstances, the Holy Spirit, and many other divine tools to bring men to Himself. Ordinarily, unsaved men are not judged on this earth, which explains why people can break the laws of God and seemingly get by with it. The judgment men receive on this earth is merely the judgment of their deeds — whatsoever they sow, they reap — but men do not receive the judgment of God until the day of judgment, with but one exception. During the last three-and-a-half years of the Tribulation Period, God will bring great judgment and calamity on mankind.

Filling Up God's Wrath

Verse 1 of our text says of the seven last plagues, "for in them is filled up the wrath of God." Verses 5 through 8 describe the judgment of God being fulfilled. Verse 1 makes it clear that this will be the last judgment before the millennial kingdom. A literal translation of verse 1 would be, "And I saw another sign in heaven, great and marvelous, seven angels having seven plagues, the last ones. . . ." When this judgment is finished, the Tribulation will be concluded and the millennium begun.

God's Purpose in This Great Tribulation

Not to understand that this impending period of great tribulation is of divine purpose and intent is to fail to understand significant truths relative to these coming events. Although we will probably not know the full extent of God's purpose for the Tribulation until we look down from heaven and see these events transpire, I would like to suggest the following four purposes as being discernible from the Scriptures:

1. To introduce a worldwide revival when, under the preaching of the 144,000 servants of God, a multitude will be gathered which no man can number (Rev. 7:9);

2. To destroy the wicked followers of Antichrist who are committed to his way, lest they pollute others and corrupt them from the truth of the Gospel, thus damning their souls;

3. To break the stubborn will of the nation of Israel, who will confess her national sin of rejecting Messiah and plead for His return;

4. To shake the earth and all things therein so that man's normal sense of security will be so disordered that he will be more prone to look to God. Crises usually cause men to look to God. The Tribulation will be a time when God creates a climate of crisis, a climate conducive for men to call upon Him while He is near.

25

The Seven Bowl Judgments

No introduction is needed for this chapter, since chapter 15 has already prefaced it. An examination of the chart on the next page will reveal the time sequence of the seven bowl judgments as being synonymous with the last half of the Tribulation Period.

The seven angels, each holding a bowl containing the judgments that are about to fall on the earth, seem reluctant to cast their bitter judgments forth. However, they are obedient to the voice of God when He speaks, saying, "Go your ways, and pour out the bowls of the wrath of God upon the earth." These bowls constitute what the Lord Jesus referred to as the "great tribulation" (Matt. 24:21), or the last forty-two months of the Tribulation Period.

Wild and fanciful ideas have been offered through the years as a means of symbolizing or spiritualizing these judgments. There is no scriptural basis for such symbolism. In fact, four of these seven judgments occurred quite literally in Egypt among the ten plagues and have never been accepted by credible Bible teachers as anything but literal. In addition, part of the sixth judgment, that of drying up the Euphrates River and producing frogs, was also literally fulfilled during the history of Israel. Frogs were generated as one of the plagues of Egypt, and both the Red Sea and Jordan River were rolled back that God's people might walk forth on dry ground. Therefore, nothing new will be transpiring when God dries up the Euphrates River that the kings of the East may march over on dry ground. If the plagues of Egypt were literal, and they certainly were, why should we not expect these awful judgments likewise to be literal? We shall now examine the judgments individually.

> And I heard a great voice out of the temple saying to the seven angels, Go your ways, and pour out the bowls of the wrath of God upon the earth. And the first went, and poured out his bowl upon the earth, and there fell a foul and painful sore upon the men who had the mark of the beast, and upon them who worshiped his image (Rev. 16:1, 2).

The Seven Bowl
Judgments

The First Bowl Judgment — Sores Upon Men

This first bowl judgment introduces grievous or painful sores upon men. Dr. Wilbur Smith notes that the same word is used by the Old Testament translators of the Greek Septuagint for boils when telling the story of the Egyptian plagues. For this reason many have called it the plague of boils. This judgment delineates two essential points:

1. The time — when Antichrist is worshiped. Further confirmation that the three judgments, the seals, the trumpets, and the vials, are sequential, not concurrent, as some Bible teachers suggest, is clarified in the time of this judgment. Antichrist will not be set up as the object of worship until the middle of the Tribulation Period. This judgment will fall on men because of their worship of Antichrist, which could only occur after the middle of the Tribulation Period as we saw in chapter 13. The time of this judgment, then, will probably commence within the first one to three months of the last half of the Tribulation Period.

2. The recipients — beast worshipers. The selection from among the peoples on the earth is clearly seen in this passage: only those containing the mark of the beast and worshiping his image will be selected for those awful sores. This would indicate that God in His marvelous grace will not bring judgment on believers during this latter half of Tribulation, but will protect them as He did the children of Israel during the plagues of Egypt. This further confirms our assumption that in the previous judgments, when He slays 25 percent and one-third of the world's population, He will exempt believers.

The Second Bowl Judgment —
the Seas Turn to Blood

"And the second angel poured out his bowl upon the sea, and it became like the blood of a dead man; and every living soul died in the sea" (Rev. 16:3). In this one short verse we encounter a catastrophe predicted for the earth that is almost beyond human comprehension. We have already seen that God will cause a third part of the sea to turn to blood during the second trumpet, but this second bowl includes the entire sea. The American Standard Version renders it, "It became blood as of a dead man"; that is, the entire sea will become corrupt, so that every living thing in the sea will die.

It does not take much imagination to see that when all living creatures in the seas die, they will float to the top, their decaying bodies discharging an unbearable stench and inaugurating potential disease. This judgment could well interfere with commercial shipping and send whole populations into confusion as man gropes for an adequate supply of water.

The Third Bowl Judgment —
Rivers and Fountains Turn to Blood

And the third angel poured out his bowl upon the rivers and fountains of waters, and they became blood. And I heard the angel of the waters say, Thou art righteous, O Lord, who art, and wast, and shalt be, because thou hast judged thus. For they have shed the blood of saints and prophets, and thou hast given them blood to drink; for they are worthy. And I heard another out of the altar say, Even so, Lord God Almighty, true and righteous are thy judgments (Rev. 16:4-7).

The third bowl, a sequel to the second, carries with it an interesting explanation as to why God permitted it. Now God will destroy the only remaining sources of water, the rivers and fountains or springs of the deep, by letting them turn to blood. Whether this means literal blood is really inconsequential, for if Christ can turn water to wine, He certainly could turn water to blood. What is significant is that it will become corrupt blood, which would breed disease and pestilence.

One of the basic needs of mankind is water. Unless God provides water from another source or engineers by some process can turn this corruption into pure water, the world will be in a state of riot and confusion, seeking this necessity of life.

The Angel of the Waters

The book of Revelation reveals interesting things from time to time about the activity of angels in this universe. It seems that, in addition to other functions which we have already noted, a special angel is assigned to the waters. This angel will speak when his waters are turned to blood, proclaiming the justification for such an awful miracle, for Antichrist will have put so many Christian martyrs to death that he will deserve exactly what he receives. His quest for the blood of Christians during the first half of the Tribulation will result in his water supply turning to blood in the last half. This is God's earthly vindication of the suffering martyrs from earliest times to the present, answering the prayers of the souls under the altar in Revelation 6.

**The Fourth Bowl Judgment —
Scorching Heat of the Sun**

And the fourth angel poured out his bowl upon the sun, and power was given unto him to scorch men with fire. And men were scorched with great heat, and blasphemed the name of God, who hath power over these plagues; and they repented not to give him glory (Rev. 16:8, 9).

The consistency of the sun, in that it rises every morning and sets every evening, producing light and heat for man according to the seasons of the year, affords a great sense of security to all people. During the Tribulation, when the fourth bowl is poured out on the earth, man will contend with a sun-induced heat wave the like of which he has never experienced. Even though a third part of the sun will be darkened, that which is left will be so powerful that it will scorch men "with great heat."

We have all lived through acute heat waves at one time or other, but we endure them because night comes to cool things somewhat, and eventually the distressing season will pass away. Even so, many deaths are occasioned through heart attack or heat stroke during such periods, and those not so afflicted are still miserably uncomfortable. Such will be the case during the Great Tribulation; but when we add the effect of this excruciating heat on the corrupt waterways and rivers, we find man almost tasting the torments of hell described by Jesus in Luke 16, without water to satiate his thirst.

One would think that this experience would drive men to their knees in repentance to the God of creation. Instead, in this chapter is found the first of three occasions, when men "blasphemed the name of God . . . and they repented not to give him glory." This illustrates the most severe rebellion and hostility to the will of God found anywhere in the annals of human history.

The best commentary on this judgment comes from the pen of Malachi the prophet who, when speaking of that same day, described it with these words:

> For, behold, the day cometh, that shall burn like an oven, and all the proud, yea, and all that do wickedly, shall be stubble; and the day that cometh shall burn them up, saith the LORD of hosts, that it shall leave them neither root nor branch. But unto you that fear my name shall the Sun of righteousness arise with healing in his wings; and ye shall go forth, and grow up like calves of the stall (Mal. 4:1, 2).

The Fifth Bowl Judgment — Darkness

And the fifth angel poured out his bowl upon the throne of the beast, and his kingdom was full of darkness; and they gnawed their tongues for pain, and blasphemed the God of heaven because of their pains and their sores, and repented not of their deeds (Rev. 16:10, 11).

The fact that the fifth bowl introduces darkness may be the singular expression of God's mercy to the rebellious citizens of the earth during the Tribulation Period. Following the great heat wave occasioned by the fourth bowl judgment, it may significantly give relief to human flesh.

This is a special judgment that seems to center on the headquarters of Antichrist, for it is poured out on "the throne of the beast, and his kingdom was full of darkness." The seat of the beast will probably be the rebuilt city of Babylon during the Tribulation Period, the center of all commerce, religion, evil, and government.

Two things would indicate that this darkness will prevail for some time upon the earth: (1) the predictions of other prophets, and (2) the effects on men.

This judgment, a repetition of the ninth plague of Egypt, is to be understood literally:

> Woe unto you that desire the day of the LORD! To what end is it for you? The day of the LORD is darkness, and not light (Amos 5:18).
>
> Who can stand before his indignation? And who can abide in the fierceness of his anger? His fury is poured out like fire, and the rocks are thrown down by him. But with an overrunning flood he will make an utter end of the place, and darkness shall pursue his enemies (Nah. 1:6, 8).
>
> That day is a day of wrath, a day of trouble and distress, a day of waste and desolation, a day of darkness and gloominess, a day of clouds and thick darkness (Zeph. 1:15).

Christ's own prediction was: "In those days, after that tribulation, the sun shall be darkened, and the moon shall not give its light" (Mark 13:24).

The effects on men, described in verse 10, "they gnawed their tongues for pain," indicate that the relief from the heat soon will produce an exasperating, frustrating darkness. If you have visited Carlsbad Caverns or Mammoth Cave, you know what true darkness really is when absolutely no light is available. We might forecast that man's ingenuity in producing electricity would solve this problem, but we must remember that the water supply produces electricity, and with the tampering of the water supply, as seen in the second and third judgments, man might be incapable of continuing to draw his electrical power and illumination from the rivers and bodies of water.

They Repented Not

These judgments are so clearly supernatural that all men will know that they descend from the God of heaven. But instead of falling down before Him to become the recipients of His mercy, they only "blasphemed the God of heaven because of their pains and their sores, and repented not of their deeds." They not only blaspheme God, but refuse to change their ways. Let it be understood that when men reject the Lord, it is not because of philosophical doubts or unexplained answers to unanswered questions, but hardness of heart and love for sin.

The Sixth Bowl Judgment — Euphrates Dried Up

And the sixth angel poured out his bowl upon the great river, Euphrates, and its water was dried up, that the way of the kings of the east might be prepared. And I saw three unclean spirits, like frogs, come out of the mouth of the dragon, and out of the mouth of the beast, and out of the mouth of the false prophet. For they are the spirits of demons, working miracles, that go forth unto the kings of the earth and of the whole world, to gather them to the battle of that great day of God Almighty. Behold, I come as a thief. Blessed is he that watcheth and keepeth his garments, lest he walk naked, and they see his shame. And he gathered them together into a place called in the Hebrew tongue Armageddon (Rev. 16:12-16).

The sixth bowl judgment really comes in two parts: (1) the drying up of the River Euphrates, which will be a preparation for the "battle of that great day of God Almighty"; and (2) the tremendous demon forces that will bring the rebellious armies of the world to the Valley of Megiddo for the purpose of opposing the Lord.

The Euphrates River, one of the most prominent rivers in the Bible, since the dawn of human history has stood as a natural barrier between east and west. To those of the western world, the peoples living east of the Euphrates River have been shrouded in darkness, while all the time their numerical superiority has been building up. The Euphrates River is the eastern border of the land God gave to Abraham (Gen. 15:18). It is about eighteen hundred miles long and so large that it forms a natural barrier against the armies of the world. Most people are not particularly conscious of the fact that it served as the eastern border of the Roman Empire. The sixth bowl judgment will dry up that river to make way for the "kings of the east."

The Kings of the East

The booming population explosion of the eastern nations has produced a new interest in Bible prophecies concerning "the kings of the east." Actually, there is very little information on the subject. The literal rendering of the word would be the kings of the "sunrising," a reference to the kings of the oriental nations of the world. Since it refers to them en masse, it would indicate that they do not amalgamate or lose their identity (for they are "kings"), but instead form a massive oriental confederacy. This confederacy may be preparing to oppose Antichrist, whose capital lies in Babylon, but due to the lying tongues of the demons we are about to study, they will be brought across the Euphrates River on the side of Antichrist in opposition to Christ.

Three Froglike Deceiving Spirits

The second part of the sixth bowl judgment reveals the three unclean froglike spirits that will come from the mouths of the devil, the Antichrist and the False Prophet. These deceiving spirits, by working miracles before the "kings of the earth and the whole world," will trick them into coming together for the "battle of that great day of God Almighty." After the five preceding judgments of God, the earth will be in a terrible dilemma. Only by this supernatural spirit of deception on the part of Satan, Antichrist, and the False Prophet will they be able to summon the kings and the armies of the world to the final conflict against God and His Christ. The timing of this event must be the very last days of the Tribulation, since the next bowl immediately concludes the Tribulation with the destruction of Babylon.

Armageddon

"The battle of Armageddon" is an expression often used to describe the decisive battle between Antichrist and his God-hating forces of the earth and Christ, who will consume them with the power of His mouth, according to Revelation 19:11-16. Actually, it is more proper to call this "the battle of that great day of God Almighty" because that is the scriptural expression. It takes place in Armageddon, which means "the Valley of Megiddo."

The Megiddo Valley, located close to the center of the land of Palestine, offered one of the most breathtaking sights my wife and I encountered in our trip through the Holy Land a few years ago. Napoleon Bonaparte is said to have stated with deep emotion after his first sight of this great valley, "This is the ideal battleground for all the armies of the world." Little did he realize that prophecy had preceded him, that it *will* be the world's great battleground. Actually, it has already served as the battleground of many major wars. There Barak defeated the Canaanites (Judg. 4:15); there Gideon defeated the Midianites (Judg. 7); there Saul and Josiah both met their deaths. Dr. M. R. Vincent in his *Word Studies in the New Testament* notes:

> Megiddo was in the plain of Esdraelon, which has been a chosen place for encampment in every contest carried on in Palestine from the days of of Nabuchodonozor, king of Assyria, unto the disastrous march of Napoleon Buonaparte from Egypt into Syria. Jews, Gentiles, Saracens, Christian crusaders, and anti-Christian Frenchmen; Egyptians, Persians, Druses, Turks and Arabs, warriors of every nation that is under heaven have pitched their tents on the plain of Esdraelon, and have beheld the banners of their nation wet with the dews of Tabor and Hermon.[20]

What could induce the kings of the earth to concentrate their forces on that one spot in such an enlightened generation? The only answer is the devastating power of the lying, froglike spirits that go forth from the satanic trinity of Satan, Antichrist and the False Prophet during the last days of Tribulation. Dr. Clarence Larkin, in *The Book of Revelation,* makes a significant statement:

> The power of a delusive and enthusiastic sentiment, however engendered, to lead to destruction great hosts of men is seen in the Crusades to recover the Holy Sepulchre at Jerusalem. If a religious fanaticism could, at nine different times, cause hundreds of thousands of religious devotees to undergo unspeakable hardships for a religious purpose, what will not the miracle working wonders of the "froglike demons" of the last days of this Dispensation not be able to do in arousing whole nations, and creating vast armies to march in all directions from all countries, headed by their Kings, for the purpose of preventing an establishment of the Kingdom of the King of Kings in His own Land of Palestine?[21]

Christ's Challenge to Tribulation Saints

Verse 15 is our Lord's challenge to any saints still living during the closing days of the Tribulation. He will come as a thief to the ungodly world not prepared for Him, and as He challenges believers of all generations to be faithful, so in those closing days He will challenge His servants whom He has supernaturally preserved from the effects of the previous judgments to continue faithful to the very end. This little parenthetical thought reminds us again of the faithfulness of our God to all of them that look to Him for the manifestation of His mercy and grace.

With the armies of the world gathering together in the Valley of Meggido, the Lord will give one last challenge to His saints; then the time will be prepared for the final judgment to be poured out upon the earth.

The Seventh Bowl Judgment — the Wrath of God

> And the seventh angel poured out his bowl into the air, and there came a great voice out of the temple of heaven, from the throne, saying, It is done. And there were voices, and thunders, and lightnings; and there was a great earthquake, such as was not since men were upon the earth, so mighty an earthquake, and so great. And the great city was divided into three parts, and the cities of the nations fell; and great Babylon came in remembrance before God, to give unto her the cup of the wine of the fierceness of his wrath. And every island fled away, and the mountains

were not found. And there fell upon men a great hail out of heaven, every stone about the weight of a talent; and men blasphemed God because of the plague of hail; for the plague was exceedingly great (Rev. 16:17-21).

When the seventh angel pours out his bowl into the air a voice will be heard from the temple of God before the throne conveying a most welcome message: *"It is done!"* It is most welcome because it signifies the consummation of Tribulation, the conclusion of the day of wrath upon ungodly men, the end of the time of Jacob's trouble.

This final judgment of God will appear in the form of the world's greatest earthquake, "such as was not since men were upon the earth." It will destroy "the great city," meaning the city of Babylon, the capital of the world at that time, dividing it into three parts. In addition, "the cities of the nations fell," meaning that the cities of the world will be wiped out. In addition, every island will vanish and the mountains will not be found. This would indicate a complete renovation of the earth, which may be a fulfillment of 2 Peter 3:10, which predicts that the entire earth will be destroyed and "the elements shall melt with fervent heat; the earth also and the works that are in it, shall be burned up."

If this were not enough catastrophe, great hailstones, "the weight of a talent" (about 135 pounds), will come down out of heaven upon men. It is difficult for us to conceive of hailstones that large, or of the devastating effect they would have upon men were they to fall. Dr. David L. Cooper, in commenting on this verse, draws attention to "what the Lord said in Job 38:22, 23. He has filled His armory full of hail and snow 'against the time of trouble, against the day of battle and war.'" More details of this catastrophe will be seen in Revelation 18 under the detailed destruction of the city of Babylon and in chapter 19 with the coming of Christ on the white horse to conquer the earth and subdue it.

Man's Perennial Rebellion Against God

Already we have seen man refuse to repent on two different occasions in the face of these judgments. The last thing to be noted in this passage of Scripture is the hardness of the unsaved, unregenerate heart. "And men blasphemed God because of the plague of the hail." It is hard to conceive of man so rebellious that he would lift his face in final defiance to God even in the face of such disaster. All hopes and dreams will be ended with the ultimate consummation because man will have chosen to worship Antichrist.

In conclusion, it is important for us to understand the purpose for all this judgment. The citizens of the Tribulation who take the mark of the beast and worship his image will break the first four of the ten commandments. Jesus said we are to love the Lord our God with all our heart, with all our soul, and with all our mind; "this is the first . . . commandment." Exodus 20 lists the commandments: (1) Have no other gods before me; (2) Thou shalt not make unto thee any graven image; (3) Thou shalt not take the name of the Lord thy God in vain; (4) Remember the sabbath day to keep it holy. None of these commandments will be kept by the inhabitants of the Tribulation. The judgments of God upon men will appear primarily because instead of worshiping Him, they worship Antichrist. Instead of worshiping God in spirit and truth through His Son Jesus Christ, they will fashion an image and fall down and worship it. Instead of worshiping in speech and word, they will "blaspheme the name of God." God has said, "I will not hold him guiltless that taketh the name of the Lord thy God in vain." The fact that they do not remember the Sabbath day or any day is further confirmation of their unregenerate, atheistic, godless hearts. Every individual that refuses to acknowledge the coming judgment of God on unregenerate men should study this chapter of Scripture. It not only clearly depicts God's intended plan for the coming tribulation people, but also reveals His plan to judge men for eternity.

26

Religious Babylon Destroyed

Revelation 17

Archaeologists tell us that Babylon is the cradle of civilization. Located on the shores of the Euphrates River, the ruins of this city have revealed some of the most ancient documents of past generations. This city begun by Nimrod, who was a rebel before the Lord, authored some of the greatest evils ever to fall on mankind. Two of these evils will be destroyed during the Tribulation Period, according to Revelation 17 and 18.

In ancient days Satan seemed to make Babylon the capital of his evil operation. From this headquarters was started false religion, man's attempt for self-government in defiance of the will of God, and city dwellings for commercial and social purposes contrary to the commandment of God to "be fruitful and multiply and replenish the earth." These great evils, which have damned the souls of millions by substituting counterfeit solutions to man's natural problems that would ordinarily lead him to God, will all be destroyed at the end of the Tribulation Period. Chapter 17 describes the coming judgment of God on the religious system that has enslaved men in superstitious darkness for centuries.

Mystery, Babylon the Harlot

And there came one of the seven angels who had the seven bowls, and talked with me, saying unto me, Come here; I will show unto thee the judgment of the great harlot that sitteth upon many waters; with whom the kings of the earth have committed fornication, and the inhabitants of the earth have been made drunk with the wine of her fornication. So he carried me away in the Spirit into the wilderness and I saw a woman sit upon a scarlet-colored beast, full of names of blasphemy, having seven heads and ten horns. And the woman was arrayed in purple and scarlet color, and bedecked with gold and precious stones and pearls, having a golden cup in her hand, full of abominations and filthiness of her fornication; and upon her forehead was a name written, MYSTERY, BABYLON THE GREAT, THE MOTHER OF HARLOTS AND ABOMINATIONS OF THE EARTH. And I saw the woman drunk with the blood of the saints, and with the blood of the martyrs of Jesus; and when I saw her, I wondered with great wonder (Rev. 17:1-6).

The first six verses of our text reveal to us a most astounding and awful scene, portraying through symbols two great forces, one religious, the other governmental.

This vision comes from "one of the seven angels who had the seven bowls." Though it is not stated by John, the context locates this judgment scene as taking place in the middle of the Tribulation Period. It is a description of the ecumenical religious system powerful enough to gain a controlling influence in the Antichrist's government.

The Vision of the Woman

Ten details delineate this woman:

1. "The great harlot"
2. "That sitteth upon many waters"
3. "With whom the kings of the earth have committed fornication"
4. "And the inhabitants of the earth have been made drunk with the wine of her fornication"
5. "A woman [in the wilderness] sitting upon a scarlet-colored beast"
6. "Arrayed in purple and scarlet"
7. "Bedecked with gold and precious stones"
8. "Having a golden cup in her hand, full of abominations and filthiness of her fornication"
9. "Upon her forehead was a name written, MYSTERY, BABYLON THE GREAT, MOTHER OF HARLOTS AND ABOMINATIONS OF THE EARTH"
10. "Drunk with the blood of the saints, and with the blood of the martyrs of Jesus."

Even before we come to the angel's interpretation of this vision, it is clear that we are not dealing with a human being, for no one woman could commit fornication with the kings of the earth, nor could a woman be "drunk with the blood of the saints and with the blood of the martyrs of Jesus." Our rule for Bible interpretation is that when the plain sense of Scripture makes common sense, seek no other sense. In this case the plain sense, "a woman," does not make common sense; therefore we must seek another sense. Fortunately, the angel gave John the interpretation to this vision, which we will consult after examining the vision of the beast.

The Vision of the Beast

Five details describing the beast are given:

1. "Full of names of blasphemy" (v. 3)
2. "Having seven heads" (v. 3)
3. "And ten horns" (v. 3)
4. "The beast that carrieth her" (v. 7)
5. "The beast . . . was, and is not, and shall ascend out of the bottomless pit, and go into perdition" (v. 8)

The Interpretation of the Beast and the Harlot

The careful Bible student will immediately begin to recognize this beast even before examining the angel's interpretation. In the first place, it is similar to the beast of Revelation 13 and doubtless represents what all beasts used symbolically represent, either a king or a kingdom that functions in opposition to the will of God. We will consider these in reverse order, just as the angel interpreted them to John.

When John "wondered with great wonder," the angel said to him, "Why didst thou wonder?" Actually, some parts of this should have been familiar to John, for it is obviously the same beast that was described in chapter 13. The angel introduced his explanation with the words, "And here is the mind which hath wisdom" (v. 9)."

The Beast Explained

1. "The seven heads are seven mountains, on which the woman sitteth." The seven mountains of this passage of Scripture have caused some to suggest that since the city of Rome is built on seven hills, she is the one designated here as the beast with seven heads. But there are good reasons for not accepting this interpretation. Geographically, it would be difficult to establish the seven hills of Rome. In addition, the context seems more to indicate that these are seven kings. It is not uncommon for mountains to designate kings or kingdoms (cf. Isa. 2).

As pointed out in the commentary on chapter 13, these seven mountains are kings: "Five are fallen, and one is, and the other is not yet come." As stated before, I am inclined to believe that the five represent five kings of the Roman Empire until John's lifetime; the existing king, Domitian, was the sixth; thus we have the five that were, the sixth that is, and the seventh who is to come, referring to Antichrist at the end time.

2. "The beast that was, and is not, even he is the eighth, and is of the seven, and goeth into perdition" (v. 11). This strongly suggests that the Antichrist is the seventh head. He will die in the middle of the Tribulation Period, duplicate the resurrection of Jesus Christ by coming back to life, but at the end of the Tribulation go "into perdition" (Rev. 19:20).

3. "And the ten horns which thou sawest are ten kings, who have received no kingdom as yet, but receive power as kings one hour with the beast" (v. 12). The ten horns coincide with the ten toes of Nebuchadnezzar's vision of Daniel 2 and the ten horns of the nondescript beast of Daniel 7 and Revelation 13. These are the ten kings who will make up the Antichrist's world confederacy of nations. Since they get their power from Antichrist, perhaps he will appoint them kings of certain countries after he has taken over world governments. Their oneness of mind is seen in verse 13 in that they "give their power and strength unto the beast"; that is, during the last three-and-a-half years of the Tribulation Period they will promise complete allegiance and cooperation to the beast.

4. The end of the beast. Looking forward to the end of the Tribulation, the angel explained to John that these ten kings will continue to function until they bring their armies to the Valley of Megiddo in the last great rebellious act of mankind against Christ, who shall "overcome them" at the battle of the great day of God the Almighty. He will overthrow them because He is Lord of lords and King of kings.

5. Full of names of blasphemy. Of the five characteristics in John's vision of the beast, the first is not interpreted here by the angel. He has already interpreted this clearly in chapter 13 when telling about this same beast, for he said, "upon his heads [is] the name of blasphemy" (v. 1), "and there was given unto him a mouth speaking great things and blasphemies" (v. 5), "and he opened his mouth in blasphemy against God, to blaspheme his name, and his tabernacle, and them that dwell in heaven" (v. 6). The blasphemous nature of world government is not limited to Nimrod's time but has been characteristic of all world governments which continue in opposition to the will of God. The one-world organization that contains the dreams and aspirations of the one-worlders of today affords a good example of this. About the only person to whom they have not granted some kind of recognition is Jesus Christ. He was excluded in the founding of the United Nations and is also excluded from the conduct of its business. That is one reason for its futility and a major reason why we can be so confident that it will continue to be futile and detrimental to humanity.

The Harlot Explained

1. The peoples the harlot sits upon — "And he saith unto me, The waters which thou sawest, where the harlot sitteth, are peoples, and multitudes, and nations, and tongues" (17:15).

The angel first explained to John the meaning of the water on which the woman was sitting: it is the peoples of the earth. Peoples, multitudes, nations, and tongues are a description used to designate all humanity in the book of Revelation. We note this in Revelation 7:9, where the 144,000 are used of the Spirit of God to harvest in "a great multitude, which no man could number, of all nations, and kindreds, and peoples, and tongues." This, then, would establish a fundamental principle in interpreting Babylon the Great, the harlot who sits on the bestial world kingdom: She is a worldwide system that has dominance on all peoples; thus she is sitting upon them.

2. The woman as a city — "And the woman whom thou sawest is that great city, which reigneth over the kings of the earth" (17:18).

Many have taken this to mean that the woman represents the capital city of Antichrist's kingdom, but this cannot be, for Antichrist himself rules over the kings of the earth. If, then, the woman is not the Antichrist, what other possible explanation could we have for such unanimous world dominance? The only answer is the one system before which all kings, dictators, and nations have been forced to bow down throughout history, that is, the Babylonian religion of idolatry. One cannot go anyplace in the world without being confronted with some semblance of the Babylonian religion of idolatry. No system in the world's history has enslaved more people than this awful religion. It has not only brought them into the decadence of superstitious ignorance, but it has darkened their understanding, making it difficult for them to grasp the simple plan of salvation as revealed in the person of God's Son, Jesus Christ.

It should not take us by surprise that this harlot woman, the religious system, is referred to as a city. The Bride, who is Christ's raptured and resurrected Church, is described in Revelation 21 as "the holy city, New Jerusalem, coming down from God out of heaven, prepared as a bride adorned for her husband." The same expression is used in verses 9 and 10. Thus we see that a city can be used as a symbol of a woman. When used symbolically, a woman is always intended throughout the Scripture to signify a spiritual or religious movement. If a good woman, it is "Jehovah's wife" or "the bride of Christ." If an evil woman, such as "a harlot," it represents the evil religious system of idolatry. Returning to the parts of the vision that are not explained in detail by the angel because they are referred to so frequently throughout Scripture, we find that such is exactly the picture. This harlot who sits upon many waters is the religious harlot of Babylonian idolatry. Taking many forms, she will have encircled the globe, causing kings of the earth to commit fornication and making the inhabitants of the earth "drunk with the wine of her fornication." The religions of the world are synonymous with depravity, debauchery, and a contemptibly low standard of morality.

In viewing the Hindus, Buddhists, Confucianists, Taoists, Mohammedans, and primitive religionists, I have found that none of them teaches the moral standards of God. Instead, their practices are based on a loose form of behavior that permits sensual activities, producing guilt complexes which the religion in turn uses to enslave its people in forms of personal sacrifice and self-abuse to atone for their own sin. The Babylonian religions of the world, whether they be Greek, Indian, African, Roman, or Chinese, are arrayed in gold, precious stones, and costly array. They use mystery and idolatry.

Being the "mother of harlots and abominations of the earth" means idolatry. Abomination in the Old Testament refers to the worship of idols, and that is exactly the form of religion Satan has used to deceive men and lead them away from God. Such religions have unanimously been opposed to "the saints" and "martyrs of Jesus."

3. Religion dominates politics — ". . . which reigneth over the kings of the earth."

The fact that the harlot is seated upon the beast and is defined as the one that "reigneth over the kings of the earth" indicates the tremendous power she will exercise over the world government. This is nothing new.

The leaders of the Babylonian idolatrous religions of the world have always vied with the political leaders for dominance over their country or the world, in distinction from the true Christian Church, which has never sought political power. Jesus said, "My kingdom is not of this world." He came the first time to establish a spiritual kingdom, to which one gains entrance by being born again (John 3:3). When He comes the second time in His glorious appearing, He will establish His earthly kingdom, but He will not need any help from those who come with Him. Instead, He will be the sole warrior, generating all the power to combat Antichrist and his cohorts. The Church, His Bride, will merely be accompanying Him on her honeymoon, prepared to rule and reign with Him for a thousand years. Whenever the church as an organization has involved herself in politics, she has forsaken the will of God. That does not rule out individual Christians being good citizens and participating in offices of government, but nowhere in Scripture is the Church taught to usurp authority from the kings of the earth. Such, however, has been the practice of Babylonian, idolatrous religion.

The People of That Period

Almost obscured by the two great personages, the beast and the harlot who rides the beast, are the millions of individuals living on the earth during the time of these events. They are referred to as the "waters," or the "peoples, and multitudes, and nations, and tongues."

All people in any age fall into one of two classifications throughout Scripture — believers or unbelievers. Such is the case in this passage. Verse 8 records for us the people living during the time of the death of Antichrist who will "wonder . . . when they behold the beast that was, and is not, and yet is." These folks are described as those "whose names were not written in the book of life from the foundation of the world." This can only refer to the unbelievers during the Tribulation who have never by faith called upon the Lord Jesus Christ to have their names written in the Lamb's book of life.

The other group cited in this passage is referred to on two occasions as "the saints" and "the martyrs of Jesus" who, because of their personal faith in Jesus Christ, will have been killed by the Babylonian religious system. We have already seen that these people "overcome the beast." In verse 14 we find that when Christ comes as King of kings and Lord of lords, He will bring with Him those who are "called and chosen and faithful." These are the individuals who have in sincere faith called upon the name of the Lord for salvation. Whether they live through the Tribulation Period or are martyred is not really important, for because of their faith in Christ they overcome the bestial Antichrist and the harlot.

The Current Identity of Babylon the Harlot

A careful examination of this passage of Scripture should make it easy for us to identify the current harlot of Babylon and predict with

some degree of accuracy what we can expect on the religious horizon.
To do so, however, we must develop a basic understanding of the biblical
meaning of Babylon. This word occurs 290 times in the Bible. The
greatest book ever written on this subject is the masterpiece, *The Two
Babylons,* by Rev. Alexander Hislop, published in 1858. This book,
containing quotations from 275 authors and to my knowledge never
refuted, best describes the origin of religion in Babylon and its present-
day function. Two more recent authors who quote heavily from this
book are likewise presented at length because they have so clearly and
simply summarized the heart of his work and provided, in few words,
the best description of these ancient events that I have found. Dr. Harry
Ironside, in his commentary on Revelation, has written:

> The woman is a religious system, who dominates the civil power, at
> least for a time. The name upon her forehead should easily enable us
> to identify her. But in order to do that we will do well to go back to
> our Old Testament, and see what is there revealed concerning literal
> Babylon, for the one will surely throw light upon the other . . .
> . . . we learn that the founder of Bab-el, or Babylon, was Nimrod,
> of whose unholy achievements we read in the 10th chapter of Genesis.
> He was the arch-apostate of the partriarchal age . . . he persuaded his
> associates and followers to join together in "building a city and a tower
> which should reach unto heaven." Not . . . a tower by which they
> might climb up into the skies . . . but a tower of renown . . . to be
> recognized as a temple or rallying centre for those who did not walk
> in obedience to the word of the Lord . . . they called their city and
> tower Bab-El, gate of God; but it was soon changed by divine judgment
> into Babel, Confusion. It bore the stamp of unreality from the first, for
> we are told "they had brick for stone, and slime had they for mortar."
> An imitation of that which is real and true has ever since characterized
> Babylon, in all ages.
> Nimrod, or Nimroud-bar-Cush . . . was a grandson of Ham, the un-
> worthy son of Noah . . . Noah had brought through the flood, the
> revelation of the true God . . . Ham on the other hand seems to have
> been all too readily affected by the apostasy that brought the flood, for
> he shows no evidence of self-judgment . . . His name . . . means
> "swarthy," "darkened," or, more literally, "the sunburnt." And the
> name indicates the state of the man's soul . . . darkened by light from
> heaven . . .
> Ham begat a son named Cush, "the black one," and he became the
> father of Nimrod, the apostate leader of his generation.
> Ancient lore now comes to our assistance, and tells us that the wife
> of Nimrod-bar-Cush was the infamous Semiramis the First. She is
> reputed to have been the foundress of the Babylonian mysteries and
> the first high-priestess of idolatry. Thus Babylon became the fountain-
> head of idolatry, and the mother of every heathen and pagan system in
> the world. The mystery-religion that was there originated spread in
> various forms throughout the whole earth . . . and is with us today . . .
> and shall have its fullest development when the Holy Spirit has departed
> and the Babylon of the Apocalypse holds sway.
> Building on the primeval promise of the woman's Seed who was to
> come, Semiramis bore a son whom she declared was miraculously
> conceived! and when she presented him to the people, he was hailed

as the promised deliverer. This was Tammuz, whose worship Ezekiel protested against in the days of the captivity. Thus was introduced the mystery of the mother and the child, a form of idolatry that is older than any other known to man. The rites of this worship were secret. Only the initiated were permitted to know its mysteries. It was Satan's effort to delude mankind with an imitation so like the truth of God that they would not know the true Seed of the woman when He came in the fullness of time. . . .[22]

Dr. Clarence Larkin, in his book *Dispensational Truth,* includes these interesting details:

Babel, or Babylon, was built by Nimrod. Gen. 10:8-10. It was the seat of the first great Apostasy. Here the "Babylonian Cult" was invented, a system claiming to possess the highest wisdom and to reveal the divinest secrets. Before a member could be initiated he had to "confess" to the Priest. The Priest then had him in his power. This is the secret of the power of the Priests of the Roman Catholic Church today.

Once admitted into this order men were no longer Babylonians, Assyrians, or Egyptians, but members of a Mystical Brotherhood over whom was placed a Pontiff or "High Priest," whose word was law. The city of Babylon continued to be the seat of Satan until the fall of the Babylonian and Medo-Persian Empires, when he shifted his Capital to Pergamos in Asia Minor, where it was in John's day. Rev. 2:12, 13.

When Attalus, the Pontiff and King of Pergamos, died in B.C. 133, he bequeathed the Headship of the "Babylonian Priesthood" to Rome. When the Etruscans came to Italy from Lydia (the region of Pergamos), they brought with them the Babylonian religion and rites. They set up a Pontiff who was head of the Priesthood. Later the Romans accepted this Pontiff as their civil ruler. Julius Caesar was made Pontiff of the Etruscan Order in B.C. 74. In B.C. 63 he was made "Supreme Pontiff" of the "Babylonian Order," thus becoming heir to the rights and titles of Attalus, Pontiff of Pergamos, who had made Rome his heir by will. Thus the first Roman Emperor became the Head of the "Babylonian Priesthood," and Rome the successor of Babylon. The Emperors of Rome continued to exercise the office of "Supreme Pontiff" until A.D. 376, when Emperor Gratian, for Christian reasons, refused it. The Bishop of the Church at Rome, Damascus, was elected to the position. He had been Bishop 12 years, having been made Bishop in A.D. 366, through the influence of the monks of Mt. Carmel, a college of Babylonian religion originally founded by the priests of Jezebel. So in A.D. 378 the Head of the "Babylonian Order" became the Ruler of the "Roman Church." Thus Satan united Rome and Babylon in one religious system.

Soon after Damascus was made "Supreme Pontiff" the "rites" of Babylon began to come to the front. The worship of the Virgin Mary was set up in A.D. 381. All the outstanding festivals of the Roman Catholic Church are of Babylonian origin. Easter is not a Christian name. It means "Ishtar," one of the titles of the Babylonian Queen of Heaven, whose worship by the Children of Israel was such an abomination in the sight of God. The decree for the observance of Easter and Lent was given in A.D. 519. The "Rosary" is of Pagan origin. There is no warrant in the Word of God for the use of the "Sign of the Cross." It had its origin in the mystic "Tau" of the Chaldeans and Egyptians. It came from the letter "T," the initial name of "Tammuz," and was used in the "Babylonian Mysteries" for the same magic purposes as the Romish Church now employs it. Celibacy, the Tonsure, and the Order of Monks and Nuns, have no warrant or authority from Scripture. The Nuns are nothing more than an imitation of the "Vestal Virgins" of Pagan Rome.[23]

After reading the above quotations, you may be inclined to think me anti-Catholic, but that isn't exactly true; I am anti-false religion. For example, I am opposed to any religious system which has enough of the truth to deceive the faithful and enough of the false to damn its followers. A false religion is worse than no religion at all.

My father was born and raised a Roman Catholic, but until he was twenty-eight years of age he never found peace in his heart before God. No one had ever explained to him that salvation was a "finished work," that it could be received freely by faith. Fortunately, six years before his death he heard to Gospel in its simplicity and received Christ by faith. Failing to bring him to God, his church had clouded the way of truth with all her Babylonian pagan innovations brought up through the centuries.

Actually, Rome is more dangerous than no religion because she substitutes religion for truth. Man would be better off with his God-given desire for truth unfulfilled that he might seek after Him. Rome's false religion too often gives man a false security that keeps him from seeking salvation freely by faith. Rome is also dangerous because some of her doctrines are pseudo-Christian. For example, she believes properly about the personal deity of Christ but errs in adding Babylonian mysticism in many forms and salvation by works.

The Pre-Christian Practices of the Roman Catholic Church

One need only turn back to chapters 5 and 6 to examine the changes made in Christianity by the Roman Catholic church. Some of these changes were referred to by the aforementioned authors. When the bishop of Rome became dominant over other church bishops, gradually "Mary-olatry" and other Babylonian practices were brought into the church. These practices had one thing in common: they existed before Christ and were not taught by Him. For example, prayers for the dead, not instituted until A.D. 300, are nowhere taught in the Scripture but are a regular part of the ancestor worship of the Chinese, who practiced it *hundreds of years before Christ.* In addition, the worship of Mary and Christ as a baby was conceived in the same form with other names by most of the major religions of the world hundreds of years before Christ. Easter and Lent observances with forty days' fasting were practiced for the benefit of Tammuz five hundred years before Christ. To prove that Tammuz was worshiped before Christ, just turn to Ezekiel 8:7-14. The worship of Tammuz was so extensive by that time that even the women of Israel were seen "weeping for Tammuz." The title "Queen of Heaven" given to Mary is certainly not Christian. In fact, good Roman Catholics should be horrified to find that the term is found in the Old Testament. Jeremiah 44:17 points out that it was used to describe the mother of Tammuz, the mother goddess of Babylon, over *five hundred years before Christ.* The practice of establishing a celibate priesthood and having nuns is not of Christian origin. Nothing in the Bible teaches this. Indeed, 1 Timothy 3:1-3 forbids it. Hundreds of years before Christ it was incorporated by the Buddhists and Hindus, who practice it to this day. Where do they get it? From Babylonian mysticism, the "mother of harlots." The sign of the cross used on the end of a pole is likewise not of Christian derivation. It was used in the worship of Tammuz five hundred years before Christ. We have already seen that confession, not taught in the Scripture, was practiced in Babylon, and we could go on to include prayer beads, purgatory, and many other pre-Christian practices of the church of Rome. Thinking people can scarcely deny the fact that Rome today is a form of Babylonian mysticism.

Rome Is Not the Only Form of Babylonian Religion

It was my privilege a few years ago to make a trip around the world. My wife and I visited some fifty temples and religious shrines of the major religions of the world. We were appalled to find the strange chords of similarity in all these forms of religion. Mystery, darkness, incense burning, superstition, ignorance, immorality, priesthood, nuns, sprinkling, idolatry, and many other Babylonian customs appeared repeatedly. I can only conclude that Rome is not the only form of Babylonian mysticism, but merely the one that has infiltrated Christianity. And she may be the one leading all forms of religions at the end time.

Ecumenical Church Unity — a Plan of the Devil

We are living in a day of ecumenical propaganda calling upon the churches of the world to amalgamate. Church unity is moving at a breathtaking pace. Twelve years ago I preached a sermon in our church entitled "The Ecumenical Church — A Sign of Our Lord's Return." During that message I stated that the day would come when Roman Catholicism and liberal Protestantism would begin moving together and make overtures to unite. That statement struck many in the church like a bombshell. I was accused of being radical and extreme. When I make that statement now, I find overwhelming agreement. The newspapers are filled with accounts of such strange things as Catholic and Protestant churches working together with the Jews on a common translation of the Scriptures, a Baptist minister participating with a Catholic priest in a marriage ceremony, and just recently a Catholic priest participating in the ordination of a Baptist minister, after which he is quoted as saying, "It was a rich and meaningful experience." As we approach the end of the age, we can expect to see liberal Protestantism, in the form of the

National Council of Churches and the World Council of Churches, being swallowed up by the church of Rome.

This unity movement should not, however, be limited to apostate Christianity. We can expect to see it move toward amalgamating all the religions of the world under Rome's headship because our text states that the religious system at the end time will be a one-world religion: "where the harlot sitteth, are peoples, and multitudes, and nations, and tongues" (v. 15). This can only mean a one-world religious system.

Finally, it need only be pointed out that the Inquisition found the church of Rome persecuting "heretics" (Christians — "saints, martyrs of Jesus") to the death.

Rome's Persecution of Christians

Protestant ecumenicists should keep in mind that Rome has a long history of persecuting Christians. Verse 6 says that the woman is "drunken with the blood of the saints and with the blood of the martyrs of Jesus." Whenever in control of a country, Rome has not hesitated to put to death all who oppose her. Rome's frantic opposition to the Reformation (caused by her pagan indulgences and corruption of the true faith) is a good example. Some passages from *Halley's Bible Handbook* will illustrate her historic brutality.

THE INQUISITION

The Inquisition, called the "HOLY OFFICE," was instituted by Innocent III, and perfected under the second following Pope, Gregory IX. It was the Church Court for the detection and punishment of heretics. Under it every one was required to inform against heretics. Anyone suspected was liable to Torture, without knowing the name of his accuser. The proceedings were secret. The Inquisitor pronounced sentence, and the victim was turned over the the civil authorities to be imprisoned for life or to be burned. The victim's property was confiscated and divided between the Church and the State. In the period immediately following Innocent III the Inquisition did its most deadly work in Southern France (see under Albigenses), but claimed vast multitudes of victims in Spain, Italy, Germany, and the Netherlands. Later on the Inquisition was the main agency in the Papacy's effort to crush the Reformation. It is stated that in the 30 years between 1540 and 1570 no fewer than 900,000 Protestants were put to death, in the Pope's war for the extermination of the Waldenses. Think of monks and priests directing, with heartless cruelty and inhuman brutality, the work of Torturing and Burning alive innocent men and women; and doing it in the Name of Christ, by the direct order of the "Vicar of Christ." The INQUISITION is the MOST INFAMOUS THING in history. It was devised by the Popes, and used by them for 500 years to maintain their power. For its record none of the subsequent line of "Holy" and "Infallible" Popes have ever apologized.

ROME'S OPPOSITION TO THE REFORMATION

In the Netherlands the Reformation was received early; Lutheranism, and then Calvinism; and Anabaptists were already numerous. Between 1513 and 1531 there were issued 25 different translations of the Bible in Dutch, Flemish and French. The Netherlands were a part of the dominion of Charles V. In 1522 he established the Inquisition, and ordered all Lutheran writings to be burned. In 1525 prohibited religious meetings in which the Bible would be read. 1546 prohibited the printing or possession of the Bible, either vulgate or translation. 1535 decreed "death by fire" for Anabaptists. Phillip II (1566-98), successor to Charles V, re-issued the edicts of his father, and with Jesuit help carried on the persecution with still greater fury. By one sentence of the Inquisition the whole population was condemned to death, and under Charles V and Phillip II more than 100,000 were massacred with unbelievable brutality. Some were chained to a stake near the fire and slowly roasted to death; some were thrown into dungeons, scourged, tortured on the rack, before being burned. Women were buried alive, pressed into coffins too small, trampled down with the feet of the executioner. Those that tried to flee to other countries were intercepted by soldiers and massacred. After years of nonresistance, under unheard of cruelty, the Protestants of Netherlands united under the leadership of William of Orange, and in 1572 began the great revolt; and after incredible suffering in 1609, won their independence; Holland, on the North became Protestant; Belgium, on the South, Roman Catholic. Holland was the first country to adopt public schools supported by taxation, and to legalize principles of religious toleration and freedom of the press.

In France. By 1520 Luther's teachings had penetrated France. Calvin's soon followed. By 1559 there were about 400,000 Protestants. They were called "Hugenots." Their earnest piety and pure lives were in striking contrast to the scandalous lives of the Roman clergy. In 1557 Pope Pius urged their extermination. The king issued a decree for their massacre, and ordered all loyal subjects to help in hunting them out. The Jesuits went thru France persuading the faithful to bear arms for their destruction. Thus hunted by Papal agents, as in the days of Diocletian, they met secretly, often in cellars, at midnight.

St. Bartholomew's Massacre. Catherine de Medici, mother of the King, an ardent Romanist and willing tool of the Pope, gave the order, and on the night of August 24, 1572, 70,000 Hugenots, including most of their leaders, were Massacred. There was great rejoicing in Rome. The Pope and his College of Cardinals went, in solemn procession, to the Church of San Marco, and ordered the Te Deum to be sung in thanksgiving. The Pope struck a medal in commemoration of the Massacre; and sent a Cardinal to Paris to bear the King and Queen-Mother the Congratulations of Pope and Cardinals. "France was within a hair-breadth of actually becoming Protestant; but France massacred Protestantism on the night of St. Bartholomew, 1572. 1792 there came to France a 'Protest' of another kind." (Thomas Carlyle.)

The Huguenot Wars. Following St. Bartholomew's Massacre the Hugenots united and armed for resistance; till finally, in 1598, by the Edict of Nantes, they were granted the right of freedom of conscience and worship. But in the meantime some 200,000 had perished as martyrs. Pope Clement VIII called the Toleration Edict of Nantes a "cursed thing"; and, after years of underground work by the Jesuits, the Edict was Revoked, 1685; and 500,000 Hugenots fled to Protestant Countries.

In Bohemia, by 1600, in a population of 4,000,000, 80 percent were Protestant. When the Hapsburgs and Jesuits had done their work, 800,000 were left, all Catholics.

In Spain. The Reformation never made much headway, because the Inquisition was already there. Every effort for freedom or independent thinking was crushed with a ruthless hand. Torquemada (1420-98), a Dominican monk, arch-inquisitor, in 18 years burned 10,200 and condemned to perpetual imprisonment 97,000. Victims were usually burned alive in the public square; made the occasion of religious festivities. From 1481 to 1808 there were at least 100,000 martyrs and 1,500,000 banished. "In the 16th and 17th centuries the Inquisition extinguished the literary life of Spain, and put the nation almost outside the circle of European civilization." When the Reformation began Spain was the Most Powerful country in the world. Its present negligible standing among the nations shows what the Papacy can do for a country.[24]

The above quotations indicate that Rome has never been noted for her toleration. To my knowledge, she has never publicly acknowledged her sin of putting these Protestants to death. Calling us "separated brethren" is just an accommodation used today to gain acceptance by Protestants. When she is established in power, you can expect additional outbreaks of the Inquisition. Look at Catholic-dominated countries today, Colombia and Spain, where Protestants are treated as heretics, their churches burned, and their religious freedom denied.

In India we find that Hinduism is so parallel to the practices of Romanism that many of the Hindus can become Roman Catholics and need not give up Hinduism. Since the religions of the world all have idolatry in common, it would be a simple thing for them to amalgamate on a common basis. What do they care whether they are worshiping Semiramis and Tammuz or Mary and Jesus, just so they have an idol before which to bow down.

The color scheme of this one-world religion as defined in verse 4 is most revealing: "And the woman was arrayed in purple and scarlet color." If you are familiar with pictures of the Vatican Council as published in national magazines, you will have observed that the bishops and cardinals wore purple and scarlet robes. You will also see that the Pope and other church leaders are "bedecked with gold and precious stones and pearls, having a golden cup in [their] hand full of abominations and filthiness of [their] fornication." The abomination and fornication is idolatry and worship of gods other than Jesus Christ. In Rome we saw all manner of idols in the very headquarters of the Roman Church. More costly surroundings can scarcely be found than in the Vatican.

The Coming Destruction of the Babylonian Harlot

Verses 16 and 17 tell us, "The ten horns which thou sawest upon the beast, these shall hate the harlot, and shall make her desolate and naked, and shall eat her flesh, and burn her with fire. For God hath put in their hearts to fulfill his will, and to agree, and give their kingdom unto the beast, until the words of God shall be fulfilled." Antichrist will permit the one-world church to govern his actions during the first three-and-a-half years of the Tribulation while he is gathering more and more power; but in the middle of the Tribulation, when he feels he can become an autocratic ruler, he and the ten kings will throw off the harlot because, in reality, while being dominated by her they "hate the harlot." None of the world's political leaders have enjoyed their subjugation to religious leaders, but have continued in a servile role only for expediency. When it is no longer necessary, the ten kings will "make her desolate and naked, and shall eat her flesh, and burn her with fire," meaning they will confiscate her temples, her gold, and her costly apparel. In so doing, they will unwittingly be the instruments of God in destroying this awful Babylonian system once and for all: "For God hath put in their hearts to fulfill his will."

What is the will of God in regard to the Babylonian system? That she be annihilated. I am not suggesting that Christians attack her and seek to exterminate her. Instead, our responsibility is to "come out from among them, and be ye separate, saith the Lord, and touch not the unclean thing" (1 Cor. 6:17), leaving her destruction to God, who will use the ten kings of the Tribulation Period as His agents. It behooves the true Church of Jesus Christ not to sink into the pitfall of the religious phobia of our day, which is "religious unity." I am reminded of a statement I once heard attributed to Charles Haddon Spurgeon, that "you cannot have unity without forsaking truth, and to forsake truth for the sake of unity is to betray Jesus Christ." May God help us to be faithful unto Him in these last days.

27

Commercial Babylon
Destroyed

Revelation 18

The destruction of Babylon described in Revelation 17 and 18 will decisively rid the world of the major evils that have plagued man for about five thousand years. We have already seen the destruction to be unleashed upon ecclesiastical or religious Babylon in the middle of the Tribulation Period. The destruction of the commercial and governmental systems will not take place, however, until the end of the Tribulation. Some Bible scholars do not distinguish between the destruction of chapter 17 and that of chapter 18, but mold them altogether. The following six reasons establish that they are not the same:

1. "And after these things. . . ." (18:1) This expression indicates that the events described in chapter 18 will not take place until after the events of chapter 17 have been fulfilled.

2. "I saw another angel come down from heaven" (18:1). Events of chapter 17 were introduced by "one of the seven angels who had the seven bowls" (17:1). The angel referred to in chapter 18 is obviously not the same as the one who introduced the events of chapter 17. Therefore, we can expect the same sequence of events that have happened all through the book of Revelation: when an angel fulfills his responsibility, another distinct judgment takes place on the earth.

3. The names in the two chapters are different. The name in chapter 18 is simply "Babylon the great" (18:2). True, the Babylon destroyed in chapter 17 has the name, "MYSTERY, BABYLON THE GREAT, THE MOTHER OF HARLOTS AND ABOMINATIONS OF THE EARTH" (17:5), but the only similarity is the location, Babylon. When both titles are used fully, the contrast of these two Babylons is clearly seen.

4. Babylon the harlot of chapter 17 will be destroyed by the kings of the earth (17:16). The Babylon of chapter 18 will be destroyed by the cataclysmic judgments of God.

5. The Babylon of chapter 17 will be destroyed by the kings of the earth, who rejoice. In the Babylon of chapter 18, the kings and merchants lament and weep for her (18:9-15).

6. If chapters 17 and 18 take place during the last days of the Tribulation, there will be no place for the Antichrist and the False Prophet to do away with all religions and substitute the worship of the Antichrist's image as described in chapter 13.

We conclude, then, that Chapter 17 describes the destruction of the religious system, whereas Chapter 18 denotes the destruction of "Satan's seat," the commercial and governmental city of Babylon, marking the prelude to the consummation of the Tribulation Period.

Babylon the Great Is Fallen

And after these things I saw another angel come down from heaven, having great power, and the earth was made bright with his glory. And he cried mightily with a strong voice, saying, Babylon the great is fallen, is fallen, and is become the habitation of demons, and the hold of every foul spirit, and a cage of every unclean and hateful bird (Rev. 18:1, 2).

Whether "another angel" is one of the seven angels who had the seven bowls we are not told. But it seems doubtful, for this angel is distinctive, with such "great power" that he lights the earth with his glory.

The message of this angel who cries with a "strong voice" is that "Babylon the great is fallen, is fallen." Since chapter 18 describes the destruction of a literal commercial city, the governmental capital of the world during the Tribulation, we naturally ask ourselves the question, "Where is that city?" Again, Bible prophecy students are not in complete agreement. I have heard men suggest that it is the city of Rome, and some years ago one suggested New York City because he felt it was the commercial center of the world. Those of us who believe that we should take the Scriptures literally whenever possible are inclined to believe that the city of Babylon will be rebuilt. Admittedly, there are good Bible teachers who do not hold that position; however, I am inclined to believe that the weight of Bible prophecy requires the literal rebuilding of Babylon.

Babylon to Be Rebuilt

The main reason for believing that Babylon must be rebuilt relates to some prophecies concerning her destruction which are yet unfulfilled.

1. Isaiah 13 and 14 and Jeremiah 50 and 51 describe the destruction of Babylon as being at the time of "the day of the Lord." A careful reading of these four chapters will reveal that the prophecies concerning the destruction of Babylon in the Old Testament use the law of double reference; that is, they refer to the overthrow of Babylon the enemy of Israel in the seventieth year of their captivity. But since Babylon is the headwaters of the world's governmental, commercial, and religious systems in opposition to the will of God, the second reference in these prophecies has to do with the day of Jehovah, or the Tribulation Period.

2. The ruins of Babylon have been used to build other cities, contrary to Jeremiah 51:26: "And they shall not take of thee a stone for a corner, nor a stone for foundations, but thou shalt be desolate forever, saith the LORD."

It is reliably reported that at least six cities bear the marks of having used parts of ancient Babylon in their building, including Seleucia, built by the Greeks; Ctesiphon, by the Parthians; Almaiden, by the Persians; and Kufa, by the Caliphs. Hillah, just a twenty-minute walk from the Babylonian ruins, was built almost entirely from the ruins of Babylon. The builders of Bagdad, fifty miles north of Babylon, also used materials from the ancient city. *The Encyclopedia of Lands and People,* Vol. 3, published by Grolier, states in reference to Babylon, ". . . they found great treasure and the materials of its wonderful buildings were used for the construction of Bagdad in 762. . . . And so, during the centuries, the greatness of Babylon and Assyria passed away. Their magnificent cities were used to supply the bricks for succeeding towns and villages, and such ruins as the barbarians left fell into decay until they became shapeless mounds whose very names were forgotten."[25] This fact alone would demand the rebuilding of Babylon, because when God destroys it in chapter 18, no part of it will ever be used to build another city.

3. The prophecies of Jeremiah and Isaiah indicate that "Babylon is suddenly fallen and destroyed" (Jer. 51:8). Isaiah 13:19 states, "And Babylon, the glory of kingdoms, the beauty of the Chaldeans' excellency, shall be as when God overthrew Sodom and Gomorrah." When taken together, these two prophecies indicate that Babylon will be destroyed by a sudden cataclysm, much the same as were Sodom and Gomorrah. History reveals that ancient Babylon was never destroyed like that.

4. Isaiah 13:20 states that the ruins of Babylon were never to be inhabited. "It shall never be inhabited, neither shall it be dwelt in from generation to generation; neither shall the Arabian pitch tent there; neither shall the shepherds make their fold there." Again, a look at history will reveal that such has not been the case with ancient Babylon. The best description of the history of Babylon, showing that this prophecy has never been fulfilled, is found in Dr. Clarence Larkin's book, *Dispensational Truth:*

> For a description of Babylon and her destruction we must turn to Isaiah, chapters 13 and 14, and Jeremiah, chapters 50 and 51. In these two prophecies we find much that has not as yet been fulfilled in regard to the city of Babylon.
> The city of Babylon was captured in B.C. 541 by Cyrus, who was mentioned "by name" in prophecy 125 years before he was born. Isaiah 44:28-45: 4, B.C. 712. So quietly and quickly was the city taken on the night of Belshazzar's Feast by draining the river that flowed through the city, and entering by the river bed, and the gates that surmounted its banks, that the Babylonian guards had forgotten to lock that night, that some of the inhabitants did not know until the "third" day

that the king had been slain and the city taken. There was no destruction of the city at that time.

Some years after it revolted against Darius Hystaspis, and after a fruitless siege of nearly 20 months was taken by strategy. This was in B.C. 516. About B.C. 478 Xerxes, on his return from Greece plundered and injured, if he did not destroy, the great "Temple of Bel."

In B.C. 331 Alexander the Great approached the city which was then so powerful and flourishing that he made preparation for bringing all his forces into action in case it should offer resistance, but the citizens threw open the gates and received him with acclamations. After sacrificing to "Bel," he gave out that he would rebuild the vast Temple of that god, and for weeks he kept 10,000 men employed in clearing away the ruins from the foundations, doubtless intending to revive the glory of Babylon and make it his capital, when his purpose was defeated by his sudden death of marsh-fever and intemperance in his thirty-third year.

During the subsequent wars of his generals Babylon suffered much and finally came under the power of Seleucus, who, prompted by ambition to build a Capital for himself, founded Seleucia in its neighborhood about B.C. 293. This rival city gradually drew off the inhabitants of Babylon, so that Strabo, who died in A.D. 25, speaks of the latter as being to a great extent deserted. Nevertheless the Jews left from the Captivity still resided there in large numbers, and in A.D. 60 we find the Apostle Peter working among them, for it was from Babylon that Peter wrote his Epistle (1 Peter 5:13), addressed "to the strangers scattered throughout Pontus, Galatia, Cappadocia, Asia, and Bithynia."

About the middle of the 5th century Theodoret speaks of Babylon as being inhabited only by Jews, who had still three Jewish Universities, and in the last year of the same century the "Babylonian Talmud" was issued, and recognized as authoritative by the Jews of the whole world.

In A.D. 917 Ibu Hankel mentions Babylon as an insignificant village, but still in existence. About A.D. 1100 it seems to have again grown into a town of some importance, for it was then known as the "Two Mosques." Shortly afterwards it was enlarged and fortified and received the name of Hillah, or "Rest." In A.D. 1898 Hillah contained about 10,000 inhabitants, and was surrounded by fertile lands, and abundant date groves stretched along the banks of the Euphrates. Certainly it has never been true that "neither shall the Arabian pitch tent there, neither shall the shepherds make their fold there." Isaiah 13:20. Nor can it be said of Babylon — "Her cities are a desolation, a dry land, and a wilderness, a land wherein no man dwelleth, neither doth any son of man pass thereby." Jeremiah 51:43.[26]

The latest information I can glean concerning the city of Hillah, in the suburbs of ancient Babylon though perhaps not within the walls of the literal city itself, is that it is growing rapidly and is considered a wealthy city. Urban and suburban Hillah have a population of about 85,000; in fact, its population is on a par with that of any prosperous city of the modern world. It seems that the Iraqi government has awakened to the fact that the ruins of Babylon make exciting attractions for the tourists of the world. In addition, the suburbs of modern Hillah are spreading out around the ancient ruins. One writer has even gone so far as to suggest that people now live in the village of Babylon. Its population has increased remarkably since 1958 because the Iraqi government is building homes and moving in workers to bring old Babylon out of her dusty grave. The ancient city of Babylon is being "resurrected."

What all of this means is not too difficult to grasp. The one-world government, the one-world religion, and the one-world banking system that make possible the commerce of the world are already gathering momentum. It is just a matter of time before they decide to locate in a single spot. That spot will be Babylon. Recently, one of the delegates at the United Nations made a strong appeal to that body that it move its facilities out of Manhattan Island because of crowded conditions, the high cost of living, and discrimination against some of the delegates. His suggestion was that the U.N. move to Geneva, which is the headquarters for the international banking institutions of the world. Having been in Switzerland on three occasions, even I can see, as lovely as it is, that it is just too small to become the headquarters of Satan during the Tribulation. Besides, the Bible teaches us that Babylon will have that dubious honor. Instead, this suggestion to the U.N. will gather momentum in view of the difficulties of life in New York — economic, racial, and moral — until eventually such a suggestion will be favorably received.

By that time the Babylonian religion under the leadership of Rome will have consumed the World Council of Churches and its ecumenical movement and will be rapidly moving toward amalgamating the major religions of the world under the headship of the one who bears the title "Pontifex Maximus." The world bankers will be more than happy to finance the rebuilding of Babylon as the greatest city of the world to accommodate the headquarters of this one-world government and one-world religion. The fact that Iraq is the most oil-rich country in the world will guarantee their investment, which, as usual, will return them a handsome profit. Railroads, river bottoms dredged to provide harbor facilities, and transatlantic air routes will make Babylon the strategic center of the world. And, like ancient Babylon in its day, it will be "the glory of kingdoms, the beauty of the Chaldeans' excellency." Unless the Lord raptures His Church soon, we can expect to see the foundation laid for the greatest city in all the world's history.

The Coming Destruction of Babylon

Once rebuilt, the great city of Babylon will serve as the seat of Satan, the governmental, religious, and commercial headquarters of the world during the Tribulation Period. In spite of her splendor and magnitude, this will be the most short-lived of the capitals of the world, for she will be earmarked for destruction by Almighty God. "In one hour is she made desolate" (Rev. 18:19).

The kings of the earth, merchants, and sailors will stand off as the city is destroyed, weeping because their great concern for making money and living to the gratification of the flesh has been cut off. No more will

they be able to make merchandise; no more will men buy from them; their riches are gone, and thus they weep in despair.

By contrast, the angel cries to heaven and instructs the holy apostles and prophets to "rejoice over her . . . for God hath avenged you on her." For centuries, spiritually dead in their quest for material gain, the merchants, religionists, and governmental leaders of the world have tried to destroy the true prophets and apostles of God. In one hour they will receive double judgment for their iniquities and works (vv. 5, 6).

This predicted judgment should certainly caution all those who put their trust in stocks and bonds, houses and lands, or the making of money, that they are trusting in the wrong things. Their trust should be wholly and completely in the Lord.

Babylon Is Millstoned

The mighty angel that casts down the great millstone symbolizes the permanence and suddenness of the destruction of Babylon, which we have already seen will be by earthquake, thunder, lightning, plagues, death, mourning and famine, and "she shall be utterly burned with fire" (18:8). The expression in verse 21 that she "shall be found no more at all" coincides with the prophecies of Isaiah 13 and Jeremiah 50 and 51, depicting the permanence of her destruction, where as with Edom and the serpent, the lifting of the curse during the millennial kingdom will not include her. Verse 22 would indicate that in addition to commerce, religion, and government, Babylon will also be the music capital of the world. If her product is similar to present-day popular music, and it no doubt will be, its noise and confusion will cease upon her fall.

The Light of Life Destroyed

The darkness with which Babylon will be perpetually enshrouded is a testimony to her lifelessness for eternity. She will be solemnly and finally judged because of her slaughter of the saints and those who would communicate God's truth to men (vv. 23, 24).

God's Merciful Call to His People

And I heard another voice from heaven, saying, Come out of her, my people, that ye be not partakers of her sins, and that ye receive not of her plagues. For her sins have reached unto heaven, and God hath remembered her iniquities (Rev. 18:4, 5).

One thing which we purposely omitted was the voice from heaven calling God's people out of the city of Babylon *before her destruction.* Who are these people referred to by the voice from heaven as "my people"? They could be tribulation saints, people who were not Christians at the time of the Rapture of the Church but who, during the Tribulation, received Christ as Savior and Lord. What they are doing in the capital city without the mark of the beast is very difficult to comprehend, but the passage indicates that some will refuse to bow their knee to Antichrist. Another suggestion is that they may be Israelites who have not yet recognized Christ and repented of their national and personal sin by turning to Him. If Babylon is to be the headwaters of commercialism, one can be sure that many Jews will be present. God's call to these people at the end of the Tribulation Period is another example of His consistent administration of mercy, as in His call to Lot and his family prior to the destruction of Sodom and Gomorrah.

One of the interesting parts of God's call to His people living in Babylon is that "ye be not partakers of her sins, and that ye receive not of her plagues." Because God works on the principle of "whatsoever a man soweth, that shall he also reap," these people are warned that if they partake of the sins of Babylon, they will be judged accordingly. His invitation to come out of her is typical of God in His call to sinners of all ages that they might turn to Him (which is repentance). Thus He forgives their sins and removes from them their judgment. The mercy of God is forever available. In every age He receives men who are willing to repent of their sin and look to Him for mercy through His Son, the Lord Jesus Christ. Only those who have done so will avoid the judgment of God that comes upon all sinners.

Part III

Christ and the
Future

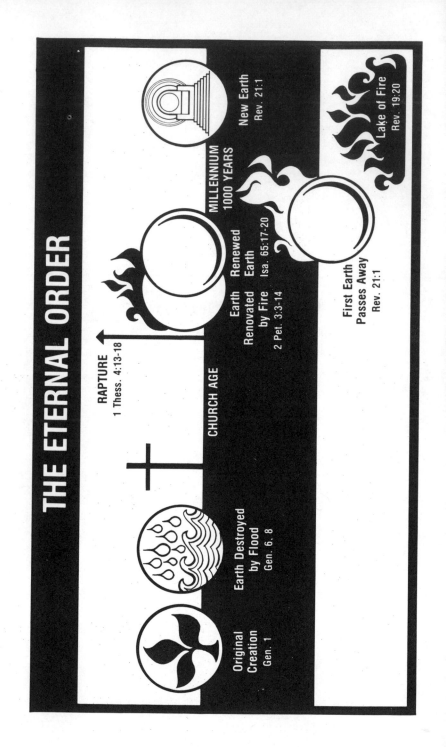

28

The Heavenly
Hallelujah Chorus

Revelation 19:1-6

And after these things I heard a great voice of many people in heaven. saying, Hallelujah! Salvation, and glory, and honor, and power, unto the Lord, our God; for true and righteous are his judgments; for he hath judged the great harlot, who did corrupt the earth with her fornication, and hath avenged the blood of his servants at her hand. And again they said, Hallelujah! And her smoke rose up forever and ever (Rev. 19:1-3).

The "Hallelujah Chorus" from Handel's *Messiah* is usually considered the most sublime expression of praise in the field of music. This paean of praise will be totally eclipsed by the magnificent heavenly hallelujah chorus of the future described here in Revelation 19, which is the source of Handel's inspiration.

We have already seen that in order to understand the book of Revelation, one must always keep in view whether the scene is depicted in heaven or on earth. The contrast between the destruction of Babylon described in chapters 17 and 18 and the rapturous songs of praise in chapter 19 can be explained in terms of the specific relationship to time and location. Chapters 17 and 18 depict the impending doom of man at the end of the tribulation on the earth. Chapter 19 gives us a view of rejoicing in heaven that God's judgment is finally settled upon the earth; no longer will men be permitted to rebel against Him.

In a vital sense the rejoicing in heaven of chapter 19 is occasioned by the final triumph of good over evil, Christ over Antichrist, God over Satan, and the Holy Spirit over the spirit of evil. Ever since the fall of Adam the angelic creatures around the throne of God have anticipated that ultimate day when the cup of man's iniquity would be filled with his abominations and God would finally judge him. This contrasts with

247

the attitude of the people in the world, who will be weeping for the doom of the harlot, Babylon. The scene in Revelation 19 offers a brief glimpse of what God intended to be the experience of man in his relationship with God, from which man fell. Man is seriously frustrated today because he is incapable, without Jesus Christ, of worshiping God as described here. His spirit of self-sufficiency and pride prohibit his abandoning himself to God; consequently he is to some degree a frustrated person. Only Christians who have voluntarily bent their knee to Jesus Christ (Phil. 2:8, 9) are really able to enjoy the blessings of true worship which is such an integral part of man's emotional desires.

Dr. Walvoord has stated that the reference to "much people" in verse 2 is to the same group as in Revelation 7:9, where "a great multitude" is a translation of the same Greek words. "Though the general reference may be to all people in heaven, the allusion seems to be to the martyred dead of the great tribulation."[27] Actually, the people of verse 1 are distinct from the other beings in heaven, as we will see, for they are singing a song that includes salvation. This would incorporate all believers — the Old Testament saints, the church age saints, and the tribulation saints. Together they join in this great chorus, proclaiming, "Hallelujah!"

Revelation 19 is the only place in the New Testament where this word "Hallelujah" is found; it appears four times. Actually, it is an Old Testament word, taken from the Psalms, and means "praise the Lord." There are many things for which men should praise the Lord, as outlined in Psalms 146 to 150, including praise to the Lord for His judgment.

Three additional words are used in the original to express this praise unto the Lord our God (the word "honor" does not appear in the best ancient manuscripts): "salvation," "glory," and "power." Walter Scott, in his exposition of the Revelation of Jesus Christ, stated, "The first of the three terms signifies deliverance, the second God's moral glory in judgment, and the third His might displayed in the execution of the judgment upon the harlot."[28]

Verse 2 establishes the cause for the judgment effected upon Babylon, here called "the Great Harlot," referring primarily to religious Babylon of chapter 17. But man has also made a religion of commercialism and government, whose destruction is described in chapter 18, so in this sense it would probably refer to all three forces that prostitute man's basic quest for God into either false religion, a lust for money and material possessions, or a lust for power through government. These three evils have characterized unregenerate men since before the flood. The destruction referred to here is most significant because it will involve more than just the city of Babylon and the commercial government and religious headquarters. It will include all that Babylon has typified since the days of Nimrod, who succeeded in carrying on the nefarious work of Cain and Lamech in the pre-flood days, when they inaugurated systems that led men away from God. In both cases these men were Satan's tools because they were unwilling to be "servants of God."

All the iniquities of past ages will be justified in this ultimate destruction when God, in righteous judgment, avenges the "blood of his servants at her hand." The extent of her judgment is seen in verse 3 in that "her smoke rolls up forever and ever," indicating that this judgment upon Babylonian religion, politics, and commerce will last forever. No wonder there is rejoicing in heaven at the realization that Satan's religious, commercial, or political systems will never again be permitted to lead men astray.

The Four and Twenty Elders

"And the four and twenty elders and the four living creatures fell down and worshiped God that sat on the throne, saying, Amen. Hallelujah!" (Rev. 19:4). The twenty-four elders mentioned in verse 4 are not strangers to us. We have seen in our exposition of chapter 4 that they are probably a special order of angelic beings who have under them thousands and thousands of angels administering the affairs of God's universe. These, plus the four living creatures also described in chapter 4, will join the redeemed men in heaven to sing praises unto God. Five times in the book of Revelation the twenty-four elders express themselves, each time in praise and rejoicing. When we read this, we find that the elders frequently break out in a chorus of praise for the Lamb and his conquests. In Revelation 4:10, 11 we see them honoring God for His creative power; in Revelation 5:8, 9 they worship the Lamb who is found worthy to take the scroll from the Father and open its seals; in Revelation 7:11, 12 they celebrate the arrival of the multitude of Gentiles in heaven; in Revelation 11:16-18 they worship God when He announces that the world has become the kingdom of Christ and He will reign forever; and now in our text we find them adding their "Amen, Hallelujah!" to God's judgment and destruction of Babylon.

> And a voice came out of the throne, saying, Praise our God, all ye his servants, and ye that fear him, both small and great. And I heard, as it were, the voice of a great multitude, and like the voice of many waters, and like the voice of many peals of thunder, saying, Hallelujah! For the Lord God omnipotent reigneth (Rev. 19:5, 6).

The voice from the throne is evidently that of an angel commanding all His servants to praise Him. All those in heaven are willing servants of God. The angels had a chance to make their choice at the fall of Satan. Some chose to leave; other passages suggest that additional angels have left since then. Men choose whether or not they will serve Him during this life. Thus in that great heavenly chorus there will be a mixture of human and celestial voices as they sing, "Praise be unto our God." They all share this in common: they have voluntarily become His servants. The whole purpose of man is to glorify God. Man was created for His good pleasure (Rev. 4:11). When man refuses to be God's servant, he does not function according to God's pleasure, thus living in disobedience. One gains entrance into heaven only by faith in Jesus Christ, involving the sublime act of yielding oneself to Him, not only as a Savior, but as Lord and Savior. Having once invited Jesus Christ into your life to be your Lord and Master, you have volunteered to become His servant.

The Lord God Omnipotent Reigneth

The united song of all those in heaven anticipates the rulership of the Lord God by His Son, Jesus Christ. This song in a sense is an announcement of what will soon occur in the prophetic sequence. For shortly after this paean of praise in heaven, Jesus Christ will come to set up His glorious kingdom. For nineteen hundred years Christians have prayed in obedience to our Lord, "Thy kingdom come, Thy will be done on earth as it is in heaven." That prayer will one day be answered when Christ comes physically to this earth to rule and to reign forever. This prophetic fact should be a cause of great rejoicing to all believers who understand and anticipate the event.

It was my privilege some years ago to preach part of the funeral service of Dr. David L. Cooper, a great Bible scholar under whom I studied for several years. At the conclusion of the service of rejoicing that this aged saint had gone on to join his dear wife and the many whom he had faithfully lead to the Savior, the organist began to play the recessional as friends came by the casket to look into the face of their departed friend. It is difficult to describe the thrill that went through me when, instead of the traditional mournful tunes I am accustomed to hearing at funerals, I heard the dynamic chords of the organ pealing out the triumphant "Hallelujah Chorus." And the best part of all is that for the child of God, it is true. That was no time for sadness, but for rejoicing and for worship of our God. His old servant was not dead but with his Lord, awaiting that great resurrection day when he will come to this earth with his Lord and all his loved ones in Christ.

29

The Marriage
Supper of the Lamb

Revelation 19:7-10

> Let us be glad and rejoice, and give honor to him; for the marriage
> of the Lamb is come, and his wife hath made herself ready. And to
> her was granted that she should be arrayed in fine linen, clean and white;
> for the fine linen is the righteousness of saints. And he saith unto me,
> Write, Blessed are they who are called unto the marriage supper of
> the Lamb. And he saith unto me, These are the true sayings of God.
> And I fell at his feet to worship him. And he said unto me, See thou
> do it not! I am thy fellow servant, and of thy brethren that have the
> testimony of Jesus. Worship God; for the testimony of Jesus is the
> spirit of prophecy (Rev. 19:7-10).

The marriage supper of the Lamb is a subject greatly misunderstood,
not because of erroneous teaching, but because it is almost neglected in
our preaching today. The main source of information concerning this
coming event is found in Revelation 19:7-10, which falls into two main
divisions: (1) the marriage of the Lamb and (2) the marriage supper of
the Lamb.

The Marriage Supper of the Lamb

The marriage supper of the Lamb was one of the themes on which the
Lord Jesus loved to dwell. In many of His stories or parables, He spoke
of marriage suppers. For instance, in the parable of the ten virgins, He
told about the preparation for the coming of the bridegroom. In Matthew
22:1-14 He spoke of the parable of the marriage of the king's son. At
this festive occasion the king sent out servants to invite people to come to
this blessed event.

Who Is the Bridegroom?

The question "Who is the Bridegroom?" has but one answer. The
Bridegroom can only be "the king's son" of Matthew 22:1-14, the Lord

Jesus Himself. In John 3:29, long after John the Baptist had introduced Jesus as "the Lamb of God, who taketh away the sin of the world" (John 1:29), John was asked to identify himself. He made it clear that he was not the Christ; in verse 29 he referred to Christ as "the bridegroom," to himself as "the friend of the bridegroom, who standeth and heareth him." From this passage we see that Christ is referred to as the Bridegroom and also as the Lamb. Thus we may conclude that Christ will be the Bridegroom at the marriage of the Lamb.

Who Is the Bride?

The answer to the question "Who is the Bride?" presents a difference of opinion. Some say that the Bride is Israel, because in Revelation 19:7 she is called "wife," just as in Isaiah 54:5 Israel is called the wife of God. But the Bride cannot be Israel because a bride is not called a wife until after the marriage has taken place. Besides, there are two wives in Scripture. The Old Testament wife was "cast off" because of the spiritual adultery committed in the worship of other gods (Jer. 3:1-20; Ezek. 16; Hos. 2; 3:1-5). It is this very difference that Paul had in mind in 2 Corinthians 11:2: "For I am jealous over you with godly jealousy; for I have espoused you to one husband that I may present you as a chaste virgin to Christ." The Church has been guilty of many sins in her nineteen hundred years of existence, but spiritual adultery is not one of them. Spiritual adultery can be defined in the Scripture as the worship of other gods. One cannot be a Christian, with the Holy Spirit as the witness in his heart, and worship anyone save the Lord Jesus Christ. This fact, of course, automatically becomes the test as to the genuineness of salvation.

One other verse of importance to consider here regarding the identity of the Bride is found in Ephesians 5:32. The Apostle Paul, speaking to husbands and wives of their relationship together, likens the husband to Christ and the wife to the Church. He sums it up in verse 32 by saying, "This is a great mystery, but I speak concerning Christ and the church," clearly indicating that the perfect picture of the relationship between the Lord Jesus and His Church is that of a bride and a bridegroom. Therefore when a person accepts Jesus Christ, he becomes a member of the Church, the true invisible Church, and is automatically espoused or engaged to Christ. This engagement will be finalized in marriage at the marriage of the Lamb.

When and Where Will This Marriage Take Place?

The marriage of the Lamb must take place in heaven, for in Revelation 19:11, after the marriage of the Lamb and the marriage supper of the Lamb, we find the Lord Jesus coming in what we call "the glorious appearing" to set up His kingdom. For this reason we must conclude that the marriage and the supper have occurred in heaven. Their location in the nineteenth chapter of the book of Revelation shows these events to have taken place at the end of the Tribulation, just before the millennial reign of Christ upon the earth. Ephesians 5:27 indicates the manner in which the Bride will be presented to Christ: "a glorious church, not having spot, or wrinkle, or any such thing; but that it should be holy and without blemish." This condition will exist only after the judgment of Christ when the believer has been completely cleansed and the Church is made whole. For that reason we believe that the judgment seat of Christ, which will take place during the Tribulation, will precede the marriage supper of the Lamb, and immediately after the judgment of reward has been presented to the last believer, the marriage of the Lamb will take place. All the Christians who have trusted in Christ during the age of grace, from the day of Pentecost to the Rapture of the Church, will make up His Bride.

How Does the Bride Make Herself Ready?

Years ago a bride usually made her own wedding dress; in fact, it is not uncommon for brides to make them today. The wedding dress, according to verse 8, made of fine linen, is defined as the righteousness of saints. This word in the Greek appears in the plural number, "righteousnesses." On that basis, then, we find that the bride makes herself ready through her righteous acts. Inasmuch as this marriage comes after the judgment seat of Christ, it would seem that the position of the individual, as a member of the Bride of Christ, would be determined by the outcome of the judgment by fire, when his works will be judged. Therefore it behooves Christians in this age to be careful to do good works (Titus 3:8). The Lord Jesus challenged Christians, "Lay up for yourselves treasures in heaven." Although Christians are reluctant to consider working for rewards, it should be borne in mind that our relationship to Christ as members of the Bride of Christ will be determined by faithful service today.

The devil is a master liar. He tells the unsaved, "Work for salvation." If his lies fail and the individual accepts Christ, the devil immediately whispers, "Now that you're saved freely by grace, you don't have to do anything." That does not agree with Ephesians 2:8-10; most Christians forget the tenth verse, "For we are his workmanship, created in Christ Jesus unto good works, which God hath before ordained that we should walk in them." The purpose of the Christian is to be available to the Lord for "good works." We may properly take periodic inventories to see if we are truly serving Christ. In that day all unfaithful Christians will rue their unfaithfulness, for it will not only keep them from the position with Christ they would desire, but will limit the extent to which they rule and reign with Christ during the millennial kingdom. The attitude of the Apostle Paul should characterize every Christian: "Lord, what wilt thou have me to do?" That kind of attitude will provide such motivation in the believer that he will not only receive a "full reward" but hear the Savior say, "Well done, thou good and faithful servant. Enter thou into the joy of thy Lord."

The Marriage Supper of the Lamb

The marriage supper, of course, is not the marriage, but the marriage feast of the Lamb. It seems a particular honor to be invited to this feast, or marriage supper, for John was instructed to write, "Blessed are they who are called unto the marriage supper of the Lamb" (Rev. 19:9). "Blessed" means happy or honored. "Called" means invited. Therefore we could read it, "Happy (or honored) are they who are invited to the marriage supper of the Lamb."

The Identity of the Guests

That guests will appear at this marriage supper can be deduced from the fact that some are called in addition to the participants of the marriage ceremony. The bride is never invited to a wedding supper; neither is the bridegroom. But the friends of the bride and groom are invited. Now who are these friends, or guests? It must be admitted that there are some differences of opinion here. It could not be the Church, for the Church is the Bride. Some try to identify the parable of the wise virgins and the parable of the marriage supper of the king's son as illustrations of the guests at this wedding supper. But these two parables only serve to illustrate the prominence of a marriage supper in the thinking of the Lord Jesus. It should be understood that both the foolish virgins and the guest who did not possess a wedding garment were left outside the wedding feast, whereas there is no place whatever for anyone to be left outside at the marriage supper of the Lamb. These two parables are "kingdom of heaven" parables, teaching that one should be prepared for the coming of the Bridegroom.

John the Baptist, one of the last Old Testament saints, indicated that he was a friend of the Bridegroom (John 3:29). These Old Testament saints will be in heaven and will have their rewards, but they are not the Church, not the Bride of Christ. They are the friends of the Bride and Bridegroom, who at this point can be seen as the ones invited as guests to the feast. So then all the believing dead from Adam until the resurrection of Christ will be guests at the feast. In addition to them will appear those who have received the Savior during the Tribulation, both Jew and Gentile, many of whom will have been martyred for the testimony of Christ.

These will comprise the guests at the feast. Some would suggest that perhaps angels will be among the guests. However, I do not feel this is probable. Angels may be spectators at the marriage supper of the Lamb, but it should be noticed that the supper is distinguished by the use of the sacrificial name of the Lord — Lamb. Angels have never been the recipients of the blessings of the redeemed. Only those who have lived a human existence, have sinned, and have been redeemed by the blood of the Lamb will be in that number, either as the Bride of Christ or as the invited guests of Christ. I do not wish to imply that the Old Testament saints are inferior to the Church, or the body of Christ, but merely to point out that this is a special blessing for the Church. Now Israel, or the guests at the wedding supper of the Lamb, have promises and relationships to Him in which we shall not share; however, the marriage supper of the Lamb is an experience reserved for the Church.

The Honeymoon of the Lamb

After weddings on this earth, the wedding party customarily has a celebration or reception, which has taken the place in the modern era of the old-fashioned marriage supper. But after the marriage supper, the bride and the bridegroom usually change into their traveling dress and slip away on a wedding trip. It is more than just coincidence that immediately after the marriage supper of the Lamb, John tells us, "I saw heaven opened and, behold, a white horse" (Rev. 19:11a). From this point he launches into a description of the glorious appearing of the Lord Jesus Christ on this earth, to set up His kingdom, when He shall come with His Bride, the Church. The earth, which is the former abode of the Church, from which the Church will have been raptured, and upon which the Lamb Himself lived and died, then will become the place of the thousand-year honeymoon. Would to God that every marriage could enjoy the fulfillment of that symbol — 1000 years of peace.

The Believer and the Millennium

Immediately after the descent of Christ to this earth, the millennial kingdom will commence. Christ will set up His kingdom and the believer will reign with Him. 2 Timothy 2:11, 12 clarifies that the believer will reign with Him. Of course, that reigning is based on the works of the believer, for Paul said, "If we endure, we shall also reign with him."

Reigning According to Faithfulness

In Luke 19:11-27 we find the parable of the pounds. This parable testifies to the quantitative element in our Christian service. The servant was given a pound; he invested that pound, and at the coming of his Lord he had earned ten pounds. It is important to note the commendation and the injunction of the Savior. In verse 17 He said, "Well done, thou good servant; because thou hast been faithful in a very little, have thou authority over ten cities." Because this servant had magnified his substance, he was given the authority of ten cities during the millennium. The same is said in verse 18 of the second servant, who had taken his pound and gained five pounds. To him was given to reign over five cities. The unfaithful servant was given nothing; in fact, the talent he had was taken away, which may well indicate that the unfaithful servants of Christ, though saved, "yet so as by fire," but who do not have any reward, will live a rather vain and barren existence during the millennium. The faithful servant, however, will be given a place of true leadership in His kingdom, a position of leadership directly in proportion to the degree of faithfulness in Christian service. What a challenge to the believer to be faithful in whatever way he can in this life, for in his service for Christ he is laying up for himself treasures in heaven that will one day determine his station and position for a thousand years.

A hymn writer challenges us to "Work for the night is coming, when man's work is done." The shades of night are falling rapidly; every Christian should be busy about the Master's business, "redeeming the time," while some light still remains.

30

The Glorious Appearing
of Jesus Christ

Revelation 19:11-16

The glorious appearing of Jesus Christ is easily the most exciting event in all Bible prophecy. Every Christian who knows anything about the Bible looks forward to that blessed day when his Lord will truly be glorified. His coming in glory will be in marked contrast to His first coming, when He fulfilled the prophecies of a Savior. On that occasion He came humbly, to be born in a manger. He suffered Himself to be abused and buffeted by men, even to the point of permitting His creatures to spit upon Him and crucify Him. The next time our Lord will not come in humility, but in "power and great glory." His glorious appearing will significantly counterpoint His humble birth almost two thousand years before.

Revelation 19:10 is the transition verse between the marriage supper of the Lamb and the glorious appearing. It could be considered in connection with either subject. After the vision John informs us that he "fell at his feet to worship him." Because the pronoun "him" has no antecedent, we can assume from the context and the divine instruction that this was the angel who revealed the vision to John. Like others who make the mistake of worshiping anyone but God, he was immediately corrected with the words, "See thou do it not: I am thy fellow servant, and of thy brethren." In the resurrection Christians will evidently be equal with angels, for in the book of Revelation they are considered as fellow servants with angels, and all bear the testimony of Jesus. Then John received this specific command: "Worship God."

This command of the angel to "Worship God" in the sense that it is used here excludes worship directed toward any other creature. It is one of the many illustrations that demonstrate the consistency of Scripture. This scene, almost at the close of the book of Revelation, coincides with the first commandment of Exodus 20, "Thou shalt have no other gods before me," teaching that God is the only object of worship. This consistency is also conveyed in establishing the personal deity of the Lord Jesus Christ. He is the only person in the Scripture who freely received worship of men without rebuke. Ten times in the New Testament Jesus was worshiped, and not once did He restrain those who worshiped Him.

That brings us to one of the most fascinating phrases in the Bible concerning Bible prophecy: "The testimony of Jesus is the spirit of prophecy." Used in this connection, we find that the "fellow servant of God" is one who holds or communicates the testimony of Jesus. Whether human or angelic, the true servants of God work indirectly or directly toward the testimony of Jesus.

The above expression gives the finest definition of the spirit of prophecy to be found in the Bible, "the testimony of Jesus." Prophecy is not solely the prediction of the future, as some say, nor is it only the declaration of ethical principles, as others claim. Prophecy receives its value and meaning from its relation to Christ, whether that relation be direct or indirect. The first prophetic utterance of God, Genesis 3:15, to the last prediction of the Revelation, the heart of prophecy, has been directed to the person of Christ. Errors of interpretation of details may be inescapable, but there need be no error in understanding the direction and purpose of prophecy; as a whole, it points to Christ.

We tend to think of prophecy as a revealing of future events, but in the New Testament we find that the prophetic gift is second only to that of the apostles and is a special form of the teaching gift. In reality, it is a making known of the divine will, and the divine will is that men humble themselves and receive His Son, Jesus Christ. Therefore, any prophecy or prophetic teaching should directly or indirectly reveal the person of Jesus Christ. The study of Bible prophecy has fallen into disrepute only when teachers have become involved in peripheral areas of date setting or rigid predictions of events that go beyond the clear teachings of Scripture and all at the expense of revealing "the testimony of Jesus."

Prophetic teaching, or preaching that testifies of Jesus, invariably warms the heart. The two disciples on the road to Emmaus acknowledged after their encounter with the resurrected Christ, "Did not our heart burn within us, while he talked with us along the way, and while he opened to us the Scriptures?" (Luke 24:32). What caused their heart to burn within them? Verse 27 gives the answer, "And beginning at Moses and all the prophets, he expounded unto them, in all the scriptures, the things concerning himself." For that reason, the study of the book of Revelation should cause our hearts to "burn within us," because it is the revelation of Jesus Christ, who forms the heart of all prophecy.

One quality that makes the Bible a literary masterpiece is its unusual simplicity. The words "And I saw heaven opened and, behold, a white horse; and he that sat upon him was called Faithful and True" present a simple introduction to the grand climax of the ages. For thousands of years it has been central to the plan of God that His Son, Jesus Christ, should reign over the earth and all things thereon. This simple expression introduces the event that shows our Lord gloriously coming to earth, fulfilling the many prophecies concerning His appearing. Since the glorious appearing of Christ is such a climactic event in the Bible, we can expect to find many references to it. In that expectation we will not be disappointed. Before we examine the text in Revelation, it would help the student to examine other Bible references to this event that he might adequately compare Scripture with Scripture and more clearly establish the proper sequence of events.

Christ Goes First to Edom

Who is this that cometh from Edom, with dyed garments from Bozrah? This that is glorious in his apparel, traveling in the greatness of his strength? I who speak in righteousness, mighty to save. Why art thou red in thine apparel, and thy garments like him who treadeth in the winefat? I have trodden the winepress alone, and of the peoples there was none with me; for I will tread them in mine anger, and trample them in my fury; and their blood shall be sprinkled upon my garments, and I will stain all my raiment. For the day of vengeance is in mine heart, and the year of my redeemed is come. And I looked, and there was none to help; and I wondered that there was none to uphold. Therefore, mine own arm brought salvation unto me, and my fury, it upheld me. And I will tread down the peoples in mine anger, and make them drunk in my fury, and I will bring down their strength to the earth (Isa. 63:1-6).

For some reason we find that our Lord will go first to Edom, where many Israelites have fled for safety from the Antichrist. He thus will vindicate the promises of God as He triumphs over the enemies of Israel. This text also describes Him as arrayed in red garments and reveals that this is the "day of vengeance." Men, having rejected the mercy of God offered through the sacrificial death of Christ on the cross, will suffer the judgment of God at the hands of the one they have rejected. This, and other texts, make it clear that Christ's glorious appearing will not be a time of joy to the unsaved but, on the contrary, a time of great sorrow because the day of God's wrath is come.

Christ's Coming Attended by Signs and Natural Phenomena

For as the lightning cometh out of the east, and shineth even unto the west, so shall also the coming of the Son of man be. For wherever the carcass is, there will the eagles be gathered together.
Immediately after the tribulation of those days shall the sun be darkened, and the moon shall not give its light, and the stars shall fall from heaven, and the powers of the heavens shall be shaken. And then shall appear the sign of the Son of man in heaven; and then shall all the tribes of the earth mourn, and they shall see the Son of man coming in the clouds of heaven with power and great glory. And he shall send his angels with a great sound of a trumpet, and they shall gather together his elect from the four winds, from one end of heaven to the other (Matt. 24:27-31).

This prediction of our Lord Himself concerning His glorious appearing is taken from the Olivet Discourse. It reveals that He will come visible and become the object of attention. The sun, moon, and stars will not give their lights, but all attention will be focused on "the sign of the Son of man in heaven," after which "the tribes of the earth [will] mourn" because they have not prepared themselves for that day. Then men will see Christ, who is the Light, "coming in the clouds of heaven with power and great glory," At this moment the second installment of the rapture will occur, when Christ will gather together His elect from the "four winds, from one end of heaven to the other."

The Second Installment of the Rapture

In Psalm 50:1-6 we find the Lord above the earth but below the heaven (v. 4), looking back up to heaven and down to the earth, calling His saints to Him. This would indicate that He will rapture the tribulation saints still living and the tribulation saints whose souls are under the altar (Rev. 6). This may include the Old Testament saints, whose resurrection may wait until the end of the Tribulation. This event may take place just before the marriage supper of the Lamb previously discussed. Now, having raptured all believers from all ages, He will come to an exclusively unsaved earth.

Christ Comes to Execute Judgment With His Saints

> And Enoch also, the seventh from Adam, prophesied of these, saying, Behold, the Lord cometh with ten thousands of his saints, to execute judgment upon all, and to convict all that are ungodly among them of all their ungodly deeds which they have ungodly committed, and of all their hard speeches which ungodly sinners have spoken against him (Jude 14, 15).

This is the only passage in the Bible telling us that Enoch was a prophet. Somehow God had revealed to him that in the unfolding of the ages Christ would come with myriads of holy ones to execute judgment on men. That judgment will begin with Antichrist and eventually will include the nations of the earth, as explained in Matthew 25.

2 Thessalonians 1:7-10 describes Christ coming in judgment to destroy Antichrist, which parallels the passage we will study in the next chapter, in which Christ casts the Antichrist into the lake of fire.

Christ Will Stand on the Mount of Olives

> Then shall the LORD go forth, and fight against those nations, as when he fought in the day of battle.
> And his feet shall stand in that day upon the Mount of Olives, which is before Jerusalem on the east, and the Mount of Olives shall cleave in its midst toward the east and toward the west, and there shall be a very great valley; and half of the mountain shall remove toward the north, and half of it toward the south. And ye shall flee to the valley of the mountains; for the valley of the mountains shall reach unto Azel; yea, ye shall flee, as ye fled from before the earthquake in the days of Uzziah, king of Judah; and the LORD, my God, shall come, and all the saints with thee (Zech. 14:3-5).

Our Lord ascended into heaven from the Mount of Olives. In Acts 1:11 the angels said, "This same Jesus, who is taken up from you into heaven, shall so come in like manner as ye have seen him go into heaven." Our Lord will not only come in "like manner," meaning visibly and physically, but He will actually come to the same place, the Mount of Olives. When His feet strike the Mount of Olives, the Mount will divide in two. Some Bible commentators have indicated that a natural division exists between the two high points on the Mount of Olives which will cleave in two, creating a new passageway from Jerusalem down to Jericho at the Jordan River. There may be a gigantic causeway from the Jordan River out to the Mediterranean. Others speak of a geological report, indicating a fault under the Mount of Olives that needs only a slight earthquake to cleave it in two. In any case, when Christ sets His feet upon the Mount, His power will be manifested in that it divides into two parts.

All of the above events, taking place in a breathtaking moment of time, will highlight the fact that our Lord has come. These passages are only some of the many that could be used to describe the great event of our Lord's glorious appearing.

The Glorious Appearing

The term "glorious appearing" is not found in the book of Revelation, but it is in Titus 2:13. There it is used to describe the physical, visible return of Christ to the earth in distinction from that "blessed hope," which is the Rapture of the Church or the secret coming of Christ for His believers prior to the Tribulation Period. Of all the descriptions of the glorious appearing in the Bible, none is more graphic than our text:

> And I saw heaven opened and, behold, a white horse; and he that sat upon him was called Faithful and True, and in righteousness he doth judge and make war. His eyes were like a flame of fire, and on his head were many crowns; and he had a name written, that no man knew, but he himself. And he was clothed with a vesture dipped in blood; and his name is called The Word of God. And the armies that were in heaven followed him upon white horses, clothed in fine linen, white and clean. And out of his mouth goeth a sharp sword, that with it he should smite the nations, and he shall rule them with a rod of iron; and he treadeth the winepress of the fierceness and wrath of Almighty God. And he hath on his vesture and on his thigh a name written, KING OF KINGS, AND LORD OF LORDS (Rev. 19:11-16).

Verse 11 introduces this dynamic scene by telling us that John "saw heaven opened." This is the second time John saw the heaven opened. The first time was in Revelation 4:1 where he was invited up into heaven and as a representative of the Church looked down on the scenes of the Tribulation Period. In chapter 19 the Tribulation has been concluded and Christ is returning to the earth, so we find the heaven opened again. This time, instead of taking a man up, heaven is opened to let the rider on the white horse out, accompanied by his armies. This rider is to be distinguished from the rider on the white horse in 6:2, who was Antichrist. This rider, with eyes "like a flame of fire," from the description can be none other than the Lord Jesus Christ. The significance of the white horse is typical of the difference between this coming and Christ's first coming. While on this earth our Lord fulfilled Zechariah 9:9, entering Jerusalem on a lowly beast of burden. Now His humiliation is done away and He will come in glory, properly using the white horse to depict His power and glory. Lest you think it strange that there are horses in heaven, I remind you that in 2 Kings 2:11 and 6:13-17 we find references to horses and chariots of fire.

Even more significant than what our Lord will do at His coming is how He is described here, for His eternal nature is revealed. "Faithful and true" presents our Lord as a contrast to the unfaithful deceivers of men, Antichrist and Satan. Our Lord has faithfully fulfilled all of His prophecies. "A day with the Lord is as a thousand years" suggests that a promise of God given a thousand years ago is as though it were given yesterday. The extent of His faithfulness, however, is not fully comprehended until He fulfills these promises. Believers accept His faithfulness now by faith, but in that moment all men will see the tangible evidence of His faithfulness. Christ is the truth; by contrast, Satan is the big lie. Christ is the true way to God; Satan is the false way, leading not to God but to hell.

The Righteous Judge

"In righteousness he judgeth." We have already seen that our Lord comes to judge this earth on the basis of what it has done concerning Himself. He is the pivot of all history and the significant factor of the ages.

The Righteous Warrior

"In righteousness he makes war." This world has known nothing but wars since it rejected God and His Son, Jesus Christ. During World War I the total number of war-related deaths was 40 million. It is estimated that the total number of deaths caused by World War II was 60 million. Most of the wars of the world have been unrighteous wars. When Christ comes, His war will consist of only one battle. He will consume all before Him, all that stand in opposition to Him, and bring every man into subjection. This will be the first righteous war in the history of mankind. The ability of Christ to wage a righteous war is not only seen in His holy nature, but in that his eyes are "like a flame of fire," indicating that He will judge according to truth. The best judge on earth cannot know all the facts of a given situation because he is limited by human frailty. Jesus Christ is not so limited. He who knows the end from the beginning will be a righteous judge, for His all-seeing eye will reveal all truth about every individual and nation.

The Righteous King

"On his head were many crowns." This would not indicate that Christ is doing a balancing act with a great number of crowns upon His head, but should be taken symbolically to mean that He will come in much authority. All through history a crown on a man's head has symbolized authority. Kings wore crowns, the Popes wear a triple crown, the Antichrist's kingdom is symbolized with crowns, even the ten kings of the Tribulation will have crowns; but when Christ comes, all power will be given unto Him as the supreme king. In fact, verses 11 and 12 of this text reveal the threefold nature of Christ in His glorious appearing. For when He comes, He will be a Warrior, a Judge, and a King.

"He had a name written, that no one knew, but he himself." Many have speculated upon this name, but it seems rather unwise to do so. A Bible name reveals the nature of the person, and there are many names that reveal facets of the nature of God and Jesus Christ. However, since He is divine, it would only seem natural that some aspects of His nature are incomprehensible to our finite minds. Therefore at least this one name will be unknown to man. J. A. Seiss made the following statement:

> This warrior, judge, and king has a name ineffable and unknowable, but it is a true and rightful name, a name of reality, which is above every name. We do not yet know all the majesty and attributes of being which belong to our sublime Savior; and when He comes forth out of heaven for the war on the beast, He will come in vast unknowableness of greatness, in heights of great majesty and glory, which no one knoweth but Himself.[29]

Verse 13 indicates, "He is arrayed in a garment sprinkled with blood" (ASV). This could well be a reference to the bloodshed caused by the battle of the great day of God Almighty as He brings forth triumphs, or it could be a symbolic reference to the fact that His garments were sprinkled with blood on Calvary's cross so that we may wear robes of righteousness.

"And His name is called The Word of God." The Apostle John was the only writer of the New Testament who used the expression "the Word of God" to describe the Lord Jesus Christ. It is a beautiful expression, coming from the Greek word *logos* and literally meaning the expression of God. Just as a word is an expression of thought, so Christ is the expression of God. As we reveal thoughts from one human mind to another through the vehicle of words, so Christ, the eternal Word of God, reveals God to men. If men would know God, they need only study about His Son, Jesus Christ, for "he hath revealed him."

The Armies of Christ

"The armies that were in heaven followed him upon white horses, clothed in fine linen, white and clean" (v. 14). The armies of heaven consist of the angelic hosts, the Old Testament saints, the Church, and the tribulation saints. The most significant truth, however, is the garb of this army. They are "clothed in fine linen, white and clean." Military men are issued fatigue uniforms for battle dress, not only for camouflage but also because war is so dirty that light-colored clothes would be severely soiled. Here, however, the Commander-in-Chief of the heavenly forces clothes His army in white, a practice unheard of in the history of warfare. The reason should not be overlooked by the reader: no member of the armies of Christ that come with Him in His glorious appearing will do battle. Not one of us will lift a finger, for the battle will be consummated by the spoken word of our Lord.

The Authority of the King of Kings

"And out of his mouth goeth a sharp sword, that with it he should smite the nations, and he shall rule them with a rod of iron." The sharp sword here has lead some to believe that it is the Sword of the Spirit, the Word of God. But Dr. John Walvoord states concerning this expression:

> The word for sword indicates a long Thracian sword, or one which is unusually large and longer than most swords. The same word is sometimes used to describe a javelin, a sword sufficiently light and long to be thrown as a spear. Here the word is used symbolically to represent a sharp instrument of war, with which Christ will smite the nations and establish His absolute rule. The expression of ruling "with a rod of iron" is also found in Psalm 2:9 and Revelation 2:27, with a similar expression, "the rod of His mouth," in Isaiah 11:4. It represents absolute, unyielding government under which men are required to conform to the righteous standards of God. [30]

The coming of Christ in His glorious appearing with the heavenly armies will not only bring to consummation the enmity of Satan, his Antichrist, the False Prophet, and the millions they deceive, but will usher in the millennial kingdom; the righteous reign of Christ upon earth. This fact is seen clearly in the name given to Christ in the next verse.

"And he hath on his vesture and on his thigh a name written, KING OF KINGS, AND LORD OF LORDS." A warrior goes into battle with his sword on his thigh. Christ's sword will be His spoken word. The word that called the world into being will call the leaders of men and the armies of all nations into control. Instead of a sword on His thigh is His name, "KING OF KINGS AND LORD OF LORDS." Christ Jesus, the living Lord, will be established in that day for what He is in reality, *King* above all kings, *Lord* above all lords. Then truly will the prophetic words of Isaiah be fulfilled, "Unto us a child is born, unto us a son is given, and the government shall be upon his shoulder; and his name shall be called Wonderful, Counselor, The Mighty God, The Everlasting Father, The Prince of Peace" (Isa. 9:6).

31

The Battle of the Great Day
of God Almighty

Revelation 19:17-21

We have already seen that the glorious appearing of Jesus Christ portrays Him as coming to be "the righteous judge, the righteous warrior, and the righteous king." This chapter, covering Revelation 19:17-21, primarily deals with Christ as the righteous warrior, for we see Him as He comes to do battle with the host of Satan's armies in what is often called "the battle of Armageddon," but which in truth is a war, or campaign, of the great day of God Almighty. This war is necessitated by the fiendishly evil ambitions of men and their evil source of power, Satan. It is doubtless the most horrible experience in the annals of human history.

Our Lord himself tells when this battle takes place in Matthew 24:29-31:

Immediately after the tribulation of those days shall the sun be darkened, and the moon shall not give its light, and the stars shall fall from heaven, and the powers of the heavens shall be shaken. And then shall appear the sign of the Son of man in heaven; and then shall all the tribes of the earth mourn, and they shall see the Son of man coming in the clouds of heaven with power and great glory. And he shall send his angels with a great sound of a trumpet, and they shall gather together his elect from the four winds, from one end of heaven to the other.

From this we conclude that the glorious appearing will take place "immediately after the tribulation of those days." Therefore we find this event takes place at the end of the Tribulation and before the millennium. Our Lord will time His coming at the most dramatic point in all history. Antichrist, the False Prophet, and Satan will inspire the armies of the world to invade Palestine in a gigantic effort to rid the world of the Jews and to fight against Christ.

This closing battle before Christ sets up His millennial kingdom is often called "the battle of Armageddon." This is a misleading expression be-

265

cause Armageddon means "Mount of Slaughter" and refers to the beautiful valley to the east of Mt. Megiddo, and the word "battle" here literally means "campaign" or "war." No war has ever been won by a single battle. In fact, it is possible to lose a battle and still win a war. The war of the great day of God Almighty will take place in a single day, and the battle of Armageddon will be just one of the battles of that war. Actually, this war will encompass more than just the Valley of Megiddo, but as we shall see, it will cover practically all of the land of Palestine. This conflict, when Christ defeats the armies of Antichrist, will be a series of at least four "campaigns"; therefore it is more properly called "the *war* of that great day of God Almighty" (Rev. 16:14). The carnage and the horror of the scene are described only generally from our text, Revelation 19: 17-21. In order to get a full picture of this horrible period, we must turn to several other passages in the Word of God.

The Battle of Armageddon

We have already seen in the previous chapter that the Lord will go first to Edom and soil His garments in a bloody battle, in which He will rescue the Israelites who have been persecuted by Antichrist and his armies. Then He probably will go to the Valley of Megiddo, where the great armies of the world will be gathered in opposition to Him. It is impossible to predict the exact sequence of the battles in this war, but since everything culminates at Jerusalem, it would seem that He would go next to the Valley of Megiddo. This conflict could literally be called the battle of Armageddon and is described in Revelation 16:12-16.

> And the sixth angel poured out his bowl upon the great river, Euphrates, and its water was dried up, that the way of the kings of the east might be prepared. And I saw three unclean spirits, like frogs, come out of the mouth of the dragon, and out of the mouth of the beast, and out of the mouth of the false prophet. For they are the spirits of demons, working miracles, that go forth unto the kings of the earth and of the whole world, to gather them to the battle of that great day of God Almighty. Behold, I come as a thief. Blessed is he that watcheth, and keepeth his garments, lest he walk naked, and they see his shame. And he gathered them together into a place called in the Hebrew tongue Armageddon.

We have already examined in chapter 25 (Rev. 16) how the Euphrates River will dry up to make possible the way of the kings of the east with their vast hordes moving like a cloud to cover the land. The satanic trinity of Antichrist, the False Prophet, and the devil himself send out "three unclean spirits like frogs" out of the mouth of the beast and out of the mouth of the False Prophet, deceiving the kings of the earth to bring them into this great battle of Armageddon, where they will fight against Christ. The importance of the Valley of Megiddo for this conflict should not be overlooked. "Armageddon," from the translated "Har-Magedon" in the American Standard Version, comes from the Hebrew which means "Mount Megiddo." This place, mentioned only in Revelation 16:16, will be the final battleground between the forces of good and evil.

> The town of Megiddo guarded the pass which formed the easiest caravan route between the Plain of Sharon and the Valley of Jezreel, and the low mountains around were silent witnesses of perhaps more bloody encounters than any other spot on earth, continuing down to recent times. Hence the appropriateness of this place for the vast conflict pictured in Revelation 16. [31]

One commentator has stated that as far back as the time of Napoleon that great valley was claimed to be the most natural battleground of the whole earth. It has been noted that many great military generals have fought there. Thothmes fought there in 1500 B.C.; Rameses, 1350 B.C.; Sargon, 722 B.C.; Sennacherib, 710 B.C.; Nebuchadnezzar, 606 B.C.; Ptolemy, 197 B.C.; Antiochus Epiphanes, 168 B.C.; Pompeii, 63 B.C.; Titus, A.D. 70; Khosru, the Persian King, A.D. 614; Omar, A.D. 637; the Crusades under St. Louis of France, A.D. 909; Saladin, who conquered Richard the Lion-hearted in A.D. 1187; and the Ottoman forces, A.D. 1616. There Satan and his hordes have met God before. Three renowned mountains overlook this valley: Carmel, Gilboa, and Tabor. It was on Mount Carmel that the contest between Elijah's God and the devil-possessed, Baal-worshiping prophets of Jezebel took place. One of the mightiest conflicts in the Old Testament, it was not a battle of one man versus a nation, but God versus Satan, for on that day "the fire of the Lord fell" (1 Kings 18:38). One day it will fall again, but on that day the fire will be accompanied by the Lord himself: "And his feet shall stand in that day upon the Mount of Olives, which is before Jerusalem on the east" (Zech. 14:4).

This great battle of Christ versus Antichrist will conclude in a display of the omnipotent Christ, for He will utterly destroy Antichrist and his armies. The carnage of this battle is well described by Ezekiel.

> And, thou son of man, thus saith the LORD GOD: Speak unto every feathered fowl, and to every beast of the field, Assemble yourselves, and come; gather yourselves on every side to my sacrifice that I do sacrifice for you, even a great sacrifice upon the mountains of Israel, that ye may eat flesh, and drink blood. Ye shall eat the flesh of the mighty, and drink the blood of the princes of the earth, of rams, of lambs, and of goats, of bullocks, all of them fatlings of Bashan. And ye shall eat fat till ye be full, and drink blood till ye be drunk, of my sacrifice which I have sacrificed for you. Thus ye shall be filled at my table with horses and chariots, with mighty men, and with all men of war, saith the LORD GOD. And I will set my glory among the nations, and all the nations shall see my judgment that I have executed, and my hand that I have laid upon them. So the house of Israel shall know that I am the LORD, their God, from that day forward (Ezek. 39:17-22).

Ezekiel 38 and 39 primarily teach the destruction of the armies of Gog and Magog who come down against Israel, which will probably take place just prior to the Tribulation. Most Bible commentators call this the battle of Armageddon, but I think they speak amiss, for the following reasons.

1. In Ezekiel 38:1-39:16 Gog's armies come against Israel and are opposed by the western confederation of nations. Armageddon will find all the armies of the earth united against Christ.

> Sheba, and Dedan, and the merchants of Tarshish, with all its young lions, shall say unto thee, Art thou come to take a spoil? Hast thou gathered thy company to take a prey, to carry away silver and gold, to take away cattle and goods, to take a great spoil? (Ezek. 38:13).

2. In the battle described in Ezekiel, Israel is living in the land of unwalled villages in a time of peace, which will not be their lot in the latter half of the Tribulation Period.

3. Also, it takes seven years to burn the implements of war left on the ground after this great battle.

> And they that dwell in the cities of Israel shall go forth, and shall set on fire and burn the weapons, both the shields and the bucklers, the bows and the arrows, and the handspikes, and the spears, and they shall burn them with fire seven years (Ezek. 39:9).

This could not be carried out during the millennium; therefore we conclude it is accomplished before the Tribulation. Whether this is before or after the Rapture of the Church is impossible to ascertain, because the Bible does not teach conclusively that the Tribulation begins immediately after the Rapture. The Tribulation, begun by the signing of the covenant between Antichrist and Israel (Dan. 9:27), may or may not commence immediately following the Rapture. Therefore Ezekiel 39:17-22 goes beyond that immediate battle when Gog's armies come down against Israel, for in this latter section it is all the armies united together, as it will be at the end of the Tribulation.

Putting these passages together (Rev. 16:13-26 and Ezek. 39:17-22), we find that when Christ meets the armies of Antichrist in the Valley of Megiddo, they will come from east and west, north and south. He then will slay them with the sword that proceedeth out of his mouth (Rev. 19:15). All that will be left of these armies is little more than a gigantic feast for the birds of prey and other parasites.

The Battle of the Valley of Jehoshaphat

> For, behold, in those days, and in that time, when I shall bring again the captivity of Judah and Jerusalem, I will also gather all nations, and will bring them down into the Valley of Jehoshaphat, and will judge them there for my people and for my heritage, Israel, whom they have scattered among the nations, and parted my land.
>
> Proclaim this among the nations, Prepare war, wake up the mighty men, let all the men of war draw near; let them come up; beat your plowshares into swords; and your pruning hooks into spears; let the weak say, I am strong. Assemble yourselves, and come, all ye nations, and gather yourselves together round about; there cause thy mighty ones to

come down, O LORD. Let the nations be wakened, and come up to the Valley of Jehoshaphat; for there will I sit to judge all the nations round about. Put in the sickle; for the harvest is ripe; come, get down; for the press is full, the vats overflow; for their wickedness is great. Multitudes, multitudes in the valley of decision; for the day of the LORD is near in the valley of decision. The sun and the moon shall be darkened, and the stars shall withdraw their shining. The LORD also shall roar out of Zion, and utter his voice from Jerusalem, and the heavens and the earth shall shake; but the LORD will be the hope of his people, and the strength of the children of Israel. So shall ye know that I am the LORD, your God, dwelling in Zion, my holy mountain; then shall Jerusalem be holy, and there shall no strangers pass through her any more (Joel 3:1, 2, 9-17).

In this great battle there are "multitudes, multitudes in the valley of decision. For the day of the LORD is near in the valley of decision." These are more of the armies of the nations who will be brought into war by the lying spirits described in Revelation 16:13. This battle is also described in Revelation 14:14-20.

And I looked and, behold, a white cloud, and upon the cloud one sat, like the Son of man, having on his head a golden crown, and in his hand a sharp sickle. And another angel came out of the temple, crying with a loud voice to him that sat on the cloud, Thrust in thy sickle, and reap; for the time is come for thee to reap; for the harvest of the earth is ripe. And he that sat on the cloud thrust in his sickle on the earth, and the earth was reaped. And another angel came out of the temple which is in heaven, he also having a sharp sickle. And another angel came out from the altar, who had power over fire, and cried with a loud cry to him that had the sharp sickle, saying, Thrust in thy sharp sickle, and gather the clusters of the vine of the earth; for her grapes are fully ripe. And the angel thrust in his sickle into the earth, and gathered the vine of the earth, and cast it into the great winepress of the wrath of God. And the winepress was trodden outside the city, and blood came out of the winepress, even unto the horse bridles, by the space of a thousand and six hundred furlongs.

These passages show that the battle will take place at the time of God's judgment, for He will put in His sickle and reap a judgment harvest upon the nations of the earth for their persecution of the nation Israel. As a result of this conflict with Christ, "the blood came out of the winepress, even unto the horse bridles by a space of a thousand and six hundred furlongs."

The Battle of Jerusalem

The final battle in the war of the great day of God Almighty will be the battle of Jerusalem. The Antichrist and what is left of his armies, or more properly the advance guard of his armies, will storm Jerusalem. This last conflict between Satan and Christ until after the millennium will find Satan making one more fiendish effort to destroy the promised seed. Satan will order his armies to destroy the entire city of Jerusalem, but Christ will come to deliver her at the last moment, as clearly seen in Zechariah 12:1-9.

The burden of the word of the LORD for Israel, saith the LORD, who stretcheth forth the heavens, and layeth the foundation of the earth, and formeth the spirit of man within him. Behold, I will make Jerusalem a cup of trembling unto all the peoples round about, when they shall be in the siege both against Judah and against Jerusalem.

And in that day will I make Jerusalem a burdensome stone for all peoples; all that burden themselves with it shall be cut in pieces, though all the nations of the earth be gathered together against it. In that day, saith the LORD, I will smite every horse with terror, and his rider with madness; and I will open mine eyes upon the house of Judah, and will smite every horse of the people with blindness. And the governors of Judah shall say in their heart, The inhabitants of Jerusalem shall be my strength in the LORD of hosts, their God.

In that day will I make the governors of Judah like an hearth of fire among the wood, and like a torch of fire in a sheaf; and they shall devour all the peoples round about, on the right hand and on the left; and Jerusalem shall be inhabited again in her own place, even in Jerusalem. The LORD also shall save the tents of Judah first, that the glory of the house of David and the glory of the inhabitants of Jerusalem do not magnify themselves against Judah. In that day shall the LORD defend the inhabitants of Jerusalem; and he that is feeble among them at that day shall be like David; and the house of David shall be like God, like the angel of the LORD before them.

And it shall come to pass, in that day, that I will seek to destroy all the nations that come against Jerusalem.

For more details of the fighting examine the following Scripture, where more graphic details are given.

And the seventh angel poured out his bowl into the air, and there came a great voice out of the temple of heaven, from the throne, saying, It is done. And there were voices, and thunders, and lightnings; and there was a great earthquake, such as was not since men were upon the earth, so mighty an earthquake, and so great. And the great city was divided into three parts, and the cities of the nations fell; and great Babylon came in remembrance before God, to give unto her the cup of the wine of the fierceness of his wrath. And every island fled away, and the mountains were not found. And there fell upon men a great hail out of heaven, every stone about the weight of a talent; and men blasphemed God because of the plague of the hail; for the plague was exceedingly great (Rev. 16:17-21).

The Return of Christ

This is the most dramatic moment in world history! After winning four successive battles, Christ will set His feet on the Mount of Olives.

Behold, the day of the LORD cometh, and thy spoil shall be divided in the midst of thee. For I will gather all nations against Jerusalem to battle; and the city shall be taken, and the houses rifled, and the women ravished; and half of the city shall go forth into captivity, and the residue of the people shall not be cut off from the city. Then shall the LORD go forth, and fight against those nations, as when he fought in the day of battle.

And his feet shall stand in that day upon the Mount of Olives, which is before Jerusalem on the east, and the Mount of Olives shall cleave in its midst toward the east and toward the west, and there shall be a very great valley; and half of the mountain shall remove toward the north, and half of it toward the south (Zech. 14:1-4).

When Christ consumes all before Him through the earthquakes, lightnings, and the sword that proceeds out of His mouth, not only will the Holy Land be destroyed but the entire country will be literally bathed in the blood of unregenerate, God-hating, Christ-opposing men. It is hard for us to envision the hordes of troops from all over the world that will oppose Christ. Who can conceive of a time when the blood of slain men will flow as high as the horses' bridles by the space of a thousand and six hundred furlongs? That is just about the length of the entire land of Palestine! Naturally many skeptics and those who do not take the book of Revelation literally find it difficult to believe that so much blood could be shed. A point to be kept in mind is that part of the destruction of the troops around Jerusalem will include a hailstorm.

"And there fell upon men a great hail out of heaven, *every stone about the weight of a talent;* and men blasphemed God because of the plague of the hail; for the plague thereof was exceeding great" (Rev. 16:21). It is estimated that a talent weighs 135 pounds. Thus millions of pieces of ice will fall to the earth weighing 135 pounds, melting in the torrid heat of Palestine and mingling with the blood of those slain until the land of Palestine will be literally bathed in a bloody liquid that is almost too horrible to describe. What a price men pay for rejecting Christ!

Men Feed Birds

And I saw an angel standing in the sun; and he cried with a loud voice, saying to all the fowls that fly in the midst of heaven, Come and gather yourselves together unto the supper of the great God, that ye may eat the flesh of kings, and the flesh of captains, and the flesh of mighty men, and the flesh of horses and of them that sit on them, and the flesh of all men, both free and enslaved, both small and great. And I saw the beast, and the kings of the earth, and their armies, gathered together to make war against him that sat on the horse, and against his army (Rev. 19:17-19).

How like the futility of man in his pent-up wrath and antagonism against God! In one moment man stands in his physical might filled with hate and bitterness, attacking the very headquarters of the Christ. The next moment his flesh is food for the ravenous birds of the heavens. What a picture of the futility of man in pitting his will against Jesus Christ. Oh, that men might see that the wisdom of man is foolishness with God, who will triumph through the one He has ordained, the Lord Jesus Christ.

None escapes the wrath of the Lord Jesus as described in verse 21: "And the remnant were slain with the sword of him that sat upon the horse, which sword proceeded out of his mouth; and all the fowls were filled with their flesh."

Not one man will escape the warrior Christ in this last great battle. Those who resist Him during the Tribulation will be slain by Him in His glorious appearing. They will then have lost whatever chance they had for eternity.

32
Satan Bound in the Bottomless Pit

Revelation 20:1-3; 19:20

The evils in this old world are caused by the devil. No living creature in the known history of the universe has brought more misery to both natural and supernatural beings. One-third of the angels in heaven and a majority of the adult population of the earth have followed him in his rebellion against God. This will earn for them eternal separation from God in what our Lord described as "everlasting fire, prepared for the devil and his angels" (Matt. 25:41). The book of Revelation is not only a book of prophecy, unfolding the future, but a book of ending. This chapter contains the doom of Antichrist, the False Prophet, and Satan.

Have you ever wondered whether or not the devil is really an individual or just a figment of the imagination? In educational circles today it is considered unrealistic to assert that there is a supernatural power conveying evil to this earth. Many would admit that the only devil is the devil within you; others would say with Goethe when he spoke through the mouth of Mephistopholes, "I am the spirit of negation."

The popular idea of the devil, or Satan, is the caricature showing him in a red suit, long tail, horns on his head, and a pitchfork in his hand. Others present him in a similar fashion in hell, shoveling the stokers for all the workers of iniquity when they suffer the torments of the damned. These humorous presentations of Satan are, no doubt, at his instigation in an effort to minimize his importance, thus giving people a false security concerning his danger.

Like other subjects of great interest to the minds of men, particularly those that delve into the spiritual realm, Satan can be understood only through the authoritative Word of God. It is obvious from the Scriptures that Satan is not just a figment of the imagination, but a living personality. Thirty-five times he is called "the devil"; fifty-two times he is called "Satan" (which means enemy or adversary).

Matthew 13:19 tells us that after a person has heard the Word of God, "then cometh the wicked one, and catcheth away that which was sown in his heart." In the same chapter the Lord Jesus tells of a farmer who sowed the good seed of the Gospel, only to have an enemy come at night and sow false seeds. The Lord Jesus said, "The enemy that sowed them is the devil; the harvest is the end of the age; and the reapers are the angels" (v. 39). (It is interesting to note that these two statements are not taken from the parable, but from Jesus' own interpretation of the parable.) Peter believed in a personal devil, for in Acts 5:3 he asked Ananias, "Why hath Satan filled thine heart to lie to the Holy Spirit?" Peter also said, "Be sober, be vigilant, because your adversary, the devil, like a roaring lion walketh about, seeking whom he may devour" (1 Pet. 5:8). Obviously Peter not only believed that he was a living person, but that he was an adversary on the march. John believed in a personal devil, for in John 13:2 he wrote, "And supper being ended, the devil . . . put into the heart of Judas Iscariot, Simon's son, to betray him." The Apostle Paul also taught the personal existence of the devil when cautioning Christians to "put on the whole armor of God," taking adequate precautions "to stand against the *wiles of the devil.*"

It is obvious from these and many other passages in the Bible that Satan is a living personality. If you disagree, you must step over Jesus Christ, the Creator of all things (John 1:3), and Peter, John, and Paul, who were used of God to write twenty of the twenty-seven books in the New Testament. The big question is, where did he come from?

The Origin of Satan

Since Satan is a living person, he must have been created. God created all things, but how could a holy God create a wicked creature like Satan? That is one of the philosophical questions of the ages. If we turn to the philosophers, we will die in confusion, for like their conclusions on other subjects, the only thing in which they are consistent is their disagreement. We are thus obliged to attend to the source of wisdom, the Word of God.

Ezekiel 28:1-19 furnishes a picture of the background of Satan. The first ten verses comprise an oracle directed against the king of Tyre. The next oracle, however, beginning in verse 12, obviously goes beyond the king of Tyre to a supernatural being, for it attributes to him things that are beyond the capability of mortal man. For example, verse 13, "Thou hast been in Eden, the garden of God." This obviously refers to and describes an Eden that is even foreign to Adam and Eve. It is not a vegetable garden, with which they would have been familiar, but a rock garden.

It is not uncommon for world rulers to be indwelt by Satan himself. History records scores of rulers who sought to make up a government contrary to the will of God. This is the embodiment of the devil's plan, pitting his will against the will of God. Ezekiel 28:3 indicates that the king of Tyre was indwelt by a supernatural power, for it tells us, "Behold, thou art wiser than Daniel; there is no secret that they can hide from thee." It is a known fact that Daniel was one of the wisest living men in the Babylonian Empire, for to him was given the gift of determining hidden secrets. He was able to recall Nebuchadnezzar's dream and interpret it when none of the soothsayers, astrologers, or wise men of the Chaldean court could do so. In addition to this, as a righteous man he had the power of God upon his life, giving him wisdom, yet the king of Tyre also had this power, and in great abundance. The reason? The king of Tyre was indwelt by Satan himself, which clarifies why the kingdom was so blessed economically, for by craftiness in knowing the future, he could guide the country in its economic plans. So we see that this oracle is divided between that which speaks against the king of Tyre himself and that which censures the power or person within the king of Tyre, the devil. It is to the latter part of the oracle we direct our attention.

Ezekiel 28 twice speaks of Satan's creation: "the day that thou wast created" (v. 13b) and "Thou wast perfect in thy ways from the day that thou wast created . . ." (v. 15). The Hebrew word translated "create" means "to bring into existence that which has had no prior form or substance." God alone has the power to create. Thus there must have been a time when Satan was not, before God brought him into being. Satan is usually considered the greatest created being. Even the archangel Michael was reluctant to bring against him any railing accusations (Jude 9).

Satan was created "the anointed cherub that covereth" (Ezekiel 28:14). This implies leadership of the angelic host in the presence of the Shekinah Glory of God. It seems that Satan was not just an angel, but the leader of the cherubim, for he was "the anointed cherub that covereth." The covering referred to here connotes "protector" or "shading." As the cherubim stand in the presence of God today, so Satan once stood in charge of them.

The abode of Satan in that day was Eden, the garden of God, as described in 28:13, where he walked up and down in the midst of the stones of fire. This mountain of God is, no doubt, the heaven that Jesus referred to. It is the headquarters of God. Although God is omnipresent (that is, everywhere at one time), He nevertheless maintains a headquarters where Jesus Christ exists today, seated at His right hand. Satan, then, was created perfect (v. 15). Not until later was iniquity found in him; verse 16 adds, "Thou has sinned." Like all God's creatures to whom is given the treasure of a free will, Satan sinned because he chose to.

The Fall of Satan

Ezekiel 28:16, 17 teaches that Satan sinned and was judged for that sin, for God said, "Thou has sinned; therefore, I will cast thee as profane out of the mountain of God, and I will destroy thee, O covering cherub, from the midst of the stones of fire." Verse 17 indicates that it was pride, pride of his beauty and wisdom, that caused him to sin.

A more detailed description of this sin can be found in Isaiah 14. Here we find another oracle delivered against an earthly king, on this occasion, the king of Babylon. After he had dealt with the king living at that time, Isaiah went on to describe a person and experiences that transcend any mortal man, again referring to Satan within the king. In verse 12 we find that Satan at one time had been called "O, Lucifer, son of the morning! how art thou cut down to the ground." Then we note his pride, for he said in his heart —

"I will ascend into heaven,
I will exalt my throne above the stars of God;
I will sit also upon the mount of the congregation, in the sides of the north,
I will ascend above the heights of the clouds,
I will be like the Most High."

This attitude on the part of Satan constituted his sin.

The Problem of Evil

We now return to the problem of evil. Since God is Holy and could not create evil, who did? To ascribe the power of creation to Satan would tend to make him a god. There is no indication in Scripture that Satan can create anything (making something from nothing), but like other of God's creatures equipped with a free will, Satan can manufacture items from the things God has created. Satan evidently took the forces of God that were given perfect, combined them in an imperfect manner, and "manufactured evil." The force of evil in the world today, directed by the person of Satan and his cohorts, is a misapplication of the perfect forces and creation of God. This can be illustrated in the chemical world, composed of over one hundred elements which, when improperly combined, can become disastrous. For example, common table salt is made up of sodium, one of the necessities of life, but by changing the mixture and introducing other elements, sodium can become the basis for a deadly poison. In this sense Satan did not create evil any more than the chemist creates poison. He merely manufactures poison out of those things which God has already created.

Evil is a matter of the will. The basic sin in the force of evil is selfishness or pride, both stemming from the same root. Satan said, "*I* will ascend," "*I* will make my throne as the throne of God." *I* will, *I* will. His will, in opposition to the will of God, constituted the great sin, and it is so still! The man who pits his will against the will of God commits evil and brings on himself the judgment of God. It is contrary to the will of God not only for men to sin, but for men to reject Jesus Christ. The Word of God tells us that "it is not the will of your Father, who is in heaven, that one of these little ones should perish" (Matt. 18:14). Likewise, "The Lord is not . . . willing that any should perish, but that all should come to repentance" (2 Pet. 3:9). Are you like Satan, in rebellion against God's will, or are you submitted to God's will? He sinned willingly against the light he possessed. Have you?

The Conflict of the Ages

"Misery likes company" is a popular expression aptly describing Satan's activities against God's special creature, man. God created man perfect (in His likeness) with a free will for His pleasure (Rev. 4:11). He placed him in an ideal garden, filled with trees containing delicious fruit and two very special trees. One was called the "tree of life," the other the "tree of the knowledge of good and evil." Man was invited to eat of every tree in the garden but forbidden to eat of the "tree of knowledge." Actually, this was a test of man's obedience to God. Had he eaten of the "tree of life," the test would have been over. Instead, he was tempted by Satan (Gen. 3) and disobeyed God, introducing sin into the human race. But God immediately promised a remedy for man's sin, a Redeemer through the seed of the woman (Gen. 3:15). From that time on Satan has tried to destroy that seed of the woman in an attempt to defy God and hinder Him in fulfilling His will. He has also tried to incite men to do his will by urging them to do their own will, regardless of what God has said.

Many illustrations could be given of this conflict down through the ages. He had Cain murder Abel, thus eliminating the first two sons of Eve. He so polluted the human race through sin that by the time of Noah, some sixteen hundred years or so after Adam and Eve, only eight people were truly seeking God. After the flood we see such evidence of this conflict as Pharaoh's attempt to exterminate the Israelites and Haman's anti-Semitic attempt to exterminate all Jews during the Medo-Persian Empire. Many times before and during the life of Christ, the true seed of the woman, Satan tried to destroy Him: Caesar Augustus' decree of taxation that carried a pregnant woman, great with child, ninety miles away to pay taxes; Herod's edict to kill all babies two years of age and under; his three temptations of Christ, seeking to make Him stoop to his fallen level; the storm on the Sea of Galilee when Jesus lay sleeping in the ship; and many others. Failing to stop Christ's perfect sacrifice for the redemption of the world, he has done everything he can to thwart the Church of Jesus Christ. Although he has kept her from fulfilling her perfect role, he has not destroyed the Church because our

Lord has kept His promise, "I will build my church, and the gates of hades shall not prevail against it" (Matt. 16:18).

Church history reveals that after three centuries of incessant attempts to destroy the Church through persecution and burning all copies of the Word of God, the Church was so powerful that she supplanted paganism as the state religion of Rome in A.D. 312. At this point Satan stumbled upon his most effective tool — indulgence or endorsement. During the next thirteen centuries the Church gradually lost her light and her spiritual power by adopting some of the satanically inspired practices of paganism contrary to the Word of God. As these practices increased, Bible light decreased, bringing on what is called the Dark Ages. No jailor ever kept his prisoner more confined than did the church of Rome keep the Bible for hundreds of years. Not until the Reformation were people again exposed to the Word of God, but again Satan made an attack. The superstitious concepts of the Roman Catholic church that by this time were little more than modernized pagan thought turned many intellectuals during the Age of Enlightenment against Christianity. History affirms that many skeptics and rationalists were educated in Jesuit colleges. Being thus exposed to a characterization of Christianity through Catholic dogma and never exposed to the living Christ, these men turned to atheism and its resultant humanism that has deified man until he is a proud, arrogant creature. The difference between John Wycliffe, John Calvin, Martin Luther, Tyndale, and other Christian intellectuals and such men as Voltaire, Rousseau, Weishaupt, Mirabeau and other atheistic thinkers was the Word of God. Had the latter group been exposed to the living Christ through the pages of the Bible, history may well have been different and the world today a far better place in which to live.

For more than four hundred years Satan's attack on humanity in general and Christianity in particular has taken many forms until today the Church seems surrounded by a host of different attacking armies of evil. The French skepticism of Voltaire and Rousseau that ultimately produced the French Revolution spread through Germany and became German Rationalism. Other evil forces and concepts stemming from it were evolution, psychiatry, illuminism, Nietzscheism, socialism, communism, liberalism, and Nazism.

Modern college professors ridicule those who believe in the "conspiratorial view of history," which is to deny both the events of history and the power of Satan to accomplish his devious attempts. Who can truthfully deny that he is subverting society by destroying Christianity in order to set up his blasphemous religion headed by the Antichrist, whom men will worship instead of God? Who can question that he is trying to destroy all national governments in favor of a one-world government which he will head through the beast, or Antichrist?

Antichrist and the False Prophet Doomed

And the beast was taken, and with him the false prophet that wrought miracles before him, with which he deceived them that had received the mark of the beast, and them that worshiped his image. These both were cast alive into a lake of fire burning with brimstone (Rev. 19:20).

According to this verse Satan's two henchmen, Antichrist and his False Prophet, will be thrown bodily into the lake of fire. This should not seem strange, for if the two witnesses can be taken up into heaven, our Lord can certainly throw two wicked tools of Satan into the lake of fire.

Satan Bound a Thousand Years

And I saw an angel come down from heaven, having the key of the bottomless pit and a great chain in his hand. And he laid hold on the dragon, that old serpent, who is the Devil and Satan, and bound him a thousand years, and cast him into the bottomless pit, and shut him up, and set a seal upon him, that he should deceive the nations no more, till the thousand years should be fulfilled; and after that he must be loosed a little season (Rev. 20:1-3).

The twentieth chapter of Revelation introduces the marvelous reign of Christ on the earth. This period of time is the utopia man has yearned for and never found. That coming kingdom age is to be an age of righteousness. History proves that the only means to secure a righteous era is for Satan to be bound; as long as he is loose, man will have trouble.

Naturally there are those who ridicule the idea of a literal angel and chain and the literal binding of Satan. As one seminary professor said, "How big a chain would it take to bind Satan and how heavy should it be? We can't take this passage literally or we introduce many problems we cannot solve." Really? What does it matter how big or heavy the chain? Is anything too hard for God? Dr. Walvoord, another seminary professor and president, has noted, "The four instances in Scripture of the word for 'chain' in Revelation 20:1 give no reason for interpreting the word in other than its ordinary sense. Whatever the physical character of the chain, the obvious teaching of the passage is that the action is so designed as to render Satan inactive."[32]

The binding of Satan will restrict him from doing the thing he does best, for the third verse says that he should deceive the nations no more till the thousand years shall be fulfilled. During the millennium Satan will not deceive men about themselves, God, Christ, or eternity. For this reason we conclude that the majority of people living then will be believers. But Satan will be released at the end of the period for one last bit of deception, after which he, too, will be cast into the lake of fire.

Satan's Final Doom

"And the devil that deceived them was cast into the lake of fire and brimstone, where the beast and the false prophet are, and shall be tormented day and night forever and ever" (Rev. 20:10). The meaning of this verse is too clear to be questioned. God, by His supernatural hand, will take Satan and cast him forever into the lake of fire. This lake of fire is synonymous with Gehenna, which Jesus referred to as the eternal abode of the lost. A detailed description of Satan being cast into hell is found in Isaiah 14:9-17. Satan will be ridiculed by the kings of the earth, who will be cast into the lake of fire later, He who was so great and had deceived them now shares their state.

Many have jokingly presented Satan as ruling over hell. This, of course, is not true. No king of hell is "tormented day and night forever and ever." We should understand that hell is eternal — forever and ever.

Those who refuse to believe in hell must remember that Jesus Christ believed in hell, for He said, "Then shall he say also unto them on the left hand, Depart from me, ye cursed, into everlasting fire, prepared for the devil and his angels" (Matt. 25:41). Unquestionably the Son of God believed and preached that there was a hell to shun.

Someone will say, "Well, for the devil and his angels, yes, but not mankind." Ah, that is the tragedy! Mankind will suffer in hell all the torments prepared for supernatural creatures, for I call again your attention to 20:10 where, at the end of the millennial kingdom, after a thousand years, the beast and the False Prophet are still in torment. They were not burned up, but are still there, obviously alluding to the fact that one does not cease to exist in hell. Also, Revelation 20:11-15 makes it clear that all men whose names are not written in the book of life will be cast into this lake of fire.

The devil, as a master of deceit, is doing everything he can to keep men from believing in hell; but hell is a literal state of existence that will be the plight of all those who reject the Lord Jesus Christ. Don't aid Satan in making the mistake that will damn your soul for eternity. Receive the Lord Jesus Christ while there is still time. Call upon Him while He is near. The good news of the Gospel of Jesus Christ offers a remedy for sin, an escape from hell. The Lord Jesus is the Savior from sin. "Verily, verily, I say unto you, He that heareth my word, and believeth on him that sent me, hath everlasting life, and shall not come into judgment, but is passed from death unto life" (John 5:24).

33

The First Resurrection

Revelation 20:4-6

And I saw thrones, and they sat upon them, and judgment was given unto them; and I saw the souls of them that were beheaded for the witness of Jesus, and for the word of God, and who had not worshiped the beast, neither his image, neither had received his mark upon their foreheads, or in their hands; and they lived and reigned with Christ a thousand years. But the rest of the dead lived not again until the thousand years were finished. This is the first resurrection. Blessed and holy is he that hath part in the first resurrection; on such the second death hath no power, but they shall be priests of God and of Christ, and shall reign with him a thousand years (Rev. 20:4-6).

One of the most treasured subjects in the whole Bible is its indisputable presentation of life after death. Practically all men dream of walking from death to an eternal state of bliss, but only the Bible gives authoritative details about it. In fact, it is mentioned so frequently that if there is no resurrection of the dead, the Bible becomes unreliable. Every promise to believers concerning an afterlife is predicated on a bodily resurrection. The expression "the resurrection from among the dead" is found forty-nine times in Scripture.

Revelation 20:4-6 is the only passage which labels the believer's resurrection." It is important to understand that just as there are two phases to Christ's second coming, (1) the Rapture of the Church and (2) the glorious appearing, so there are three phases to the resurrection of believers: (1) the Church, (2) seven years later the Old Testament saints, and finally (3) the tribulation saints. John merges them all together when he says "Blessed and holy is he that hath part in the first resurrection."

Church Age Saints — Phase 1

The saints of the church age will be resurrected in the first phase of the first resurrection, as outlined in 1 Thessalonians 4:13-18. This passage describes the Rapture of the Church, when all Christians will be resurrected. This resurrection, according to Paul's writing, will concern only "the dead in Christ" and those "who sleep in Jesus"; thus it will be limited to the church age. Consisting solely of those who are born-again believers, the Rapture will include no Old Testament saints. "In Christ" is uniformly used in the New Testament wherever it has theological meaning as a reference to those who have been baptized by the Spirit into the body of Christ and is used in reference to saints after the day of Pentecost.

Old Testament Saints — Phase 2

Dr. Walvoord notes that the Old Testament seems to place the resurrection of Israel after the Tribulation. In Daniel 12, immediately after the description of the Tribulation in the preceding chapter, deliverance is promised Israel at the close of the Tribulation.[33]

> And at that time shall Michael stand up, the great prince which standeth for the children of thy people, and there shall be a time of trouble, such as never was since there was a nation even to that same time; and at that time thy people shall be delivered, every one that shall be found written in the book. And many of those who sleep in the dust of the earth shall awake, some to everlasting life, and some to shame and everlasting contempt. (Dan. 12:1, 2).

The suggestion that Israel will be resurrected prior to the tribulation saints results from a comparison of Revelation 19:7-9 with Psalm 50:1-6. At the marriage supper of the Lamb, Israel will be in attendance as friends of the Bridegroom. Since the marriage supper will occur just prior to the glorious appearing, we may assume that Israel will be resurrected *before* the glorious appearing, tribulation saints *during* or *at* His glorious appearing.

Tribulation Saints — Phase 3

Revelation 6:9-11 presents a picture of the tribulation saints who have been martyred for the testimony of the Lamb, waiting for the resurrection, for they were told to wait "yet for a little season, until their fellow servants also . . . should be fulfilled." This is an obvious reference to the end of the Tribulation Period, at which time, when Christ comes in His glory to set up His millennial kingdom, the tribulation saints will be resurrected.

This accords with our text:

> And I saw thrones, and they sat upon them, and judgment was given unto them; and I saw the souls of them that were beheaded for the witness of Jesus, and for the word of God, and who had not worshiped the beast, neither his image, neither had received his mark upon their foreheads, or in their hands; and they lived and reigned with Christ a thousand years (Rev. 20:4).

In order to live, the tribulation saints must be resurrected; this evidently will take place while the angel is binding Satan, just prior to or at the beginning of the millennial kingdom.

A chart of these three phases appears below.

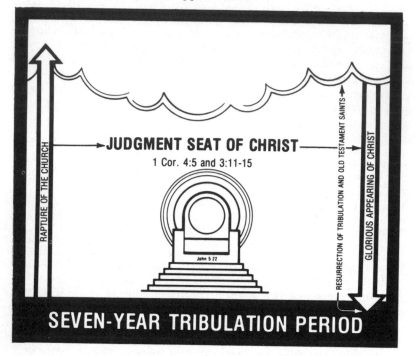

JUDGMENT SEAT OF CHRIST
1 Cor. 4:5 and 3:11-15

RAPTURE OF THE CHURCH

RESURRECTION OF TRIBULATION AND OLD TESTAMENT SAINTS

GLORIOUS APPEARING OF CHRIST

John 5:22

SEVEN-YEAR TRIBULATION PERIOD

The Happy and Holy Ones

Verse 6 describes the eternal state of those taking part in the first resurrection as "blessed and holy." "Blessed" means "happy"; caused by the blessing of God, such happiness is linked with holiness.

Man cannot enjoy uninterrupted blessing today because of sin. All those resurrected in the first or believer's resurrection will be resurrected holy. Thus the blessing of God, His original intent for man, will never be withheld, because man will live eternally holy and therefore eternally happy.

Those who partake of this first resurrection will be unusually happy because, according to verse 6, "on such the second death hath no power." Fear of death is one of the primary causes of present unhappiness. Man today can escape mentally from it or try to amuse himself until he is unaware of it, but if he thinks at all, it disrupts his happy state of mind. No Christian should fear death. The book of Revelation clarifies that our Lord and Savior holds the keys of death and hades (Rev. 1:18), and thus the second death, or lake of fire (Rev. 20:14, 15), has no power over us. No wonder the believer is happy. His participation in the first resurrection has made him impervious to the second death.

The Unbelieving Dead

Who are these who are called "the rest of the dead"? About this there is no question. They are the unbelievers of all ages. Luke 16:19-31 demonstrates that upon death they exist in hades. We shall see in our study of the last part of this chapter that they will be brought out of hades and judged, then cast alive into the lake of fire, which is the second death.

Since these unbelievers are not resurrected to life but to death, a state of separation from God, they are referred to as having part in the "second death." The second resurrection, then, is a resurrection to death.

The chart below sharply contrasts the nature of the two resurrections.

The First Resurrection	*The Second Resurrection*
Involves witnesses of Jesus (Rev. 20:4)	Involves those deceived by Satan (Rev. 20:8) and unbelievers (Rev. 21:8)
Will occur before the millennium (Rev. 20:4)	Will occur after the millennium (Rev. 20:11)
"And they lived" (Rev. 20:4)	"The dead" (Rev. 20:12)
Judged (Rev. 20:4)	Judged (Rev. 20:13)
Become priests and rulers with God and Christ (Rev. 20:6)	Tormented day and night (Rev. 14:10, 11)
God's sons (Rev. 21:7)	There was found no place for them (Rev. 20:11)
Over them the second death has no power (Rev. 20:6)	Cast into the lake of fire, which is the second death (Rev. 20:14, 15)
Enjoy life eternal (Matt. 25:46)	Suffer everlasting punishment (Matt. 25:46)
Happy and holy (Rev. 20:6)	Weeping and gnashing of teeth (Matt. 25:30)

What Determines Your Resurrection?

The answer to this question signifies clearly your relationship to the one who does the resurrecting. I can never consider 1 Thessalonians 4:13-18 without pointing out the condition of verse 14, "if we believe that Jesus died and rose again . . ." The condition of being a part of this resurrection of the believer rests in personal acceptance of Christ's death for our sins according to the Scripture and His resurrection on the third day according to the Scriptures. Right here it would be good to ask yourself, "Am I ready for that resurrection? Have I met the condition? Will I be a part of it?" If your answer is negative, may I encourage you to accept Christ now? Call upon Him, assured of His promise that "whosoever shall call upon the name of the Lord shall be saved" (Rom. 10:13).

Just as John announced, "Blessed and holy is he that hath part in the first resurrection," so it follows that tragic and horrible is he that has part in the second resurrection. For to have part in the second resurrection is to be eternally lost. At any cost, avoid that resurrection by calling upon the Lord Jesus today that you might partake of the first resurrection — that you might be one of Christ's at His coming. When I think of all these momentous events taking place at the end of time, I can't think of anyone I would rather belong to than Jesus Christ!

34

The Millennium and Church History

Revelation 20:1-6

And I saw an angel come down from heaven, having the key of the bottomless pit and a great chain in his hand. And he laid hold on the dragon, that old serpent, who is the Devil and Satan, and bound him a thousand years, and cast him into the bottomless pit, and shut him up, and set a seal upon him, that he should deceive the nations no more, till the thousand years should be fulfilled; and after that he must be loosed a little season.

And I saw thrones, and they sat upon them, and judgment was given unto them; and I saw the souls of them that were beheaded for the witness of Jesus, and for the word of God, and who had not worshiped the beast, neither his image, neither had received his mark upon their foreheads, or in their hands; and they lived and reigned with Christ a thousand years. But the rest of the dead lived not again until the thousand years were finished. This is the first resurrection. Blessed and holy is he that hath part in the first resurrection; on such the second death hath no power, but they shall be priests of God and of Christ, and shall reign with him a thousand years (Rev. 20:1-6).

The twentieth chapter of Revelation is one of the most controversial chapters in the Bible, not because it contains anything essentially complex, but because it touches on a subject of preconceived bias.

The Kingdom of Christ in Relation to His Coming

The first seven verses of this twentieth chapter refer six times to the kingdom of Christ lasting "one thousand years." This has triggered a major controversy, not because there is any question about the accuracy of the original text, but because it conflicts with concepts held by many theologians down through the years. This is the only place in the Bible that establishes the length of time for the coming kingdom of Christ. That there is to be a kingdom age during which Christ will rule on earth is really unquestioned by sincere Bible students who believe the Bible to be the Word of God, for it is one of the most frequently mentioned subjects in the entire Bible.

This kingdom period is often labeled "the *millennium,*" a term derived from the Latin words *mille* (one thousand) and *annum* (year). It is unfortunate that this term "millennium," meaning the one thousand years, has replaced the more scriptural term "kingdom." This period of time will literally fulfill the prayer our Lord taught His followers to pray, "Thy kingdom come." The point of controversy throughout church history regarding the kingdom essentially concerns whether Christ will come before the kingdom is ushered in or whether the world will get better and better and Christ will come to a righteous earth. By spiritualizing the Scripture, some have even tried to explain away the millennium. Three concepts, known as premillennialism, postmillennialism, and amillennialism, define the area of conflict. Before examining the nature of the kingdom itself, we must first review the content of these views, note when they were introduced into the church, and examine them in the light of Scripture.

Premillennialism — the Oldest View

The premillennial view is the view that holds that Christ will return to earth, literally and bodily, before the millennial age begins and that, by His presence, a kingdom will be instituted over which He will reign. In this kingdom all of Israel's covenants will be literally fulfilled. It will continue for a thousand years, after which the kingdom will be given by the Son to the Father when it will merge with His eternal kingdom. The central issue in this position is whether the Scriptures are to be fulfilled literally or symbolically. In fact, this is the essential heart of the entire question.[34]

Generally speaking, man's view of interpreting the Scriptures determines whether or not he is a premillennialist. For the most part, all who believe the Bible to be literal are premillennialists. Some Bible scholars, however, separate prophecy from other passages. They interpret the rest of the Bible literally, but whenever they come to prophecy, and particularly the book of Revelation, they tend to spiritualize it. Only in taking the Bible other than literally can a person be anything but a premillennialist.

The early Christians were almost unquestionably premillennialists. The New Testament itself indicates that the apostles expected the Lord to return and set up His kingdom in their lifetime. In Acts 1:6, just before our Lord ascended into heaven, the disciples asked a question that revealed their understanding: "Lord, wilt thou at this time restore again the kingdom to Israel?" The Lord did not deny that He would set up a kingdom, but He told them, "It is not for you to know the times or the seasons, which the Father hath put in his own power." So we find the disciples and those whom they taught anticipating the return of Christ and the establishment of His Kingdom. Many of the detractors of the premillennial position suggest that it is a relatively new theory, having come on the scene during the days of John Darby and others. The truth of the matter is that premillennialism held sway during the first three centuries of the early church and was known as "chiliasm." Dr. Pentecost quotes Lewis Sperry Chafer in his *Systematic Theology:*

> Chiliasm, so named from . . . *(chilioi)* — meaning "one thousand" — refers in a general sense to the doctrine of the millennium, or kingdom age that is yet to be, and as stated in the *Encyclopedia Britannica* (14th ed., S.V.) is "the belief that Christ will return to reign for a thousand years. . . ." The distinctive feature of this doctrine is that He will return *before* the thousand years and therefore will characterize those years by His personal presence and by the exercise of His rightful authority, securing and sustaining all the blessings on the earth which are ascribed to that period. The term *chiliasm* has been superseded by the designation *premillennialism;* and . . . more is implied in the term than a mere reference to a thousand years. It is a thousand years which is said to intervene between the first and second of humanity's resurrections. . . . In this thousand years . . . every earthly covenant with Israel will be fulfilled. . . . The entire Old Testament expectation is involved, with its earthly kingdom, the glory of Israel, and the promised Messiah seated on David's throne in Jerusalem.[35]

An additional definition of premillennialism appears in the writings of John Walvoord,

> Premillennialism generally holds to a revival of the Jewish nation and their repossession of their ancient land when Christ returns. Satan will be bound (Revelation 20:2) and a theocratic kingdom of righteousness, peace, and tranquillity will ensue. The righteous are raised from the dead before the millennium and participate in its blessings. The wicked dead are not raised until after the millennium. The eternal state will follow the judgment of the wicked. Premillennialism is obviously a viewpoint quite removed from either amillennialism or postmillennialism. It attempts to find a literal fulfillment for the prophecies in the Old and New Testament concerning a righteous kingdom of God on earth. Premillennialism assumes the authority and accuracy of Scriptures and the hermeneutical principle of a literal interpretation wherever this is possible.[36]

Some in the early church taught that since there were six literal days of creation after which God rested, so there would be six thousand-year periods of time given to man upon the earth, after which he would rest for a thousand years of peace. This view was revived somewhat during the nineteenth century but has not been given wide acceptance, probably because modern science teaches that there are millions of years of human history. It would not be surprising if this ancient theory were revived as we approach the year 2000, which will then total six thousand years of biblical history. This theory may become appealing in that it would parallel the many signs of the end of the age rapidly approaching — signs that are so obvious to the careful student of prophecy.

Toward the end of the third century the spiritualizing and allegorizing of Scripture began to take over theological thought, and together with the merging of ecclesiastical and governmental Rome under Constantine, premillennialism fell into disrepute. With the advent of Augustine and other Catholic theologians, theology and philosophy supplanted the study of Scriptures. The Dark Ages are well named, for the Word of God, which is the light of life, was hidden from men by the church that was entrusted with the responsibility of propagating it. As the light of God's Word was extinguished, the hope of the Church, the literal return of Christ to the earth, was eclipsed. Not until after the Reformation was there a revival of premillennialism. The first generation of reformers, such as John Calvin and Martin Luther, did not pursue the study of the second coming particularly but were heavily influenced by the theology of Augustine. Martin Luther had been a priest of the Augustinian order prior to his withdrawal from Rome, and thus his interpretation was affected by his previous training. The second generation of reformation Bible scholars saw a rise in the literal interpretation of Scripture, which in turn produced a reemphasis on the ancient "chiliasm," now given the more modern title of premillennialism.

J. Dwight Pentecost refers to some of the great post-Reformation scholars holding the premillennial view. "Among them will be found the greatest exegetes and expositors that the church has known, such as Bengel, Steir, Alford, Lange, Fausset, Keach, Bonar, Ryle, Lillie, MacIntosh, Newton, Tregeles, Ellicott, Lightfoot, Westcott, Darby, to mention only a few."[37] Even the critics of premillennialism suggest that the Brethren Movement arising in England and Ireland during the first part of the nineteenth century was largely responsible for popularizing the dispensational view of the Lord's return. It was sometimes called "Darbyism" because of the popular and practical writings of John Nelson Darby (1880-1882), one of its leaders.

After the turn of the century, Bible institutes sprang up throughout America with a heavy emphasis on a literal interpretation of the Bible. These schools have overwhelmingly advocated the premillennial view — not by premeditation, but because they are biblical literalists. No doubt the most important influence in popularizing the premillennial viewpoint has been the *Scofield Reference Bible*. (A new edition of the Scofield Bible has recently been printed, correcting the archaic words of the King James but retaining the beautiful style and dignity.) According to Dr. Walvoord,

> This edition of the Bible, which has had unprecedented circulation, has popularized premillennial teachings and provided ready helps of inter-pretation. It has probably done more to extend premillennialism in the last half century than any other volume. This accounts for the many attempts to discredit this work . . . The reputation of the Scofield Bible is curious because each succeeding writer apparently believes that his predecessors have not succeeded in disposing of this work once and for all. This belief apparently is well-founded, for the Scofield Bible continues to be issued year after year in greater numbers than any of its refuters.[38]

It is probable that the premillennial view, though subject to many attacks, will remain a dominant influence upon the Church until the Lord returns.

Amillennialism

Amillennialism holds that there will be no literal millennium on the earth following the second coming of Christ. It tends to spiritualize all the prophecies concerning the kingdom and attributes to the Church those prophecies relating to Israel. "Its adherents are divided on whether the millennium is being fulfilled now on the earth (Augustine) or whether it is being fulfilled by the saints in heaven (Kliefoth). It may be summed up in the idea that there will be no more millennium than there is now, and that the eternal state immediately follows the second coming of Christ."[39]

This view believes that Satan was bound at the first coming of Christ. Those who hold the amillennial point of view concede that it was first suggested by Augustine, who is said more than any other to have "molded the doctrines of the church of the Middle Ages."[40] Augustine was preceded by a dangerous philosophy introduced into the church by Clement of Alexandria and his student, Origen, who trained Dionysius. Together these three established the Alexandrian emphasis on spiritualizing the Scriptures. Due to the Greek emphasis on Platonic philosophy and Plato's allegorical teaching methods learned by these Alexandrian scholars, the third century ended in serious controversy. Although these men did not teach amillennialism, they did condition the brilliant-minded Augustine with the spiritualization of Scripture, and he produced it. His view of amillennialism became the accepted viewpoint of the church of Rome, which eventually took over most of the Church and thus propagated his view.

In his book, *The City of God,* Augustine presented the present age as a state of continual conflict between the "City of God" and the "City of Satan." This was ultimately to climax in the victory of the Church over the world. He felt that Satan was bound on the earth by Christ, according to Luke 10:18, and he considered the Roman government's endorsement of Christianity as a state religion evidence that the church was winning the conflict in his day. When this was completed, Christ would return and the eternal order would be established. "In arriving at his conclusion regarding the millennium Augustine used the principle of spiritualizing Scripture freely."[41]

Augustine is widely regarded as a brilliant theologian and thinker by evangelical Christians. That his teachings have left an indelible mark on the Church cannot be doubted, but that it has been a mark for good can very well be questioned. "His view of what the City of God is led him into teachings that have given rise to unspeakable misery, the very greatness of his name accentuating the harmful effects of the error he taught.

He, beyond others, formulated the doctrine of salvation by the Church only, by means of her sacraments."[42] This doctrine, plus his amillennialism and his conception of extreme predestination at the choice of God, would certainly give us a right to question the true value of Augustine's contribution to Christianity.

Naturally amillennialism during the age of Rome's dominance of the Christian scene waxed supreme. The early reformers took their cue from Augustine and similarly adopted amillennialism. This view was accepted by Calvin, Luther, Melanchthon, and many others. Amillennialism flourished during the early Reformation Period, particularly in the formalistic churches, until today it is "without question a majority view of professing Christians." Dr. Walvoord points out that the large number of amillennialists at present come from three sources: those who have become disenchanted with postmillennialism, those who came out of the church of Rome, and those identified with twentieth-century liberalism.[43] It is not right to say that all amillennialists are liberal, but it is correct that all liberals are amillennialists. One cannot hold the amillennial point of view without unusual spiritualization of Scripture, which is a most dangerous interpretation to follow.

Postmillennialism

Postmillennialism, the most recent of the three major views concerning the establishment of the millennium, is almost extinct at the present time. Postmillennialism basically suggests that the world will get better and better until the whole world is Christianized, at which time Christ will return to a kingdom of peace. This view was originated by Daniel Whitby (1638-1726), a Unitarian controversialist in England. Although he was censored for some of his heretical views, particularly on the subject of the Trinity, "many conservative theologians rapidly embraced and propagated his viewpoint on the millennium."[44]

Although this view was quite popular before the turn of the century and was given some impetus during the great revival movement of the Wesleys, Finney, Moody, and others, it has been almost eliminated as a result of the two great world wars, the great depression, and an overwhelming rise in moral evil. One theological professor I heard years ago observed, "The postmillennialist does not have a post to lean on." Many of those who once held the postmillennial view have changed to the amillennial position.

Reasons for Accepting the Premillennial View

There are many reasons for accepting the premillennial view of our Lord's return to this earth. Dr. Clarence Larkin, in his masterful book *Dispensational Truth,* offers the following evidence:

> 1. When Christ comes He will raise the dead, but the Righteous dead are to be raised before the Millennium, that they may reign with

Christ during the 1000 years, hence there can be no Millennium before Christ comes. Revelation 20:5.

2. When Christ comes He will separate the "tares" from the "wheat," but as the Millennium is a period of universal righteousness the separation of the "tares" and "wheat" must take place before the Millennium, therefore there can be no Millennium before Christ comes. Matthew 13:40-43.

3. When Christ comes Satan shall be bound, but as Satan is to be bound during the Millennium, there can be no Millennium until Christ comes. Revelation 20:1-3.

4. When Christ comes Antichrist is to be destroyed, but as Antichrist is to be destroyed before the Millennium there can be no Millennium until Christ comes. 2 Thessalonians 2:8; Revelation 19:20.

5. When Christ comes the Jews are to be restored to their own land, but as they are to be restored to their own land before the Millennium, there can be no Millennium before Christ comes. Ezekiel 36:24-28; Revelation 1:7; Zechariah 12:10.

6. When Christ comes it will be unexpectedly, and we are commanded to watch lest He take us unawares. Now if He is not coming until after the Millennium, and the Millennium is not yet here, why command us to watch for an event that is over 1000 years off?[45]

These are only some of the reasons why we anticipate the coming of Christ before the millennium. In addition, it is the clear teaching of the Bible. Revelation 19 pictures Christ coming literally to the earth, slaying Antichrist and casting him alive into the lake of fire. After Satan is bound, Christ will rule with His saints. A literal interpretation of Scripture will invariably point one to the premillennial return of Christ to the earth.

35

The Coming Kingdom
of Christ

Revelation 20:1-10

There can be no doubt as to the scriptural evidence for the coming kingdom of Christ. There are literally hundreds of verses in the Bible that predict an earthly kingdom of God on this earth, ruled by the Son of God and superseding all the kingdoms of the world. Most of the prophets treat this subject at length, often holding it out as a source of encouragement to the children of Israel in their most desperate days. In this chapter we will seek to give an exposition of some of the longer passages. The following chapter will contain a description of the millennium from some of the shorter passages; then the texts will be briefly compared in order to develop a composite picture of life during the millennium.

The Kingdom According to Daniel

In Daniel 2:31-35 we find the vision of Nebuchadnezzar recalled by Daniel, the great prophet. He sums up this description of the four world empires with these words:

> Thou sawest until a stone was cut out without hands, which smote the image upon its feet that were of iron and clay, and broke them to pieces. Then were the iron, the clay, the bronze, the silver, and the gold, broken to pieces together, and became like the chaff of the summer threshing floors; and the wind carried them away, that no place was found for them; and the stone that smote the image became a great mountain, and filled the whole earth (Dan. 2:34, 35).

The interpretation of this vision is provided by Daniel in verses 36-45. After describing the parts of the great image as four world kingdoms — (1) the head of gold as Babylon; (2) the breast and arms of silver representing the Medo-Persian Empire; (3) the belly and thighs of bronze representing the Greek Empire; and (4) legs of iron signifying the Roman Empire — he describes the ten toes and the feet of iron and clay as representing the ten kingdoms that will cooperate in establishing the Antichrist in his power during the Tribulation Period. In verse 44 we find the interpretation of the stone cut without hands, which grinds to powder the rest of the image.

> And in the days of these kings shall the God of heaven set up a kingdom, which shall never be destroyed; and the kingdom shall not be left to other people, but it shall break in pieces and consume all these kingdoms, and it shall stand forever. Forasmuch as thou sawest that the stone was cut out of the mountain without hands, and that it broke in pieces the iron, the bronze, the clay, the silver, and the gold, the great God hath made known to the king what shall come to pass hereafter; and the dream is certain, and the interpretation of it sure (Dan. 2:44, 45).

From this prophecy and the interpretation we see that a coming kingdom will pulverize all the known kingdoms of the world and expand until it "consume all these kingdoms, and it shall stand forever." This can be none other than the kingdom of God, for God shall "set up a kingdom, which shall never be destroyed." This, then, is the kingdom of God ruled over by Christ, who is symbolized in the Bible as a rock. His kingdom will be firmly established, filling the whole earth. We have already seen in Revelation 17 and 18 that nothing is more detrimental to humanity than religion and government. Man looks on government as a panacea to solve all of his ills. By contrast, the Bible teaches that a government without a benevolent despot of supernatural origin as its leader cannot be a happy experience, but a source of man's misery. The utopian kingdom predicted in this passage of Scripture will be the kingdom established on earth when Christ, the only truly benevolent despot who has already demonstrated His love for mankind, shall return.

The Coming King

The second Psalm, written by David under inspiration of the Holy Spirit, prophesies a day when the world's leaders will become so atheistic and antagonistic to God that they will pit their wills against Him in a gigantic atheistic, anti-Semitic conflict. The reaction of God, however, is laughter; He holds them in derision. This event evidently will take place in the middle of the Tribulation, when man's pride is so filled with his own importance that he thinks he can actually defy God. In so doing, he will incur the wrath of God, but first he will incur the laughter of God (v. 4). Verse 5 predicts His anger in these words: "Then shall he speak unto them in his wrath, and vex them in his great displeasure. Yet have I set my king upon my holy hill of Zion" (Ps. 2:5, 6).

God will establish His king in His holy place in His due time, regardless of the atheistic antagonism of men. A description of that kingdom follows in verses 7 through 9:

> I will declare the decree: The LORD hath said unto me, Thou art my Son; this day have I begotten thee. Ask of me, and I shall give thee the nations for thine inheritance, and the uttermost parts of the earth for

thy possession. Thou shalt break them with a rod of iron; thou shalt dash them in pieces like a potter's vessel.

This passage speaks of an absolute kingdom stretching to the uttermost parts of the earth. He will rid the world of all those kings who oppose Him. Verses 10 through 12 of this great Psalm conclude with God's challenge to world leaders concerning their present attitude: "Be wise now, therefore, O ye kings; be instructed, ye judges of the earth. Serve the LORD with fear, and rejoice with trembling. Kiss the Son, lest he be angry, and ye perish from the way, when his wrath is kindled but a little. Blessed are all they who put their trust in him."

If the world leaders responded that way today, this world would be an entirely different place in which to live.

Ezekiel's Prophecies of a World Kingdom

The prophecies of Ezekiel take on logical progression when in chapters 36 and 37 we find the restoration of the nation of Israel to the land of Palestine. Chapters 38 and 39 contain the abortive attempt of Russia to come down against Israel in the latter days just prior to the Tribulation. Then in chapters 40 through 48 we encounter a description of the millennial kingdom, particularly the temple and conditions for worship during the thousand-year period. Ezekiel goes into great detail regarding the matter of worshiping in the temple, even pointing out that the sacrificial systems will be reestablished. These sacrifices during the millennial kingdom will be to the nation Israel what the Lord's Supper is to the Church today: a reminder of what they have been saved from. No meritorious or efficacious work will be accomplished through these sacrifices. Instead, they will remind Israel repeatedly of their crucified Messiah, just as the Passover Feast reminded the nation of Israel for centuries that God delivered them from the land of Pharaoh by blood.

The Millennial Kingdom According to Zechariah the Prophet

Zechariah 14 contains an easily interpreted prophecy concerning the coming kingdom.

And it shall be, in that day, that living waters shall go out from Jerusalem; half of them toward the former sea, and half of them toward the hinder sea; in summer and in winter shall it be.

And it shall come to pass that every one that is left of all the nations which came against Jerusalem shall even go up from year to year to worship the King, the LORD of hosts, and to keep the feast of tabernacles. And it shall be that whoever will not come up of all the families of the earth unto Jerusalem to worship the King, the LORD of hosts, even upon them shall be no rain. And if the family of Egypt go not up, and come not, that have no rain, there shall be the plague, with which the LORD will smite the nations that come not up to keep the feast of tabernacles. This shall be the punishment of Egypt, and the punishment of all nations that come not up to keep the feast of tabernacles.

In that day shall there be upon the bells of the horses, HOLINESS UNTO THE LORD: and the pots in the LORD's house shall be like the bowls before the altar. Yea, every pot in Jerusalem and in Judah shall be holiness unto the LORD of hosts; and all they that sacrifice shall come and take of them, and boil in them; and in that day there shall be no more a Canaanite in the house of the LORD of hosts (Zech. 14:8, 16-21).

These verses make it clear that Jerusalem will serve as headwaters for the religious life of the people, the source of the waterways of the world: "living waters shall go out from Jerusalem" (v. 8). This refers to the "living waters" that Jesus promised the woman at the well in Samaria, indicating that the way of redemption and new life would be supplied from Jerusalem, the headquarters of the King. It also refers to the physical waters provided during that age from Jerusalem. It will be, then, the headwaters for both spiritual and physical waters. Verse 16 indicates that all people will come to Jerusalem to worship the king every year. Not to do so will be to incur the animosity of God "in the form of a plague." Verse 20 refers to the holiness of the kingdom. We have already seen that Satan will be bound during this millennial kingdom (Rev. 20:1-3); when Christ rules, it will be a true kingdom of holiness. The world has never known an era of holiness when standards were not established through the practices of men but by the mandate of God. During those days God's standards will be the law. Violators of that law will be severely punished.

The Millennium According to the Prophet Isaiah

The prophet Isaiah referred to the coming kingdom of Christ many times. The last two chapters in Isaiah contain specific information concerning that period.

> For, behold, I create new heavens and a new earth, and the former shall not be remembered, nor come into mind. But be glad and rejoice forever in that which I create; for, behold, I create Jerusalem a rejoicing, and her people a joy. And I will rejoice in Jerusalem, and joy in my people; and the voice of weeping shall be no more heard in her, nor the voice of crying. There shall be no more in it an infant of days, nor an old man that hath not filled his days; for the child shall die an hundred years old, but the sinner, being an hundred years old, shall be accursed. And they shall build houses, and inhabit them; and they shall plant vineyards, and eat the fruit of them. They shall not build, and another inhabit; they shall not plant, and another eat; for like the days of a tree are the days of my people, and mine elect shall long enjoy the work of their hands. They shall not labor in vain, nor bring forth for trouble; for they are the seed of the blessed of the LORD, and their offspring with them. And it shall come to pass that, before they call, I will answer; and while they are yet speaking, I will hear.
>
> The wolf and the lamb shall feed together, and the lion shall eat straw like the bullock, and dust shall be the serpent's food. They shall not hurt nor destroy in all my holy mountain, saith the LORD. (Isa. 65: 17-25).

This passage reveals some of the most descriptive details known of the millennium. Such information is given to show that Jerusalem will be the place of rejoicing; no more weeping will be heard within the city. Jerusalem has known much heartache throughout its many centuries. One if its walls is famous today as a place of wailing — wailing for the future restoration of the greatness of Israel. This will be fulfilled during the millennium.

Verse 20 indicates that the life span of man will be increased as in the days before the flood. Believers will evidently live until the end of the millennium, some almost a thousand years. However, unsaved people will be given a hundred years in which to receive Christ. If they reject Him, they will die on their hundredth birthday.

Economic stability will be the standard during that period. For instance, men will not build houses and let others occupy them due to death or sickness. It will be a stable time when people can enjoy the fruits of their efforts. "They shall not labor in vain, nor bring forth for trouble" (Isaiah 65:23).

The text also indicates that God will answer His people speedily during the millennial kingdom, even while they are in the midst of praying, and sometimes "before they call." God will anticipate the needs of the people, supplying those needs in many cases before they call upon Him.

The curse will be lifted from the animals, who will enjoy peace one with another, for "the wolf and the lamb shall feed together." The only exception seems to be the serpent, which will continue to crawl on his belly and eat dust.

The Renovation of the Earth by Fire

Most prophetic teachers acknowledge that the earth will be renovated by fire, but for some reason they insist on locating the event at the end of the millennium. Verse 17 of this text, preceding the description of the millennium, indicates that God will "create new heavens and a new earth" *before* the kingdom is established. That means He will create a new atmospheric heaven around the earth and reestablish the earth on a far better basis. We learn from other passages that the waste areas of the world will be recreated. Today three-quarters of the earth is wasted by water, making much of the earth unusable. At that time vast mountain ranges will be leveled, and the earth will enjoy a complete resurfacing before the millennium.

The same period of time is referred to in 2 Peter 3:1-16. The apostle predicted that in the last days scoffers would come, "walking after their own lusts" and suggesting that since no changes have occurred in creation since the beginning, there is no reason to believe the fact of His coming. They reject the change of the flood and the destruction of Sodom and Gomorrah. The apostle pointed out to believers that they are not so limited by such biased concepts. He further stated that "one day is with the Lord as a thousand years," meaning that God's promises of two thousand years ago are only two days old. Then he predicted that the day of the Lord would usher in a time of cataclysmic change upon the earth. His terms indicate that the earth will be dissolved, meaning the surface of the earth in the day of the Lord. The day of the Lord, then, will dawn with the destruction of this old earth and the refurbishing of its surface, upon which God will establish His kingdom of righteousness.

The times described by Peter are upon us. Certainly every child of God today should heed His words: "Seeing, then, that all these things shall be dissolved, what manner of persons ought ye to be in all holy living and godliness, looking for and hasting unto the coming of the day of God . . ." (2 Pet. 3:11, 12a).

Satan's Final Conflict

And when the thousand years are ended, Satan shall be loosed out of his prison, and shall go out to deceive the nations which are in the four quarters of the earth, Gog and Magog, to gather them together to battle; the number of whom is as the sand of the sea. And they went up on the breadth of the earth, and compassed the camp of the saints about, and the beloved city; and fire came down from God out of heaven, and devoured them. And the devil that deceived them was cast into the lake of fire and brimstone, where the beast and the false prophet are, and shall be tormented day and night forever and ever (Rev. 20:7-10).

We have already seen that at the beginning of the millennial kingdom Satan was bound by a great angel in the bottomless pit (20:1-3). That means that men will not be tempted by Satan for a thousand years. Today there are three forces of temptation: the world, the flesh, and the devil. During the millennial kingdom men will only be tempted by the flesh. Because the world will be a kingdom of righteousness, administered by the Lord, the righteous judge, no lewd, suggestive, worldly temptations can mislead men. Neither will they be tempted of Satan, for he will be chained. Therefore the only source of temptation will be the flesh. In such an environment the overwhelming number of people will no doubt be saved.

Isaiah 65:20 casts some interesting light on this future time of great world blessing: "There shall be no more in it an infant of days, nor an old man that hath not filled his days; for the child shall die an hundred years old, but the sinner, being an hundred years old, shall be accursed."

This verse suggests that believers will live after birth to the end of the millennium, since a man will be reckoned a child when he is a hundred years old. But it also indicates that if a person reaches a hundred years of age and is not a believer, he will be accursed, or die. In other words, those living during the millennium are given a hundred years to make a decision to receive Jesus Christ as Savior and Lord. If they do so, they will continue living to the end of the millennium, paralleling the age of man before the flood. If they do not receive Jesus Christ, they will die at a hundred years of age. If we add to this the absence of worldly temptation and the absence of satanic temptation, plus the fact that the whole world will know the Gospel of Christ in that day, we can reasonably conclude that this will be the most ideal environment in which to raise children.

Like Adam and Eve and others after them until the flood, couples in the millennium can have children not only the first hundred years but for hundreds of years thereafter. Since it will be a time of unprecedented blessing and food supply, a couple will conceivably have as many children as they desire. The conclusion seems justifiable, then, that the overwhelming majority of people on the earth during the last nine hundred years will be Christians. Of course, many born during that age will reject Christ and die by their hundredth birthday. And even though they die at a hundred years of age, there will be ample time for these unsaved to propagate a generation of unbelievers to follow Satan when he is released at the end of the kingdom age. "And shall go out to deceive the nations which are in the four quarters of the earth, Gog and Magog, to gather them together to battle; the number of whom is as the sand of the sea" (Rev. 20:8).The statement "the number of whom is as the sand of the sea" does not necessarily mean that the overwhelming majority of the world population at that time will follow Satan. Instead, it indicates that a fantastic population explosion will occur during the millennium and that many born during the last century will follow him. Comparatively speaking, this will be a youth movement, since all who follow Satan in his last rebellion will be under a hundred years of age.

The Massive Millennial Soul Harvest

It is most encouraging to realize that many times more people will be converted during the millennial kingdom than will be lost. Because the millennial population will undoubtedly exceed the total world population during the whole of biblical history, and since the majority living at that time will be Christians, it follows that there will be more people in heaven than in hell. Consequently, God will achieve His grand purpose for the majority of mankind — their salvation (2 Pet. 3:9).

Another truth revealed in verse 8 concerns the consistency of the work of Satan in every generation. After being incarcerated for a thousand years, he will immediately proceed to do what he has done for centuries — *deceive the nations*. Satan is the master deceiver of men. His conflict-of-the-ages program, as previously outlined, is just a sample of the extent of his consistent deception. He will inspire Antichrist to be a master deceiver during the Tribulation (2 Thess. 2:9, 10). This deception always finds itself in opposition to the will of God. Whenever man rebels against God, whether he be Cain, Lamech, Nimrod, Pharaoh, Judas, Voltaire, Thomas Paine, or Robert Ingersoll, he is deceived by the devil. In a practical sense Satan tries two basic approaches with man today: he either gets him to turn against Christ because he loves unrighteousness, or he gets him to rebel against God by willfulness. It is most practical here to pause and ask you, reader, if you have received

Jesus Christ as your personal Lord and Savior. If you have not, then you are deceived by the devil. You may dress up your deception with a host of excuses and a long list of reasons, but it is nothing more than Satan's deception. It would be well for you to contemplate the final outcome of Satan's own rebellion lest you share it with him. "And the devil that deceived them was cast into the lake of fire and brimstone, where the beast and the false prophet are, and shall be tormented day and night, forever and ever" (Rev. 20:10). God, in His infinite wisdom, did not cast Satan into the lake of fire at the time He cast in his two chief tools, the beast and the False Prophet. They were cast in at the end of the Tribulation, before the millennium began (Rev. 19:20). He saved Satan out of that judgment because He wanted to give the last generation who would not live to be a hundred years of age a final choice. This will make unanimous the experience of all men who have ever lived, from the time of Adam and Eve to the very end of human history. All men have been tempted of Satan and have had to decide whether to respond to God or Satan. All men have sinned, but God through the gift of His Son, Jesus Christ, on Calvary's cross has given men a second chance. That second chance, available only on this earth, involves the acceptance of God's gift of salvation in the person of His Son. If you have never made that decision, you are making a contrary decision right now.

It should be pointed out here that although the beast and the False Prophet, or Antichrist and the False Prophet, were cast into the lake of fire a thousand years before the devil, they remained there, for the passage says, "where the beast and the false prophet are." Since these are men, suffering the torments of the damned for a thousand years, we may clearly discern the capability of man to suffer that length of time. The plight of Satan for eternity as given in verse 10 is the same plight as that shared by all those who have been deceived by him: he "shall be tormented day and night forever and ever." There is no reason to symbolize these simple words. The same words used to describe the eternal blessings of those who receive Christ and the eternal nature of God are used to describe the plight of the lost — "forever and ever." If God is eternal and believers will enjoy Him eternally, why should we arbitrarily suggest that it is not possible for man and Satan to be tormented day and night forever and ever?

36

The Great
White Throne

Revelation 20:11-15

And I saw a great white throne, and him that sat on it, from whose face the earth and the heaven fled away, and there was found no place for them. And I saw the dead, small and great, stand before God, and the books were opened; and another book was opened which is the book of life. And the dead were judged out of those things which were written in the books, according to their works. And the sea gave up the dead that were in them; and they were judged every man according to their works. And death and hades were cast into the lake of fire. This is the second death. And whosoever was not found written in the book of life was cast into the lake of fire (Rev. 20:11-15).

You have just read the most awesome passage found anywhere in the Bible. It confronts man with the sobering truth of his ultimate encounter with God. The story is told of the great statesman Daniel Webster, toward the twilight of his life, attending a luncheon meeting with some younger government leaders. The chairman of the group turned to Mr Webster and asked, "What is the greatest thought that has ever passed through your head?" Quick as a flash Daniel Webster replied, "My accountability to God." Nowhere is man's accountability to God more clearly defined than in this passage of Scripture.

One truth must be emphasized at the outset of this study: this ultimate judgment of the Great White Throne is for unbelievers only. Who are these "dead, small and great"? They are *dead* now in trespasses and sins because of their rejection of Jesus Christ, and they will be resurrected in order to appear at this judgment. Revelation 20:5 states, "The rest of the dead [that is, those who were not raised before the thousand years begin] lived not again until the thousand years were finished." It is noteworthy that in verse 12 the dead are referred to as "small and great." This would mean the "small and great" intellectually, physically, financially, positionally, and in every other way. This group will include

300

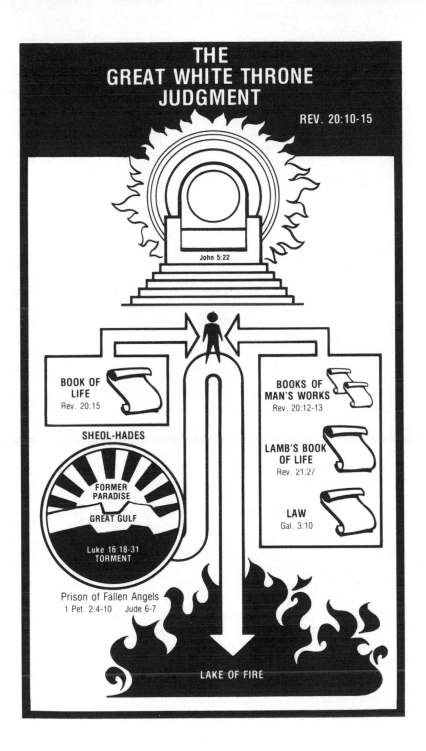

all the dead without Jesus Christ. Verse 13 adds further information: "The sea gave up the dead that were in it, and death and hades delivered up the dead that were in them." The sea will give up all those who were drowned or buried at sea, never having accepted Jesus Christ. Death represents the grave, hades the place of torment where their spirits have gone. What these two verses teach is that we may expect a physical resurrection uniting the dead, whether their ashes are in the grave, in a mausoleum, on the earth, or in the sea. Those ashes will be resurrected and united with the soul and spirit as they arise from the place of torment, and in this resurrected form they will stand before the throne.

The Book of Life Opened

At this point we find a set of books and a book being opened. Notice the wording in verse 12: "and the books were opened; and another book was opened, which is the book of life."

For the identity of these books we must look beyond our immediate text to another passage in the Word of God. Galatians 3:10 contains the description of the second book by which man will be judged. Those who have lived under the hearing of the law of God will be judged by it. Unless man accepts the mercy of God in the person of His Son, there is no way he can be found righteous, because "all have sinned, and come short of the glory of God" (Rom. 3:23).

Revelation 20:12 indicates that some of the books at this Great White Throne Judgment will be the books of man's works, for "the dead were judged out of those things which were written in the books, according to their works." The same thing is said in the latter part of verse 13. In some way every man must have a recording angel who in this life is tabulating everything he does. In connection with this thought it is well to consider Ecclesiastes 12:14: "For God shall bring every work into judgment, with every secret thing, whether it be good, or whether it be evil." In this final hour the books of man's works, or his deeds, will be open.

If man today is able by the means of photography to capture the action of a man's life and by the means of plastic recordings to record a man's voice, certainly Almighty God can play His divine film and recording at the judgment. Not only will the actions and words of man be recalled at this judgment, but "every secret thing." This would indicate that God has a special x-ray camera that takes photographs of the thoughts and intents of the heart, which will be revealed in that day.

D. L. Moody, the famous evangelist, used to say that if a man ever invented a camera that could take a picture of the human heart, he would starve to death, for people would refuse to have this revealing picture exposed. In that awesome day all the secret thoughts and intents of the heart will be revealed by the projection of God's special x-ray, taken from the books of man's deeds.

Verse 12 indicates not only that the dead will be judged out of the books according to their works, but that another book is opened, which is the Book of Life. Here we discover that a recording angel maintains a book called the Book of Life. The New Testament refers to this Book of Life eight times; and although the Old Testament does not call it the Book of Life, three times it mentions a book in which names are written. To properly understand the Book of Life, you must realize that there are really two Books of Life. One is called the Book of Life, the other, the Lamb's Book of Life. These are definitely not the same! The Book of Life contains the names of the living. The Lamb's Book of Life is a book belonging to the Lord Jesus Christ, the "Lamb of God which taketh away the sin of the world." The book, then, is His. Jesus Christ came into the world to save sinners and, as He repeatedly said, "to give unto them eternal life." Very clearly, then, the Lamb's Book of Life is the book of Jesus Christ in which are entered the names of those who have received His eternal life (Rev. 13:8). I am personally inclined to believe that in this book will appear only the names of the believers who have lived since the cross.

Revelation 13:8 indicates that during the Tribulation Period the people who will worship the Antichrist are those whose names are *not* written in the Book of Life of the Lamb slain from the foundation of the world. Revelation 21:27 tells us that the only people who will enter into the Holy City are "they who are written in the Lamb's book of life." It is therefore absolutely essential that one have his name written in this book.

There are two major differences between the two books. First, the Book of Life seems to contain the names of all living people, whereas the Lamb's Book of Life includes only the names of those who call upon the Lamb for salvation. Second, and without doubt most important, it is possible to have one's name blotted out of the Book of Life, but not out of the Lamb's Book of Life. In Revelation 3:5 we find that "He that overcometh, the same shall be clothed in white raiment; and I will not blot his name out of the book of life." An overcomer here is one clothed in the white garments of Christ, for he is a believer to whom is imputed the righteousness of Christ. Therefore his name will not be blotted out of the Book of Life. In Exodus 32:33 we find, "The LORD said unto Moses, Whosoever hath sinned against me, him will I blot out of my book." It is therefore possible to have one's name blotted out of the Book of Life because of sin. But it is impossible to have one's name removed from the Lamb's Book of Life.

> And if any man shall take away from the words of the book of this prophecy, God shall take away his part out of the book of life, and out of the holy city, and from the things which are written in this book (Rev. 22:19, KJV).

Some try to tell us that this reference to God taking away a man's "part" out of the Book of Life suggests that anyone who detracts from the book of Revelation and its prophecy will lose his rewards; but this cannot be, for the only "part" we have in the Book of Life is our name. We have no indication in Scripture that anything but our name is written in the Book of Life, for the deeds of a man are not recorded there, but in the books of our works.

We see, then, that there are three reasons for having one's name blotted out of the Book of Life: (1) for sinning against God, (2) for not being clothed in the righteousness of Christ through the new birth, and (3) for taking away from the words of the book of this prophecy.

Revelation 20:15 establishes the importance of the Book of Life, for it tells us, "And whosoever was not found written in the book of life was cast into the lake of fire." In a sense this is God's double check at the Great White Throne Judgment, for as a man comes forward, he will be judged by the book of law, by the Lamb's book of life, and by the deeds done in the flesh taken from the books of his works. Then, just before he is cast into the lake of fire, he is given a double check. The recording angel will look through this book, "and whosoever was not found written in the book of life was cast into the lake of fire."

This double check in the Book of Life points out a consistent scriptural principle — that there are only two kinds of people. The Bible repeatedly refers to believing or unbelieving, saved or unsaved, condemned or not condemned, righteous or unrighteous, just or unjust, wise or unwise. This principle is maintained here: there are those whose names are written and others whose names are not written in the Book of Life. In that hour there will be no hesitation, no indecision, for either a man's name is written or it is not written in the Book of Life. It must be one way or the other.

One does not need to have his name entered in the Book of Life, for if he is alive it is already there; God is "not willing that any should perish, but that all should come to repentance" (2 Pet. 3:9). But to keep it there, he must also have his name written in the Lamb's Book of Life.

Jesus Christ said, "I am the bread of life; he that cometh to me shall never hunger, and he that believeth on me shall never thirst" (John 6:35). The Lord Jesus repeatedly invited men to come to Him, for He alone is the way, the truth, and the life. John 5:24 tells us, "verily, verily, I say unto you, He that heareth my word, and believeth on him that sent me, hath everlasting life, and shall not come into judgment, but is passed from death unto life." The steps of salvation here are very clear: (1) "he that heareth my word" and (2) "believeth on him that sent me." That means trusting in Him. Trust that Jesus Christ is the way of salvation, the one who has come to seek and to save that which was lost, including you. The man who trusts has everlasting life. Those whose names are written in the Lamb's Book of Life are those who have received this everlasting life. *Have you?*

Revelation 20:11-15 includes two books of vital importance. Your name is already written in the Book of Life, but is it written in the Lamb's Book of Life? That depends entirely on what you have done with the Lord Jesus Christ. If you have accepted Him, it is; if you have not accepted Him, it is missing. The answer to the question determines your eternal destiny.

37

The New Heaven
and New Earth

Chapter 21 of Revelation introduces the eternal future planned by
God, the ultimate purpose of God for man. Not much space in Scripture
is given to this eternal state, but enough is revealed to assure every
believer's heart about the future. Revelation 21 and 22 provide
more details of this state than can be found anywhere else in the Bible.

Seven New Things

There are seven new things revealed in these two chapters that form
a fitting introduction to the eternal future God has prepared for those
who love Him.

a new heaven (21:1)	a new paradise (22:1-5)
a new earth (21:1)	a new source of light (22:5)
new Jerusalem (21:2)	a new place for God's
new things (21:5)	throne (22:3)

The Destruction of This Earth

Three destructions of the earth are described in the Bible, one past
and two yet to come. The first destruction came when the flood covered
the earth in the days of Noah, sparing only eight just persons (Gen. 6-8).
In one of the best-known promises in the Old Testament, however, signified
by the rainbow, God promised Noah that He would never again destroy
the earth by flood.

Nevertheless, two passages in the Bible predict that God will yet
destroy the earth. One destruction will come by fire, after which He
will restore all things. Isaiah 65:17-20 speaks of a restored earth, and
2 Peter 3:4-14 describes the judgment of fire reserved or kept in store
"against the day of judgment." The other destruction is described in our
text (Rev. 21:1). Many Bible scholars seem to identify Isaiah 65:17-20

306

and 2 Peter 3:4-14 with Revelation 21:1. This presents some serious problems. A thorough examination of the two passages would suggest that since death appears in the Isaiah 65 passage, Isaiah was obviously not talking about the eternal order, but the millennial kingdom. And since 2 Peter 3:10 refers to the day of the Lord, I am inclined to believe that he meant the second catastrophic event that will come upon the earth, producing a refurbished earth to begin the millennium. We have already examined Revelation 20 concerning the final insurrection of Satan, when again the heaven and the earth will be polluted by the rebellion of Satan. Therefore the words of our Lord, "Heaven and earth shall pass away, but my words shall not pass away" (Matt. 24:35), evidently will be fulfilled when the prophecy of Revelation 21:1 is completed: "And I saw a new heaven and a new earth; for the first heaven and the first earth were passed away, and there was no more sea."

The Destruction of Heaven

Why will God destroy the heaven? Very simply, because the atmospheric heavens are filled with evil. Whenever we read about heaven in the Bible, we should keep in mind that there are three heavens: the atmospheric heaven around the earth; the stellar heaven, which contains the great galaxies that we view on a starry night; and the third heaven, or the throne of God, as referred to in 2 Corinthians 12:2 and Revelation 4 and 5. Our text in no way indicates that God will destroy the stellar heaven, or the place of His headquarters, but the atmospheric heaven, which is the abode of Satan. Ephesians 6:12 indicates that Satan, who is the "god of this earth," and his emissaries are performing spiritual wickedness in heavenly places. Therefore, after the final rebellion of Satan, God will destroy this earth that is so marred and cursed by Satan's evil. He will include the atmospheric heaven to guarantee that all semblance of evil has been cleared away.

The New Heaven and the New Earth

Because it is God's plan for man to inhabit the earth forever in fulfillment of His promises, after He does away with this planet as we know it, He will create a new heaven and a new earth better than anything this world has ever known, including the Garden of Eden. Many changes will be made, as seen in verse 1: "And there was no more sea." Two-thirds of the present earth's surface is covered with water; the remaining one-third includes a large area rendered worthless due to mountains and deserts. Thus only a small percentage of the earth's surface is inhabitable. Nothing in the text indicates a new earth limited to the twenty-five thousand miles in circumference and eight thousand miles in diameter of the present earth. It may be much larger; the Bible just does not say. But one thing is certain — the new earth will be the Christian's heaven. When the Christian talks about going to heaven, he means in the soul state, provided he dies before the Rapture. After the resurrection of the body, believers will come to earth to reign with Christ during the millennium. After that thousand years we will live forever on the new earth described in our text. Although it will have a river and an abundance of water, it will not have land surface wasted by seas.

"And I, John, saw the holy city, new Jerusalem, coming down from God out of heaven, prepared as a bride adorned for her husband" (Rev. 21:2). The Holy City which our Lord went to prepare for His saints (John 14:1-3) will come down from heaven to this earth. This new Jerusalem, fully described in the chapter, will be the city of righteousness, prepared by God for the enjoyment of His people. The expression "prepared as a bride adorned for her husband" is a symbolic reference to the preparation of a virtuous young woman for the day of her marriage. God has been preparing the city for almost 2,000 years. Since Christ instantly called worlds and universes into being, one can scarcely imagine the glories of this city which has been so long in preparation.

"Behold, the tabernacle of God is with men, and he will dwell with them." Another outstanding characteristic of this new city is that God's tabernacle will no longer be in the third heaven, for He will move His headquarters to the new earth and will literally take up His abode in the new Jerusalem. We simply do not have the mental capacity to comprehend the significance of living in an economy where God Himself exists.

"And they shall be his people, and God himself shall be with them, and be their God." The people who inhabit the new eternal earth will be those who voluntarily received Christ by faith — before the flood, before Abraham, before Christ, during the church age, throughout the Tribulation and millennium. As indicated in our study of the millennium, far more people will inhabit heaven than hell. God has a special love for mankind. That love will have all eternity to express itself upon His obedient creatures. To the true Christian heaven is not just a place where all things are new, but a place where he can enjoy unbroken fellowship with God.

"And God shall wipe away all tears from their eyes." The wiping away of all tears, means that the normal reaction of present life, sorrow, will be eliminated. As Job tells us, "Man is born unto trouble, as the sparks fly upward" (Job 5:7). Trouble produces sorrow, sorrow produces tears. But these tears will be wiped away. The passage may also indicate that we will lose the power to remember loved ones who rejected Jesus Christ. With the keenness of mind which we will possess in the resurrection, doubtless the compassionate heart of God's people would burst with sorrow and heaven would be ruined were they to contemplate the lost plight of their loved ones condemned for eternity. God in His marvelous mercy will wipe away all tears from their eyes. That probably means He will erase all remembrance of the unsaved from the minds of believers.

"There shall be no more death." The specter of death, the natural result of sin, will at last be removed.

". . . neither sorrow, nor crying, neither shall there be any more pain." Since sin produces death and sickness, a sinless eternity will not admit these miseries.

"And he that sat upon the throne said, Behold, I make all things new." This is almost a certain indication that God will enter into a dimension that we cannot yet comprehend. He plans an entirely new way of life for us. For instance, many have wondered about the marital status of Christians during the millennium, but I think that whatever remorse we experience when thinking of life for eternity without marriage can easily be offset by faith when we accept the fact that all things will be new. As marvelous as a good Christian marriage is today, it will be totally eclipsed by sheer delight and unquenchable joy during the eternal future in whatever experience that newness possesses.

The Lord Reiterates His Earthly Offer

"And he said unto me, It is done. I am Alpha and Omega, the beginning and the end. I will give unto him that is athirst of the fountain of the water of life freely" (Rev. 21:6). When the Lord Jesus walked this earth, He said to the people of His day, "If any man thirst, let him come unto me, and drink. He that believeth on me, as the scripture hath said, out of his heart shall flow rivers of living water" (John 7:37, 38). To the woman at the well, who was drinking natural water, He said, "Whosoever drinketh of the water that I shall give him shall never thirst, but the water that I shall give him shall be in him a well of water springing up into everlasting life" (John 4:14). The Lord Jesus is the same yesterday, today, and forever. Two thousand years after He made these promises we find Him prophetically reiterating the same thing to man. "I will give unto him that is athirst of the fountain of the water of life *freely*."

Man's Thirst for God

Anyone who has ever traveled will testify that the ancient civilizations and present cultures are extremely religious. Man's religious inclination is a testimony of his thirst for God. Man will not thirst in the eternal state, but will be satisfied over and above all that he can ever ask or think. His thirst will be supplied by Christ Himself. If nothing else, this speaks of the complete satisfaction of the place that lasts forever.

Only Believers Will Inhabit the Eternal Order

"He that overcometh shall inherit all things, and I will be his God, and he shall be my son" (Rev. 21:7). One of the most wonderful concepts in the Bible is the father-son relationship between God and a Christian. This verse indicates that it will go on forever in heaven as on earth.

The Eternal State of the Lost

But the fearful, and unbelieving, and the abominable, and murders, and fornicators, and sorcerers, and idolaters, and all liars, shall have their part in the lake which burneth with fire and brimstone, which is the second death (Rev. 21:8).

Since God has been talking about the eternal state of the blessed, He contrasts that with the eternal state of the lost, described more fully in 20:11-15. Here He refers to them as those that have part in the second death. These are the individuals who through fear or unbelief or a lust for sin rejected Jesus Christ.

The location of verse 8 in the eternal plan of God revealed in this book should be carefully examined. It once and for all repudiates the suggestion of many that there is a second chance for sinners after death. This unscriptural concept is made to appease the conscience of those libertines who have rejected Jesus Christ and prefer sin. But not one shred of evidence in the Bible substantiates it! And certainly the location of this verse pronounces an everlasting death sentence on the idea. Here in the eternal order men are pictured already in their eternal state as based on their own personal decision about God; He refers to them one last time, revealing that they will have their part in the "lake which burneth with fire and brimstone, which is the second death."

Only Two Kinds of People

Verses 7 and 8 confirm the consistent presentation throughout the entire Bible that God sees only two kinds of people, believers and unbelievers. Either they are overcomers who have part with God eternally or unbelievers who have their part in the lake of fire. You who read this chapter should examine yourselves to see which kind of person you represent. Are you one who has trusted Jesus Christ and thus through Him will inherit all things, or are you among those who have rejected Him? If so, you will have your part in the lake of fire. It is not too late to heed the Savior's call: "I will give unto him that is athirst of the fountain of the water of life freely." He will receive you right now if you will call on Him. If there is any question in your mind as to whether you have ever invited Jesus Christ into your life, may I urge you to get down on your knees right now and ask Him to save you.

38

The New Jerusalem

Revelation 21:9-27

The dazzling glory of the new city of Jerusalem that is to come down from God out of heaven is beyond man's ability to comprehend. It is pictured in Revelation as the ultimate preparation of God for man's habitation. This same difficulty of comprehension may be observed in the ministry of many of our missionaries. As they live amid a primitive tribe for a period of time and try to communicate to them scenes of the outside world, the natives look at them in bewilderment. How can one describe an electric stove to a native who has never seen anything but an open wood fire? How can one describe refrigeration to a native who has known nothing but the cool of the mountain stream that runs by his thatched hut? Only by comparing the unknown with the known is the missionary able to convey facts of the outside world or, more importantly, the eternal truths of God. Thus it is with us as we try to comprehend the glories God has prepared in the Holy City for them that love Him. He has used terms and descriptions with which we are familiar to describe the things that are beyond our finite frame of reference.

The New Jerusalem — the Bride of Christ

And there came unto me one of the seven angels who had the seven bowls full of the seven last plagues, and talked with me, saying, Come here, I will show thee the bride, the Lamb's wife. And he carried me away in the Spirit to a great and high mountain, and showed me that great city, the holy Jerusalem, descending out of heaven from God, having the glory of God; and her light was like a stone most precious, even like a jasper stone, clear as crystal (Rev. 21:9-11).

Inviting John to a high mountain, the angel showed him the Bride, the Lamb's wife. But the Bride is described in the tenth verse as that great city, the holy Jerusalem. This does not suggest that the Bride of Christ is a city. Since chapter 19 described the marriage of the Lamb

311

to the Bride, we find that the Bride is not a physical city but the Church. The Holy Spirit here is telling us about that city which the Lord promised His disciples in John 14 when He said, "I go to prepare a place for you." Now that prepared city is coming to the earth, and the inhabitants of it are the members of the Bride. When this city comes to the earth, it will be a people-filled city — people in their resurrected bodies after the millenium, prepared to dwell with Christ for eternity. That is why this city, which surpasses the splendor of anything comprehended by man, is called the Bride, the Lamb's wife. A city is more than buildings and streets, for these are merely the means of providing for the inhabitants which compose the real city. As we shall see, others will be permitted into the city, but the city, which will be the capital of the eternal order of God, is "the bride, that great city, the holy Jerusalem."

"Having the glory of God." This city is the crowning feature of the creation of God, the unique habitation of the redeemed for eternity. To emphasize the glory of God, the verse pictures a dazzling light "like a jasper stone, clear as crystal." Someone has suggested that perhaps the city will be surrounded with a ball of crystal light; just as the earth is round, this square city would have a round sphere of light. Certainly it will reflect the glory of God.

The City Foursquare (Rev. 21:12-21)

"And had a wall great and high." The great wall around this city suggests that it will be an exclusive city. It will not be built for protection, of course, since no enemies will threaten in the eternal order, but it will stand as a visual reminder that all men do *not* have access to God.

". . . and had twelve gates, and at the gates twelve angels, and names written on the gates, which are the names of the twelve tribes of the children of Israel." Obviously the number twelve takes on great significance in this city. Since the Bible is inspired by God, we can expect, in spite of the various authors and the length of time engaged in its writing, that there would be an unusual, even supernatural continuity in the use of numbers. Students of Bible numerology point out this thrilling thread of consistency that attests to divine authorship. For example, it is suggested that the number *one* stands for unity, *two* for union, *three* for the Trinity; *four* is the number of the earth (four directions: east, west, north, south), *five* the divisional number (five wise and five foolish virgins), *six* the number of man. Everything in the Bible that has to do with man seems to be in the realm of six. For instance, "Six days shalt thou labor." The height of the average man is about six feet. The Antichrist uses for his number three sixes, called the number of man. *Seven* seems to be the perfect number, or God's number. He instructed Solomon to put seven steps in the throne of the temple. He established the divine calendar on the basis of seven days, and He has described seven millennia of time relating to man's activity on earth. *Twelve* seems to be the governmental or administrative number. Thus we find multiples of twelve in the administration of God's universe — twenty-four thrones around the altar and one hundred forty-four thousand outstanding Christians, as described in Revelation 14, who will probably gain special leadership positions during the millennial kingdom. Note the many references to twelve in this picture of the Holy City that will come down from heaven.

Twelve gates. Twelve entrances will always be open for God's people to have access to the city. Verse 13 indicates there will be three gates on each of the four sides of this gigantic city.

Twelve angels. Again we see the relationship of angels in the eternal order and their work with man.

The names of the twelve tribes. These indicate clearly that the children of Israel will have ready access to this splendid heavenly city. Since angels are mentioned, it seems that each of the tribes has its angel, just as each of the churches, according to Revelation 2 and 3, has its angel.

Twelve foundations. The foundation walls will be magnificent beyond comprehension. In verses 19 to 21 they are described as "garnished with all manner of precious stones." Dr. Walvoord described the twelve foundations as follows:

> The various foundations are represented as layers built upon each other, each layer extending around all four sides of the city.
>
> *Jasper* — gold in appearance but like clear glass in substance, namely, glass with a gold cast to it;
>
> *Sapphire* — a stone similar to a diamond in hardness and blue in color;
>
> *Chalcedony* — an agate stone from Chalcedon (in Turkey), thought to be sky blue with other colors running through it;
>
> *Emerald* — introduces a bright green color;
>
> *Sardonyx* — a red and white stone;
>
> *Sardius* — refers to a common jewel of reddish color, also found in honey color which is considered less valuable. The Sardius is used with Jasper in Revelation 4:3 in describing the glory of God on the throne;
>
> *Chrysolyte* — a transparent stone, golden in color, according to the ancient writer Pliny, and therefore somewhat different from the modern pale green Chrysolyte stone;
>
> *Beryl* — is sea green;
>
> *Topaz* — is yellow-green and transparent;
>
> *Chrysoprasus* — introduces another shade of green;
>
> *Jacinth* — is a violet color;
>
> *Amethyst* — is commonly purple.
>
> Though the precise colors of these stones in some cases are not certain, the general picture here described by John is one of unmistakably beauty, designed to reflect the glory of God in a spectrum of brilliant color. The light of the city within shining through these various colors in the foundation of the wall topped by the wall itself composed of the crystal-clear Jasper forms a scene of dazzling beauty in keeping with the glory of God and the beauty of His Holiness. The city is undoubtedly far more beautiful to the eye than anything man has ever been able to create, and it reflects not only the infinite wisdom and power of God but also His grace as extended to the objects of His salvation.[46]

". . . and in them the names of the twelve apostles of the Lamb." The foundation stones contain the names of the apostles, indicating that the Holy City will contain the redeemed by the blood of Christ, who heard the Word through the faithful witnessing of the servants of God in the first century, the apostles. The gates of the city contain the names of the twelve tribes, clearly indicating that they were the vehicles through which the oracles of God were revealed in the Old Testament days, and to whom Messiah came. Both the Old Testament saints and the Church will have access to this city, but each time they enter they will be reminded of their debt to the nation Israel and to the apostles.

> And he that talked with me had a golden reed to measure the city, and the gates of it, and its wall. And the city lieth foursquare, and the length is as large as the breadth; and he measured the city with the reed, twelve thousand furlongs. The length and the breadth and the height of it are equal (Rev. 21:15, 16).

Most Bible scholars agree that the root meaning of the Greek word for furlong indicates that each side of this city is approximately fifteen hundred miles long. Thus the city itself would stretch from about the eastern seaboard of the United States to the Mississippi River on one side and from the Canadian border to the Gulf of Mexico on the other. In addition to the length and breadth, the city will be the same in height. Bible scholars do not agree as to whether this will be a square-shaped or a pyramid-shaped city. Even though the pyramid concept seems more in keeping with our understanding, the literal interpretation of the text would suggest that it will be square. The great size, of course, will afford sufficient space for a habitation of the saints of all ages. Can you imagine the view from your apartment house overlooking the Holy City and extending as far as the éye can see from an elevation of fifteen hundred miles?

"And the twelve gates were twelve pearls." Every gate will be one pearl, large enough to cover the gateway to this hugh city, so they will be larger than men. In addition, the streets of the city will be "pure gold, as it were, transparent glass," clearly indicating that we will walk on gold. In our mind's eye, gazing at this city with its fantastically beautiful and expensive stones for foundations, its gigantic pearl gates, and its gold streets, we are impressed with the superiority of this city over anything known to man. Today we use concrete and stone for foundations, scarcely the most beautiful material on earth, but selected because of its durability, supply, and low cost. Our streets are made of concrete or blacktop for the same reasons. By comparison, the Holy City of God will be so magnificent that we will literally walk on precious metals that today are used for costly bracelets, necklaces, and rings. The city's foundation will consist of precious stones that today are used for ornaments only and, due to their expense, are very small. This presentation, when taken literally, emphasizes the phenomenal omnipotent power of our God.

No Temple in the City

"And I saw no temple in it; for the Lord God Almighty and the Lamb are the temple of it" (Rev. 21:22). From the very beginning of man's creation God has chosen to fellowship with man. He fellowshiped with Adam and Eve before they sinned. After the fall, a place of sacrifice had to be established. In Genesis 4, we find that Cain and Abel both knew about building an altar on which to place a sacrifice. The antediluvian and postdiluvian patriarchs also used this approach to God through sacrifice. In the days of Moses God established the tabernacle, where He would come to tabernacle in the midst of the people in what is known as the Holy of Holies. Under the reign of Solomon this was transferred to the temple, but due to Israel's apostasy they lost this choice position with God. Finally the Lord Jesus Christ came to tabernacle with men and to become the complete sacrifice. When He departed, He sent His Holy Spirit to tabernacle in the bodies of believers.

In the millennial kingdom a memorial temple will provide a place for men to worship God because they will still be in the deciding process, exercising their free will to worship God or reject Him. However, in the eternal order there will no longer be a need for a "temple," or dwelling place of God, as the Greek word implies. Instead, God Himself will be there with His Son and with the Holy Spirit. This would make not only the Holy City one grand and glorious temple or place of worship but the eternal earth. This coincides with Hebrews 11:9, 10 where Abraham specifically is described as looking for a city, meaning the heavenly Jerusalem. This will be realized by Abraham and the sons of Abraham who have responsed to Jesus Christ their Messiah (Heb. 12:22-24). One can scarcely visualize the Holy City without the resurrected Abraham because of that passage of Scripture. This certainly indicates that though the Holy City is referred to as the Bride of the Lamb, it will be inhabited not just by the Church, but all those who have been redeemed through His blood.

God Is the Light of the City

The Bible teaches us that "God is light, and in him is no darkness at all (1 John 1:5). Therefore the sun and the moon will no longer be needed in the eternal order. God Himself will provide sufficient light by His very presence. Several times this text declares that God will be the light of this city. One of the most beautiful statements I have ever read on this subject came from the pen of Dr. Lehman Strauss.

> In that city which Christ has prepared for His own there will be no created light, simply because Christ Himself, who is the uncreated light (John 8:12), will be there. . . . The created lights of God and of men are as darkness when compared with our Blessed Lord. The light He defuses throughout eternity is the unclouded, undimmed glory of His own Holy presence. In consequence of the fullness of that light, there shall be no night.[47]

Think of it! No darkness forever!

Everyone Has Access to the Holy City

And the nations of them which are saved shall walk in the light of it, and the kings of the earth do bring their glory and honor into it. And the gates of it shall not be shut at all by day; for there shall be no night there. And they shall bring the glory and honor of the nations into it (Rev. 21:24-26).

Some have suggested that because nations and kings are referred to here, during the eternal order God will continue to separate the people by nations. This could well be His intent and meaning, fully in accord with His planned purpose for man since Genesis 10. However, hundreds of years transpired before the flood when He apparently did not interject difference of nationalities. The word "nations" comes from the root word "Gentiles" and is so translated in many places in the Bible. Therefore this reference could be to Gentiles who have received Christ. The kings would be saved men who were kings or world leaders, men of renown, who during the eternal order will come into the Holy City and give their glory to Christ. If this is the interpretation, it would concern men who have come to God, not on the basis of being kings, but as poor lost sinners who need a Savior. I am inclined to believe that this is the best interpretation, indicating that the Holy City will contain the Old Testament saints and the Church, plus the tribulation saints who are redeemed from every tongue and tribe and nation (Rev. 7:9). It will also include the people of many nationalities who become believers during the millennial age. This could reach back into the days of Israel, when God had His witnesses in other nations of which we have little or no record. Many of these people no doubt responded to God but, knowing nothing of Israel, were thus not Jewish proselytes.

One of the fascinating things about this city is that there will be no night there and that the gates of it shall not be shut at all by day. No time will be wasted in sleep, but we will be able to enjoy all the eternal ages to come. There will never be a closing of the pearly gates, for man will forever have access to the presence of God and the Holy City.

Those Excluded From the Holy City

"And there shall in no way enter into it anything that defileth, neither he that worketh abomination, or maketh a lie, but they who are written in the Lamb's book of life" (Rev. 21:27). As a reminder of God's consistent pattern in dealing with men, those who reject His Son will not be admitted to His city. For we learn that "anything that defileth" or "he that worketh abomination, or maketh a lie" will not be admitted. That would include everyone in human history who has not received Christ. Thus all those who die in their defilement and lies and abominations are excluded from the city. In essence, only by acceptance of Jesus Christ does man have access to the ultimate blessing that God has prepared for him. This closing scene of chapter 21, with its inspired presentation of the glories that God has established for men in the eternal order, should inspire every man to receive Jesus Christ and thus have his name written in the Lamb's Book of Life.

39

Heaven on Earth

Revelation 22

The last chapter of the book of Revelation contains a final description of that heavenlike earth which God has prepared for them that love Him. It also contains a final challenge of a loving Savior who came into this world to die for the sins of man and has consistently sent His Spirit through His servants to convey His loving Gospel message to them.

It is a fitting way to end not only this greatest of all books on prophecy, *The Revelation of Jesus Christ,* but also the library of God's Word. The Bible opens and closes with basically the same type of setting. In the first two chapters of Genesis we encounter God's description of creation and the heavenlike conditions on the earth prepared for man. That last two chapters of Revelation describe the eternal heaven that God will re-establish for man. All the chapters between contain the great conflict of the ages as man turns his back upon God and as He seeks to draw man unto Himself. In all these books man is consistently presented with the opportunity to worship God freely by faith or reject Him by rebellion of will.

The first five verses of our text contain six challenging descriptions of the heavenlike earth. As you bear in mind the heavenly city and the new earth described in chapter 21, we turn now to additional details to make this utopian state even more ideal.

"And he showed me a pure river of water of life, clear as crystal, proceeding out of the throne of God and of the Lamb" (22:1). Man cannot live without water in this life or seemingly in the life to come. A study of history shows that man has always looked for water. The ideal fortress cities of the world have been located on high points of ground which had an adequate water supply. Many have died and nations have had to change their homeland because there was no adequate water supply. In the eternal paradise God has planned for man, an abundance of water will proceed out of the throne of God Himself, indicating that God will be the source of that life-giving substance.

". . . the tree of life, which bore twelve kinds of fruits, and yielded her fruit every month" (22:2). When Adam and Eve sinned, God forbade them to eat of the Tree of Life. Genesis 3:22-24 states,

> And the LORD God said, Behold, the man is become as one of us, to know good and evil; and now, lest he put forth his hand, and take also of the tree of life, and eat, and live forever; therefore the LORD God sent him forth from the garden of Eden, to till the ground from where he was taken. So he drove out the man; and he placed at the east of the garden of Eden cherubim, and a flaming sword which turned every way, to guard the way of the tree of life.

This text clarifies that the eating of the Tree of Life makes man live forever. Man was forbidden to eat of that tree because he had first taken of the Tree of the Knowledge of Good and Evil, but in the eternal future he will be able to eat of it; this testifies of the eternity of man's blessed future state.

The fruit of this tree will spring forth all year. In our backyard we have two avocado trees that yield fruit alternately every six months. In the paradise of God trees will continually bring forth fruit twelve months of the year, possibly with a variety of fruit. These two verses make it clear that we will be able to eat and drink in the eternal future. Whether we will eat meat or not isn't mentioned, but we will be able to eat fruit.

One aspect of the Tree of Life has brought some controversy relative to the expression "and the leaves of the tree were for the healing of the nations" (22:2). It would be better to translate the word "healing" as health, not indicating that anyone will be sick during the eternal order, but that the Gentiles or nations that have been inhuman to each other throughout their known history will be healed in their relationship toward each other and will thus live equitably and fairly.

"And there shall be no more curse, but the throne of God and of the Lamb shall be in it, and his servants shall serve him" (22:3). The curse that God placed on the earth as a result of the sin of man in the Garden of Eden will be partially lifted during the millennium, but completely lifted during the eternal order. Therefore, the unlimited potential of the planet God gave to man will be realized for the first time. As proof that it will be an uncursed earth, God will place His throne here. His angelic hosts and men will be with Him as His servants. No rebellious servants of God will exist in the eternal order.

"And they shall see his face; and his name shall be in their foreheads" (22:4). The seal of God in the forehead of man is an indication that he is the blood-bought child of God through faith in Jesus Christ. The superiority of the future status of man in relationship to God is seen in the fact that man will actually be able to see God. Today we know that "no man has seen God at any time"; in that order we will literally see God.

"And there shall be no night there; and they need no lamp, neither light of the sun; for the Lord God giveth them light" (22:5). As expressed in chapter 21, God Himself, who is light, will be the light of that eternal order, suggesting a consistency of heat and light. Today we are dependent on the sun for light and heat, changing our apparel or place of residence or habits of agriculture in accordance with the cycle of the sun. At that time we will not be limited to external objects, for God Himself will provide a consistent pattern of light that is ideally suited for man.

These first five characteristics bring beauty and warmth into the heaven-like condition of the new order. The description in chapter 21 of the stone city with golden streets, pearl gates, and rock foundations does not suggest the warmth that the water, vegetation, and light described in this chapter convey. This indicates that it will not be a cold city, like some of our concrete jungles, but a city furnishing the warmth of natural life that is so advantageous to human beings. Ecology-minded Christians will be happy to know that.

". . . and they shall reign forever and ever" (22:5). Just as we rule with Christ for a thousand years, so we will reign with Him forever. Whether that will involve universes, galaxies, and other planets can only be guessed at. But one thing is for certain: we will reign with Him forever.

Since the Bible does not in any one passage offer a complete presentation of God's plan for man's activities during the eternal order, it would be good to examine the characteristics delineated by Dr. Pentecost in his book *Things to Come.*

A. *A life of fellowship with Him.*

For now we see through a glass, darkly; but then face to face (1 Cor. 13:12).

Beloved, now are we the sons of God, and it doth not yet appear what we shall be: but we know that, when he shall appear, we shall be like him; for we shall see him as he is (1 John 3:2).

I will come again, and receive you unto myself, that where I am, there ye may be also (John 14:3).

And they shall see his face (Rev. 22:4).

B. *A life of rest.*

And I heard a voice from heaven saying unto me, Write, Blessed are the dead which die in the Lord from henceforth: Yea, saith the Spirit, that they may rest from their labours; and their works do follow them (Rev. 14:13).

C. *A life of full knowledge.*

. . . now I know in part; but then shall I know even as also I am known (1 Cor. 13:12).

D. *A life of holiness.*

And there shall in no wise enter into it any thing that defileth, neither whatsoever worketh abomination, or maketh a lie: but they which are written in the Lamb's book of life (Rev. 21:27).

E. *A life of joy.*

And God shall wipe away all tears from their eyes: and there shall be no more death, neither sorrow, nor crying, neither shall there be any more pain: for the former things are passed away (Rev. 21:4).

F. *A life of service.*
And there shall be no more curse: but the throne of God and of the Lamb shall be in it; and his servants shall serve him (Rev. 22:3).

G. *A life of abundance.*
I will give unto him that is athirst of the fountain of the water of life freely (Rev. 21:6).

H. *A life of glory.*
For our light affliction, which is but for a moment, worketh for us a far more exceeding and eternal weight of glory (2 Cor. 4:17).
When Christ, who is our life, shall appear, then shall ye also appear with him in glory (Col. 3:4).

I. *A life of worship.*
And after these things I heard a great voice of much people in heaven, saying Alleluia; Salvation, and glory, and honour, and power unto the Lord our God (Rev. 19:11).
After this I beheld, and, lo, a great multitude, which no man could number, of all nations, and kindreds, and people, and tongues, stood before the throne, and before the Lamb, clothed with white robes, and palms in their hands; And cried with a loud voice, saying, Salvation to our God which sitteth upon the throne, and unto the Lamb . . . Blessing and glory, and wisdom, and thanksgiving, and honour, and power, and might, be unto our God for ever and ever. Amen (Rev. 7:9-12).[48]

Christ's Last Message to Man

Verses 6 through 9 take us back to the early part of the book of Revelation, when the faithful and true witness told us that He would send his angel to convey His message concerning the things that must come to pass. For the second time John bowed before the angel but was forbidden to do so in verse 9, for the consistent pattern in the Word of God is that men worship God only. Again we remind you that the Lord Jesus would have to be God or a crass impostor, for ten times He accepted the worship of man without rebuking him. Since angels refuse to accept the worship of man, certainly the only excuse Jesus Christ would have for accepting their worship is that He is the Son of God.

"Behold, I come quickly" (22:7). Three times we find this expression in the last verses of this book. Some have been confused about the literal meaning of the expression because it was uttered almost two thousand years ago. It would have been more accurately translated, "Behold, I come suddenly." It does not refer to an appointed time soon to come but means that His coming will take place suddenly and without warning.

Significant details are given in association with each of these promises of our Lord.

Verse 7 contains the promise, "Blessed is he that keepeth the words of the prophecy of this book." This could be a reference to the Rapture of the church. "Happy are those" who are sufficiently aware of the prophecy of this book to be ready when that day arrives.

"And, behold, I come quickly, and my reward is with me, to give every man according as his work shall be" (22:12). Added to His promise of a second coming, this verse proclaims a reward by way of judgment, a standard part of the state of believers after the resurrection. On the basis of this reward men will reign with Christ forever.

"And he saith unto me, Seal not the words of the prophecy of this book; for the time is at hand" (22:10). How different is the commandment of God to John from that which He gave to Daniel at the close of his book. The Lord spoke to Daniel and said, "But thou, O Daniel, shut up the words, and seal the book, even to the time of the end" (Dan. 12:4). The reason for the difference in the instructions is that one lived after the time of Christ's crucifixion, the other before. In John's day it was possible to see the unfolding of the events prophesied. In Daniel's day they were a long way off.

A Severe Warning to Detractors From This Prophecy

For I testify unto every man that heareth the words of the prophecy of this book, If any man shall add unto these things, God shall add unto him the plagues that are written in this book; and if any man shall take away from the words of the book of this prophecy, God shall take away his part from the tree of life, and out of the holy city, and from the things which are written in this book (Rev. 22:18, 19).

This is one of the most awesome challenges in the Word of God against tampering with Holy Writ. Far too many today glibly ridicule, detract from, and cast disparaging remarks upon holy Scripture. This is their day of opportunity, but their judgment will come upon them swiftly in God's good time. It is a fearful thing to disbelieve God, and it is unbelief that causes man to detract from His Holy Word. Although this is not a reference to Bible-believing commentators of the Word who mistakenly translate some passage and inadvertently minimize it, it does serve as a soul-stirring challenge to those of us who have taken in hand to write and preach on this marvelous book. I can well appreciate the attitude of the late Dr. Joseph A. Seiss, who wrote in his book, *The Apocalypse:*

With an honest and ever-prayerful heart, and with these solemn and awful warnings ever before my eyes, I have endeavored to ascertain and indicate in these lectures what our gracious Lord and Master has been so particular to make known and defend. If I have read into this Book anything which he has not put there, or read out of it anything which he has put there, with the profoundest sorrow would I recant, and willingly burn up the books in which such mischievous wickedness is contained. If I have in anything gone beyond the limits of due subjection to what is written, or curtailed in any way the depth and measure of what Jesus by his angel has signified for the learning of the Churches, I need not the condemnation of men to heap upon me the burden of censure which I deserve. If feebleness, or rashness, or overweening confidence in my own understanding has distorted anything, I can only deplore the fault, and pray God to send a man more competent to unfold to us the mighty truths which here stand written. . . . If I err, God forgive me! If I am right, God bless my feeble testimony! In either case, God speed His everlasting truth![49]

The Lord Jesus' Last Invitation to Man

"And the Spirit and the bride say, Come. And let him that heareth say, Come. And let him that is athirst come. And whosoever will, let him take the water of life freely" (Rev. 22:17). The Lord Jesus Christ, ever concerned for the souls of lost men, closes His great revelation to the churches with a challenge for individual men to call upon His name. He indicates that there are two who invite men to come to Him, the "Spirit" and the "bride." In addition, He will even use "him that heareth." God the Holy Spirit will use the printed page as well as men who are just repeating what they have heard but may not even believe what they are saying. He also uses the "bride," which indicates that the primary ministry of the church of Christ during the entire church age is to tell men about the Savior. All Christians everywhere should be engaged in saying to men, "Let him that is athirst, come. And whosoever will, let him take the water of life freely." Jesus Christ, of course, is the water of life. The closing verses of the Bible make it perfectly clear that salvation is a matter of the will. Whosoever *will* may come. This would clearly imply that whosoever wills *not* to come is lost. This teaching abounds throughout the Scriptures.

In contrast to those who reject Christ, we encounter the state of the blessed described in verse 14. Those who have washed their robes in the righteousness of Christ have a right to the Tree of Life and thus are entitled to live forever. He describes their state as "blessed," meaning "happy."

Every individual wants happiness. The way to eternal happiness is to receive Christ as Lord and Savior, which entitles you to entrance into the holy city, access to the Tree of Life, and the marvelous blessings of a loving God. If there is any question in your mind as to whether or not you have received the living Christ, I urge you, on the basis of His challenge, to change your will and receive Him as your Lord and Savior today.

FOOTNOTES

1. Henry H. Halley, *Halley's Bible Handbook,* 24th ed. (Grand Rapids: Zondervan Publishing House, 1965), p. 758.

2. Loraine Boettner, *Roman Catholicism* (Philadelphia: Presbyterian and Reformed Publishing Co., 1962), p. 8.

3. Harry A. Ironside, *Lectures on the Book of Revelation,* 12th ed. (Neptune, New Jersey: Loizeaux Brothers, 1942).

4. Boettner, pp. 8, 9.

5. Ironside, pp. 80, 81.

6. Quoted in William R. Newell, *The Book of the Revelation* (Chicago: Moody Press, 1935), p. 374.

7. Ironside, pp. 81-83.

8. Newell, p. 374.

9. J. Vernon McGee, *Reveling Through Revelation* (Los Angeles: Thru the Bible Books Foundation, 1962), I, 82.

10. Ironside.

11. Lehman Strauss, *The Book of Revelation* (Neptune, New Jersey: Loizeaux Brothers, 1964), p. 228.

12. McGee, II, 2.

13. Ironside, pp. 203, 204.

14. Joseph A. Seiss, *The Apocalypse* (Grand Rapids: Zondervan Publishing House, 1957), p. 318.

15. Clarence Larkin, *Dispensational Truth* (Philadelphia: Rev. Clarence Larkin Estate, 1920), p. 120.

16. David L. Cooper, "An Exposition of the Book of Revelation: The Great Parenthesis (11:15 – 15:8)," *Biblical Research Monthly, XIX* (May, 1954), p. 84.

17. Newell, p. 209.

18. Ibid., p. 210.

19. McGee, II, pp. 542, 543.

20. Marvin R. Vincent, *Word Studies in the New Testament* (Wilmington, Delaware: A. P. & A., 1972), II, pp. 542, 543.

21. Clarence Larkin, *The Book of Revelation* (Philadelphia: Rev. Clarence Larkin Estate, 1919).

22. Ironside, pp. 287-291.

23. Larkin, *Dispensational Truth*, p. 140.

24. Halley, pp. 291, 292.

25. "Babylon," *Encyclopedia of Lands and People* (New York: The Grolier Society, Inc., 1960), III, 221.

26. Larkin, *Dispensational Truth,* p. 142.

27. John F. Walvoord, *The Revelation of Jesus Christ* (Chicago: Moody Press, 1966), p. 268.

28. Walter Scott, *Exposition of the Revelation of Jesus Christ,* 4th ed. (London: Pickering & Inglis Ltd., n.d.), p. 375.

29. Seiss, p. 436.

30. Walvoord, *The Revelation of Jesus Christ,* p. 277.

31. Merrill C. Tenney, ed., *The Zondervan Pictorial Bible Dictionary* (Grand Rapids: Zondervan Publishing House, 1963), p. 71.

32. Walvoord, *The Revelation of Jesus Christ,* p. 291.

33. Ibid., p. 298.

34. Dwight J. Pentecost, *Things to Come,* (Grand Rapids: Zondervan Publishing House, 1958), p. 372.

35. Pentecost, p. 370.

36. John F. Walvoord, *The Millennial Kingdom* (Grand Rapids: Zondervan Publishing House, 1959), pp. 5, 6.

37. Pentecost, p. 390.

38. Walvoord, *The Millennial Kingdom,* p. 12.

39. Ibid., p. 6.

40. Halley, p. 764.

41. Walvoord, *The Millennial Kingdom,* p. 51.

42. E. H. Broadbent, *The Pilgrim Church* (London: Pickering and Inglis Ltd., 1931), p. 26.

43. Walvoord, *The Millennial Kingdom,* p. 8.

44. Ibid.

45. Larkin, *Dispensational Truth,* pp. 10, 11.

46. Walvoord, *The Revelation of Jesus Christ,* p. 325.

47. Strauss, p. 355.

48. Pentecost, p. 581.

49. Seiss, p. 527.

BIBLIOGRAPHY

Boettner, Loraine. *Roman Catholicism*. Philadelphia: Presbyterian and Reformed Publishing Company, 1962.

Bradbury, John W., ed. *Hastening the Day of God*. Wheaton, Illinois: Van Kampen Press, 1953.

Broadbent, E. H. *The Pilgrim Church*. London: Pickering and Inglis Ltd., 1931.

Cooper, David L. "An Exposition of the Book of Revelation: The Great Parenthesis (11:15 – 15:8)," *Biblical Research Monthly, XIX* (May, 1954), 84-85, 89.

——————. "An Exposition of the Book of Revelation: The Pouring Out of the Bowls of God's Wrath (16:1 – 21)," *Biblical Research Monthly, XIX* (October, 1954), 186, 187.

DeHaan, M. R. *Revelation: 35 Simple Studies on the Major Themes in Revelation*. Grand Rapids: Zondervan Publishing House, 1946.

Grant, F. W. *The Revelation of Christ*. New York: Loizeaux Brothers, n.d.

Halley, Henry H. *Halley's Bible Handbook*, 24th ed. Grand Rapids: Zondervan Publishing House, 1965.

Ironside, Harry A. *Lectures on the Book of Revelation*, 12th ed. New York: Loizeaux Brothers, 1942.

LaHaye, Tim F. *The Beginning of the End*. Wheaton, Illinois: Tyndale House Publishers, 1972.

Larkin, Clarence. *The Book of Daniel*. Philadelphia: Rev. Clarence Larkin Estate, 1929.

——————. *The Book of Revelation*. Philadelphia: Rev. Clarence Larkin Estate, 1919.

——————. *Dispensational Truth*. Philadelphia: Rev. Clarence Larkin Estate, 1920.

McGee, J. Vernon. *Reveling Through Revelation*, 2 parts. Los Angeles: Thru the Bible Books Foundation, 1962.

Newell, William R. *The Book of the Revelation*. Chicago: Moody, 1935.

Ottman, Ford C. *The Unfolding of the Ages in the Revelation of St. John*. New York: "Our Hope," 1905.

Pentecost, J. Dwight. *Things to Come*. Grand Rapids: Zondervan Publishing House, 1958.

Scott, Walter. *Exposition of the Revelation of Jesus Christ*, 4th ed. London: Pickering and Inglis Ltd., n.d.

Seiss, Joseph A. *The Apocalypse*. Grand Rapids: Zondervan Publishing House, 1957.

Strauss, Lehman. *The Book of Revelation*. Neptune, New Jersey: Loizeaux Brothers, 1964.

Talbot, Louis T. *An Exposition of the Book of Revelation*. Grand Rapids: Wm. B. Eerdmans Publishing Company, 1937.

Tenney, Merrill C. *Interpreting Revelation*. Grand Rapids: Wm. B. Eerdmans Publishing Company, 1957.

Walvoord, John F. *The Millennial Kingdom*. Grand Rapids: Zondervan Publishing House, 1959.

——————. *The Revelation of Jesus Christ*. Chicago: Moody, 1966.